CSR, Sustainability, Ethics & Governance

In recent years the discussion concerning the relation between business and society has made immense strides. This has in turn led to a broad academic and practical discussion on innovative management concepts, such as Corporate Social Responsibility, Corporate Governance and Sustainability Management. This series offers a comprehensive overview of the latest theoretical and empirical research and provides sound concepts for sustainable business strategies. In order to do so, it combines the insights of leading researchers and thinkers in the fields of management theory and the social sciences and from all over the world, thus contributing to the interdisciplinary and intercultural discussion on the role of business in society. The underlying intention of this series is to help solve the world's most challenging problems by developing new management concepts that create value for business and society alike. In order to support those managers, researchers and students who are pursuing sustainable business approaches for our common future, the series offers them access to cutting-edge management approaches. CSR, Sustainability, Ethics and Governance is accepted by the Norwegian Register for Scientific Journals, Series and Publishers, maintained and operated by the Norwegian Social Science Data Services (NSD).

Clea Beatriz Macagnan
Editor

Corporate Governance in Capital Markets

Navigating Governance Systems of Publicly Traded Firms

Springer

Editor
Clea Beatriz Macagnan
Federal University of Paraíba
João Pessoa, Paraíba, Brazil

ISSN 2196-7075 ISSN 2196-7083 (electronic)
CSR, Sustainability, Ethics & Governance
ISBN 978-3-031-94750-6 ISBN 978-3-031-94751-3 (eBook)
https://doi.org/10.1007/978-3-031-94751-3

This Springer imprint is published by the registered company Springer Nature Switzerland AG
The registered company address is: Gewerbestrasse 11, 6330 Cham, Switzerland

Foreword

"Corporate Governance in Capital Markets: Navigating Governance Systems of Publicly Traded Firms" is a valuable contribution to the field of corporate governance, offering a comparative analysis of governance systems across ten nations. This book is particularly significant for executives and business students as it fills a crucial gap in the existing literature, which has been heavily focused on the corporate governance practices of the United States and the United Kingdom. By providing insights into the governance frameworks of countries like Germany, China, Japan, and India, this book broadens the understanding of how corporate governance operates in different legal, cultural, and economic environments.

The importance of this theme cannot be overstated. In today's globalized economy, executives need to navigate complex governance challenges that go beyond their home country. This book equips them with the knowledge to understand and manage these challenges, making it an essential reader for anyone involved in international business or corporate management. For business students, the comparative approach offers an invaluable opportunity to learn how governance practices differ and sometimes converge across various regions.

While the book succeeds in providing detailed country-specific insights, it could benefit from an introduction that better ties the chapters together, highlighting the commonalities and differences across nations. A more cohesive introduction would underscore key themes, such as the contrast between shareholder-centric and stakeholder-centric models, the varying roles of regulatory bodies, and the global trend toward integrating environmental, social, and governance (ESG) factors. For instance, countries like Germany and Japan adopt stakeholder models that emphasize employee participation in governance, while nations like the USA and UK focus more on shareholder value. Regulatory frameworks also differ significantly, with civil law countries like Germany and Italy offering more statutory-driven governance, while common law countries like Australia rely on self-regulation through governance codes.

In sum, "Corporate Governance in Capital Markets: Navigating Governance Systems of Publicly Traded Firms" is a groundbreaking work expanding corporate governance literature's scope. It provides executives and business students with a nuanced understanding of governance practices across diverse countries, while also identifying areas where the global convergence of governance trends is taking place. A stronger, integrative introduction would enhance the book's impact by clearly delineating these key insights, making it even more accessible and insightful for its intended audience.

Instituto de Tecnologia de Massachusetts – MIT
Cambridge, MA, USA

Rodrigo Verdi

Contents

Chapter 1
Introduction

Clea Beatriz Macagnan

Corporate governance has become a cornerstone of modern business practice, shaping how companies interact with "Corporate Governance in Capital Markets: Navigating Governance Systems of Publicly Traded Firms," shareholders, stakeholders, and regulators across the globe. This book comprehensively analyzes corporate governance systems across diverse nations and highlights how these frameworks are deeply rooted in unique economic, legal, and cultural contexts. "Corporate Governance in Capital Markets: Navigating Governance Systems of Publicly Traded Firms" is particularly valuable for executives and business students, as it provides a global perspective on governance, equipping readers with the knowledge necessary to navigate and manage corporate governance challenges in today's interconnected world.

The book delves into the governance systems of ten countries: Australia, China, Germany, Hong Kong, Italy, India, Japan, Russia, Singapore, and Spain. Significant differences and striking similarities in corporate governance are highlighted through the lens of these nations. Such aspects provide essential insights into how governance structures are shaped in response to distinct legal frameworks, market conditions, and cultural influences. The book does not present chapters on the governance system in the United States and the United Kingdom, as they are the best-known systems due to their size and are also at a reference stage in developing capital markets in other countries.

Key Insights and Themes Divergent Corporate Governance Models: Shareholder vs. Stakeholder Focus Regulatory Bodies and Legal Systems.

C. B. Macagnan (✉)
Federal University of Paraiba, João Pessoa, Paraiba, Brazil

C. B. Macagnan (ed.), *Corporate Governance in Capital Markets*, CSR, Sustainability, Ethics & Governance,
https://doi.org/10.1007/978-3-031-94751-3_1

One of the most prominent distinctions in global corporate governance is the difference between shareholder-centric and stakeholder-centric models. Countries like the United States and the United Kingdom represent shareholder models, where the primary focus of governance is maximizing shareholder value. By contrast, countries like Germany and Japan adopt stakeholder models, focusing on balancing the interests of a broader group of stakeholders, including employees, suppliers, and the community.

In Germany, for example, the system of *codetermination* allows for employees' representation on supervisory boards, giving workers a formal voice in corporate decisions. Such employee's representation contrasts sharply with the shareholder-driven approach prevalent in countries like the United States and the United Kingdom, where employees do not have active representation in governance matters.

Similarly, Japan's *keiretsu* system—a network of interlocking business relationships and shareholdings—creates a stakeholder-oriented governance structure that fosters long-term relationships between banks, corporations, and suppliers. This stakeholder-centric approach emphasizes stability and consensus over short-term profits.

While these models differ in emphasis, a common goal across all systems is to create a governance framework that promotes transparency, accountability, and fairness. Whether focused on shareholders or stakeholders, corporate governance aims to foster trust among investors, employees, and the broader society.

1.1 The Role of Regulatory Bodies and Legal Systems

Another significant difference across nations is the role of regulatory bodies and legal frameworks in shaping corporate governance. In countries under civil law, such as Germany, Japan, and Italy, governance practices are heavily influenced by statutory laws and detailed regulations. Germany's governance system is tightly controlled by formal regulations, like the Stock Corporations Act and the German Corporate Governance Code, which set guidelines for corporate transparency and accountability.

Such control contrasts the judicial precedents and self-regulation present in countries under the common law system, like the United States, Australia, and the United Kingdom. Australia, for instance, follows a "comply or explain" model under the Australia Stock Exchange (ASX) Governance Code, where companies are encouraged to adopt best practices, but deviations do not lead to penalties if adequately explained.

In emerging markets like India and China, regulatory bodies such as the *Securities and Exchange Board of India (SEBI)* and the *China Securities Regulatory Commission (CSRC)* play crucial roles in governance reform. Both countries have undertaken significant reforms to enhance corporate transparency and protect minority shareholders, reflecting their evolving roles in the global economy. Despite this progress, these markets still face challenges, such as concentrated ownership and state influence, which can undermine the effectiveness of governance structures.

1.2 Ownership Structures: Concentration vs. Dispersion

Ownership concentration is another major differentiating factor in corporate governance systems. In countries like Russia, India, and China, ownership tends to be highly concentrated, often in the hands of families, state-owned enterprises (SOEs), or a small group of insiders. This concentration can lead to governance challenges, such as conflicts of interest, reduced accountability, and limited protection for minority shareholders.

In *Italy* and *Spain*, on the other hand, businesses are predominantly family-owned, and the interests of controlling families often influence governance and management decisions. This type of business faces unique challenges in balancing family control with the demands of capital markets, especially regarding transparency and succession planning.

Still, in countries like the *United States, **Australia, and **Germany*, ownership is spread among institutional investors, pension funds, and individual shareholders. Ownership dispersion typically increases concerns about minority shareholders' protection. Consequently, governance frameworks in dispersed ownership environments tend to be designed to mitigate conflicts between managers and shareholders.

Despite these differences, a common aspect is the increasing global focus on enhancing *shareholder rights* and protecting minority investors. Even in countries with concentrated ownership structures, there are ongoing reforms aimed at improving transparency and curbing the influence of controlling shareholders.

1.3 Corporate Governance Codes and Global Convergence

A remarkable trend across the countries encompassed in this book is the growing importance of corporate governance codes, which provide companies with a set of best practices to be followed. These codes align increasingly with international standards, such as the **G20/OECD Principles of Corporate Governance. For example, **Singapore's* Corporate Governance Code and *Hong Kong's* governance framework were designed to attract international investors by promoting transparency and adherence to global standards.

Meanwhile, there is a global convergence toward a more *sustainable approach* to corporate governance. Countries like Australia and Germany have integrated *environmental, social, and governance (ESG)* criteria into their corporate governance frameworks, reflecting a broader recognition that companies must consider financial performance and their impact on society and the environment.

Regulatory reforms and market pressures foster this convergence as investors increasingly demand greater transparency and accountability from companies on non-financial matters. Despite the different pace and scope of these changes among countries, the movement toward more responsible and sustainable governance is discussed worldwide.

1.4 Final Considerations

"Corporate Governance in Capital Markets: Navigating Governance Systems of Publicly Traded Firms" highlights the complex, evolving corporate governance landscape, shaped by each country's specific legal, economic, and cultural framework. For executives and business students, understanding these differences is critical to navigating the global business environment. Whether operating in a shareholder-centric or stakeholder-centric system, or governed by statutory laws or self-regulatory codes, the principles of transparency, accountability, and fairness remain the foundation of corporate governance practices.

By comparing governance systems of diverse nations, this book illustrates distinct ways companies can be managed and controlled, offering valuable lessons to the most recent global trends of corporate governance. Whether you are an executive making strategic decisions or a business student preparing to enter the corporate world, this book provides essential insights into the governance frameworks that influence the success and sustainability of modern businesses.

Chapter 2
Germany

Corporate Governance in Germany: Issues, Systems, Characteristics, and Regulations

Reiner Quick, Ísis Beltrão Pereira, and Clea Beatriz Macagnan

2.1 Introduction

Akerlof (1978) and Arrow (1978) addressed the asymmetry of information that occurs when one of the parties has more than the other. If there is information asymmetry, conflicts of interest are likely, and at least one party may be willing to take risks, which can lead to opportunism and increased conflict costs (Jensen & Meckling, 1976; Williamson, 1975). Conflicts of interest arise when there is a possibility that agents may not act in the best interest of the principal, for example, the shareholders. The agents, for example, the directors, might take risks if they believe that others will bear the consequences. In the context of the German setting, the key agent is the management board, and the principals are the shareholders, the supervisory board, creditors, employees, and the state. Good corporate governance can help reduce opportunism, conflicts of interest, and related costs. Corporate governance refers to how corporations and their managers are directed and controlled (Holmstrom & Kaplan, 2001). This system aims to protect investors and other stakeholders from expropriation by insiders (La Porta et al., 2000). Thus, corporate governance may foster investor confidence in the company and its management. As a result, the share price of listed companies reflects investors' collective assessment of the quality of corporate governance (Morck, 2005).

R. Quick (✉)
Technische Universität Darmstadt, Darmstadt, Germany
e-mail: reiner.quick@tu-darmstadt.de

Í. B. Pereira
Brazilian Air Force University, Rio de Janeiro, Brazil
e-mail: isisibp@fab.mil.br

C. B. Macagnan
Federal University of Paraiba, João Pessoa, Paraiba, Brazil

C. B. Macagnan (ed.), *Corporate Governance in Capital Markets*, CSR, Sustainability, Ethics & Governance,
https://doi.org/10.1007/978-3-031-94751-3_2

There are two principal corporate governance models: the shareholder and the stakeholder model (Berglöf, 2000; Chhillar & Lellapalli, 2015). In the shareholder model, which is prevalent in countries like the United States and the United Kingdom, institutional control is primarily exercised by the company's shareholders. In contrast, the stakeholder model, applied in countries, such as Germany and Japan, involves a broader range of stakeholders, including banks and employees, which participate in control (Berglöf, 2000). Many other countries apply hybrid models that combine elements of both. These models differ fundamentally in their objectives. The shareholder model focuses on maximizing shareholder profits, while the stakeholder model seeks to balance profit with the well-being of employees, suppliers, funding sources, and society at large (Rahman & Carpano, 2017).

The importance of corporate governance is highlighted by many and varied fraud scandals causing adverse effects on investors and stakeholders. A notable example is the Enron bankruptcy at the beginning of the twenty-first century. More recently, Germany has faced significant scandals of its own (Peemöller et al., 2020), like the Siemens bribery scandal, the Volkswagen emission scandal, and the Wirecard accounting scandal with the disappearance of 1.9 billion Euros.

The objective of this chapter is to analyze the corporate governance of Germany, with a focus on its structure and functioning. The primary contribution is its exploration of the unique features of the German corporate system, including the separation of responsibilities between management (Management Board) and control (Supervisory Board), as well as codetermination, which grants employees a specific role within this framework.

The remainder of the chapter is organized as follows. Sections 2.2 and 2.3 explore the financing system of the German economy. Section 2.4 provides an overview of the relevant German company law. Then, Sect. 2.5 delves into the board structure of stock corporations as regulated by the Stock Corporations Act. Section 2.6 discusses the German Corporate Governance Code, which complements the provisions of the Stock Corporation Act. Section 2.7 points out the particularities of codetermination in Germany. The following Sects. 2.8 and 2.9, are dedicated to financial accounting and auditing in the German setting. The final section summarizes the chapter and concludes.

2.2 Sources of Financing

According to The Federal Statistical Office (Destatis), Germany's population in 2023 was 83.3 million (Destatis, 2024a). Considering the country's large-scale acceptance of refugees from conflict areas and immigrants from diverse backgrounds, more than 12 percent of the population consists of foreigners, totaling 13.9 million. Another critical item of data for understanding the country's economic structure is its economically active population of 46.1 million, representing 55% of its people, and an employment rate of 80.4%, (Destatis, 2024b). Additionally, the country's strong economy can be expressed through its gross domestic product

(GDP), which grew by 0.1% in the third trimester of 2024 compared to the same period of the previous year. To see this in perspective, in absolute numbers, the GDP of Germany was about 4.19 trillion Euros in 2023 (Destatis, 2024c). Despite the war in Ukraine, the current inflation rate, in November 2024, is at 2.2% (Destatis, 2024d). Furthermore, Germany's export-oriented economy has regained momentum after the crises of the early twenty-first century, and consequently, unemployment rates have dropped (Rühmkorf et al., 2019). The unemployment rate in November 2024 was 5.9% (Bundesagentur für Arbeit, 2024).

Unlike the US and UK markets, stock financing is less prevalent in the German economy. Instead, banks are essential in funding, resulting in the so-called bank-centric corporate governance model (Goergen et al., 2008a). Consequently, banks strongly influence the corporate governance of financed companies. Chhillar and Lellapalli (2015) classify financial systems into market-based and bank-based. In this manner, the market or the banks that sustain the operations influence the functioning of corporations. Therefore, banks are highly relevant to the German economy (Quick & Sayar, 2021). The German model is a decentralized universal bank-based financial system (Elsas & Krahnen, 2004; Hardie & Howarth, 2009) with three pillars: privately owned banks, banks with government involvement, and regionally focused savings banks and small credit cooperatives (Hackethal, 2004).

Universal banks offer various financial services and provide a significant finance share through debt and equity holding. In Germany, bank borrowing is the most important external source of finance, primarily via long-term loans (Hackethal et al., 2005; Deutsche Bundesbank, 2012). In this so-called house-bank model, the relationships between banks and their corporate clients are close (Behr & Schmidt, 2015). For instance, banks are represented on companies' Supervisory Boards, and often control large blocks of shareholder voting rights. These voting rights derive from direct ownership of the shares and proxy powers, as banks operate a stock-broking service that includes an option for proxy rights management to passive investors, as part of the share purchasing service (Franks & Mayer, 2001; Becht & Boehmer, 2003).

Consequently, banks can often elect their managers to corporate boards (Dittmann et al., 2010), manage most issues of marketable securities, frequently place them with their customers, and/or serve as financial intermediaries or investment advisory services to and on behalf of a firm. For all these reasons, banks play a significant role in the structure of German corporate governance (Cable, 1985; La Porta et al., 2000; Chirinko & Elston, 2006; Goergen et al., 2008b). For example, Fohlin (2005) found a strong presence of financing and control of large banks regarding listed companies in Germany. However, this was less evident in smaller companies, which tend to have family control blocks.

Moreover, banks are not the only financial institutions to invest resources in companies (Favara, 2003). According to the International Monetary Fund (2016), Germany's insurance sector also plays an essential role as a capital provider. Additionally, the asset management sector is the third largest in Europe, measured by assets under management, and comprises a broad range of management companies and funds.

2.3 Capital Market

The Deutsche Börse Group is the German stock exchange management institution, which disclosed in its 2023 annual review report net revenues of 5.1 billion euros, with a net profit attributable to shareholders in the period of more than 1.7 billion euros. It is headquartered in the financial center of Frankfurt, *Rhein-Main* (Frankfurt Metropolitan Region) (Deutsche Börse Group, 2024a), Germany. However, it operates in cities worldwide, such as Luxembourg, Prague, London, Zug, New York, Chicago, Hong Kong, Singapore, Beijing, Tokyo, and Sydney. It has more than 14,000 employees in 61 locations worldwide (27 countries). This way, the organization claims to work for fair, transparent, and safe markets for investors and companies (Deutsche Börse Group, 2024b).

In Europe, there are two forms of access to capital markets: (1) a regulated market governed by public law and (2) a market governed by private law (Open Market). The Regulated Market follows the European Union Securities Trading Law. Admission to the Open Market is possible for stocks not admitted to the Regulated Market, configuring access to the stock market, especially for small and medium-sized enterprises (Deutsche Börse Group, 2024d). Thus, the "General Terms and Conditions" of Deutsche Börse Group regulate conditions for the inclusion and accompanying duties of securities listed for the Open Market on the Frankfurt Stock Exchange (*Frankfurter Wertpapierbörse*) (Deutsche Börse Group, 2023). The Regulated Market includes the prime and general standards. According to November 2024 Deutsche Börse Group data, the German market has 275 prime standard companies and 103 general standard companies (Deutsche Börse Group, 2024g). Companies accepted for general standard must fulfill the legal requirements for the regulated market. In contrast, prime standard companies must meet further requirements (e.g., concerning transparency and disclosure).

The Deutsche Börse Group has the DAX index as its primary stock market index. It comprises the 40 largest companies according to the market capitalization listed on the Frankfurt Stock Exchange. Therefore, the DAX index is an essential indicator of the German economy. Furthermore, this index indicates capital concentration in these 40 large companies, which comprise approximately 80 percent of the nominal capital of listed companies (Deutsche Börse Group, 2024c). Other important stock market indices are the MDAX (50 largest companies regarding market capitalization below the DAX), the TecDAX (30 largest technological companies), SDAX (70 largest companies below the MDAX), and the GEX (medium-sized owner-managed companies, i.e., managers hold between 25 and 75% of the shares; going public within the last 10 years) (Deutsche Börse Group, 2024c, 2024e).

Ownership of listed German companies is highly concentrated (Edwards et al., 2009; Goergen et al., 2008a) and mainly in the hands of public households, banks, and other companies (Quick et al., 2018). Groups of blockholders, such as banks, family owners, or other corporations, strongly influence companies in Germany (Tuschke & Luber, 2012). Bottenberg et al. (2017) clarified that these blockholders are more committed to a specific company than is the case for other shareholders.

For example, banks often show more substantial involvement in making a company's strategic decisions than other financial investors because they are interested in stable, long-term relationships (Bottenberg et al., 2017). Thus, Bottenberg et al. (2017) concluded that banks overlap interests as shareholders and business partners of the companies in which they invest. Quick et al. (2018) argued that opportunism and interest-conflict costs in this scenario might be lower, because investors may have access to vital information to the extent that they participate in the management board.

Minority shareholders are less widespread in Germany than in other markets, which might explain their low protection and power level (La Porta et al., 2000; Gul et al., 2013; Rühmkorf et al., 2019). Thus, minority shareholders are more exposed to the possibility of expropriation by majority shareholders in the German stakeholder-centric model than in shareholder-focused models (Chhillar & Lellapalli, 2015; Lazarides & Drimpetas, 2010). In this context, the problems of information asymmetry, opportunism, and the possibility of conflicts of interest become more evident, drawing attention to the importance of establishing regulations that emphasize the importance of disclosing information and establishing corporate governance mechanisms that mitigate these problems between majority and minority.

In Germany, trading within the exchanges is monitored by three institutions: (1) Trading Surveillance Office (TSO); (2) Exchange Supervisory Authority of the Federal States, and (3) Federal Financial Supervisory Agency (Deutsche Börse Group, 2024f). The German market is monitored by the Trading Surveillance Office (TSO), an independent supervisory body of the exchange, which supervises trading activities (Deutsche Börse Group, 2024f). The Exchange Supervisory Authority of the Federal States also acts at the state level. It ensures that participants admitted to exchange trading adhere to Exchange Act regulations and may impose sanctions on market participants, if infringements of rules occur. Finally, the German Federal Financial Supervisory Agency (*Bundesanstalt für Finanzdienstleistungsaufsicht*–BaFin) supervises banks, financial service providers, insurance undertakings, and securities trading. It operates in the public interest and ensures the proper functioning, stability, and integrity of the German financial system, that is, it ensures the ability of banks, financial service institutions, and insurance undertakings to meet their payment obligations. Furthermore, its supervision of the markets aims to safeguard fair and transparent market conditions and thereby to protect customers (BaFin, 2024).

2.4 Company Law

Legal systems can either follow common law, which is based on previous court decisions, or civil law, which provides laws for application (La Porta et al., 1997; Chhillar & Lellapalli, 2015). Common law is a body of unwritten laws based on legal precedents established by the courts. Thus, in common law systems, judges and lawyers play an important role, and judges act as true protagonists in the construction of law and its application to practical cases. In contrast, civil law systems, also called *continental* or *Romano-Germanic* legal systems, are typically codified systems of law, which is the primary source of law, and judges must follow it. It holds case law secondary and subordinate to statutory law. Law codes are laws enacted by the legislature. The German legal system is an example of a civil law system (Kaske, 2002).

Figure 2.1 provides an overview of the primary legal forms for entities. Apart from sole proprietorships, there are two principal types of legal forms, commercial partnerships (*Personenhandelsgesellschaften*) and limited liability companies (*Kapitalgesellschaften*) (for details see, e.g., Raiser, 1988; Grundei & Talaulicar, 2002). There are two critical differences between these principles. The owners are involved in corporate management in the case of commercial partnerships, which reduces opportunism and interest conflict problems, but not in limited liability companies. On the other hand, the owners of commercial partnerships are also liable to make compensation from their private assets. In contrast, the liability of limited liability companies is restricted to the company's assets. Two types of commercial partnerships are available (Wellisch et al., 2002), namely, the limited commercial partnership (*Kommanditgesellschaft*–KG; §§ 161 et seq. HGB; for details see, e.g., Steding, 2003) and the general partnership (*Offene Handelsgesellschaft*–OHG; §§ 105 et seq. HGB). Both are regulated by the Commercial Code (*Handelsgesetzbuch*–HGB). The limited commercial partnership differs between the two types of owners. General partners (*Komplementäre*) manage the company, and their liability is unlimited. In contrast, limited partners (*Kommanditisten*) are not involved in the management, and their liability is limited (§ 161 (1), 164, 170, and 171 (1) HGB). In a general partnership, all owners manage the company and are exposed to unlimited liability (§105 (1), 126 (1) HGB). OHG has a good reputation due to its

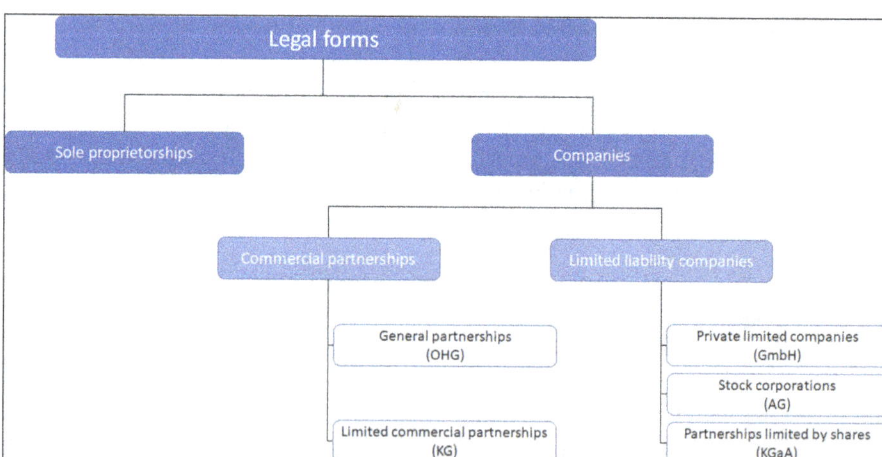

Fig. 2.1 Principle legal forms

unlimited liability. However, a KG could more easily increase equity without a direct impact on the management of its business.

Regarding limited commercial partnerships, there are (Rühmkorf et al., 2019) private limited corporations (*Gesellschaft mit beschränkter Haftung*–GmbH) and stock corporations (*Aktiengesellschaft*–AG), which are governed by different laws, the Private Limited Companies Act (*Gesetz betreffend die Gesellschaften mit beschränkter Haftung*–GmbHG) and the Stock Corporations Act (*Aktiengesetz*–AktG). Compared to the GmbH, the AG is regulated in greater detail and has stricter rules. However, the GmbH cannot be listed, meaning better access to equity for the AG. Additionally, there is a further legal form also belonging to the category of limited liability companies, the partnership limited by shares (*Kommanditgesellschaft auf Aktien*–KGaA), which combines elements of a stock corporation and a limited commercial partnership (for details, see e.g., Lahmann, 1999). It is also regulated in the AktG and can be listed, but this legal form is rarely applied. Figure 2.1 summarizes the types of companies in the German market.

For harmonization reasons, the European Union also offers the *Societas Europaea* (SE), which can choose between a one-tier and a two-tier system and is regulated through a separate law, the law on the implementation of the European Directive 2157/2001 (*Gesetz zur Ausführung der Verordnung (EG) Nr. 2157/2001 des Rates vom 8. Oktober 2001 über das Statut der Europäischen Gesellschaft*–SEAG). Due to the outstanding economic importance of stock corporations and the typically large number of owners, corporate governance is critical to them. Therefore, the subsequent explanations primarily refer to this legal form.

2.5 Two-Tier Corporate Governance Model

The board structure is a crucial element of corporate governance and is intended to align the interests of management and capital providers. It is either characterized as a one-tier or two-tier board system. The one-tier system originates from common law, whereas the two-tier system prevails in civil law countries. Instead of having only one body, the two-tier system relies on a supervisory board, which controls the management board (Rose, 2005). German companies are assigned to the two-tier system and follow a stakeholder approach (Wulf et al., 2014). The management board is responsible for managing the company.

In contrast, the supervisory board appoints, advises, and monitors the management board and is also responsible for the soundness of the financial statements (Quick & Schmidt, 2018). The advantage of a two-tier system is that it may strengthen the supervisory board's independence. However, non-executive directors in one-tier systems are closer to the firm's operations and management decisions and have more access to information than the supervisory board members (Hohenfels & Quick, 2020). Therefore, monitoring efficiency may be higher in a one-tier system.

The management board is responsible for managing the company and consists of one or more people. Two board members are required if the share capital exceeds three million euros. For listed companies with more than three management board members, at least one member must be female, and at least one member must be male (§ 76 AktG). The supervisory board appoints management board members for a maximum 5-year period. A reappointment is possible. If the supervisory board appoints more than one management board member, it is possible to appoint a board chairperson. The supervisory board can revoke appointments for valid reasons (§ 84 AktG). It also must ensure appropriate remuneration of the management board and, in the case of a listed company, implement a clear and understandable remuneration system (§§ 87, 87a AktG). The management board must report to the supervisory board on the company's intended business policy, business planning, profitability, course of business and business situation, and transactions with significant impacts on profitability or liquidity (§ 90 AktG). The management board is responsible for financial accounting and must implement a system for early identification of ongoing concerns and risks. In the case of listed companies, the management board must also implement internal control and a risk management system (§ 91 AktG). Board members shall conduct the company's business as responsible and conscientious managers and are personally liable in case of misconduct (§ 93 AktG).

The supervisory board monitors the management board‘s business conduct (§ 111 (1) AktG). It consists of three members, but the by-law of the company can determine a more substantial number. The maximum number of members is nine in case of a share capital not exceeding 1.5 million Euro, 15 in cases of share capital above 1.5 million Euro and not exceeding 10 million Euro, and 21 in case of share capital above 10 million Euro (§ 95 AktG). Supervisory board members represent shareholders and, in the case of co-determined supervisory boards, also employees. For co-determined supervisory boards of listed companies, at least 30% of the members must be female, and at least 30% must be male (§ 96 AktG). Recently, the Council and European Parliament reached a provisional political deal on a new EU law promoting a more balanced gender representation on the boards of listed companies. Listed companies should aim to have at least 40% of their non-executive director positions held by members of the underrepresented sex by 2026. If member-states apply the new rules to executive and non-executive directors, the target would be 33% of all director positions by 2026 (European Council, 2022). Individuals cannot have more than ten supervisory board seats (§ 100 (2) AktG).

Supervisory board members representing shareholders (for employee representatives, see Sect. 2.7) are elected by the general meeting (§ 101 (1) AktG) for a maximum term of 4 years (§ 102 (1) AktG). A supervisory board member is not entitled to simultaneously be a management board member (§ 105 (1) AktG). The board must elect a chairperson and a vice-chairperson among its members, who can form committees like an audit committee. An audit committee supervises the financial reporting process and deals with the effectiveness of the internal control system, the risk management system, the internal auditing system, and the external audit (§ 107 AktG). For public interest entities (in Germany, capital-market-oriented companies, banks, and insurance companies), an audit committee is mandatory; at least one member must have accounting, and another one must have audit expertise.

Moreover, the audit committee must have industry expertise (§ 107 (4) AktG in conjunction with § 100 (5) AktG).

The remuneration of supervisory board members shall be appropriate concerning their tasks and the company's economic position. It is determined by the company's by-laws or the general meeting and shall be re-determined at the latest after 4 years if the company is listed (§ 113 AktG). In addition to appointing the supervisory board members, the general meeting of shareholders decides on the remuneration system, and the remuneration report of the members of management and the supervisory board (§ 120a AktG). It also decides on the formal dismissal of management and supervisory board members (§ 120 AktG), the distribution of retained earnings, the appointment of the statutory auditor, the amendment of the by-laws, measures for acquiring and reducing capital, the appointment of special auditors for the assessment of facts relating to the incorporation or management of the company and the dissolution of the company (§ 119 AktG). Figure 2.2 concisely illustrates the management system of German corporations.

Quick and Henrizi (2019) indicated that, despite the separation of administration and oversight, there is considerable criticism of the efficiency of supervisory boards, such as those members who work on too many supervisory boards (§ 100 (2) AktG allows simultaneous membership in up to ten boards), the lack of full-time mandates, the low frequency of meetings (Roe, 1998), and also doubtful technical competences of supervisory board members, particularly of the representatives of employees (Du Plessis, 2004; Cromme, 2005).

Additionally, Quick and Henrizi (2019) also indicated that it is a commonplace for former management board members to migrate to the supervisory board, which

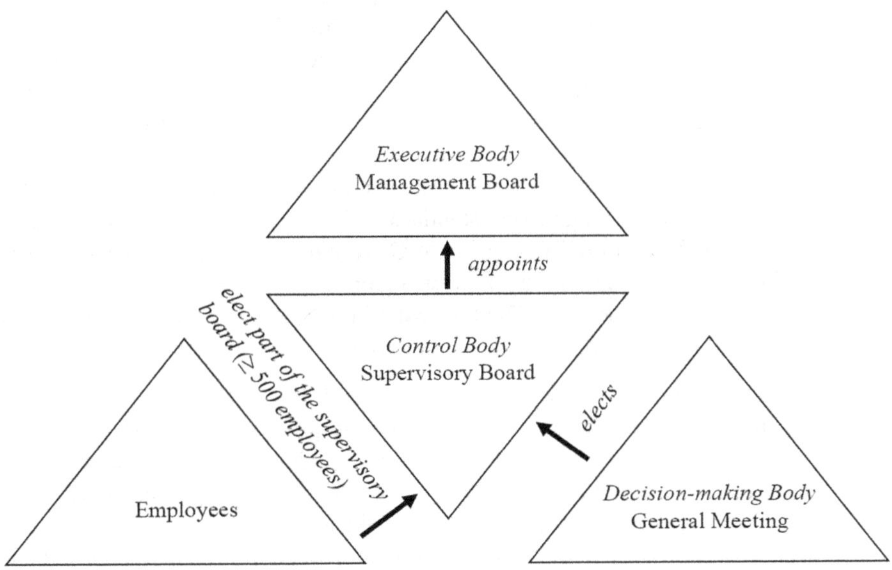

Fig. 2.2 Bodies of (co-determined) Stock Corporations

may reflect potential for conflicts of interest, even considering the cooling-off period of 2 years required by law (§ 100 (2) AktG). Consequently, the independence of the supervisory board from the management board may be threatened. Finally, supervisory boards are used as platforms to cultivate business relations between suppliers, clients, and creditors. Therefore, the division between the two boards becomes blurred, and the supervisory board's independence is negatively affected by many interests (Hopt & Leyens, 2004; Jungmann, 2006).

2.6 Corporate Governance Code

Created in 2002, the German Corporate Governance Code, currently version 2022, which has, in comparison to the prior version, a greater focus on sustainability (Beckmann, 2022), provides a regulatory framework for managing and supervising companies listed in the German capital market or companies with access to capital markets. The German Corporate Governance Code is sub-statutory and acts with principles, recommendations, and suggestions to the management and the supervisory boards to ensure that companies are managed optimally (Regierungskommission, 2022).

The German Code clarifies that the principles reflect relevant legal requirements for responsible governance and are used to inform investors and other stakeholders. The code's recommendations are indicated in the text using "shall." Companies can deviate from the suggestions, but in this case, they must disclose and explain any deviations each year in the logic of "comply or explain" why they did not follow the guidance of the code. That allows companies to consider specific characteristics of the industry or the company. Contrary to what it may seem, justified deviations from the code's recommendations may be in the interest of corporate governance. Finally, the code contains "suggestions" from which companies can move away without disclosure; suggestions are indicated in the text with "should" (Regierungskommission, 2022).

The German Corporate Governance Code contains nationally and internationally recognized corporate management standards (Regierungskommission, 2022), according to the G20 and OECD Corporate Governance Principles (2016), and is organized into 26 principles, as well as 66 recommendations and/or suggestions oriented to seven areas of activity. The following items summarize each of the seven areas with crucial principles and recommendations:

(a) Management and Supervision: on the one hand, the governance tasks of the management board include developing the enterprise strategy, coordinating it with the supervisory board, and ensuring its implementation; stipulating target values for the share of women in the management levels under the management board; ensure responsible management of risks arising from business activities through an appropriate and effective risk management system and internal control system; and, disclose information on the enterprise's current and future business development, financial condition, and earnings situation in a timely, comprehensive, and understandable manner. On the other hand, the supervision tasks of the supervisory board include appointing and discharging the members of the management board; supervising and advising the management board in the management of the enterprise; being involved in decisions of fundamental importance to the enterprise; and ensuring that the enterprise is managed in its best interests, considering the interests of the shareholders, the enterprise's workforce, and other stakeholders. Finally, the general meeting's function includes directing resolutions on the appropriation of net profit; approbating the actions of the management and the supervisory boards by way of discharge; electing the shareholder representatives to the supervisory board and the external auditors; adopting resolutions on the company's legal principles; and discussing the remuneration system for the management and the supervisory boards.

(b) Appointments to the Management Board: The supervisory board determines the number of the management board members, the required qualifications, and the appointment of suitable candidates for individual positions. This board also ensures that gender participation is legally required on the management board and defines target values for compliance with the percentage of women on the management board according to the framework of legal requirements. Those guidelines are within legal and statutory provisions. The code recommends that the management board consider diversity when appointing members and that the first appointment of management board members shall be for at most 3 years.

(c) Composition of the Supervisory Board: The supervisory board consists of shareholder representatives and employee representatives, if applicable. In this context, shareholders and employee representatives must act in the enterprise's best interests. The composition of the supervisory board must ensure that its members collectively have the knowledge, skills, and professional expertise required to perform their duties properly. Finally, the legal gender quota must be considered when appointing members to the supervisory board. One of the most important recommendations in this section is the independence of the supervisory board members. For that purpose, the supervisory board member shall be independent of any controlling shareholder and independent from the company and its management board to reduce conflicts of interest.

(d) Supervisory Board procedures: The supervisory board shall adopt its own procedure rules and publish these on the company's website. The code also argues that the management and the supervisory boards must cooperate on a trust basis in order to benefit the enterprise. Good corporate governance requires an open dialogue between the supervisory board and the management board and between the members of these individual boards. Likewise, cooperation with external auditors is also a code principle. The external auditors support the supervisory board and, if necessary, the audit committee in monitoring the management, especially in the accounting review and the risk management systems area. The external auditors advise the capital market about financial reporting compliance with generally accepted accounting principles. Furthermore, comprehensive observance of confidentiality is paramount in this regard.

(e) Conflicts of interest: Members of the management board and supervisory board must act in the best interests of the enterprise and avoid pursuing personal interests or exploiting business opportunities that belong to the enterprise. Management board members must also comply with non-compete clauses during their appointment. Each supervisory and management board member must immediately disclose any conflicts of interest to the relevant parties. The supervisory board must inform the general meeting of any conflicts of interest and how they were addressed. Conflicts of interest with a member of the supervisory board that are not temporary must result in the termination of that member's mandate. Members of the management board must obtain approval from the supervisory board before assuming any sideline activities, especially supervisory board mandates outside the enterprise.

(f) Transparency and external reporting: The company must ensure equal treatment of all shareholders regarding information. The group management report consolidated financial statements, and interim financial information must inform shareholders and third parties. The company must disclose to shareholders all new material facts available to financial analysts and similar addresses. The consolidated financial statements and the group management report should be disclosed to the public within 90 days from the end of the financial year. The management and supervisory board must provide information about the company's corporate governance in their corporate governance statement annually. The corporate governance statement must specify what code recommendations were not applied due to overriding legal stipulations. The company must keep previous corporate governance statements and Declarations of Compliance regarding the recommendations of the code available on its website for at least 5 years.

(g) The Management Board and Supervisory Board: The supervisory board must decide on a clear and comprehensible system for the remuneration of management board members and determine the actual remuneration for each member based on this system. The general meeting usually adopts advisory resolutions on approving the remuneration guidelines for the management board members prepared by the supervisory board. It proposes resolutions on approving the remuneration report for the preceding financial year. The remuneration structure of listed companies must be oriented toward long-term development and company sustainability. The remuneration of the management board members must promote the corporate strategy and support the company's long-term development. The remuneration shall be offset if the management board members are also members of intra-group supervisory boards. If supervisory board memberships are assumed at non-group entities, the board shall decide if and to what extent the remuneration from such memberships shall be considered. The remuneration of supervisory board members shall consider, appropriately, the higher time commitment of the chair, the deputy chair of the supervisory board, the chair, and the members of committees (Regierungskommission, 2022).

The German Corporate Governance Code's Government Commission (*Regierungskommission*) discloses recommendations and suggestions. It reviews whether they continue to comply with best corporate governance practices or need adjustments annually. Commission members are representatives from the management and supervisory boards of capital market-oriented companies and their stakeholders. Thus, it also encompasses representatives of institutional and non-professional investors, academia, labor unions, and auditors (Regierungskommission, 2022). The commission shall have at least 10 members, but at most, 15 (currently 14) (Regierungskommission, 2024). They are appointed and dismissed by the Federal Ministry of Justice. The commission must keep the code up-to-date and maintain a dialogue with companies, stakeholders, politicians, and the public. Two forums that enable this constant dialogue are the public consultation process and the Annual Conference of the Corporate Governance Code (Regierungskommission, n.d.).

2.7 Codeterminations

Codetermination means that workers play an official role in corporate governance. The German setting encompasses the principle of shared governance, that is, worker representation on the supervisory board and work councils as a further method of worker-management cooperation (Hayden & Bodie, 2021).

Supervisory boards comprise shareholders and employee representatives. The codetermination law (*Mitbestimmungsgesetz*–MitbestG) applies to all limited liability companies with over 2000 employees (§ 1 (1) MitbestG). These companies must form a supervisory board even if they are not obliged to do so by other laws (§ 6 (1) MitbestG). Supervisory boards of companies with not more than 10,000 (more than 10,000 up to 20,000; more than 20,000) employees comprise six (eight; ten) representatives of shareholders and six (eight, ten) representatives of employees. The latter include two (2; 3) representatives of trade unions (§ 7 (1) and (2) MitbestG). The supervisory board elects a chairperson and a vice-chairperson among its members by a two-thirds majority. However, if this majority is not reached, the chairperson will be elected by the shareholder representatives, and the vice-chairperson by the employee representatives (§ 27 MitbestG). Supervisory board decisions require a simple majority of the votes. The chairperson's vote decides in case of a tie (§ 29 MitbestG). Consequently, there is a slight predominance of shareholders, and thus not genuine parity. Thus, the chairperson's vote inhibits the equality of codetermination since the chairperson typically represents the shareholders (Rahman & Carpano, 2017; Rühmkorf et al., 2019).

There is a separate codetermination law for limited liability companies from the coal and steel industry with more than 1000 employees (*Montanmitbestimmungsgesetz*–MontanMitbestG). Here, the supervisory board comprises 11 members (four shareholder representatives plus a further member, four employee representatives plus another member, and a further member). Additional members cannot represent a trade union or an employee in the organization, must not have worked or served as an employer and shall not have an economic interest in the company (§ 4 MontanMitbestG). The eleventh (further) member is neutral and elected on the recommendation of the other members. Thus, full parity exists in this industry.

The One-Third Participation Act (*Drittelbeteiligungsgesetz*–DrittelbG) applies to limited liability companies, mutual insurance associations, and cooperatives with more than 500 employees not covered by the MitbestG and the MontanMitbestG (§ 1 (1) DrittelbG). At least one-third of the supervisory boards must consist of employee representatives (§ 4 (1) DrittelbG).

A work council must be elected in firms with at least five employees (§ 1 (1) *Betriebsverfassungsgesetz*–BetrVG [Work Constitution Act]). The size of the work council depends on the number of employees (§ 9 BetrVG). The critical task of a work council is to monitor the application of regulations in favor of employees. The work council also promotes gender equality, the compatibility of work and family, the integration of disabled persons, the employment of older employees, and the integration of foreign employees (§ 80 (1) BetrVG). To accomplish these tasks, the work council has comprehensive information rights (§ 80 (2) BetrVG). In addition, the work council participates in social affairs (§ 87 BetrVG), consults in personnel affairs (§§ 92 ff. BetrVG), and can negotiate work agreements.

In summary, German law ensures that strategic decisions involve employees on the supervisory board. This may yield efficiency benefits in the context of corporate bargaining and balance the interests of shareholders and employees (Sandrock, 2015). Additionally, codetermination ensures that the employee representatives have access to the same information as shareholder representatives. This mitigates or eliminates information asymmetries, potentially avoids opportunism, and conflicts of interest costs like costly strikes (Frege, 2002; Dammann & Eidenmüller, 2021). Furthermore, codetermination facilitates cooperation between employers and employees, pacifies labor, and enhances competitive logic (Paster, 2012).

Moreover, codetermination may foster employee motivation and loyalty to the firm and encourage employee investment. Above and beyond this, the possibility of exchanging ideas and information with workers and the experience of joint decision-making capable of providing capital and work opportunities may build a better, more reliable, and more cooperative relationship and even increase productivity (FitzRoy & Kraft, 2005; Harcourt et al., 2020). Codetermination can also reduce divergence between capital and labor interests (Rühmkorf et al., 2019) and positively affect corporate social responsibility (Scholz & Vitols, 2019).

On the other hand, divided loyalties within the supervisory board may adversely affect its functioning. Furthermore, codetermination may be an obstacle to the market for corporate control and discourage certain types of risk-taking (Dammann & Eidenmüller, 2021). According to the power-distributive logic, power-sharing with labor limits the capacity of owners and executives to make decisions that would be most effective in strengthening the firms' competitiveness, that is, codetermination may result in an inefficient allocation of resources caused by over-staffing or a slow-down in decision making (Paster, 2012).

2.8 Accounting System

Capital-market-oriented parent companies that are obliged to prepare consolidated financial statements according to the German Commercial Code must present consolidated accounts using the International Financial Reporting Standards (IFRS) (§ 315e HGB). Parent companies not active in the capital market can optionally apply the IFRS or the German Accounting Standards to prepare their consolidated financial statements. In contrast, German Accounting Standards are mandatory for individual financial statements. However, it is possible to alternatively fulfill a company's publication requirements by disclosing individual financial statements that comply with the IFRS (§ 325 (2a) HGB). However, two sets of individual financial statements would be costly (Hennrichs, 2008). Therefore, in practice, the application of this option is limited to parent companies preparing their consolidated accounts according to the IFRS, because they must adopt the individual financial statements of the group companies to IFRS for consolidation purposes anyway.

The primary addresses of financial reporting are creditors, who must be protected. Therefore, the overarching German accounting principle is the principle of prudence, which means that values must be determined prudently, from which the realization and the imparity principles are derived (§ 252 (1) Nr. 4 HGB). According to the realization principle, profits may only be recognized if economic transactions realize them. In contrast, the imparity principle says that risks and losses that arise up to the balance sheet date must be recognized even if they are not realized. Consequently, only the cost model can be applied for measuring assets, and historical costs minus depreciation is the upper limit for measurement (§ 253 (1) HGB).

In contrast, the IFRS mainly addresses shareholders and must provide an accurate and fair view of the economic situation of the company reporting. Therefore, the accrual principle (IAS 1.27-28) is dominant, and the IFRS includes alternative measurement models such as the revaluation model (e.g., IAS 16.31-42) or the fair value model (IFRS 13), which allows exceeding the historical cost. Another key feature of the German Accounting Standards is the existence of different accounting options regarding recognition, for example, regarding self-created fixed intangible assets (§ 248 (2) HGB), and measurement, for example, regarding production costs to which administration costs, social costs, and borrowing costs can optionally be included (§ 255 (2) HGB). Consequently, German companies can build hidden reserves by using such accounting options. Hidden reserves reduce the information value and thereby the decision usefulness of financial statements but protect uninformed creditors. However, the problem with hidden reserves is that their release can conceal adverse business developments.

A specific element of financial reporting not covered in the IFRS is the management report, which large and medium-sized limited liability companies must prepare (§§ 264 (1) HGB). It includes a presentation of the course of the business and the company's position and a report on the company's probable development, including material changes and risks. The management report also informs us on risks and risk management regarding financial instruments, research and development, and subsidiaries (§ 289 (1–2) HGB). Furthermore, large, limited liability companies must disclose the most important key non-financial performance indicators (§ 289. (3) HGB). In addition, capital market-oriented companies must also inform on the principal characteristics of their internal control and risk management system regarding accounting processes (§ 289 (4) HGB). Finally, large capital market-oriented companies must also add a corporate social responsibility report (§ 289b HGB), and companies listed on the regulated market must prepare a corporate governance statement (§ 289f HGB). The Corporate Sustainability Reporting Directive of the European Union requires more companies to prepare sustainability reports than before. All large corporations and all small- and medium-sized entities which are public interest entities will be obliged for sustainability reporting. Moreover, companies must engage an assurance provider to attest these reports (European Parliament and Council, 2022).

Only limited liability companies must disclose their financial statements and management reports in the *Elektronischer Bundesanzeiger*—electronic Federal Gazette (§ 325 (1) HGB). However, there are concessions for companies that are not large. Medium-sized companies can disclose the balance sheet and the notes in simplified form (§ 327 HGB). Small companies must only disclose the balance sheet and the notes, both in an even more simplified form, however, not the income statement (§ 326 (1) HGB), and tiny companies only need to submit their balance sheet to the operator of the Federal Gazette without publication (§ 326 (2) HGB). Companies belong to a specific size category if they fulfill two of three criteria (see Table 2.1) in two subsequent financial years (§§ 267 and 267a HGB). Thus, companies' financial statements of different legal forms are not publicly available.

However, if these companies are very large, they must disclose their financial statements. To belong to this category, companies must fulfill two out of three size categories in three subsequent years (§ 1 (1) PublG = *Publizitätsgesätz* = Publicity Act). Table 2.2 shows that large company also has other parameters.

Only parent limited liability companies must prepare consolidated financial statements and a group management report (§ 290 HGB). They must also disclose both in the electronic Federal Gazette (§ 325 (3) HGB). Similar requirements for preparation and disclosure apply for large parent companies according to §§ 11 (1) and 15 PublG.

Table 2.1 Company size categories (§ 267 HGB)

	Balance sheet total [€]	Turnover [€]	Employees
Very small	Up to 450,000	Up to 900,000	Up to 10
Small	Up to 7,500,000	Up to 15,000,000	Up to 50
Medium	Up to 25,000,000	Up to 50,000,000	Up to 250
Large	Over 25,000,000	Over 50,000,000	Over 250

Table 2.2 Exceptionally very large companies (§1 (1) PublG)

	Balance sheet total [€]	Turnover [€]	Employees
Very large	Over 65,000,000	Over 130,000,000	Over 5000

2.9 Auditing

There are information asymmetries (Jensen & Meckling, 1976) between management (the agent) and shareholders, and other stakeholders (the principals), that is, management has more, better, and earlier information. Consequently, external interest groups cannot wholly assess management performance (hidden action), and management could use its informational advantage to maximize its own benefit instead of shareholders (moral hazard). Financial statements include information and potentially reduce information asymmetries. However, management prepares financial statements, and there is again a hidden action problem. Hence, the primary function of statutory audits is to reduce opportunism and to address conflicts costs by providing additional information in the auditor report, thereby increasing the credibility of financial reporting (Ng, 1978).

Germany's large and medium-sized limited liability companies must engage an external auditor (§ 316 (1) HGB). If a limited liability parent company is obliged to prepare consolidated financial statements, it must engage a group auditor (§ 316 (2) HGB). Very large unlimited liability companies are essential to the German economy and must therefore also have a statutory auditor (§ 6 PublG). The same applies to consolidated financial statements of unlimited liability companies (§ 14 (1) PublG) if they exceed the same size criteria as those for individual financial statements (§ 11 (1) PublG). Above and beyond that, external audits are mandatory for all banks (§ 340k HGB), insurance companies (§ 341k HGB), and cooperatives (§ 53 GenG, *Genossenschaftsgesetz*–Cooperative Act). Statutory audits can be performed by certified public accountants (*Wirtschaftsprüfer*) or public accounting firms (*Wirtschaftsprüfungsgesellschaften*). Small GmbHs can also be audited by so-called *vereidigte Buchprüfer* (a lower qualification in auditing that still exists for historical reasons) and related firms. In addition, cooperatives and savings banks have a particular external auditing system (Marten et al., 2020).

According to § 317 HGB, the audit covers the financial statements comprising the balance sheet, income statement, and notes, and in the case of group audits, the cash flow statement and equity analysis. Moreover, the auditor must check whether the management report accurately presents the company's situation. In the case of a listed company, the auditor must also check whether the management board has implemented an internal control and a risk management system and whether these systems are effective. In contrast, the company's long-term ability to continue as a going concern, its economic situation, and the quality of management are not subject to statutory audits (§ 317 (4a) HGB).

The German Commercial Code lists situations incompatible with a statutory auditor's function to ensure auditor independence, for example, providing certain non-audit services (financial accounting, internal auditing, management, financial, and valuation services; § 319 (3) HGB). Moreover, there is a mandatory audit partner rotation after 5 years for audits of public interest entities (§ 43 (6) WPO, *Wirtschaftsprüferordnung*–Public Accountants Act). For audits of public interest entities, additional independence-related restrictions are provided by the EU

Table 2.3 Civil liability caps

	Civil liability cap [€]	
	Ordinary Negligence	Gross Negligence
Capital market-oriented companies	16,000,000	Unlimited
Non-capital market-oriented banks and insurance companies	4,000,000	32,000,000
Others	1,500,000	12,000,000

Regulation 537/2014. Specifically, there is a cap for non-audit service fees (70% of the audit fees earned from that client), and there is audit firm rotation after 10 years.

Auditors and audit firms that perform statutory audits must undergo external quality controls performed by peers (§ 57a WPO). In addition, if an auditor or an audit firm performs statutory audits of public interest entities, they are covered by inspections conducted by the auditor oversight board (§ 62b WPO). The German auditor oversight system is considered less strict than that in the United States (Eilifsen et al., 2018). Prior research has shown that audit quality increases with an increased liability exposure of auditors.

In Germany, however, auditors' civil liability is capped in cases of negligent misconduct (see Table 2.3), which is one reason for the low investor protection (Quick, 2021).

2.10 Summary and Conclusion

To understand Germany's economic structure, it is necessary to consider its economically active population of 46.1 million individuals, constituting 55% of the total population. The nation boasts an impressive employment rate of 80.4%, underscoring the vitality of its labor force. The robust German economy is further evident in its Gross Domestic Product (GDP), which grew by 0.1% in the third trimester of 2024 compared to the same period of the previous year, despite facing challenges. In absolute terms, Germany's GDP in 2023 reached approximately 4.19 trillion Euros, according to (Destatis 2024c).

Within this context, Germany applies a stakeholder model of corporate governance. Capital from the stock exchange is less relevant than in Anglo-Saxon countries, and banks are an important source of finance for the German economy. Consequently, there is a bank-centric corporate governance model, and these institutions influence the governance system. The capital market is monitored by three institutions: the Trading Surveillance Office; the Exchange Supervisory Authority of the Federal States, and the Federal Financial Supervisory.

German corporate governance is grounded on a Civil Law system and applies a two-tier corporate governance model. Within this model, a supervisory board controls the management board responsible for managing the company and separating management and control. In addition, banks play an essential role in companies' supervisory boards. In addition to the legal system, the German Corporate Governance Code is a sub-statutory guide with principles, recommendations, and suggestions on how to manage best and supervise companies listed in the German capital market.

Using a two-tier system has the advantage of strengthening the independence of the supervisory board. However, non-executive directors have more proximity to operations and management decisions and greater access to information than supervisory board members in single-level systems. Therefore, the effectiveness of monitoring can be superior in a one-tier system.

In Germany, minority shareholders have a smaller presence than in other markets, which may explain their reduced protection and influence. As a result, minority shareholders are more susceptible to expropriation by majority shareholders in the German model, compared to shareholder-oriented models. In this context, the challenges related to information asymmetry, opportunism, and potential conflict of interest become more evident, highlighting the crucial need to establish regulations emphasizing the importance of information disclosure. In addition, it is necessary to implement corporate governance mechanisms that mitigate the problems of relations between majority and minority.

Moreover, another particularity of German corporate governance is the codetermination model, which means that employees participate in decisions and control. On the one hand, they are represented on the supervisory boards. On the other hand, they take part via work councils. In this way, the German model encourages strategic decision-making that involves employee participation on the supervisory board, resulting in potential efficiency gains. In addition, the principle of codetermination ensures that employee representatives have access to the same information that is available to shareholder representatives. This mechanism helps mitigate information asymmetries, potentially preventing opportunism and reducing conflict costs such as costly strikes. Furthermore, codetermination facilitates collaboration between employers and employees, promoting a harmonious approach to labor relations.

Despite various reforms with the intent of harmonization, there are still particularities of the German financial accounting system, which is dominated by the objective of creditor protection and the principle of prudence. An essential characteristic of auditing in Germany is the capped liability of auditors. Finally, this chapter has highlighted some strengths and weaknesses of the German corporate governance model, which, nevertheless, may be well suited for the future, for example, because of a growing focus on corporate social responsibility.

References

Akerlof, G. A. (1978). The market for "lemons": Quality uncertainty and the mechanism market. *Uncertainty in Economics, 84*(3), 235–251.

Arrow, K. J. (1978). Uncertainty and the welfare economics of medical care. In *Uncertainty in economics* (pp. 345–375). Academic Press.

BaFin, Federal Financial Supervisory Authority. (2024). *About BaFin*. Retrieved December 3, 2024, from https://www.bafin.de/EN/DieBaFin/diebafin_node_en.html

Becht, M., & Boehmer, E. (2003). Voting control in German corporations. *International Review of Law and Economics, 23*(1), 1–29.

Beckmann, K. M. (2022). Green and more: deutlicher Nachhaltigkeitsfokus im Entwurf des DCGK 2022. *Die Wirtschaftsprüfung, 75*(8), 479–486.

Behr, P., & Schmidt, R. H. (2015). *The German banking system: Characteristics and challenges*. SAFE White Paper No. 32.

Berglöf, E. (2000). Reforming corporate governance: Redirecting the European agenda. *Economic Policy, 12*(24), 91–123.

Bottenberg, K., Tuschke, A., & Flickinger, M. (2017). Corporate governance between shareholder and stakeholder orientation: Lessons from Germany. *Journal of Management Inquiry, 26*(2), 165–180.

Bundesagentur für Arbeit. (2024). *Arbeitslosenquote & Arbeitslosenzahlen 2024*. Retrieved December 7, 2024, from https://www.arbeitsagentur.de/news/arbeitsmarkt

Cable, J. (1985). Capital market information and industrial performance: The role of west German banks. *The Economic Journal, 95*(March), 118–132.

Chhillar, P., & Lellapalli, R. V. (2015). Divergence or convergence: Paradoxes in corporate governance? *Corporate Governance, 15*(5), 693–705.

Chirinko, R. S., & Elston, J. A. (2006). Finance, control, and profitability: The influence of German banks. *Journal of Economic Behavior & Organization, 59*(1), 69–88.

Cromme, G. (2005). Corporate governance in Germany and the German corporate governance code. *Corporate Governance: An International Review, 13*(3), 362–367.

Dammann, J., & Eidenmüller, H. (2021). Codetermination: A poor fit for U.S. corporations. *Columbia Business Law Review, 2020*(3), 870–941.

Destatis, Federal Statistical Office. (2024a). *Einwohner Deutschlands und seiner Nachbarstaaten im Jahr 2024*. Retrieved December 7, 2024, from https://de.statista.com/statistik/daten/studie/1331425/umfrage/bevoelkerung-der-nachbarlaender-deutschlands/

Destatis, Federal Statistical Office. (2024b). *Europäische Union: Erwerbsquoten in den Mitgliedstaaten, aufgeschlüsselt nach Geschlecht im 2. Quartal 2024*. Retrieved December 7, 2024, from https://de.statista.com/statistik/daten/studie/188794/umfrage/erwerbsquote-in-den-eu-laendern/

Destatis, Federal Statistical Office. (2024c). *National accounts, domestic product Gross domestic creation (GDP)*. Retrieved December 7, 2024, from https://www.destatis.de/EN/Themes/Economy/National-Accounts-Domestic-Product/Tables/gdp-bubbles.html

Destatis, Federal Statistical Office. (2024d, November 28). *Pressemitteilung Nr. 448 vom*. Retrieved December 7, 2024, from https://www.destatis.de/DE/Presse/Pressemitteilungen/2024/11/PD24_448_611.html#:~:text=Harmonisierter%20Verbraucherpreisindex%2C%20November%202024%3A&text=Wie%20das%20Statistische%20Bundesamt%20(Destatis,2024%20um%200%2C2%20%25

Deutsche Börse Group. (2023). *General Terms and Conditions of Deutsche Börse AG for the Regulated Unofficial Market (Freiverkehr) on Frankfurter Wertpapierbörse*. Retrieved December 3, 2024, from https://www.deutsche-boerse-cash-market.com/resource/blob/297574/97b037404b632f5c731fe7313e26c9f5/data/2023_10_10_dbag_agb_freiverkehr_en.pdf

Deutsche Börse Group. (2024a). *Annual report 2023*. Retrieved November 10, 2024, from https://deutsche-boerse.com/resource/blob/3812002/b934c928e41adafe176865bd66c5fead/data/annual-report-2023_tug_jahresfinanzbericht_de.pdf

Deutsche Börse Group. (2024b). *Unser purpose*. Retrieved December 3, 2024, from https://www.deutsche-boerse.com/dbg-de/ueber-uns/gruppe-deutsche-boerse/purpose

Deutsche Börse Group. (2024c). *DAX – Benchmark and barometer for the German economy*. Retrieved December 3, 2024, from https://www.deutsche-boerse.com/dbg-de/media/news-stories/explainers/DAX-Index-Benchmark-und-Barometer-f-r-die-deutsche-Wirtschaft-148654

Deutsche Börse Group. (2024d). *Our markets*. Retrieved December 3, 2024, from https://www.deutsche-boerse-cash-market.com/dbcm-en/primary-market/going-public/markets

Deutsche Börse Group. (2024e). *GEX German Entrepreneurial Index*. Retrieved December 3, 2024, from https://www.deutsche-boerse.com/dbg-en/about-us/contact/glossary/glossary-article/GEX-246202

Deutsche Börse Group. (2024f). *Market Surveillance in Germany*. Retrieved December 3, 2024, from https://www.deutsche-boerse-cash-market.com/dbcm-en/about-us/organisation-of-the-fwb/market-surveillance-in-germany

Deutsche Börse Group. (2024g). *Listed companies*. Retrieved December 7, 2024, from https://www.deutsche-boerse-cash-market.com/dbcm-de/instrumente-statistiken/statistiken/gelistete-unternehmen

Deutsche Bundesbank. (2012). Die langfristige Entwicklung der Unternehmensfinanzierung in Deutschland – Ergebnisse der gesamtwirtschaftlichen Finanzierungsrechnung. *Monatsberichte der Deutschen Bundesbank, 64*(1), 13–28.

Dittmann, I., Maug, E., & Schneider, C. (2010). Bankers on the boards of German firms: What they do, what they are worth, and why they are (still) there. *Review of Finance, 14*(1), 35–71.

Du Plessis, J. (2004). The German two-tier board and the German corporate governance code. *European Business Law Review, 15*(5), 1139–1164.

Edwards, J. S., Eggert, W., & Weichenrieder, A. J. (2009). Corporate governance and pay for performance: Evidence from Germany. *Economics of Governance, 10*(1), 1–26.

Eilifsen, A., Quick, R., Schmidt, F., & Umlauf, S. (2018). Investors' perceptions of nonaudit services and their type in Germany: The financial crisis as a turning point. *International Journal of Auditing, 22*(2), 298–316.

Elsas, R., & Krahnen, J. P. (2004). Universal banks and the relationship with firms. In J. P. Krahnen & R. H. Schmidt (Eds.), *The German financial system* (pp. 197–232). Oxford University Press.

European Council. (2022). *Council and European Parliament agree to improve gender balance on company boards*. Retrieved December 3, 2024, from https://www.consilium.europa.eu/en/press/press-releases/2022/06/07/council-and-european-parliament-agree-to-improve-gender-balance-on-company-boards/

European Parliament and Council. (2022). *Directive (EU) 2022/2464 of the European Parliament and of the Council of 14 December 2022 amending Regulation (EU) No 537/2014, Directive 2004/109/EC, Directive 2006/43/EC and Directive 2013/34/EU, as regards corporate sustainability reporting*. Retrieved December 3, 2024, from https://eur-lex.europa.eu/legal-content/EN/TXT/PDF/?uri=CELEX:32022L2464

Favara, M. G. (2003). *An empirical reassessment of the relationship between finance and growth* (Vol. 03, p. 1). International Monetary Fund.

FitzRoy, F., & Kraft, K. (2005). Co-determination, efficiency, and productivity. *British Journal of Industrial Relations, 43*(2), 233–247.

Fohlin, C. (2005). The history of corporate ownership and control in Germany. In *A history of corporate governance around the world* (pp. 223–277). National Bureau of Economic Research.

Franks, J., & Mayer, C. (2001). Ownership and control of German corporations. *The Review of Financial Studies, 14*(4), 943–977.

Frege, C. M. (2002). A critical assessment of the theoretical and empirical research on German work councils. *British Journal of Industrial Relations, 40*(2), 221–248.

Goergen, M., Manjon, M. C., & Renneboog, L. (2008a). Is the German system of corporate governance converging towards the Anglo-American model? *Journal of Management & Governance, 12*(1), 37–71.

Goergen, M., Manjon, M. C., & Renneboog, L. (2008b). Recent developments in German corporate governance. *International Review of Law and Economics, 28*(3), 175–193.

Grundei, J., & Talaulicar, T. (2002). Company law and corporate governance of start-ups in Germany: Legal stipulations, managerial requirements, and modification strategies. *Journal of Corporate Governance, 6*, 1–27.

Gul, F. A., Zhou, G. S., & Zhu, X. K. (2013). Investor protection, firm informational problems, Big N auditors, and cost of debt around the world. *Auditing: A Journal of Practice & Theory, 32*(3), 1–30.

Hackethal, A. (2004). German banks and banking structure. In J. P. Krahnen & R. H. Schmidt (Eds.), *The German financial system* (pp. 71–105). Oxford University Press.

Hackethal, A., Schmidt, R. H., & Tyrell, M. (2005). Banks and German corporate governance: On the way to a capital market-based system? *Corporate Governance: An International Review, 13*(3), 397–407.

Harcourt, M., Gall, G., Wilkinson, A., Croucher, R., & Lam, H. (2020). Using the endowment effect to explain managerial resistance towards codetermination: Implications for employment relations from the German case. *Human Resource Management Journal, 30*(1), 149–163.

Hardie, I., & Howarth, D. (2009). Die Krise but not La Crise? The financial crisis and the transformation. *Journal of Common Market Studies, 47*(5), 1017–1039.

Hayden, G. M., & Bodie, M. T. (2021). Codetermination in theory and practice. *Florida Law Review, 73*(2), 321–358.

Hennrichs, J. (2008). IFRS und Mittelstand – Auswirkungen der Gmbh-Reform und Zukunft der Kapitalerhaltung. *Zeitschrift für Unternehmens- und Gesellschaftsrecht, 73*(2–3), 361–380.

Hohenfels, D., & Quick, R. (2020). Non-audit services and audit quality: Evidence from Germany. *Review of Managerial Science, 14*(5), 959–1007.

Holmstrom, B., & Kaplan, S. (2001). Corporate governance and merger activity in the United States: Making sense of the 1980s and 1990s. *Journal of Economic Perspectives, 15*(2), 121–144.

Hopt, K. J., & Leyens, P. C. (2004). Board models in Europe–recent developments of internal corporate governance structures in Germany, the United Kingdom, France, and Italy. *European Company and Financial Law Review, 1*, 135–168.

International Monetary Fund. (2016). *Germany: Financial sector assessment program. Financial system stability assessment*. Retrieved December 3, 2024, from https://www.imf.org/external/pubs/ft/scr/2016/cr16189.pdf

Jensen, M. C., & Meckling, W. H. (1976). Theory of the firm: Managerial behavior, agency costs, and ownership structure. *Journal of Financial Economics, 3*(4), 305–360.

Jungmann, C. (2006). The effectiveness of corporate governance in one-tier and two-tier board systems – Evidence from the U.K. and Germany. *European Company and Financial Law Review, 3*(4), 426–474.

Kaske, T. (2002). The co-existence of common law systems and civil law systems in modern society: A comparison between the legal system s of New Zealand and Germany. *Canterbury Law Review, 8*, 395–424.

La Porta, R., Lopez-de-Silanes, F., Shleifer, A., & Vishny, R. W. (1997). Legal determinants of external finance. *The Journal of Finance, 52*(3), 1131–1150.

La Porta, R., Lopez-de-Silanes, F., Shleifer, A., & Vishny, R. (2000). Investor protection and corporate governance. *Journal of Financial Economics, 58*(1–2), 3–27.

Lahmann, D. (1999). Rechtsformen im Vergleich. Die KGaA als Alterntive. *Going Public*, Sonderausgabe Praxis, 14–16.

Lazarides, T., & Drimpetas, E. (2010). Corporate governance regulatory convergence: A remedy for the wrong problem. *International Journal of Law and Management, 52*(3), 182–192.

Marten, K.-U., Quick, R., & Ruhnke, K. (2020). *Wirtschaftsprüfung. Grundlagen des betriebswirtschaftlichen Prüfungswesens nach nationalen und internationalen Normen* (6th ed.). Schäffer-Poeschel-Verlag.

Morck, R. K. (Ed.). (2005). *A history of corporate governance around the world*. National Bureau of Economic Research - NBER.

Ng, D. (1978). An information economics analysis of financial reporting and external auditing. *The Accounting Review, 53*(4), 910–920.

OECD. (2016). *G20/OECD principles of corporate governance*. OECD Éditions. https://doi.org/10.1787/9789264236882-en. Retrieved December 3, 2024, from https://www.oecd-ilibrary.org/governance/g20-oecd-principles-of-corporate-governance-2015_9789264236882-en,

Paster, T. (2012). Do German employers support board-level codetermination? The paradox of individual support and collective opposition. *Socio-Economic Review, 10*(3), 471–495.

Peemöller, V. H., Krehl, H., Hofmann, S., & Jack, J. (2020). *Bilanzskandale: Delikte und Gegenmaßnahmen*. Erich Schmidt Verlag.

Quick, R. (2021). Maßnahmen zur Steigerung der Jahresabschlussprüfungsqualität – derzeitige Regulierungsdiskussion und wissenschaftliche Evidenz. *RWZ – Zeitschrift für Recht und Rechnungswesen, 31*(7–8), 222–231.

Quick, R., & Henrizi, P. (2019). Experimental evidence on external auditor reliance on the internal audit. *Review of Managerial Science, 13*(5), 1143–1176.

Quick, R., & Sayar, S. (2021). The impact of assurance on compliance management systems on bank directors' decisions. *International Journal of Auditing, 25*(1), 3–23.

Quick, R., & Schmidt, F. (2018). Do audit firm rotation, auditor retention, and joint audits matter?—An experimental investigation of bank directors' and institutional investors' perceptions. *Journal of Accounting Literature, 41*(1), 1–21.

Quick, R., Schenk, N., Schmidt, F., & Towara, T. (2018). The impact of corporate governance on auditor choice: Evidence from Germany. *Journal of Management and Governance, 22*(2), 251–283.

Rahman, M., & Carpano, C. (2017). National corporate social policy, corporate governance systems, and organizational capabilities. *Corporate Governance: The International Journal of Business in Society, 17*(1), 13–29.

Raiser, T. (1988). The theory of enterprise law in the Federal Republic of Germany. *American Journal of Company Law, 36*(1), 111–129.

Regierungskommission. (2022). *German Corporate Governance Code*. Retrieved December 3, 2024, from https://www.dcgk.de/files/dcgk/usercontent/de/download/kodex/220517_Deutscher_Corporate_Governance_Kodex_2022.pdf

Regierungskommission. (2024). *Members of the Regierungskommission Deutscher Corporate Governance Kodex*. Retrieved December 3, 2024, from https://www.dcgk.de/en/kommission-33/members.html

Regierungskommission. (n.d.). *Geschäftsordnung*. Retrieved December 3, 2024, from https://www.dcgk.de//files/dcgk/usercontent/de/download/geschaeftsordnung/140414_Geschaeftsordnung_RegKom.pdf

Roe, M. J. (1998). German codetermination and German securities markets. *Columbia Business Law Review, 1*, 167–183.

Rose, C. (2005). The composition of semi-two-tier corporate boards and firm performance. *Corporate Governance: An International Review, 13*(5), 691–701.

Rühmkorf, A., Spindler, F., & Samanta, N. (2019). Evolution of German corporate governance (1995-2014): An empirical analysis. *Corporate Governance, 19*(5), 1042–1062.

Sandrock, O. (2015). German and international perspectives of the German model of codetermination. *European Business Law Review, 26*(1), 129–146.

Scholz, R., & Vitols, S. (2019). Board-level codetermination: A driving force for corporate social responsibility in German companies? *European Journal of Industrial Relations, 25*(3), 233–246.

Steding, R. (2003). Rechtsformen des Gesellschaftsrechts. Kommanditgesellschaft (KG). *Betrieb und Wirtschaft, 57*, 469–471.

Tuschke, A., & Luber, M. (2012). Corporate governance in Germany: Converging towards shareholder value-orientation or not so much? In *The convergence of corporate governance* (pp. 75–92). Palgrave Macmillan.

Wellisch, D., Neidhardt, L., & Zeitz, M. (2002). Praxisorientierte Informationen zur Unternehmensgründung. Teil I: Rechtsformalternativen und deren Eignung für Unternehmensgründer. *Betrieb und Wirtschaft, 56*(7), 299–307.

Williamson, O. E. (1975). *Markets and hierarchies: Analysis and antitrust implications: A study in the economics of internal organization*. University of Illinois at Urbana-Champaign's Academy for Entrepreneurial Leadership Historical Research Reference in Entrepreneurship.

Wulf, I., Niemöller, J., & Rentzsch, N. (2014). Development toward integrated reporting, and its impact on corporate governance: A two-dimensional approach to accounting with reference to the German two-tier system. *Journal of Management Control, 25*, 135–164.

Chapter 3
Singapore

Corporate Governance in Singapore

Luciano Bohn and Ding Jun Toh

3.1 Introduction

Singapore is a small city-state (approximately 710 square kilometers in size) made up of one main island, where most of the population dwells, and approximately 60 small islands; most of which are uninhabited or used for military purposes. Strategically located at the southern end of the Malay Peninsular and blessed with natural deep waters, Singapore has historically been a crucial entrepot for trade flowing east to west, and from west to east. In 1819, Sir Stamford Raffles (British) founded a trading and shipping outpost on the island. The entire island subsequently became a British colony in 1824 (Ann, 2016). This remained the case until the Second World War when the island was occupied by the invading Japanese forces from 1942 to 1945. After the war, the British re-took control of the island. In 1963, Singapore ceased to be a colony of England, and together with Malaya, North Borneo, and Sarawak, formed the Federation of Malaysia. Shortly thereafter, in 1965, Singapore became an independent nation from Malaysia, with the main reason for the split being the racial tensions that were simmering between the Chinese (the racial majority in Singapore), and the Malays (the racial majority in Malaysia).

Prime Minister Lee Kuan Yew, leader of the People's Action Party (PAP), governed the country until 1990 and, together with the rest of his cabinet, shaped the trajectory of Singapore's economic and political development. Through an uncompromising insistence on incorruptibility, transparency, and accountability, as well as

L. Bohn (✉)
Dom Bosco College, Porto Alegre, Brazil
e-mail: luciano@faculdadedombosco.edu.br

D. J. Toh
National University of Singapore, Singapore, Singapore
e-mail: toh_dj@nus.edu.sg

C. B. Macagnan (ed.), *Corporate Governance in Capital Markets*, CSR, Sustainability, Ethics & Governance,
https://doi.org/10.1007/978-3-031-94751-3_3

focusing intense efforts to modernize the economy and keeping it open to foreign investments, the PAP government has enabled Singapore to progress from a developing to a developed country within 30 years of the country's independence from Malaysia. This stands in contrast to other Southeast Asian countries, which are still considered developing countries (Gracia & Siregar, 2021).

Today, Singapore has a cosmopolitan outlook with a stable multiracial society, with a population size of almost 6 million people (DOS, 2024). Singapore has four main racial communities: Chinese (the majority), Malays, Indians, and Eurasians. Due to her multiracial and multi-religious character, the country has adopted policies to promote and ensure racial and religious harmony. For example, English was adopted as the official language as part of the government's effort to bridge the social divides that then existed between the different races, where each had their mother tongue. Another example is the existence of the Maintenance of Religious Harmony Act 1990, which was enacted to safeguard the separation of religion and politics and to ensure moderate religious influences in Singapore (SSO, 2024a).

Singapore has a parliamentary democracy system, with the ruling party, the PAP, being in power for almost 60 consecutive years. Singapore has three branches of government: the legislature, which is elected by the population and is tasked with law-making; the executive, which implements the law; and the judiciary, which is responsible for interpreting and applying the law (SSO, 2024b). Additionally, the country is a member of the Association of Southeast Asian Nations, along with countries like Thailand, the Philippines, Malaysia, Indonesia, Brunei, Vietnam, Myanmar, Laos, and Cambodia. Singapore's nominal GDP in 2023 was S$673.3 billion (DOS, 2023).

At the heart of Singapore's economic success is its regulators' "continuous commitment to keeping pace with the highest global standards of corporate governance" (Lan, 2022). Since its independence in 1965, Singapore has faced many economic crises and corporate mismanagement scandals—for example, the Pan-Electric crisis of 1985 which resulted in the closure of the then Stock Exchange of Singapore (the predecessor to the current Singapore Exchange, also known as SGX), the first and only time in its history (MAS, 2024); as well as the Global Financial Crisis of 2008. More recently, Singapore's regulators had to deal with the poor corporate governance and mismanagement of local companies Hyflux Ltd (The Straits Times, 2022) and Hin Leong Trading Pte Ltd (Reuters, 2020).

Financial crises often shock policymakers and regulators out of their slumber and complacency, to swing into regulatory action, due to the sheer extent of individuals affected. This occurred in the aftermath of the 2008 Global Financial Crisis. In Asia, the Asian Financial Crisis of 1997, precipitated by the speculative attack on the Thai Baht, was the watershed event that triggered many Asian countries to undertake corporate governance reforms, as the prevailing standards were found to be not only inadequate but also had exacerbated the adverse impact of the subsequent fallout (Nam & Nam, 2004). Key governance concerns included a general lack of financial disclosures, low transparency, and weak legal protection for minority shareholders. In response, national regulators across the region have made sustained efforts to improve governance standards by introducing various governance codes, guidelines, mechanisms, and best practices (Ramachandran et al., 2020).

The purpose of this chapter is to analyze Singapore's corporate governance practices which, like many Asian countries, gained momentum as a direct consequence of the Asian Financial Crisis. Singapore's first Code of Corporate Governance, seen as the bedrock and foundation of corporate governance in Singapore, was introduced in 2001 and came into effect in 2003 (SID, 2011). For this chapter, "corporate governance" is defined as "the system by which companies are directed and controlled" (Cadbury, 1992). This definition is to be broadly construed—it encompasses the combination of laws, regulations, listing rules, and voluntary private sector practices that enable the corporation to attract capital, perform efficiently, achieve the corporate objective, and meet both legal obligations and general societal expectations (Gregory, 2000). Like the experiences of other Asian countries, Singaporean companies largely have a concentrated ownership structure that is either controlled by the family or the state (Dixit et al., 2021). This, in turn, allows such owners (especially those held by families) to blur the lines between corporate and familial interests and pursue their private interests at the expense of minority shareholders (Nam & Nam, 2004). This chapter therefore aims to mainly analyze capital market regulation, corporate control, and the level of protection provided to shareholders.

This chapter has been structured in the following order: Part 2 introduces Singapore's capital market, Part 3 states the corporate forms and corporate ownership that can be found in Singapore, Parts 4 and 5 lays out the relevant legislation and rules that apply to publicly listed companies, Part 6 introduces the corporate governance structure found in publicly listed companies in Singapore, Part 7 examines the auditing standards that apply to publicly listed companies in Singapore. To the extent possible, primary sources have been referred to. This is accompanied by secondary information from academic articles found through a systematic literature review.

3.2 Capital Market (Regulatory Bodies and Stock Exchange)

The Monetary Authority of Singapore (MAS), Singapore's closest equivalent to the Financial Conduct Authority in the United Kingdom, is Singapore's central bank and integrated financial regulator. It is responsible for administering various statutes relating to currency, banking, insurance, securities, and the financial sector in general. Beyond this role, MAS has also been given the power to act as a banker and financial agent of the Singapore government, as well as being entrusted with the responsibility of promoting monetary stability in Singapore's economy. Thus, MAS' mission is "to promote sustained non-inflationary economic growth, and a sound and progressive financial center" and, in this regard, seeks to "support and foster a culture of zero tolerance towards fraud and other misconduct" (MAS, 2021a).

Singapore's Ministry of Finance (MOF) is responsible for managing fiscal policies and the structure of the country's economy. It works to maintain international standards and best practices in areas such as company law, accounting standards, and corporate governance. MOF thus plays a key role in upholding and constantly reviewing the relevant regulatory statutes such as the Accountants Act 2004, Accounting Standards Act 2007, Business Names Registration Act 2014, Companies Act 1967, Limited Partnerships Act 2008, and the Limited Liability Partnerships Act 2005. For example, in 2007, the MOF set up a steering committee to carry out a fundamental review of the Companies Act 1967, intending to modernize the statute's provisions to provide a conducive, effective, and efficient regulatory framework for setting up and doing business in Singapore; keep pace with relevant international legal developments and technological advances; provide flexibility and clarity to directors and management of enterprises in the operation of corporate entities, without harming the interests of stakeholders and the public; maintain an appropriate balance in the use of statutory provisions and non-statutory standards in regulating corporate behavior; and to promote greater accountability and transparency while keeping compliance costs low and manageable (MOF, 2011). This review ultimately resulted in the largest number of amendments being made in 2014 to the Companies Act since it was first enacted in 1967 (ACRA, 2014). Finally, MOF is also responsible for formulating the country's annual budget, all the while ensuring that Singapore's financial reserves are optimally managed to ensure the government's fiscal sustainability in the medium to long term (MOF, 2021).

Therefore, the MOF and MAS play a direct role in influencing the debate on corporate governance in Singapore and shaping corporate governance reforms. However, it is essential to highlight that other organizations contribute to Singapore's formal institutional system, such as the Securities Industry Council (SIC); the Accounting and Corporate Regulatory Authority (ACRA); the Inland Revenue Authority of Singapore (IRAS); the Institute of Singapore Chartered Accountants (ISCA); the Singapore Institute of Directors (SID); and the Singapore Exchange Limited (SGX). Each of these organizations will be discussed in turn.

The Securities Industry Council, or SIC, rules the non-statutory Singapore Code on Takeovers and Mergers (Take-over Code)(SIC, 2021). It has powers under the law to investigate any deal with securities that relates to a takeover or a merger transaction. SIC also reviews takeover rules and practices periodically and recommends changes for promulgation by the MAS. Additionally, the SIC issues guidance notes on the application of specific principles or rules found within the Take-over Code (MAS, 2019a). The Take-over Code is issued by the MAS according to section 321 of the Securities and Futures Act 2001. It primarily applies to listed public companies, listed registered business trusts, and real estate investment trusts. Unlisted public companies and unlisted registered business trusts with more than 50 shareholders or unitholders (as the case may be), and with net tangible assets of S$5 million or more must also observe the letter and spirit of the Take-over Code where appropriate (MAS, 2019b), although the former (unlisted companies) may seek a waiver of the Take-over Code's application under the Practice Statement on the Waiver of the Application of the Singapore Code on Takeovers and Mergers to Unlisted Public Companies (MAS, 2019c). For completeness, the Takeover Code does not apply to takeovers or mergers of other unlisted public companies and unlisted business trusts, or private companies.

The Takeover Code does not have the force of law due to its non-statutory nature. Its primary objective is to promote the fair and equal treatment of all shareholders in takeovers or mergers. In this regard, it states that shareholders in the company subject to a take-over offer must be given sufficient information, advice, and time to consider and decide on the offer. Thus, the Takeover Code can be better understood as ensuring procedural fairness, rather than substantive fairness, for example, whether the transaction is financially or commercially advantageous. Notwithstanding the fact that the Takeover Code has no force of law, if the SIC finds that the Take over Code has been breached, it may issue a private reprimand or public censure or, in a more severe case, take further action, including penalties designed to deprive the offender temporarily or permanently of its ability to enjoy the facilities of the securities market.

The Accounting and Corporate Regulatory Authority, or ACRA, Singapore's closest equivalent to the Financial Reporting Council in the United Kingdom, is the regulator of business registration, financial reporting, public accountants, and corporate service providers. It is also responsible for developing the accountancy sector and setting the accounting standards for companies, charities, cooperative societies, and societies in Singapore. Ultimately, ACRA seeks to "foster a vibrant and trusted business environment that enables innovation and growth" (ACRA, 2021a).

The Inland Revenue Authority Singapore, or IRAS, collects income tax, goods and services tax, property tax, property sale/purchase tax, gambling tax, and inheritance tax (IRAS, 2021). The fundamental tenet of Singapore's tax policy is to keep tax rates competitive both for corporations as well as individuals. The country's maximum marginal corporate tax rate is 17%. There is no tax payable on dividends paid to shareholders nor any tax on capital gains resulting from the sale of shares. Therefore, unlike in some significant economies (i.e., the USA), the high tax rate or differing tax treatment between capital gains and dividends in Singapore does not create friction costs (Ganguli et al., 2020). By granting income tax exemption on dividends, Singapore creates a highly competitive environment from a business perspective, in terms of her taxation regime as compared to other ASEAN countries such as the Philippines, Indonesia, and Thailand (Oktavia, 2020).

The Institute of Singapore Chartered Accountants, or ISCA, is the national accountancy body in Singapore. Starting in 1963 as the Singapore Society of Accountants, ISCA was first reconstituted as the Institute of Certified Public Accountants of Singapore under the Accountants Act 1987, before changing to its current name in 2013 (ISCA, 2024). ISCA's stated mission is to, first, represent their members on matters affecting and of interest to the profession; second, influence the development of the accountancy profession and ecosystem positively; third, serve the public interest by helping to instill sound values and ensuring right ethical standards among their members and the profession; and finally, enable their members to achieve their professional aspirations (ISCA, 2024).

The Singapore Institute of Directors, or the SID, is the national association for company directors. Established in 1998, following the Asian Financial Crisis in 1997, the SID makes it their mission to transform boards and empower board directors to be champions of good governance by building competencies and capabilities to enhance the boardroom skills of directors for informed decision-making. In advocating for good governance, the SID advances thought leadership on corporate governance and directorship issues. The SID is also at the forefront of efforts to drive climate action on boards (SID, 2024a). In 2024, it officially launched its SID Director Accreditation program to encourage directors to build their competencies in eight important domains: governance; director duties and practices; financial proficiency; risk management; strategy development; digital proficiency; human capital; and finally, sustainability fundamentals (SID, 2024b).

Singapore's stock exchange is operated by the Singapore Exchange Limited, also known as the SGX, an investment holding company that provides full service for equities, fixed income, derivatives, commodities, and foreign currency exchange. Singapore Exchange Limited itself is a publicly traded company listed on the stock exchange it manages. In 1999, the merger of three separate entities—the Stock Exchange of Singapore, the Singapore International Monetary Exchange, and the Securities Clearing and Computer Services Pte Ltd resulted in the creation of the SGX. SGX lists equities, bonds, options contracts, foreign exchange, and commodities products after it acquired the Singapore Commodity Exchange Ltd in 2008. Although located in Singapore, SGX has a global reach with holdings in several regional exchanges worldwide (Chen, 2021). Top listings on the SGX Mainboard include real estate, banking, shipping, and oil and gas companies, although significant representation exists in the consumer staples and healthcare sectors. Besides the Mainboard, SGX also allows fast-growing companies to list on its Catalist platform. Catalist adopts a sponsorship system, i.e., a listing applicant can be listed so long as its full sponsors deem it fit to do so (SGX, 2024a). DBS Bank, Singtel, CapitaLand Investment, UOB Bank, and Yangzijiang Shipbuilding (Holdings) Ltd are among the top listed companies on the SGX Mainboard in terms of market capitalization (Chen, 2021). According to its Market Statistics Report, as of June 2024, SGX had a total of 623 listed securities with a total market capitalization of close to S$800 billion (SGX, 2024b).

The SGX plays a crucial role in the corporate governance of listed companies, through the promulgation of the SGX Mainboard Rules, as well as the SGX Catalist Rules. Both sets of rules are broadly similar. As various provisions will subsequently be discussed in greater detail, in Part 5 of this chapter, it suffices for present purposes to state that the rules are largely concerned with ensuring that trading on the SGX is conducted in a fair, orderly, and transparent manner. Important rules include those governing prospectuses, continuing obligations which listed companies come under, interested person transactions, significant transactions, as well as takeovers.

Taken together, the MOF, the MAS, and other previously mentioned regulatory bodies have enabled Singapore to develop an attractive corporate governance framework, making it a trusted venue for trade to take place. Singapore's political and economic stability, low corruption, pro-business policies, favorable tax structure, well-established legal system, market transparency, and bureaucratic efficiency have resulted in the country being seen as Southeast Asia's de facto financial hub, with certain observers calling her "The Switzerland of Asia" (Hsieh & Nieh, 2010). As the only stock exchange based in Singapore, the SGX has certainly benefited from this climate, leading it to be considered one of Asia's leading exchanges (Lim & Cheong, 2017).

3.3 Corporate Forms and Corporate Ownership

This part first examines the diverse corporate structures that businesses in Singapore can adopt. It thereafter examines corporate ownership in Singapore. A comprehensive understanding of these aspects is fundamental to understanding the corporate governance system, which is designed to mitigate problems of information asymmetric, opportunism, and conflict of interest.

3.3.1 Corporate Forms

There are five main types of corporate form that a business may be established in Singapore:

(1) Sole proprietorships (one owner);
(2) General partnerships (two or more owners);
(3) Limited partnerships;
(4) Limited liability partnerships; and
(5) Companies.

The use of a company as a business vehicle is now the most popular choice around the world. Singapore is no exception. Five common features can be found in most companies. First, it has a separate legal personality. Second, it has limited liability, which means that the company's shareholders' assets are protected from being seized by the company's creditors—absent any independent wrongdoing on the part of the shareholders, the company's creditors are only entitled to satisfy their claims against the company's assets. Third, the company has transferable shares. Fourth, the company's day-to-day business is conducted by the management, rather than its shareholders. Finally, the company is owned by its shareholders, i.e., investor ownership.

In Singapore, a company may be limited by shares, limited by guarantee, or an unlimited company (section 17(2), Companies Act 1967). Most companies in Singapore are limited by shares. A limited company can be identified using "Ltd." in its name (section 27(8), Companies Act 1967). A company is either a private or public company—under the law, a company can be incorporated as a private company if: first, it restricts the right to transfer its shares; and second, does not have more than 50 members (section 18(1), Companies Act 1967). If it has no such share transfer restrictions, or if it has more than 50 members, then such a company must be incorporated as a public company. Thus, a public company limited by shares is identified as "X Ltd", while a private company limited by shares is identified as "X Pte Ltd."

Every company must have at least one member (section 20A, Companies Act 1967). It must also have "at least one director who is ordinarily resident in Singapore" (section 145(1), Companies Act 1967). A director, ordinarily resident in Singapore or otherwise, must have attained the age of 18 years and have full legal capacity (section 145(2), Companies Act 1967). It is thus possible for a company to have one member, who is also its director.

3.3.2 *Corporate Ownership*

Shareholder concentration in Singapore is high, with family businesses and state-owned companies often having controlling shareholders who hold a large block of shares. Most companies listed in Singapore have a block shareholder of 15% or more (OECD, 2017).

Through their ownership of shares in the company, shareholders are given certain rights against the issuing company. For instance, shareholders have the right to dividends when it is declared. Other rights include but are not limited to, the right to attend any general meeting of the company and to speak on any resolution before the meeting (section 180(1), Companies Act 1967); the right to appoint directors by ordinary resolution passed at a general meeting, unless the corporate constitution provides otherwise (section 149B, Companies Act 1967); and the right to remove directors (section 152, Companies Act 1967).

The types of shares that a company may issue are not generally restricted by the Companies Act 1967. Therefore, it is possible to create different classes of shareholders which have different rights, such as different voting rights, different dividends rights, or different rights to surplus capital on a winding-up (Tjio et al., 2015). There are generally six types of shares that may be issued by the company in Singapore (ACRA, 2021b):

1. **Ordinary shares** are the most common type of share; they normally carry voting rights but do not give the shareholders the right to receive or demand dividends. Ordinary shareholders also receive less than dividends as compared to shareholders who hold preferred shares. Companies may divide their ordinary shares into different classes (e.g., "A" and "B") with different rights assigned to each class. Ordinary shareholders are also the residual claimants of the company in the company's winding up (Tjio et al., 2015).
2. **Preference shares** confer certain preferential rights on the holder, superior to ordinary shares. Whether preference shares are accompanied by voting rights

depends on the terms of the preference shares, i.e., it is very much a contractual issue (Tjio et al., 2015). Normally, the preferential rights are in relation to the right to fixed dividends, priority to dividends over ordinary shares, and a return of capital when the company is liquidated.

3. **Redeemable preference shares** are one of two special types of preference shares, with the other being convertible preference shares. The company may redeem these shares at an agreed value on a specified date or at the board's discretion. This is on condition that the company is a going concern. Any redemption can be paid out of the company's capital using proceeds from a fresh issue of shares. The directors must lodge a solvency statement with ACRA under the "Notice of Redemption of Redeemable Preference Shares" transaction via BizFile+ (ACRA's online filing and information retrieval system).
4. **Convertible preference shares** usually carry rights to a fixed dividend for a particular term. At the end of the term, the company can convert it into ordinary shares or leave them as they are. Conversion prices, or rate of exchange, must be specified in the company's constitution and must be fixed at the time of issuance.
5. **Treasury shares** are the company's ordinary shares that have been acquired from shareholders. The company will be listed as the owner of the shares but is not allowed to exercise the right to attend or vote at meetings (section 76J(2) & (3), Companies Act 1967), and no dividends may be paid to the company (section 76J(4), Companies Act 1967). The treasury shares that a company holds must not exceed 10% of the total number of shares in that class (section 76L (1) & (2), Companies Act 1967). Any treasury shares of more than 10% must be cancelled or disposed of within 6 months (section 76L (3), Companies Act 1967). The company may sell, cancel, or transfer treasury shares (section 76K (1), Companies Act 1967).
6. **Dual-class shares (DCS)** are common shares that give the right to multiple votes per share. Safeguards, as listed on SGX's website (SGX, 2021a), to address specific risks associated with DCS include: (a) requiring an enhanced voting process where all shares carry one vote each regardless of class, for the appointment and removal of independent directors and/or auditors, variation of rights attached to any class of shares, a reverse takeover, winding-up or delisting; (b) requiring most of the audit committee, the nominating committee, and the remuneration committee, and each of their respective chairmen, to be independent directors; (c) limiting each multiple voting shares to 10 votes per share and limiting the holders of shares to named individuals or groups of permitted holders whose scope must be specified in the initial public offering (IPO); and (d) require sunset clauses whereby multiple voting shares will be automatically converted into ordinary voting shares in circumstances that the company must stipulate at the time of the IPO.

Dual-class shares have become one of the hottest topics of discussion in current capital markets and corporate governance debates. In recent years, academics, regulators, legislators, and stock exchanges worldwide have discussed whether companies should be allowed to go public with two-class shares and, if so, which restrictions should be imposed (Gurrea-Martínez, 2021). In Singapore, while companies listed on the SGX Mainboard have been able to go public with dual class shares since June 2018, none of the companies that went public in 2018 and 2019 adopted these share structures. Only AMTD International, a Hong Kong-based company listed on the New York Stock Exchange, had a secondary listing on SGX with a dual-class share structure. One type of restriction may require stock exchange approval after a thorough assessment of the "suitability" of the company interested in going public with dual-class shares. This approach has been adopted in Singapore, and SGX may consider permitting a company to adopt a two-class share structure after a consideration of the following factors: (a) the business model of the issuer, e.g., whether the issuer has a conceptualized long-term plan that contemplates ramping up growth at a fast pace; (b) track record, including operating track record, of the issuer, group or business; (c) the role of contribution of intended multiple-vote shareholders to the success of the issuer or business and, in the case of a permitted holder group, its relevance to the issuer or business; (d) participation by sophisticated investors; (e) if the permitted holder group is a trust or corporate vehicle, the suitability of the arrangement, including an assessment of whether sunset features or other safeguards are in place to govern the holding structure; and (f) other features of the issuer or business that requires the adoption of such a structure. This approach provides public investors with an additional layer of protection since the stock exchange would be fulfilling the filtering function that, in countries with highly sophisticated capital markets such as the United States, is performed by the market itself (Gurrea-Martínez, 2021).

For listed companies on the SGX, the issuing company must ensure that at least 10% of the total number of issued shares excluding treasury shares (and excluding preference shares and convertible equity securities) in a class that is listed is at all times held by the public (rule 723, SGX Mainboard Listing Rules). As soon as the 10% threshold is breached, i.e., the free float falls below 10%, the issuing company must, as soon as practicable, announce this, and SGX may suspend trading of the class, or all the securities of the issuer (rule 724(1), SGX Mainboard Listing Rules). That being said, SGX may allow the company 3 months, or longer, to restore the 10% threshold (rule 724(2), SGX Mainboard Listing Rules).

3.3.3 Government-Owned and Government-Linked Companies

The Singapore economy has two main government-owned companies in GIC Private Limited (GIC) and Temasek Holdings (Private) Limited (Temasek). They were incorporated under the Companies Act 1967 and are wholly owned by the Singapore government. Both companies are responsible for managing a certain aspect of Singapore's past reserves. While appearing to be outwardly similar, GIC and Temasek have distinct historical starting points.

Temasek was incorporated in 1974 following the Singapore government's decision that its rightful role was to manage the national economy and not individual enterprises. Before this decision, the Singapore government was the direct shareholder in various economically important companies such as DBS Bank, Singapore Airlines, Neptune Orient Lines, Keppel Shipyard, and Sembawang Holdings. Temasek was thus set up as an asset manager to take over ownership of these companies on behalf of the Singapore government, freeing up scarce government resources to focus on national governance. In the years since then, Temasek has sold its shareholding in many of these companies by listing them on the SGX, e.g., Singapore Airlines, although in many cases it still retains a significant shareholding block, e.g., Singapore Telecommunications Limited, where Temasek still retains a 51% shareholding (Temasek, 2024a). In certain rare cases, such as Singapore Power Limited (a company operating in the energy sector), Temasek continues to wholly own the company.

GIC was incorporated later, in 1981, as the brainchild of Goh Keng Swee, then Singapore's Deputy Prime Minister and Chairman of the MAS, to manage the country's foreign reserves. GIC was tasked to invest the reserves in a globally diversified portfolio of asset classes to deliver good long-term returns (GIC, 2020). In this regard, GIC can better be understood as Singapore's sovereign wealth fund.

Temasek is more significant domestically given its ownership of many companies that form the commanding heights of Singapore's economy such as banking, finance, and defense, as well as companies that are responsible for the provision of public goods and services such as public transport and electricity. In 2016, a rare privatization exercise was undertaken by Temasek to privatize the train operator SMRT Corporation, which was previously publicly listed on the SGX in 2000, following the failure of the company to properly maintain its assets in an attempt to maximize profits, resulting in various massive rail failures from 2011 to 2015 (The Straits Times, 2020).

Despite the common criticism that state-owned and/or state-linked companies can be a drain on taxpayers' money, as the government might be required to subsidize such companies' operations, this is not the case in Singapore. Many of the state-linked companies have independent boards and decision-making processes, and commercial decisions are made without the Singapore government's input. Indeed, many of the government-linked companies that were privatized in the 1990s and 2000s were already competitive before their privatizations. This is because such companies have always competed with foreign companies, which has forced Singapore's government-linked companies to become more efficient than those observed elsewhere (Sam, 2013).

Additionally, as holding companies, GIC and Temasek are largely left to make their own commercial strategies and decisions (Temasek, 2024b). Singapore's model of governing Temasek has been praised as a model for reform in China (Chen, 2016). As evidenced by the empirical data in the work of Chen (2016), the Temasek model shows that good public governance might lead to good corporate governance.

Indeed, from the very beginning, the Singapore government was aware of the risks of political interference in the corporate governance of government-owned and government-linked companies. As a result, it developed a highly visible and well-tailored regulatory framework to explicitly prevent politics from influencing the corporate governance of such companies. This framework has been successful as such companies "are professionally managed with limited interference from the government" and have performed exceptionally well for decades (Cheng-Han et al., 2014).

An examination of the historical evolution of Singapore's governance over government-owned and government-linked companies illustrates that a successful economy and corporate governance system can be built on a foundation of corporations that have the government as the main controlling shareholder. Crucially, this feature of Singapore's corporate governance has been maintained even as Singapore moved from a developing to a developed nation.

3.4 Legislation and Corporate Regulation

In terms of corporate legislation and regulation, among the main statutes in Singapore are:

1. Securities and Futures Act 2001 (SFA): The SFA relates to the regulation of activities and institutions in the securities and derivatives industry, including trading in leveraged foreign exchange, financial benchmarks, and clearing mechanisms, and for matters related thereto. The SFA also prescribes statutory prospectus requirements and disclosure obligations of directors, chief executive officers, and major shareholders of a listed company in relation to their interests in securities (MAS, 2021b).
2. Companies Act 1967 (CA): This is the main legislation applicable to all companies (private and public) incorporated in Singapore and, in some limited cases, to foreign corporations with commercial operations in Singapore. The current version of the CA, while structurally based upon the United Kingdom's Companies Act 1948, currently reflects influences and legal transplants from New Zealand, Australia, Canada, and the United States. This is a result of reforms over the last decade, especially those recommended by the Company Legislation and Regulatory Framework Committee (Puchniak, 2015).
3. Insolvency, Restructuring and Dissolution Act 2018 (IRDA): This is an omnibus act to deal with matters related to both personal and corporate insolvencies. In relation to corporate insolvency, the statute provides both substantive and procedural rules governing winding-up, judicial management and schemes of arrangement. It also regulates insolvency practitioners. Many of the provisions found in the IRDA were previously a part of the CA, e.g., winding-up and dissolution, but have since been consolidated as part of the IRDA.

Singapore's legal system is based on the English common law. La Porta et al. (2002) stated that investors in common law countries have the strongest legal protection, i.e., legal origins theory. However, as argued by Puchniak (2015), Singapore's lack of shareholding dispersion calls into question the controversial theory of legal origins, which portrays all common law countries, especially economically successful ones, in the same light and suggests a causal link between common law minority shareholder protections, dispersed holdings, and economic prosperity. In Singapore, the presence of genuinely independent directors is limited, the corporate control market lacks vitality, and the government, primarily through its sovereign wealth fund, holds paramount importance as a shareholder in the market. Indeed, Singapore's strong common law heritage, concentration of shareholdings, and a recent acclamation as the world's most efficient economy turns the theory of legal origins on its head. The Singapore judiciary is well recognized for its efficiency and quality, and Singapore law is rapidly becoming one of the most applied sets of laws used in regional transactions and disputes as Singapore grows in stature as a hub for international and ad hoc arbitration in Asia (Puchniak, 2015).

3.4.1 Minority Shareholder Rights

Overall, Singapore ranks first and second globally regarding the ease of doing business and investor protection, respectively. According to the Heritage Foundation, Singapore ranks second in the Index of Economic Freedom. In practice, the index measures the legal framework and security of property rights, credit regulation, labor, and business (Ganguli et al., 2020). Singapore ranks first in East Asia and the Pacific region for legal protection and the administration of justice. It is in the top four globally among 97 countries. Regarding the rule of law, corruption, and risk of expropriation, Singapore is placed third, after the United States and the United Kingdom, among the British common law origin countries. The country ranked the fifth least corrupt country in the world out of 176 countries on the Transparency International Corruption Perception Index in 2012 (Ganguli et al., 2020).

Section 216 of the CA is the main mechanism in Singapore company law for protecting minority shareholders against unfair treatment. This mechanism, commonly known as the "oppression remedy," provides a direct solution to any member of a company who can prove that there was a non-equal treatment, or a treatment considered 'commercially unfair' (Puchniak, 2015). Besides this, minority shareholders may also avail themselves of the statutory derivative action in section 216A of the CA, as well as apply for the winding up of the company on the basis that it would be "just and equitable" to do so, under section 125(1)(i) of the IRDA.

Statutory derivative action is widely recognized as an important part of corporate law and governance. It is a lawsuit against officers or directors brought by shareholders on behalf of the company. In other words, the statutory derivative action is brought in the company's name (the former two remedies are brought in the aggrieved shareholder's name). Any recovery, thus, belongs rightfully to the company rather than the individual shareholder. Among the Commonwealth jurisdictions, Singapore was one of the first countries to adopt statutory derivative action in 1993, adopting the Canadian provisions on the same. This has contributed to

Singapore's position as a world leader in protecting minority investors in corporate indices.

Initially, the statutory derivative action excluded Singapore-incorporated companies listed in Singapore because it was thought that such companies were already monitored by various regulatory authorities and disgruntled shareholders of such companies have an avenue to sell their shares in the open market. Extending the remedy to listed companies, it was feared, would have led to "unscrupulous people [making] frivolous applications to harass listed companies and thereby attempt to manipulate the share price" (MOF, 2011). It was, however, later normalized in 2014 by a law reform, which was hailed as a radical shift towards improved corporate governance by reformers (Tang, 2020). The reason for this extension was an attempt to make the law on statutory derivative action consistent, such a remedy was already available to Singapore-incorporated companies listed overseas (MOF, 2011).

Finally, the minority shareholder can also avail itself of the "just and equitable" winding up remedy. The basis for this remedy is one of unfairness. However, it is a distinct remedy from the oppression remedy. Nevertheless, to the extent that the unfair conduct complained of is oppressive, the "just and equitable" winding up remedy does overlap with the oppression remedy. One crucial distinction, however, must be noted. Unlike the oppression remedy, the 'just and equitable' winding up remedy does not require the applicant to establish fault on the part of the defendant. Thus, the "just and equitable" winding up remedy can be used to wind up a company should there be acrimony and irreconcilable differences among the company's shareholders, such that there is an irretrievable breakdown and/or deadlock within the company.

The report *Survey of Corporate Governance Frameworks in Asia*, managed by OECD in 2017, lists several non-profit institutions that promote best corporate governance practices, including the Securities Investors Association Singapore (SIAS). It is a public charity and the most significant organized investor group in Asia, with nearly 12,000 retail investors as members (SIAS, 2024). An elected management committee composed of volunteer professionals leads SIAS. It actively promotes investor education, corporate governance, and transparency and advocates for investor rights. SIAS is the "voice" of minority shareholders, and it has already been involved in disputes with companies that do not comply with good corporate governance practices. However, their preferred approach to resolving investor rights issues is to do so in the boardroom rather than in court. Annually, SIAS tracks and evaluates listed companies for their corporate governance practices and rewards those that have excelled with the Singapore Corporate Governance Award (SIAS, 2024).

With specific and limited exceptions, Singapore corporate law offers no legal mechanism for shareholders to obtain direct access to or inspect the company's books and records generally. No listing rules, nor does company law create any right or even possibility for shareholders of listed companies to inspect their books and records. The first explanation, from the perspective of information seekers, is that Singapore's controlling shareholder-dominated landscape generates little demand for greater shareholder information rights. In Singapore's controlling shareholder dominated listed companies, controlling shareholders can normally use their formal legal rights and informal tactics to access whatever information they require. The second explanation, from the perspective of information holders, rests on the fact that as the government, through Temasek, is the largest controlling shareholder in Singapore, it may not be sufficiently incentivized to expand inspection rights to allow shareholders greater access to the information of its government-linked companies (Puchniak & Tang, 2021).

However, this factor may be deceiving as the Singapore government has a history of voluntarily going beyond its formal legal obligations to provide access to information regarding its management of government-linked companies and has specifically limited its shareholder rights to ensure that such companies are effectively governed. Temasek voluntarily discloses a considerable amount of information about its financial performance, corporate governance, and stewardship activities in the Temasek Review. Given that the Singapore government is the sole shareholder of Temasek, shareholder inspection rights are not at issue in Temasek. Most importantly, shareholder information rights have yet to become established as a significant indication of "good corporate governance" by globally influential actors. As such, at least for now, the Singapore government has not needed to supply the formal law to send a signal of good corporate governance by meeting a prominent global standard for inspection rights, because such a standard does not yet exist (Puchniak & Tang, 2021).

3.4.2 Accounting System and Dividend Policy

The Accounting Standards Committee (ASC) is the official accounting standards-setting body in Singapore, established under the Accounting Standards Act 2007 for companies, charities, cooperative societies, and societies incorporated or registered in Singapore (ASC, 2021). The ASC is currently a committee in the ACRA, having been previously an independent body before 2023. Such accounting standards consist of the Singapore Financial Reporting Standards (International) (SFRS(I)), the Financial Reporting Standards (FRS), and the Singapore Financial Reporting Standard for Small Entities (SFRS for Small Entities).

Singapore has adopted all effective IFRS Standards, except IFRIC 2 (Shares of Members in Cooperative Entities and Similar Instruments), and made several changes to the transition provisions and the effective dates of the IFRS Standards adopted. The ASC has a formal process for endorsing IFRS Standards as and when issued by the board. The standards, known as the Singapore Financial Reporting Standards (SFRS), are aligned with IFRS standards. Failure to adopt IFRIC 2 does not affect companies incorporated in Singapore (both listed and non-listed companies).

The Companies Act 1967 states that incorporated companies should use the accounting standards prescribed by the ASC in their consolidated and separate financial statements. In addition, all foreign companies listed on SGX are authorized to apply IFRS following the SGX Mainboard Listing Rules. Specifically, foreign companies whose equity securities have a primary listing must apply SFRS, IFRS Standards, or US GAAP. In contrast, those with a secondary listing are only required to reconcile their financial statements to SFRS, IFRS Standards, or US GAAP. IFRS Standards are permitted for companies incorporated in Singapore if approval for the use of IFRS Standards is granted by ACRA, or in the case of a company incorporated in Singapore that is listed on the SGX and a stock exchange outside Singapore, if the latter requires the use of IFRS standards (IFRS Foundation, 2021).

According to section 403 of the Companies Act 1967, dividends should only be declared if there are profits available at the time of declaration. Every director or chief executive officer of a company who willfully pays or permits to be paid any dividend in contravention of this provision shall: first, be guilty of a criminal offense and, upon conviction, be liable to pay a fine not exceeding S$5,000 or to an imprisonment term not exceeding 12 months; and second, be liable to the creditors of the company for the amount of the debts due by the company to them to the extent by which the dividends so paid have exceeded the company's profits.

The Singapore Code of Corporate Governance 2018 requires companies listed on the SGX to establish and disclose a dividend policy. Moreover, if any company listed on the SGX chooses not to declare dividends, it must provide reasons for adopting this decision. Companies listed on SGX follow a stable dividend policy, and there is a positive association between company value and dividends. This is because Singapore provides investors with a favorable business environment and legal protection. The capacity for investors to receive dividends from companies serves as confirmation of the company's realization of free cash flow entitlements and aligns with the broader assurance of property rights security, a key component of a country's economic freedom index.

Overall, the dividend policy of Singaporean companies is consistent with a proper corporate governance practice of protecting investor rights which, in turn, is consistent with the global rating and perception of the country regarding the security of property rights (Ganguli et al., 2020; Ahmed et al., 2020).

3.5 The Code of Corporate Governance

Since the Asian Financial Crisis in 1997, the Anglo-American model of corporate governance has been transplanted into many of the large Asian economies in the Far East, but changes in practice have been gradual (Chen et al., 2018).

Singapore's unique economic, political, and institutional environment does not lend itself to easy understanding, as Singapore regularly features at the top of global rankings in terms of economic competitiveness and efficiency of its corporate regulatory environment despite most public listed companies having a powerful controlling shareholder (Wee & Puchniak, 2012; Puchniak, 2015).

In 2001, the government of Singapore formed three private sector committees to recommend improvements in corporate governance, disclosure, accounting standards, company regulation, and regulatory framework (Eng & Mak, 2003). The code was first issued by the Corporate Governance Committee (CGC) in March 2001, which was then revised in July 2005 (public consultation) and again in May 2012. The code became the responsibility of the Monetary Authority of Singapore (MAS) and the Singapore Exchange (SGX) as of September 2007. In February 2017, the Corporate Governance Council was established to review the code. In August 2018, the council submitted its recommendations to MAS, with the latter accepting all recommendations and issuing a revised code (2018 Code) applicable to annual reports covering financial years beginning January 1, 2019. The introduction section of the 2018 Code explains the "comply or explain" approach, stating that the code should not be seen as "burdensome but should help companies by giving clear direction on good board and management practices that will help build investor and stakeholder confidence." In February 2019, MAS established the Corporate Governance Advisory Committee (CGAC) as a permanent industry-led body to uphold good corporate governance practices among Singapore-listed companies. Under the SGX Mainboard Rules, listed companies must disclose their corporate governance practices and must provide explanations for any deviations from the 2018 Code in their annual reports (rule 710, SGX Mainboard Rules).

The 2018 Code contains 13 principles, supplemented by provisions, which relate to board matters (Principles 1 to 5), remuneration matters (Principles 6 to 8), accountability and auditing (Principles 9 and 10), shareholder rights and engagement (Principles 11 and 12), and engagement with stakeholders (Principle 13). The 2018 Code reinforces the focus on board independence. Certain independence tests have been edited out of the 2012 Corporate Governance Code and added to the SGX Mainboard Rules for mandatory compliance. The Practice Guidance elaborates on the 2018 Code's principles and provisions, and companies are not required to disclose or explain deviations from the Practice Guidance (MAS, 2021c).

Among the listing rules of the SGX, rule 710 states that companies must describe their corporate governance practices concerning the principles and provisions of the 2018 Code, detailing how the company's practices comply with the principles. In addition, under the Listing Manual, issuers are required to disclose any information known to the issuer about the issuer or any of its subsidiaries or associated companies that is necessary to prevent the establishment of a false market or that could materially affect the price or value of their bonds (rule 703, SGX Mainboard Rules). Law enforcement of disclosure requirements under section 203 of the Securities and Futures Act 2001 creates a statutory obligation for an issuer and others to comply with SGX's ongoing disclosure requirements. Other listing rules include:

- Rule 210(5)(a) requires that any director who has not had prior experience as a director of a listed company undergo training in the roles and responsibilities of a director of a listed company.
- Rule 210(5)(c) requires independent directors to constitute at least one-third of the board.

- Rule 210(5)(d) (iv) states that a director will not be independent if he has been a director for an aggregate period of more than 9 years (whether before or after listing). This requirement was phased in on January 11, 2023 and is intended to encourage an even more rigorous assessment of long-tenured directors' independence in Singapore (Cassim, 2021). It has been reported that the director with the longest tenure on the board of a listed company in Singapore was 59 years and that approximately 42% of companies listed in Singapore had at least one independent director who has served on the company's board for more than nine years (Tan, 2018).
- Rule 210(5)(e) requires companies to establish one or more committees as necessary to perform the functions of an audit committee, a nominating committee, and a remuneration committee, with written terms of reference that set out the authority and duties of the committees.
- Rule 720(5) states that an issuer must have all directors submit themselves for re-nomination and re-appointment at least once every 3 years.
- Rule 1207(10A) requires the board to disclose the relationship between the chairman and the chief executive officer if they are immediate family members.
- Rule 1207(10B) states that all directors, including their designations (i.e., independent, non-executive, executive, etc.) and roles (as members or chairman of the board or board committees), must be identified in the annual report.

SGX requires sustainability reporting (rules 711A and 711B) as a listing rule. SGX justified the need for mandatory sustainability reporting by pointing to broader environmental concerns and international duties, specifically the Paris Agreement on Climate Change and the UN Sustainable Development Goals, of which Singapore is a signatory (Liu et al., 2019).

In the guidelines on the applicability of these rules concerning an issuer that is a Real Estate Investment Trust (REIT), it is stipulated under the Securities and Futures Act 2001 that the manager of an authorized REIT must act in the best interest of all investors as a whole and give priority to their interests over the manager's interests in the event of a conflict. The regulations and notices made under the Securities and Futures Act 2001 stipulate requirements for the composition of a REIT management board, the establishment of an audit committee, and the circumstances in which a director of the REIT management is independent (SGX, 2021b). The REIT market began to flourish between 2002 and 2007, during which time 20 REITs were listed and traded on the SGX due to improved tax transparency and refinement of regulations for REITs (Ramachandran et al., 2018). Asian REIT regulators must apply stringent corporate governance rules and regulations to govern the existing structure of externally administered REITs in Asia (Chong et al., 2017). Asian REITs are prone to agency problems, which arise from the unequal distribution of power to sponsors (mostly banks or construction companies) that results from the external management structure. Greater sponsor ownership aligns the interests of sponsors and minority shareholders and improves the performance of Asian REITs, but this effect diminishes as sponsors become more entrenched. Developer-sponsored REITs drive the incentive alignment effect and the entrenchment effect, and the presence of institutional investors mitigates agency issues and increases company performance. Singapore REITs tend to have relatively high dividends when compared to the price per share (0.078%) (Tang & Mori, 2017).

Singapore hosts the region's most developed collective investment industry, and investment funds are also heavily invested in the equity markets. The MAS has been responsible for regulating mutual funds since 1999. MAS introduced the Business Trusts Act 2004 to regulate business trusts. Offshore mutual funds and investment funds have been able to offer units to Singapore residents since July 2002. In addition, Singapore has liberalized the inflow of foreign-based funds. As a result, Singapore holds a dominant position in serving the needs of private customers in the Southeast Asian region, one of the fastest growing in the world in terms of new net cash flows. Many wealthy individuals tend to hold substantial assets in Singapore (Walter & Sisli, 2007).

3.6 Corporate Governance Structure

SGX's listing rules state that companies listed on the SGX must "describe in its annual report its corporate governance practices with specific reference to the principles and the provisions of the [2018] Code." If there is any deviation from such principles and provisions, then the onus is on the company to explicitly state, in its annual report, the provision from which it has varied, explain the reason for the variation, and explain how the practices adopted are consistent with the intent of the relevant principle.

The 2018 Code expressly states that the board "has the dual role of setting strategic direction, and of setting the company's approach to governance." The board's role is, therefore, broader than providing oversight. In this regard, the board must have an appropriate level of independence, diversity of thought, and experience and have a lead independent director to provide leadership in situations where the chairman is in conflict. The chairman and chief executive officer must be separate persons to ensure an appropriate balance of power, and non-executive directors must constitute most of the board (Code of Corporate Governance, 2018). An "independent" director is one who is independent in conduct, character, and judgment and has no relationship with the company, its related corporations, its substantial shareholders, or its officers that could interfere, or be reasonably perceived as interfering, with the director's exercise of independent business judgment in the best interest of the company (Rahmat et al., 2020). The term "related corporation", in relation to the company, has the same meaning as currently defined in the Companies Act 1967—a company that is the company's holding company, subsidiary, or fellow subsidiary.

To ensure that the board has a formal and transparent process for directors' appointment and re-appointment, the board must establish a nominating committee (NC) to make recommendations related to the following matters: review of succession plans for directors, particularly the appointment and/or replacement of the chairman, the chief executive officer and key management personnel; the process and criteria for evaluating the performance of the board, its committees, and directors; the review of training and professional development programs for the board and its directors; and finally, the appointment and re-appointment of directors.

The NC is composed of at least three directors, most of whom, including the NC's chairman, are independent. In addition, the lead independent director, if any, is a member of the NC. The company must disclose, in its annual report, the process for selecting, appointing, and re-appointing directors to the board, including the criteria used to identify and evaluate potential new directors and the channels used to search for suitable candidates (Code of Corporate Governance, 2018). The NC is also responsible for ensuring that new directors are aware of their duties and obligations, as well as the responsibility for determining if a director is able to and has been adequately carrying out his or her duties as a director of the company.

To ensure that the board has a formal and transparent procedure for developing policies on director and executive remuneration, and for fixing the remuneration packages of individual directors and key management personnel, the board must establish a remuneration committee (RC) to review and make recommendations to the board on: first, a remuneration framework for the board and key management personnel; and second, the specific remuneration packages for each director and key management personnel.

The RC should be composed of at least three directors. All RC members are non-executive directors, the majority of whom, including the RC's chairman, are independent. The company must disclose in its annual report the policy and criteria for setting remuneration, as well as names, amounts, and breakdowns of: (a) each director and the chief executive officer; and (b) at least the top five key management personnel who are not directors or the chief executive officer in bands no wider than S$250,000 and in aggregate the total remuneration paid to these key management personnel.

SGX has since gone above and beyond what is recommended by the 2018 Code. For annual reports prepared for the financial years ending on or after 31 December 2024, rule 1207(10D) of the SGX Listing Manual now requires companies to furnish the names, amounts, and breakdown of remuneration paid to each director and the chief executive officer by the company and its subsidiaries. Such a breakdown must include (in percentage terms) base or fixed salary, variable or performance-related income or bonuses, benefits in kind, stock options granted, share-based incentives and awards, and other long-term incentives. As the force of this rule is now grounded in the SGX Listing Manual rather than the 2018 Code, a listed company's failure to comply with the provision might result in SGX taking disciplinary action against it.

Additionally, under the 2018 Code, the company must disclose the names and remuneration of employees who are substantial shareholders of the company or are immediate relatives of a director, the chief executive officer, or a substantial shareholder of the company, and whose compensation exceeds S$100,000 during the year, in bands not exceeding S$100,000, in its annual report. The disclosure must clearly state the employee's relationship with the relevant director, chief executive officer, or major shareholder (Code of Corporate Governance, 2018).

The board is also responsible for risk governance and has the responsibility of ensuring that management maintains a sound system of risk management and internal controls, to safeguard the interests of the company and its shareholders. As part of this principle, the 2018 Code states that companies may establish a board risk committee to assess appropriate means to fulfill their responsibility to oversee the company's risk management framework and policies. A risk management committee is required for banks incorporated in Singapore and major direct insurers under the Banking (Corporate Governance) Regulations 2005 and Insurance (Corporate Governance) Regulations 2013 respectively. In addition, systematically important financial market infrastructure, such as approved exchanges, clearing houses, licensed trade repositories and approved holding companies, are required to have a risk management committee pursuant to the Securities and Futures (Corporate Governance of Approved Exchanges, Approved Clearing Houses, Licensed Trade Repositories and Approved Holding Companies) Regulations 2024.

Finally, the board also should establish an audit committee (AC). Out of all the committees discussed thus far, the AC is unique, in that it has a statutory footing, i.e., it is the only committee mandated by law. Thus, section 201B (1) of the Companies Act 1967 states that "[e]very listed company must have an audit committee." The AC is a very important governance mechanism established under the Companies Act 1967 for listed companies to manage the agency problem arising from the conflict of interests between shareholders and management (Chu et al., 2021).

The duties of the AC include: first, reviewing the significant financial reporting issues and judgments so as to ensure the integrity of the financial statements of the company and any announcements relating to the company's financial performance; second, reviewing at least annually the adequacy and effectiveness of the company's internal controls and risk management systems; third, reviewing the assurance from the chief executive officer and the chief financial officer on the financial records and financial statements; fourth, making recommendations to the board on the proposals to the shareholders on the appointment and removal of external auditors and the remuneration and terms of engagement of the external auditors; fifth, reviewing the adequacy, effectiveness, independence, scope and results of the external audit and the company's internal audit function; and sixth, reviewing the policy and arrangements for concerns about possible improprieties in financial reporting or other matters to be safely raised, independently investigated and appropriately followed up on.

The AC comprises at least three directors, all of whom are non-executive and the majority of whom, including the AC's chairman, are independent. At least two members, including the AC chairman, must have recent and relevant knowledge or experience in accounting or related financial management (Code of Corporate Governance, 2018). The AC should not include former partners or directors of the existing auditing firm or auditing corporation: (a) within 2 years commencing on the date of their ceasing to be a partner of the auditing firm or director of the auditing corporation and (b) in any event, for as long as they have any financial interest in the auditing firm or auditing corporation. The 2018 Code thus sets a much higher standard for the AC's composition when compared to the statutory requirements found under section 201B of the Companies Act 1967, which only mandates that the AC be made up of three or more directors of whom a majority must not be: (a) executive directors of the company or any related corporation; (b) a familial member of an executive director of the company or any related corporation; or (c) any person having a relationship which, in the opinion of the board, would interfere with the exercise of independent judgment in carrying out the functions of an audit committee.

In this regard, a study conducted by Kusnadi et al. (2016) found that financial reporting quality increases when the AC consists of members who possess other skill sets in terms of finance of supervisory expertise. Additionally, the authors there found that so long as most of the AC consisted of independent directors, the addition of one more independent director, i.e., incremental independence, did not result in higher financial reporting quality. This suggests that ACs with the most independent directors possessed sufficient independence to monitor their companies' financial reporting process. Their findings resulted in them casting doubts over the need for an all-independent AC.

In 2016, Stewardship Asia, a Singapore private entity with the stated mission of promoting stewardship in Singapore and Asia, introduced the "Stewardship Principles for Responsible Investors" (Singapore Stewardship Code) which was inspired by the United Kingdom's Stewardship Code that was first published in 2010. In late 2018, Stewardship Asia also introduced the "Stewardship Principles for Family Businesses" (Family Stewardship Code), a version of the Singapore Stewardship Code developed for family companies. However, Puchniak and Tang (2020) argue that Singapore adopted a stewardship code as a form of "halo signaling" to demonstrate Singapore's commitment to Anglo-American-cum-global standards of good corporate governance. Even without the stewardship code, Singapore already had "good stewards" in the form of Temasek and family controlling shareholders—backed by an institutional architecture and public enforcement mechanisms—which effectively controlled the problem of systematic wealth-reducing private benefits of control. This form of "halo signaling" demonstrates Singapore's commitment to strong corporate governance as, by releasing the first stewardship code, Singapore took control of this regulatory space and prevented more bottom-up approaches of shareholder stewardship—which could have been more unpredictable and potentially disruptive to Singapore's successful corporate governance model—from developing. This form of "pre-emptive corporate governance" has allowed Singapore to maintain the existing system of corporate governance and its position as a global corporate governance leader by embracing "shareholder stewardship" (Puchniak & Tang, 2020).

The corporate governance structure found in Singapore's publicly listed companies has, therefore, allowed Singapore to top many corporate governance rankings. This, in turn, suggests that it may be a poster child for the global American model of good corporate governance—which is built on the notion that the shareholder-centric, Berle-Means corporation is the pinnacle of efficiency. However, if one digs a little below the rankings, it quickly becomes apparent that Singapore's corporate governance model is distinctly non-American at its core. The dispersed, shareholder-centric Berle-Means corporation is virtually non-existent in Singapore. By contrast,

Singapore's corporate governance system is built almost entirely on companies owned by concentrated block shareholders. Furthermore, empirical evidence suggests that as Singapore's wealth increased, so did its stock concentration—the opposite of what proponents of the American model of corporate governance might have predicted (Cheng-Han et al., 2014). In conclusion, the unique variety of corporate governance found in Singapore's listed companies must be considered together with the country's politico-socio-commercial environment before it can be properly understood.

3.7 External Audits

A company in Singapore must appoint an auditor within 3 months of being incorporated unless it is exempt from having its accounts audited if it qualifies as a "small company" (section 205C, Companies Act 1967). Generally, a company qualifies as a small company if (Thirteenth Schedule, Companies Act 1967):

- It is a private company throughout the financial year; and
- It satisfies any two of the following criteria for each of the two financial years immediately preceding the financial year—the revenue of the company for each financial year does not exceed S$10 million; the value of the company's total assets at the end of each financial year does not exceed S$10 million; and/or it has at the end of each financial year not more than 50 employees.

Auditing standards in Singapore are called the Singapore Standards on Auditing (SSAs), which are written in the context of an external audit of financial statements (i.e., historical financial information) by an independent auditor (ISCA, 2022). The standards are based on the International Standards on Auditing (ISAs) issued by the International Auditing and Assurance Standards Board (IAASB), an independent standard-setting board of the International Federation of Accountants (IFAC). Standard No. SSA 200 *Overall Objectives of the Independent Auditor and the Conduct of an Audit by Singapore Standards on Auditing* explains that the main objective of an external audit is to enable the auditor to express an opinion on whether the financial statements are prepared (in all material respects) under an identified financial reporting framework (SSA 200, p. 3) and whether the financial statements give a true and fair view of the financial position and performance of the company (section 207(2)(a)(ii), Companies Act 1967). However, the users of audited financial statements cannot assume that the opinion is an assurance as to the future viability of the entity nor the efficiency or effectiveness of with which management has conducted the affairs of the entity, and the auditor cannot be held responsible for the prevention of fraud or error, as explained in Standard No. SSA 240 *The Auditor's Responsibilities Relating to Fraud in an Audit of Financial Statements* (Kan, 2013).

In Singapore, ACRA regulates the audit profession, which also considers complaints made against public accountants who are registered with the authority. The board of directors and the management of the entity are responsible for preparing and presenting the financial statements, with the oversight of those charged with governance, who also assume primary responsibility for preventing and detecting fraud and error. External audits are generally carried out annually, which coincides with the financial reporting cycle of most organizations. This ensures that shareholders receive current and accurate financial information promptly. The external auditor's opinion on the financial statements does not relieve those charged with management and governance of any of their responsibilities, but the examination and opinion of an external auditor gives credibility to the financial statements (Kan, 2013).

According to the 2018 Code, the Audit Committee (AC) must meet with the external and internal auditors, without the presence of the company's management, at least annually (paragraph 10.5, Code of Corporate Governance 2018). In addition, the AC must review the independence of the external auditors and should state in the company's annual report (a) the aggregate amount of fees paid to the external auditors and (b) a breakdown of the fees paid in total for audit and non-audit services, respectively. In addition, the 2018 Code recommends diversity of expertise in the AC, consisting of accounting experts and members with finance and supervisory expertise, resulting in an improved board monitoring and higher quality financial reports (Kusnadi et al., 2016).

3.8 Final Considerations

This chapter's main objective was to provide an overview of the current stage of corporate governance in Singapore. Asian firms were severely criticised for having failed to monitor and check the power of controlling families and/or predatory states, which led to the Asian Financial Crisis in 1997. To recover from the crisis, the Singapore government imported American capital market logic and its associated corporate governance structures as "gold standards" and enacted them as regulations. The government has worked hard to make the country attractive to investors by reviewing and improving corporate governance (Tsui-Auch & Yoshikawa, 2015).

The resulting institutional change has been gradual. Due to large family businesses, Chinese business groups in Singapore, for example, have begun to recruit more non-familial professional managers (Selekler-Goksen & Öktem, 2009). In 2022, the SGX mandated listed companies to "maintain a board diversity policy that addresses gender, skills, and experience, and any other relevant aspects of diversity." Thus, in their annual report, listed companies must now describe their board diversity policy, including (a) targets to achieve diversity on its board; (b) accompanying plans and timelines to achieve such targets; (c) progress toward achieving such targets; and (d) description of how the combination of skills, talents, experience and diversity of its directors serves the needs and plans of the company. This development comes 5 years after an OECD Report (2017) highlighted Singapore's non-requirement of gender disclosure in the composition of the board.

Since independence, Singapore has enjoyed great economic success and has built a strong and stable nation. As evidenced in the work of Sam (2013), Singapore is often regarded as an economic success, having transformed from a low-income economy in the 1960s to being described as an economic miracle. Its real Gross Domestic Product (GDP) has grown at an average of 10.5% (1961–2009), with the real per capita GDP rising from S$1567 in 1965 to S$51,656 in 2009 (at the current market price). As a result, the city-state has been labelled as a quintessential development state where the state's legitimacy is derived from its ability to develop the country economically (Sam, 2013).

Singapore was ranked first out of 130 countries and territories globally in the corporate governance category of the 2019 "FM Global Resilience Index" which ranks countries based on the overall resilience of their business environments (Cassim, 2021). Singapore is known for its strong law enforcement against graft and corruption. It also took the number one spot in the World Bank's Ease of Doing Business Ranking (out of 189 economies) in 2013 and 2014 (Chen, 2016).

All this evidence demonstrates the strength of public sector governance in Singapore. This may also support arguments that strong law enforcement of corporate and contract law may be a necessary step towards diffused ownership and good corporate governance (Chen, 2016). Singapore is extremely adept when it comes to corporate law and governance, at ensuring its formal law meets or exceeds the important global norms of good corporate governance—which have increasingly been recognized as playing a prominent role in shaping the evolution of corporate law around the world (and, particularly, in Asia) (Puchniak & Tang, 2021).

Today, Singapore is one of the wealthiest countries in the world. With virtually no natural resources, effective governance has been the key to Singapore's success. While corporate governance measures are shaped by investor preferences, particularly those placed by global financial investors of repute, their enforcement (both public and private) is considerably strong in Singapore (Cheng-Han et al. 2014).

At first blush, Singapore's common law heritage, robust shareholder remedies, and efficient economy appear to confirm the controversial legal origins theory. However, on closer examination, the Singapore story turns the legal origins theory upside down and suggests that the classical American model of corporate governance may not be the only way to achieve corporate governance success (Puchniak, 2015). Over the last 40 years of Singapore's miraculous economic growth, its shareholder market has become more concentrated, and family-owned firms have remained dominant. This has occurred during a period when Singapore has transformed into a global financial center known for its English-speaking population, vibrant multiculturalism, and increasingly Westernized society (Wee & Puchniak, 2012).

References

Accounting and Corporate Regulatory Authority (ACRA). (2014). *Key Amendments to the Companies Act*. Retrieved July 25, 2024, from https://www.acra.gov.sg/legislation/legislative-reform/companies-act-reform/companies-amendment-act-2014/key-amendments-to-the-companies-act

Accounting and Corporate Regulatory Authority (ACRA). (2021a). *Who we are*. Retrieved November 13, 2021, from https://www.acra.gov.sg/who-we-are/overview-of-acra

Accounting and Corporate Regulatory Authority (ACRA). (2021b). *Shares and updating share information*. Retrieved November 18, 2021, from https://www.acra.gov.sg/how-to-guides/shares-and-updating-share-information/different-types-of-shares

Accounting Standards Council Singapore (ASC). (2021). *About us*. Retrieved November 18, 2021, from https://www.asc.gov.sg/AboutUs

Ahmed, S., Shah, Z. A., & Bhatti, A. A. (2020). Roles of corporate governance and ownership structure in dividend smoothing behavior of Asian firms.

Ann, L. S. (2016). Governance and economic change in Singapore. In *Singapore's economic development: Retrospection and reflections* (pp. 17–33). World Scientific Publishing.

Cadbury, A. (1992). *Report of the committee on the financial aspects of corporate governance* (Vol. 1). Gee.

Cassim, R. (2021). A comparative analysis of director tenure in South Africa and Selected International Jurisdictions (2021) 54 (1) Comparative and International Law Journal of Southern Africa 1-37. *Comparative and International Law Journal of Southern Africa*.

Chen, C. (2016). Solving the puzzle of corporate governance of state-owned enterprises: The path of the Temasek model in Singapore and lessons for China. *Northwestern Journal of International Law & Business, 36*, 303.

Chen, J. (2021). *Singapore Exchange (SGX)*. Retrieved November 19, 2021, from https://www.investopedia.com/terms/s/singapore_exchange.asp

Chen, C., Wan, W. Y., & Zhang, W. (2018). Board Independence as a panacea to tunneling? An empirical study of related-party transactions in Hong Kong and Singapore. *Journal of Empirical Legal Studies, 15*(4), 987–1020.

Cheng-Han, T., Puchniak, D. W., & Varottil, U. (2014). State-owned enterprises in Singapore: Historical insights into a potential model for reform. *Columbia Journal of Asian Law, 28*, 61.

Chong, W. L., Ting, K. H., & Cheng, F. F. (2017). The performance of externally managed REITs in Asia: Further evidence from free cash flow and agency costs. *Journal of Property Investment & Finance*.

Chu, M. K., Ho, Y. K., & Yeap, L. H. (2021). Tracking the development of audit committees in Singapore listed companies. *Managerial Auditing Journal*.

Code of Corporate Governance. (2018). *Code of Corporate Governance*. Retrieved November 13, 2021, from https://www.mas.gov.sg/regulation/codes/code-of-corporate-governance

Department of Statistics Singapore. (2024). *Population and population structure*. Retrieved July 25, 2024, from https://www.singstat.gov.sg/find-data/search-by-theme/population/population-and-population-structure/latest-data

Department of Statistics Singapore (DOS). (2023). *Gross domestic product dashboard*. Retrieved July 25, 2024, from https://www.singstat.gov.sg/find-data/search-by-theme/economy/national-accounts/visualising-data/gross-domestic-product-dashboard

Dixit, J., Singh, P., & Haldar, A. (2021). Investor protection: Effects of takeover convergence. *International Journal of Organizational Analysis*.

Eng, L. L., & Mak, Y. T. (2003). Corporate governance and voluntary disclosure. *Journal of Accounting and Public Policy, 22*(4), 325–345.

Ganguli, S. K., Dawar, V., & Arrawatia, R. (2020). Corporate dividend policy, minority shareholders right and equity value of firm: Evidence from Singapore. *Journal of Public Affairs, 20*(2), e2039.

GIC. (2020). *Investing Singapore's Foreign Reserves*. Retrieved July 25, 2024, from https://www.gic.com.sg/wp-content/uploads/2021/04/GIC-ThinkSpace-Investing-Singapores-Foreign-Reserves.pdf

Gracia, O., & Siregar, S. V. (2021). Sustainability practices and the cost of debt: Evidence from ASEAN countries. *Journal of Cleaner Production, 300*, 126942.

Gregory, H. J. (2000). The globalization of corporate governance. *Global Counsel, 5*, 52–65.

Gurrea-Martínez, A. (2021). Theory, evidence, and policy on dual-class shares: A country-specific response to a global debate. *European Business Organization Law Review*, 1–41.

Hsieh, J., & Nieh, C. C. (2010). An overview of Asian equity markets. *Asian-Pacific Economic Literature, 24*(2), 19–51.

IFRS Foundation. (2021). *Jurisdiction profile: Singapore*. Retrieved November 18, 2021, from https://www.ifrs.org/content/dam/ifrs/publications/jurisdictions/pdf-profiles/singapore-ifrs-profile.pdf

Inland Revenue Authority Singapore (IRAS). (2021). *What we do*. Retrieved November 13, 2021, from https://www.iras.gov.sg/who-we-are/what-we-do/taxes-in-singapore/the-singapore-tax-system

Institute of Singapore Chartered Accountants (ISCA). (2022). https://www.isca.org.sg/standards-guidance/auditassurance/standards-and-guidance/singapore-standards-on-auditing-(ssas)

Institute of Singapore Chartered Accountants (ISCA). (2024). *About us*. Retrieved July 27, 2024, from https://www.isca.org.sg/about-us/about-the-institute-of-singapore-chartered-accountants/our-history

Kan, E. (2013). *Audit and assurance-principles and practices in Singapore*. CCH Asia Pte Ltd.

Kusnadi, Y., Leong, K. S., Suwardy, T., & Wang, J. (2016). Audit committees and financial reporting quality in Singapore. *Journal of Business Ethics, 139*(1), 197–214.

La Porta, R., Lopez-de-Silanes, F., Shleifer, A., & Vishny, R. (2002). Investor protection and corporate valuation. *The Journal of Finance, 57*(3), 1147–1170.

Lan, L. L. (2022). *Corporate governance in Singapore – The road thus far*. European Corporate Governance Institute-Law Working Paper, (667).

Lim, P. S. S., & Cheong, M. H. (2017). *Value investing in Asia: The definitive guide to investing in Asia*. Wiley.

Liu, F. H., Demeritt, D., & Tang, S. (2019). Accounting for sustainability in Asia: Stock market regulation and reporting in Hong Kong and Singapore. *Economic Geography, 95*(4), 362–384.

Ministry of Finance (MOF). (2011). *Report of the Steering Committee for Review of the Companies Act*. Retrieved July 25, 2024, from https://www.mof.gov.sg/docs/default-source/default-document-library/news-and-publications/press-releases/annex-a-sc-report-complete-2.pdf

Ministry of Finance (MOF). (2021). *Who we are*. Retrieved November 18, 2021, from https://www.mof.gov.sg/who-we-are/overview

Monetary Authority of Singapore (MAS). (2019a). *Securities Industry Council*. Retrieved July 25, 2024, from https://www.mas.gov.sg/securities-industry council#:~:text=The%20Securities%20Industry%20Council%20(SIC,(Take%2Dover%20Code)

Monetary Authority of Singapore (MAS). (2019b). *The Singapore code on take-overs and mergers*. Retrieved July 25, 2024, from https://www.mas.gov.sg/-/media/mas/resource/sic/the_singapore_code_on_take_overs_and_merger_24-january-2019.pdf

Monetary Authority of Singapore (MAS). (2019c). *The Singapore code on take-overs and mergers*. Retrieved July 25, 2024, from https://www.mas.gov.sg/-/media/mas/resource/sic/practice-statements/practice-statement-on-the-waiver-of-the-application-of-the-code-to-unlisted-public-companies.pdf

Monetary Authority of Singapore (MAS). (2021a). *About us*. Retrieved November 13, 2021, from https://www.mas.gov.sg/

Monetary Authority of Singapore (MAS). (2021b). *Securities and Futures Act (Cap. 289)*. Retrieved November 18, 2021, from https://www.mas.gov.sg/regulation/acts/securities-and-futures-act

Monetary Authority of Singapore (MAS). (2021c). *Code of Corporate Governance*. Retrieved November 18, 2021, from https://www.mas.gov.sg/regulation/codes/code-of-corporate-governance

Monetary Authority of Singapore (MAS). (2024). *MAS Staff Paper No. 32, Case Study on pan-electric crisis*. Retrieved July 25, 2024, from https://www.mas.gov.sg/-/media/MAS/resource/publications/staff_papers/MAS_Staff_Paper_No32_Jul_2004.pdf

Nam, S. W., & Nam, S. U. (2004). *Corporate governance in Asia: Recent evidence from Indonesia, Republic of Korea, Malaysia, and Thailand (No. 6)*. Asian Development Bank Institute.

OECD. (2017). *OECD survey of corporate governance frameworks in Asia.*

Oktavia, O. (2020). *Independent corporate governance organs' activities, tax avoidance, and country tax environment: Evidence from ASEAN countries.*

Puchniak, D. W. (2015). Multiple faces of shareholder power in Asia: Complexity revealed. In *Research handbook on shareholder power* (pp. 511–534). Edward Elgar.

Puchniak, D. W., & Tang, S. S. (2020). Singapore's puzzling embrace of shareholder stewardship: A successful secret. *Vanderbilt Journal of Transnational Law, 53*, 989.

Puchniak, D. W., & Tang, S. (2021). *Limited shareholder inspection rights in Singapore: Worrying legal gap or unnecessary for rankings?* Available at SSRN 3918900.

Rahmat, M. M., Ahmed, K., & Lobo, G. J. (2020). Related party transactions, value relevance, and informativeness of earnings: Evidence from four economies in East Asia. *Review of Pacific Basin Financial Markets and Policies, 23*(01), 2050005.

Ramachandran, J., Chen, K. K., Subramanian, R., Yeoh, K. K., & Khong, K. W. (2018). Corporate governance and performance of REITs: A combined study of Singapore and Malaysia. *Managerial Auditing Journal.*

Ramachandran, J., Alam, N., & Goh, C. E. (2020). A win-win situation for both managers and shareholders: A study of ASEAN corporate governance. *Managerial Finance, 46*(8).

Reuters. (2020). *Exclusive: Head of oil trader Hin Leong didn't disclose $800 million losses - Court filing*. Retrieved April 25, 2024, from https://www.reuters.com/article/us-singapore-oil-hinleong-exclusive/exclusive-head-of-oil-trader-hin-leong-didnt-disclose-800-million-losses-court-filing-idUSKBN2210EK/

Sam, C. Y. (2013). Partial privatisation and the role of state-owned holding companies in China. *Journal of Management & Governance, 17*(3), 767–789.

Securities Industry Council (SIC). (2021). *About the Securities Industry Council*. Retrieved November 18, 2021, from https://www.mas.gov.sg/securities-industry-council

Securities Investors Association Singapore (SIAS). (2024). *About us*. Retrieved November 17, 2024, from https://sias.org.sg/about-us/

Selekler-Goksen, N. N., & Öktem, Ö. Y. (2009). Countervailing institutional forces: Corporate governance in Turkish family business groups. *Journal of Management & Governance, 13*(3), 193–213.

SGX. (2021a). *SGX launches rules for listing of dual class shares companies*. Retrieved November 13, 2021, from https://www.sgx.com/media-centre/20180626-sgx-launches-rules-listing-dual-class-shares-companies

SGX. (2021b). *Practice Note 4.2 corporate governance requirements for real estate investment trusts and business trusts*. Retrieved November 18, 2021, from http://rulebook.sgx.com/rulebook/practice-note-42-corporate-governance-requirements-real-estate-investment-trusts-and

SGX. (2024a). *Catalist*. Retrieved July 25, 2024, from https://www.sgx.com/securities/catalist

SGX. (2024b). *Market statistics report June 2024*. Retrieved July 25, 2024, from https://api2.sgx.com/sites/default/files/2024-07/SGX%20Monthly%20Statistics%20Report%20Update%20%28For%20the%20month%20of%20Jun%202024%29%20_FA.pdf

Singapore Institute of Directors (SID). (2011). *Adrian Chan "The Singapore Code of Corporate Governance – Its evolution"*. Retrieved July 25, 2024, from https://www.sid.org.sg/common/Uploaded%20files/eGuide/SporeCodeCorporateGovernance-Evolution.pdf

Singapore Institute of Directors (SID). (2024a). *About SID*. Retrieved July 25, 2024, from https://www.sid.org.sg/Web/About/About_SID.aspx

Singapore Institute of Directors (SID). (2024b). *Accreditation*. Retrieved July 25, 2024, from https://www.sid.org.sg/Web/Web/Professional_Development/Accreditation.aspx?hkey=781dbb25-fffb-402b-ae4d-59f00f6ed016

Singapore Statutes Online (SSO). (2024a). *Maintenance of Religious Harmony Act 1990. Accreditation*. Retrieved July 25, 2024, from https://sso.agc.gov.sg/Act/MRHA1990

Singapore Statutes Online (SSO). (2024b). *Constitution of the Republic of Singapore*. Retrieved July 25, 2024, from https://sso.agc.gov.sg/Act/CONS1963?ProvIds=P18-#pr93

Tan, A. (2018, August 7). *Nine-year cap on Independent Directors to Kick in from 2022*. The Business Times. Retrieved March 12, 2022, from https://www.businesstimes.com.sg/government-economy/nine-year-cap-on-independent-directors-to-kick-in-from-2022

Tang, S. S. (2020). The anatomy of Singapore's statutory derivative action: Why do shareholders sue–or not? *Journal of Corporate Law Studies, 20*(2), 327–357.

Tang, C. K., & Mori, M. (2017). Sponsor ownership in Asian REITs. *The Journal of Real Estate Finance and Economics, 55*(3), 265–287.

Temasek. (2024a). *Our portfolio*. Retrieved July 25, 2024, from https://www.temasek.com.sg/en/our-investments/our-portfolio

Temasek. (2024b). *FAQs*. Retrieved July 25, 2024, from https://www.temasek.com.sg/en/about-us/faqs#portfolio-companies

The Straits Times. (2020). *SMRT's privatisation: 9 things to know about the deal*. Retrieved November 17, 2024, from https://www.straitstimes.com/business/companies-markets/smrts-privatisation-9-things-to-know-about-the-deal

The Straits Times. (2022). *Hyflux and its directors, including Olivia Lum, under criminal investigation for corporate governance breaches*. Retrieved April 25, 2024, from https://www.straitstimes.com/business/companies-markets/hyflux-and-its-directors-including-olivia-lum-under-criminal

Tjio, H., Koh, P., & Lee, P. W. (2015). *Corporate law*. Singapore Management University School of Law Research Paper, (54).

Tsui-Auch, L. S., & Yoshikawa, T. (2015). Institutional change versus resilience: A study of incorporation of independent directors in Singapore banks. *Asian Business & Management, 14*(2), 91–115.

Walter, I., & Sisli, E. (2007). The asset management industry in Asia: Dynamics of growth, structure, and performance. *Financial Markets, Institutions & Instruments, 16*(1), 1–77.

Wee, M. S., & Puchniak, D. W. (2012). Derivative actions in Singapore: Mundanely non-Asian, intriguingly non-American and at the forefront of the commonwealth. In D. Puchniak, H. Baum, & M. Ewing-Chow (Eds.), *The derivative action in Asia: A comparative and functional approach (International corporate law and financial market regulation)* (pp. 323–368). Cambridge University Press.

Chapter 4
China

Corporate Governance in China: Issues, Systems, Characteristics, Regulations

Caroline de Oliveira Orth and Clea Beatriz Macagnan

4.1 Introduction

For several decades, China remained a closed-planned economy (Li et al., 2021). However, the reform-and-open policy implemented since 1978 have given China worldwide attention and the title of the largest developing country (Xu et al., 2018). Since then, China has experienced considerable economic growth, surpassing Japan, rising to the second-largest economy in terms of GDP (Duchin et al., 2020; Xu et al., 2018), and the world's second-largest stock market (Ding et al., 2022; Liu et al., 2019; Chen et al., 2020b). In addition, it became the world's largest investor, with \$5.9 trillion in investments in 2018, compared with \$4.3 trillion in the United States and \$1.2 trillion in Japan (Carpenter et al., 2021). However, its stock market shares many common patterns with other developing countries (Li et al., 2021). In addition, the institutional differences between China and developed economies continue to establish an essential debate on the impact of standard governance mechanisms on the performance of Chinese markets and companies (Mutlu et al., 2018).

Thus, for all its history of growth and the debate promoted by the rules adopted by the country, and for entering the era of decentralized equity (Zheng, 2022), China has become the focus of investors and international regulators (Carpenter et al., 2021). That increases the importance of a clear understanding of the governance rules of this country because corporate governance is an essential determinant of corporate performance. Moreover, poor corporate governance can harm shareholders'interests and cause business collapse (Li et al., 2021). These factors

C. de Oliveira Orth (✉)
Federal University of Rio Grande do Sul, Porto Alegre, Brazil
e-mail: caroline.orth@ufrgs.br

C. B. Macagnan
Federal University of Paraiba, João Pessoa, Paraiba, Brazil

C. B. Macagnan (ed.), *Corporate Governance in Capital Markets*, CSR, Sustainability, Ethics & Governance,
https://doi.org/10.1007/978-3-031-94751-3_4

require constant updating of knowledge regarding (1) corporate governance rules formally established by China and (2) the effectiveness of such rules for investor security.

This chapter describes the stage of China's Corporate Governance. We achieve this objective by confronting the rules formally established by the Governance Code issued by the China Securities Regulatory Commission (CSRC) with empirical literature (by conducting a systematic literature review), as well as exploring the OECD's view (through the analysis of the document entitled Corporate Governance of Companies Listed in China).

This chapter is structured as follows: first, we present a brief history of corporate governance in China, the role of the Shanghai and Shenzhen stock exchanges and the performance of the regulatory body, and a short analysis of corporate rules, governance, and accounting standards. Next, we explain the sources of financing for Chinese companies and how the separation between ownership and management occurs. We present the main challenges inherent to conflict of interest and information asymmetry. We also address the primary rights of shareholders, board performance, and executive compensation. Finally, we present our conclusions.

4.2 History of Corporate Governance in China

Until 1978, most Chinese companies were state-owned enterprises (SOE). That year, a reform initiated the gradual implementation of corporate governance in China (Mutlu et al., 2018; OECD, 2011; Wang, 2018; Wang et al., 2019; Yang et al., 2020; Yeung & Lento, 2020). This process had five phases:

Phase 1 (From 1978 to 1984): the beginning of the decentralization of management. China's subsidies to loss-making state enterprises (SOEs) reached high levels in the late 1980s. At that time, it became clear that more profound structural changes in the government-to-company relationship were necessary. Since then, Chinese authorities have identified corporate governance as the central element of the "modern business system" designed to promote business performance and correct incentive problems (Mutlu et al., 2018; OECD, 2011; Wang, 2018.

Phase 2 (1984–1992): There was a change in how SOEs are distributed. It is a transition period from a planned economy to a market-based economy. In 1990, the Shanghai and Shenzhen Stock Exchanges were established (OECD, 2011; Chen et al., 2020c). We highlight that Shanghai, since 1860, was considered a financial center with stock trading, but in 1949, operations were closed and only resumed in 1990 (Goetzmann & Koll, 2005). Stock exchanges were essential vehicles for the privatization of the issuance of shares of Chinese SOEs in the early 1990s. This privatization process is considered the largest global one and still profoundly influences governance in the Chinese economy. Privatizations have led to substantial progress in relocating control rights to private owners. However, depending on the privatization method, respring government influence continued to a greater or lesser extent (Gan et al., 2018).

In other words, the central government's strategy was to retain control over a small number of large corporations and privatize the many small- and medium-sized state enterprises, especially those deficient. And the rest of the companies were restructured through the expansion of equity systems or selling to stakeholders. Also, to attract foreign investment, China allowed foreign investors to cooperate with Chinese state-owned companies and form joint ventures (Weng, 2017). However, the pace and patterns of these changes were decided by local bureaucracies, which calculated their strategies based on local resources and political interests. That led to a new property rights division of SOEs, reflecting China's center-local relations (Wang, 2018; Gan et al., 2018). Thus, the reform's implementation made it difficult for the stock market and corporate governance to function properly (Huang, 2017). It was during this period that the pyramidal structures intensified. These structures are currently considered the main mechanisms of imbalance between cash flow rights and responsibilities for equity participation and generate negative externalities such as resource tunneling and low performance. The formation of a pyramidal holding structure with companies listed as subsidiaries was not only due to corporate financing needs. Still, it was also related to policies introduced by the Chinese government in restructuring state-owned enterprises and adjusting the industrial structure (Zheng, 2022).

Phase 3 (From 1993 to 2003): The Company Law, enacted in December 1993, provided legal support for establishing a modern business system. As a result, some SOEs were restructured and began to have their capital listed on the stock exchange. In 2001, China joined the World Trade Organization (WTO) and pledged to adopt the Organization for Economic Cooperation and Development (OECD) Corporate Governance Principles and improve the corporate governance of its listed companies. WTO membership further accelerated the development of the financial market on the continent, including granting more autonomy in investment decision-making and credit allocation to state financial institutions, removing restrictions on their ownership structure, and relaxing geographical and legal restrictions on the entry of new financial intermediaries (Wang, 2018; Chen et al., 2020a, 2020b, 2020c).

In 2001, the Chinese government tried to sell its stakes in listed companies, but the plan failed after solid protests from private investors, who were concerned that the sale of state shares would flood the market and stock prices would plummet (Huang, 2017). That year, it was also mandatory to present independent advisors on the boards of listed companies (Meng et al., 2018). CSRC and the National Commission on Economics and Commerce jointly issued the Corporate Governance Code of listed companies in early 2002 (OECD, 2011; Yeung & Lento, 2020). To fulfill the commitment to a financial opening in two agreements that same year, the government launched the RMB Qualified Foreign Institutional Investor program (RQFII). Only foreign institutional investors qualified by the government could invest in China's financial markets (Chen et al., 2020a, 2020b, 2020c).

Phase 4 (From 2004 to the present—in April 2005). The Chinese government again tried to sell its shares using the market mechanism. In this process, government officials and public investors negotiated the terms of state reform plans, including compensation paid by non-negotiable shareholders to negotiable shareholders. This process was known as Split-Share Structure Reform (SSSR) (He & Kyaw, 2018; Huang, 2017; Jia et al., 2018; Zhang & Greve, 2018; Yeung & Lento, 2020). According to Carpenter et al. (2021), this reform expanded the investor base and improved Chinese bond price information. However, Titman et al. (2021) found that insiders use split-share to manipulate the stock price. 2006, the Company Law and the Securities Act were revised to strengthen investor protection, especially for minority investors (OECD, 2011). By June 2012, 1336 companies had implemented the SSSR. As of December 2013, there were 2489 listed companies and 2574 shares traded in China, and negotiable shares account for about 80% of the total market capitalization (Huang, 2017).

Even after all these reforms, the financial system and its capital markets are still less developed than those of advanced economies' international stock exchanges (Li et al., 2019; Chen, 2017). Moreover, Chinese corporate governance is also poorly designed and weak (Huang & Sattar, 2021; Cui et al., 2021; Weng, 2017). The main factor is that local governments continue to interfere in the functioning of the market. This interference occurs by targeting certain loans, grants, or stock listings (Wang, 2018; Huang & Sattar, 2021). In addition, the improvement in corporate governance, especially related to the ownership and control of state-owned enterprises, has not improved after the SSSR as the stock market had hoped. That is because the benefits of privatization wiped out the controlling shareholders of the government, not minority investors (Huang, 2017).

Phase 5: As of 2015, the average participation rate of the Chinese capital market's most prominent shareholder of companies listed is less than 33.3%. That means the Chinese capital market is no longer characterized by a shareholder structure dominated by controlling shareholders but has transitioned to the so-called era of decentralized equity. In parallel, the fourth industrial revolution, with high-technology companies, brings new aspects to be considered by corporate governance arrangements. Some examples of these arrangements are (a) excessive nomination of directors by major shareholders, (b) employee stock ownership plans, c) shareholder agreements, (d) control arrangement logic for limited partnership structures, (e) different rights for different classes of actions, and (f) social connections between councilors (Zheng, 2022).

Even after all these reforms, the financial system and its capital markets are still less developed than those of international stock exchanges in advanced economies (Li et al., 2019; Chen, 2017). Chinese corporate governance is also underdeveloped and weak (Huang & Sattar, 2021; Cui et al., 2021; Weng, 2017). The main factor lies in the pyramid structures that allow the tunneling of resources, causing imbalances between the participation in the rights to cash flow and the responsibilities related to equity for the shareholder that holds control (Zheng, 2022). It is also remarkable that local governments continue to interfere in market functioning. This interference occurs by targeting certain loans, subsidies, or stock listings (Wang, 2018; Huang & Sattar, 2021). The improvement in corporate governance, especially concerning ownership and control of SOEs, did not improve after the SSSR as the stock market had expected. The benefits of privatization ended up with the government's controlling shareholders, not minority investors (Huang, 2017).

However, despite the criticism of inferior performance against privileged information and market manipulation by controlling shareholders (Ali et al., 2018; Ding et al., 2010), Chinese stock exchanges have stood out in the world market, as explained in the following section.

4.3 Shanghai Stock Exchange and Shenzhen Stock Exchange and China Securities Regulatory Commission (CSRC)

The Shanghai Stock Exchange (SSE) was founded on November 26, 1990, and the Shenzhen Stock Exchange (SZSE) on December 1, 1990. Both are independent legal entities directly governed by the CSRC. They provide centralized securities trading locations and facilities, organize and supervise securities trading, and exercise self-regulatory management. Its functions include developing business rules, accepting and organizing listings, organizing and monitoring trading securities, regulating listed members and companies, and managing and disseminating market information.

According to statistics from the World Federation of Exchanges, SSE is the fourth largest stock exchange in the world in terms of market capitalization ($3.9 trillion) and the second in terms of raised capital ($92.93 billion). At the same time, SZSE is in fifth place with $59.11 billion in raised capital and is one of the 30 most significant exchanges in the world. In China, the capital market is divided into more than one category: first, the central council (SSE and SZSE); second, the Small and Medium-Sized Enterprise (SMEs) council; and third, the over-the-counter market.

As part of innovation and market opening, in November 2014, Shanghai-Hong Kong Stock Connect (SHHKSC) was launched to facilitate cross-border investment. Subsequently, in December 2016, the Shenzhen Hong Kong Stock Connect program was launched. These programs enable investors in both markets to trade with each other (Ali et al., 2018). Furthermore, in June 2019, SSE launched the Science and Technology Innovation Council (SSE STAR Market) and the pilot registration based on the IPO system on the Shanghai Stock Exchange. This project aims to make Shanghai an international financial center and a center of science and innovation and constantly improve the bases of the domestic capital market.

Additionally, listed Chinese companies have several classes of stocks traded. Some stocks are traded by domestic investors: A share. There are stocks denominated in foreign currencies reserved for foreign investors: B shares. There are also stocks of companies listed or listed abroad, mainly H shares listed in Hong Kong. Domestic investors were not allowed to trade B shares until March 2001, when the China Securities Regulatory Commission (CSRC) lifted restrictions on their trading. As mentioned, pronounced state participation is a hallmark in the Chinese stock market. The state holds the shares to maintain control over companies listed and managed by government agencies (Huang, 2017; Chen et al., 2020c).

The China Securities Regulatory Commission (CSRC), in October 1992, created a ministerial-level government agency under the State Council. In 2006, the CSRC was approved to be governed under the Public Servant's Law of the People's Republic of China. The regulatory agency operates under the authority granted by laws, regulations, and the Council of State, aiming to regulate and safeguard the market of bonds and futures throughout the Chinese national territory (CSRC, 2020). CSRC has sanctioning power and operates through regional offices that report to the head office (OECD, 2011). Although it is an essential institutional pillar that regulates the capital market, it is a necessary institutional foundation, just like the S.E.C. in the United States.

Stock exchanges and other capital market-related entities such as China Securities Finance Corporation Limited (CSF), China Corporation Limited Futures Market Monitoring Center (CFMMC), Capital Market Statistics and Monitoring Center Corporation Limited (CMSMC), among others, are organizations under CSRC rules and as such complement CSRC's regulatory programs in the task of monitoring and enforcing self-regulatory regulations to its members and participants, listed and admitted companies, and the securities and futures activities thereof (OECD, 2011). These bodies regulate and are part of China's institutional corporate governance system. A governance system that, as in other countries, is driven by social changes in the respective society where it is located and by the capital market.

4.4 National Legislation and International Accounting Standards (IFRS)

The regulatory framework governing Corporate Governance in China is in the following laws (called basic laws): Company Law (2006), Securities Law (2006); Criminal Law Amendment Act (6) (2006), Law on the State-Owned Assets of Enterprises (2009), and Accounting Law (2000). With the basic laws, it is also necessary to understand the administrative regulations issued by the Council of State. They are Opinions on the Promotion of the Reform, Opening, and Constant Growth of Capital Markets, Circular of the Council of State on its Approval of the Opinion of the CSRC on the Improvement of the Quality of Listed Companies (OECD, 2011).

In addition, the departmental provisions are created by ministries, commissions, the People's Bank of China, the Audit Administration, and other agencies with administrative jurisdiction under the supervision of the Council of State. Finally, self-disciplinary rules refer to stock exchanges'Stock Listing Rules and Trading Rules (OECD, 2011). Even if there is no lack of laws and regulations, evaluating the quality of government policies is necessary. Specifically, the quality of bureaucrats and politicians who make them, according to Wang (2018), is a critical impact factor on the performance of Chinese companies.

Regarding laws and regulations, it is essential to note that market entry regulations, taxation, and lending decisions are part of the government toolkit to influence the direction of structural transformation. In addition, the literature on China's local state corporatism highlights the different roles of regional governments as producers, planners, and regulators of local economies (Wang, 2018). However, more efficient coercion mechanisms should be added for proper compliance with the existing regulatory system.

From this perspective, the legal system's effectiveness, which guarantees the effectiveness of these laws, is another worthy aspect. China is undeveloped and often falls short of practices, imposing insufficient or excessive regulation on Chinese companies. In addition, the lack of legislation in some cases and the frequent review of policies in others bring great uncertainty to the legal environment, which explains why Chinese companies are less likely to seek legal support. Even if companies start lawsuits, the results are very uncertain. Another situation companies face when resorting to the judicial system is government interference in the judicial process (Qin et al., 2020). Thus, it cannot be said that law is the primary determinant of China's financial market development (Chen et al., 2017a).

The legal strengthening of minority shareholders would theoretically make it possible, if not to eliminate, but at least to reduce the illegitimate expropriation they suffer by controlling shareholders (Jia et al., 2018; Ding et al., 2010). Boateng and Huang (2017) find that the contestability of multiple non-controlling large shareholders relative to controlling shareholders reduces the adoption of excess leverage policies and tunneling and enhances capital investment.

However, this theoretical solution is complicated to achieve in vast emerging markets. That is because the Rule of Law remains underdeveloped, and controlling shareholders often hold enormous economic and political power to undermine efforts to establish and/or enforce these laws. Thus, not eliminating expropriation but giving minority shareholders certain decision-making rights to carry out activities that could increase the company's value and help them capture some value (Jia et al., 2020; Sun et al., 2017).

Even though the Companies Law (2006) was formalized to protect these rights through the standardization and organization of companies, to safeguard the socio-economic order and promote the development of a market economy, in practice, its objectives have not yet been fully achieved (Jia et al., 2020; Sun et al., 2017). This legislation governs the incorporation and organizational structure of various business organizations since its constitution, structure, issuance, and transfer of shares. It also regulates the qualifications and obligations of directors, supervisors, and executives, corporate securities, corporate finance and accounting, mergers of companies, mergers, capital increases and reductions, dissolution and liquidation of companies, branches of foreign companies, and legal responsibilities (OECD, 2011). A breakthrough in this legislation is related to the role played by supervisory boards (Ding et al., 2010; Yeung & Lento, 2020).

Another legal provision is Amendment VI to the Criminal Law (2006). This amendment is designed to give a complete definition of legal responsibilities and insecurities, improve the laws governing the securities market, and promote healthy development. The amendment governs corporate governance related to the following violations: disclosure violations, non-disclosure of essential information, breach of trust and damage to the interests of the listed company, insider trading, and insider trading and manipulation of securities or futures market information (OECD, 2011). Even so, the Chinese market is still a fertile arena for these crimes, especially the risk of expropriation by insiders (Chen et al., 2017b; Ding et al., 2010), tunneling practices (Ali et al., 2018), and high levels of information outcome management and asymmetry (Han et al., 2022).

From the accounting perspective, Chinese accounting standards meet recognized international standards. Article 8 of the Accounting Law states that China would implement a uniform accounting system prepared and issued by the Ministry of Finance. On February 15, 2006, the Ministry of Finance of China enacted the new Accounting Standards system, which entered into force for companies listed on January 1, 2007 (OECD, 2011). However, before that, Chinese companies with type B shares were already required to report according to international standards. In addition, companies that owned type A and B shares, even if they had an obligation to produce their financial reports using the Chinese Accounting Standards (CAS), also needed to provide additional accounting information compiled according to IFRS (Pasko et al., 2021).

In China, accounting standards comprise 39 items covering accounting changes for economic transactions and matters applicable to various companies (OECD, 2011). Therefore, such changes toward IFRS were significant, as this set of rules is more principle-based than the old Chinese accounting standards, which were more rule-based and industry-specific (Yeung & Lento, 2020). On the one hand, listed companies recorded a significant export increase after convergence with IFRS. Still, this effect only occurred when companies traded with IFRS-compliant countries and were non-state companies (Xie et al., 2021). On the other hand, there was a decrease in the information on profits (Chan et al., 2021), a reduction in accounting conservatism (Pasko et al., 2021), and an increase in creative accounting or accounting innovation (Zhang et al., 2022). Thus, as well as corporate governance rules in general, accounting rules are considered high quality in theory but may need to be better understood for their practical effectiveness.

China's corporate governance institutional framework encompasses three parts: the CSRC, the agency responsible for securities and futures markets; Government agencies related to corporate governance, such as the Ministry of Finance, the Committee on Supervision and Administration of Assets and Employees, and The General Administration of Industry and Trade, the Banking Regulatory Commission of China (BRCC) and the Insurance Regulatory Commission of China (IRCC); and stock exchanges and companies registering and liquidating securities (OECD, 2011). Thus, because it is an important global financial center and has attracted many foreign investors (Han et al., 2022), our research seeks to elucidate the level of corporate governance in China. Therefore, we conducted a Systematic Literature Review to achieve our goal, and our parameters are described below. In addition, Chinese companies must comply with the Code of Good Corporate Governance Practices, which is the main rule described in the following section.

4.5 Corporate Governance Code

The Corporate Governance Code of Publicly Held Companies: "The Code" was implemented in 2002. The document is largely based on regulations of the United States and European nations. It can be said that the code contains the basic principles of corporate governance, determining the means of investor protection and the basic rules of conduct of executives and directors. The code also guides the board's structure, responsibilities, transparency, and disclosure of information. The document also addresses the board's features, such as board size, directors' experience, and structures for effective decision-making (Yeung & Lento, 2020).

China faces the ongoing challenge of ensuring that its corporate governance laws and regulations are enforced, meaning the rules and laws on paper must be effectively implemented to make a difference. It is known that this is a plan, the results of which will be observed over time and not in the short term. Thus, the main aspects of corporate governance established in the Code of Governance, the evaluation of the OECD, and the empirical literature on the subject stand out. Thus, we listed out the aspects inherent to governance in seven major topics, namely: (3.1) Sources of Funding, (3.2) Separation of ownership and management, (3.3) Information Asymmetry, (3.4) Shareholders' Rights, Board of Directors, Remuneration Policy, and (3.5) Accounting System and Independent Audit. These subjects are presented below:

4.5.1 Sources of Funding

In China, private and state-owned enterprises (SOEs) differ in both funding sources and investment policy (Carpenter et al. (2021). Despite programs to accommodate foreign investment in A-shares, foreign investors still hold only 3% of the market, which means that after the reforms, the state remains the primary source of financing for companies because state banks represent the main instrument of centrally planned investment policy (Carpenter et al., 2021). In addition, block holders who control the state often have excessive control rights to facilitate the encapsulation of resources out of listed companies, usually by institutionalizing a pyramidal structure (Zheng, 2022). Thus, listed companies often bear the burden of subsidizing local companies due to their association with the government and transfer profits to their state-owned relatives to finance their loss-making operations (Zhang, 2018).

Companies that open capital or finance themselves through bank shares or loans, directly or indirectly, are subject to the intervention of the government of China. This occurs because they are forced to keep a government agent at the top of management by the bonds created through political connections, called guanxi. Guanxi means connecting two people through the exchange of favors instead of the exchange of feelings. It establishes a relationship of reciprocity in this exchange of favors, and the relationships established through fulfilling reciprocal obligations tend to be continued.

Private companies also use guanxi to obtain advantages and/or government resources (Ali et al., 2018; Huang, 2017; Jia et al., 2018; Yang et al., 2017). Consequently, the boundaries between state and private enterprises are nebulous since both respond to the institutional matrix, which establishes preferential treatment of the state and close ties with the government and the party (Yu, 2019). 75% of Chinese listed companies, both state-owned (SOEs) and non-state companies, have received government subsidies in the last decade (Huang, 2019).

Another difference in China's institutional financing environment is that commercial banks cannot acquire company shares (Commercial Banking Law of 1995, revised in 2003). This prohibition generated a scenario where companies became shareholders of banks. In other words, it is the companies that become bank holdings. To do this, specific qualification criteria must be met. Thus, bank-holding companies have grown rapidly with government support, which leaves room for Chinese companies to build connections (guanxi) between banks and companies in a different way than in other countries (Wang et al., 2020a).

China also has mixed ownership, with a particular ownership structure of state and non-state shareholders (Yin et al., 2018). Many of these investments generate minority state ownership and aim to supply state investment funds for emerging ventures from the initial stage to the public offering (Wang et al., 2018). In addition, the Initial public offering (IPOs) market is well-restricted and controlled by China's China Securities Regulatory Commission (CSRC). The CSRC restricts the IPO process to micromanage the total number of listed companies. Given the long IPO process, private companies that want to become public often opt for a reverse merger because it involves fewer administrative steps and is much faster. The reverse merger process takes place through the acquisition of shares of small, listed companies, which are targeted by larger companies that do not wish to engage in an IPO to become public (Liu et al., 2019). This contributes significantly to the institutional pyramid structure (Zheng, 2022).

Even though the state is the primary funding source for Chinese companies, it is necessary to point out that there is no equal access to resources even among state-owned companies. There are two types of state-owned enterprises: local state-owned enterprises (LSOES) and central state-owned enterprises (CSOEs). Local governments maintain significant autonomy over operating and distributing revenues from LSOEs. Still, there is a tendency for social and political objectives to conflict with the profit objectives of these companies, therefore ending up being fertile ground for predation and income search by local bureaucracies. CSOEs, on the other hand, benefit from various preferential policies and treatments in areas ranging from taxation and technology transfer to material supplies and state bank loans that would otherwise be impossible (Wang, 2018). Moreover, employees at different levels of government, local or central, have other objectives and exert other institutional pressures on state-owned enterprises, shaping their corporate governance (Teng et al., 2018).

Another characteristic of Chinese culture is the networks of relationships known as Guanxi. Guanxi means contracting based on relationships; one consequence is reducing incentives and the usefulness of corporate disclosure (Schiavini et al. 2012). China also has a weak external monitoring role played by debt creditors (Huang et al., 2018). Furthermore, Song et al. (2020) found that large shareholders and institutional investors are less likely to participate in monitoring due to management maneuvers, opportunism and conflicts of interest, or collusion with controlling shareholders.

As the Chinese capital market is characterized by the concentration of shares with the controlling block, the major concern is to create protection for the minority shareholder. Since 2008, there has been a regulation on dividend commitment in firm bylaws. This regulation is also very characteristic in China, as it differs from the mandatory dividend adopted by many emerging countries. In this respect, Yang et al. (2020) found that the level of dividends is negatively associated with the cost of debt. That suggests that the payment of dividends influences investors and reduces their required returns. In other words, the commitment to pay dividends not only benefits minority investors but also reduces required returns, thus reducing the cost of capital for the company. Even so, Carpenter et al. (2021) present evidence that Chinese companies face a higher cost of equity than U.S. companies.

4.5.2 Separation Between Ownership and Management

The design of the shareholding and control structure is the main institutional arrangement of corporate governance that coordinates the opportunism of managers and conflict between minority shareholders and shareholding control. The shareholding structure determines the concentration or dispersion of equity. Until 2015, China was characterized by having a highly concentrated capital market, whether in the hands of families or the government. However, from 2015 onward, it began to experience the era of decentralized equity (Zheng, 2022). This fact, combined with the peculiar institutional characteristics of China, leads to different aspects to be considered regarding the separation of ownership and management. However, historians have shown that in Chinese businesses that had strong family influence, control of heritage was rarely separated from management control (Zheng, 2022). Succession disputes were important for the company's continuity. Culturally, this difficulty of separating control and management also applies to corporate companies, but now, it is between the state and companies (Goetzmann & Koll, 2005; Zhang, 2018).

Chapter 6 of the Corporate Governance Code issued by the CSRC (2019) prescribes rules for controlling shareholders and their related parties: companies invested in. The rules are divided into (a) Code of Conduct, (b) Independence, and (c) Related Parties. They aim for equity between the legitimate rights and interests of the company and other shareholders. The code of conduct for controlling shareholders states that they must not use their control power to harm other parties.

Controllers must always observe laws and regulations. Important decisions must be made at the shareholders' meeting or the board of directors.

Furthermore, controlling shareholders must comply with commitments. Concerning independence, controlling shareholders do not deal with personal matters related to the company's affairs and should not assume burdens of trust in more than one group of company. There is no relationship of subordination between a publicly held company and its controlling shareholders or effective controllers at all levels of the corporate structure. Transactions with related parties must be formalized by contract, observing transparency and conditions of equality with any unrelated party without favoritism.

An important feature of Chinese companies is the dual-principal phenomenon in which they are owned by the government and non-state shareholders, especially after the reform of the split-share structure of 2005 (Huang, 2017). Before the reform, approximately 60% of the shares belonged to the state. After the reform, state participation fell to 30% (Yang et al., 2017). Even so, state-appointed managers influence any listed company‘s management (Ali et al., 2018). In addition, Article 5 of the Corporate Governance Code states that every listed company must allow and create conditions for party activities: "Organizations of the Communist Party of China (the Party) should be established in a listed company under the Company Law to conduct the Party's activities. In addition, listed companies should provide necessary conditions for the activities of the Party organizations (CSRC, 2019)." Therefore, while the governance code provides for government participation, listed Chinese companies are unlikely to be independent of government influence.

In the case of SOEs, the separation of ownership and control differs entirely from Western companies. First, state-owned industry executives have significant power to run and operate the company in any way they see fit. The restriction mechanism ensures that it acts in the company's or country's best interests is weak. Second, in addition to economic objectives, state-owned enterprises have political or social goals (Zhang, 2018). The obligation to consider political and social objectives is expressed in the Corporate Governance Code: "State-controlled listed companies should incorporate requirements related to the Party building work into their articles of association under the Company Law and relevant regulations, and by giving due consideration to the companies' actual situations such as ownership structure and business management (CSRC, 2019)." The Chinese governance code has advanced on several points, according to the OECD analysis; however, the mandatory influence of the party, both in publicly traded and state-owned companies, still needs to be improved.

The Chinese governance code has advanced on several points, according to the OECD analysis; however, the mandatory influence of the party, both in publicly traded and state-owned companies, still needs to be improved. Even though Chap. 3 of the Governance Code establishes that a listed company must establish a formal and transparent procedure for appointing directors and that the election is open, fair, and impartial, especially in SOEs, its practice is questionable. The power of senior executives does not come from the company's board of directors or a general meeting of shareholders but from a staff appointment through the Communist Party of China (CPC's) Top Standing Committee. The research by Yu et al. (2020) warns that this fact leads to nepotism and the potential network of corruption between political organizations and the state. Chinese state-owned enterprises are going through the process of incorporating party organizations into the traditional corporate governance structure (Wang et al., 2020b).

In theoretical terms, corporate governance is designed to operate in the three boards format, composed of the (a) general shareholders' meeting and responsible authority, which allows the appointment of the (b) board of directors and the (c) supervisory board (OECD, 2011). The general shareholders' meeting is the power and decision-making organ of the company, and it has decision-making power concerning major issues. The board of directors is a decision-making body responsible for appointing senior management, determining internal management systems, convening shareholder meetings, and making certain decisions. The supervisory board functions as a monitoring body, and responsibilities prescribed by the Company's Law include financial review, supervising directors and managers, proposing temporary shareholder meetings when necessary, and reporting annually to the shareholders' meeting Beltratti et al. (2012). In addition, since 2002, the CSRC has required listed Chinese companies to appoint independent directors and establish audit committees under the board of directors (Yeung & Lento, 2020), as shown in the Fig. 4.1

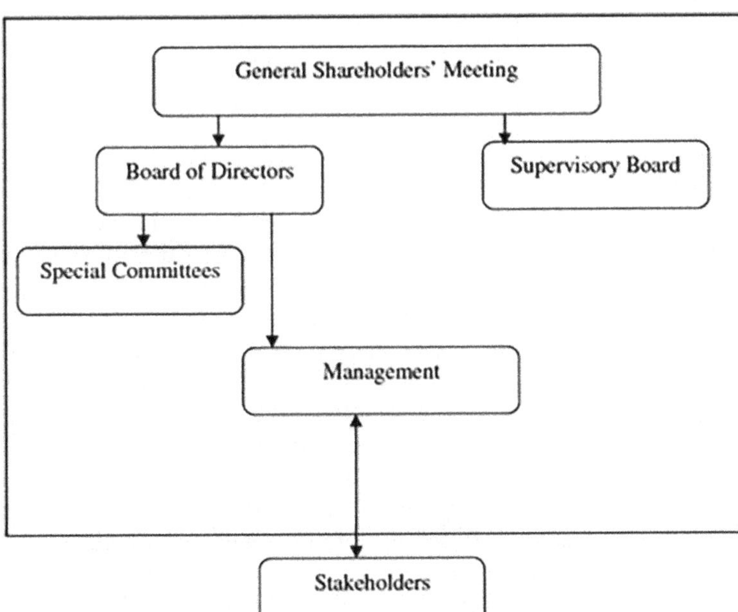

Fig. 4.1 The Corporate Governance Framework in China. Source: OECD-China Policy Dialogue on Corporate Governance - Corporate Governance of Listed Companies in China, 2011

Although property rights reform is key to alleviating government intervention, large-scale property transfers cannot be achieved due to China's socialist economic nature. A more realistic approach is to increase the distance between governance and the state. One solution found was the creation of a pyramidal structure (Su et al., 2018). This would increase the autonomy and risk-taking of state-owned companies.

However, in practice, a substantial pyramid-shaped corporate shareholder structure was formed, consisting of some listed companies and many unlisted companies, in many companies with state-owned backgrounds. Thus, through this chain of actions mechanism, the royal controllers built huge financial empires at the top of the pyramid (Zheng, 2022). This is because the pyramidal structure often leads to an imbalance between the rights to cash flow and the responsibilities for shareholding, causing the controller himself to enjoy more rights and fewer responsibilities (Zheng, 2022). In practice, the solution found to give greater autonomy to listed companies ended up harming minority shareholders.

4.5.3 *Information Asymmetry Relation Can Create Opportunism*

The last of China's corporate governance codes was updated in 2019. The update aims to improve the corporate governance of listed companies, protect investors' legitimate rights and interests, and promote the steady and solid development of China's capital markets (CSRC, 2019). In many relevant respects, it is perceived as a code well aligned with those of the Anglo-Saxon system (Yeung & Lento, 2020).

However, the rules are not always adjusted for the peculiarities of the local capital market. Adopting certain symbolic principles within the Chinese governance structure may signal compliance with institutional rules and norms in form but not substance (Mutlu et al., 2018). For example, Wang et al. (2020c) identified significant differences between the design and performance of the internal control early warning system of different sectors. Internal controls are critical rules for an effective governance system, but they may not work if seen as mere formalities (Chen et al., 2020a). The so-called Chinese-style internal control is reinforced by the pyramid structure and social connections (Guanxi). This phenomenon is characterized by executives who use real control power, usually more significant than the ability to bear responsibilities, to make decisions for their benefit. The consequences of such choices are paid by shareholders (Zheng, 2022).

Thus, in addition to the fact that the empirical literature shows that in many respects, the prescribed corporate governance differs from practice, in China, it is essential to take into account the existence of asymmetric information relation create at least three types of possibilities for the emergence opportunism and conflicts of interest: (a) the majority/minority conflict, also known as "principal-principal"; (b) conflict of three layers found in the state-owned enterprises (SOEs) and (c) the conflicts generated by the mixed property. In the following paragraphs, we explain these three ownership structure possibilities that may give rise to conflicts of interest.

Regarding the opportunism and the possibility of conflict of interest between majority shareholders and minority shareholders, we can say that even in the era of decentralized equity, most Chinese companies have a concentrated ownership structure behind the pyramid structure. This characteristic generates potential opportunisms and the possibility of conflict of interest between majority and minority shareholders and remains a central issue of corporate governance (Sun et al., 2017; Wang, 2018; Huang, 2017; Zheng, 2022). In addition, the array of shareholders is quite heterogeneous. For example, some shareholders are ordinary citizens, almost administrative agents, and even centrally controlled companies.

Usually, shareholders are considered intermediate for the different final controllers. The latter often imposes specific goals and priorities on companies that affect their market value (Wang, 2018; Zheng, 2022). For some non-core subsidiaries, the controller pays much more attention to capital operation and market speculation than corporate governance and operations management. The controller often speculates on asset replacement, new equity issuance, mergers and acquisitions, and even name changes. In this context, a market for privileged information is formed (Zheng, 2022). This allows opportunism and the emergence of conflicts and interests, reducing the efficiency of the capital market.

Given the possibilities of opportunism and conflict of interest, the Chinese market is mainly disputed by individual retail investors with little knowledge or speculative investors, and it is characterized by high volatility and low quality of information on stock prices (Qin et al., 2020; Carpenter et al., 2021; Titman et al., 2021; Zeng, 2021). In addition, one of the most characteristic aspects of the Chinese capital market is its spectrum of governance models ranging from fully private companies that can presume to maximize profit to SOEs, which supposedly pursue additional or alternative objectives such as maximizing employment, GDP, or strategic value for the government (Carpenter et al., 2021).

The second structure relation type is the presence of SOEs, which have two aspects: (a) between the party-state in its role as controlling shareholder and the minority of public (non-state) shareholders; (b) the absence of a true "principal," given that citizens on whose behalf state-owned enterprises are theoretically owned are unable to monitor or influence government agents given the exacerbated authoritarian regime (Milhaupt, 2020). Thus, the main-agent relationship in Chinese SOEs is characterized by at least three layers, i.e., (1) the State and its citizens, (2) a government representative (an official) who chairs the board, and (3) business managers who are based on the council (Guan et al., 2021). That means this part is a representation, not the real owner.

Senior executives of the state-owned enterprises are not from the market of free administrators but instead from the management of the Communist Party system. Therefore, governance mechanisms such as the board of directors, the board of supervisors, and incentives and restrictions for managers according to the perspective of the foreign companies have limited effect on the corporate governance of Chinese state-owned enterprises. Moreover, the remuneration structure of these executives has been criticized for being insensitive to the company's performance since its remuneration is linked to political power (Zhang et al., 2018).

The third structure relation is the mixed-owned property, officially proposed at the 18th National Congress of the Communist Party of China in 2012 and is currently being implemented. However, there is no consensus on the effectiveness of this reform. For some, mixed ownership has evolved regarding how the state sector expropriates private property, or privileged people expropriate state assets, making competition less equitable. In addition, many recently revealed that severe corruption is related to mixed property (Zhang, 2018). At the same time, other companies argue that mixed-owned companies are more efficient business organizations than state-owned enterprises (Yin et al., 2018). The study by Wang et al. (2018) reveals the hostile intention of minority state ownership in privately controlled companies in the IPO. They attribute this negative signaling of the state's presence, even if it is a minority, to the weak monitoring capacity, limited supply of resources, and political interdependence between private controllers and minority state owners.

In an economy dominated by state-owned enterprises, there is no fair competition between state and private companies and no such thing as private companies. That is because when state-owned enterprises have privileges, certain connected private companies will use guanxi (connections) with state-owned enterprises to engage in profitable activities, leaving private companies without these special connections in a disadvantageous position. This type of example can be found throughout China (Yu, 2019; Zhang, 2018).

Thus, concentrated ownership, decisive state intervention, and weak legal institutions are considered the reason why the expropriation of minority shareholders occurs (Wang, 2018; Zhang, 2018). Such expropriations in literature are called tunneling (Huang, 2017; Jia et al., 2020). However, the Chinese Corporate Governance Code expressly prohibits tunneling practices. Central government agencies are less inclined than local government agencies and private entities to tunnel through listed subsidiaries. In addition, they infer that the possible collusion between administrators and controlling shareholders of local agencies is what enables the tunnels. Finally, private companies are receptive to legal and regulatory institutions, but subnational institutions are less effective at curbing the opportunism of local government officials (Hu & Sun, 2019). This fact may be explained by the uncertainty in the legal environment or by too much political influence since local governments have received unequal political concessions and the right to "interpret" and adapt the national regulations to their contexts. They often use this authority to promote and protect local economic interests, producing substantial non-compliance with core directives. When a government mandate is issued in an institutional environment characterized by increased application uncertainty, pressures for organizational compliance with government regulations are not sufficiently coercive (Jones & Zou, 2017; Xie et al., 2020).

Therefore, laws and regulations can generate significant variation in organizational compliance (Xie et al., 2020). Nevertheless, there is no lack of rules and regulations in China that deal with corporate governance. Still, it lacks a more reliable legal environment and an alignment of the Chinese-style regulatory State, whose duality between a regulatory state and a changing state whose integrated and unequal fragmentation, decentralization, and internationalization of state applications directly imply the adoption of governance rules (Jones & Zou, 2017). Moreover, the opportunism of controlling shareholders is widespread in China due to the initial design of the stock market (Hu & Sun, 2019).

The Chinese institutional environment is conducive to the existence of information asymmetry that creates the possibility of opportunism and conflict of interest (Titman et al., 2021). China's corporate governance environment can be considered relatively mature in terms of formal but poorly practiced rules. This context has developed a fruitful research flow that addresses alternative monitoring mechanisms: Chizema et al. (2020) study the effect of mutual fund monitoring on tunneling behavior, Zhou and Lan (2018) and Cao et al. (2020) study the influence of institutional investors on the efficiency of the company, Zhang et al. (2017), Anderson et al. (2019) and Wang et al. (2019) study how monitoring takes place through foreign institutional investors that large non-controlling shareholders play the role of alternative monitoring and Chen et al. (2018); Deng and Gao (2018); Ni and Yin (2020) study the disciplinary effects of short selling. Shahab and Ye (2018) note that both the presence of institutional owners and independent directors and the size of the board positively influence the increased disclosure of ESG and the adherence to ESG guidelines.

4.5.4 *Rights of Minority Shareholders, Board of Directors, and Remuneration Policy*

This subchapter reviews the rights of minority shareholders, the board of directors, and the remuneration policy. Three critical aspects typically receive attention when establishing a corporate governance structure, considering the focus on mitigating opportunism and the chances of conflict of interest emerging between those involved.

4.5.4.1 Rights of Minority Shareholders

Both the Chinese governance code and the literature address the primary rights of minority shareholders, such as voting rights and dividends, and deal with the need for board independence. Regarding the right to vote, in January 2002, the CSRC issued the Code of Governance, which states that "the election of directors must adequately reflect the opinions of minority shareholders, and the Cumulative Voting System (CVS) should be promoted at the shareholders' meeting." Companies listed with a controlling shareholder that holds more than 30 percent of the outstanding shares must adopt CVS, which was also provided for in the Company Act of 2006 (Yuan et al., 2018). Yugang et al. (2019) found that debt financing costs are reduced when the CVS coexists with the staggered council elections in listed Chinese companies.

Dividend regulation in China began in 2008 and followed the "issue-assessment-supplement/review-evaluation" steps. As of Decree No. 57 (CSRC, 2008), the CSRC determined that all listed Chinese companies should include a commitment to pay dividends in their bylaws to ensure the continuity and stability of the distribution of profits. In November 2011, the CSRC added that IPO companies should include the commitment of dividends in their prospectuses (Yang et al., 2020).

In May 2012, the CSRC required listed companies to increase the disclosure of information related to the dividend commitment. In 2013, CSRC called on listed companies to indicate whether differentiated dividend policies among shareholders were allowed. The same year, the General Office of the Council of State (GOSC) declared that listed companies violating their commitment to dividends in their statutes would be penalized and recorded in dishonesty files. This fact would harm them in future external financing. The following year, the CSRC issued the Guidelines for the Statutes of Listed Firms (CSRC Guideline No. 47 of 2014, which was updated in 2019) in an additional effort to monitor dividend commitments in the bylaws (Yang et al., 2020).

4.5.4.2 Board of Directors

Listed Chinese companies have two types of boards: a board of directors and a supervisory board. However, the Chinese supervisory board has only investigative and inspection rights and in such conditions the directors are not able to properly perform their monitoring role, let alone make the board of directors socially responsible (Weng, 2017). The beginning of Chinese stock exchange was established in the early 1990s, and the recently amended Corporations Act (version 2006) made the independent board mandatory for listed companies. In other words, the legislation establishes that the positions of Chairman of the Board and the CEO/General Manager should be held by different people (Ding et al., 2022; Yeung & Lento, 2020).

The board's independence is one of the corporate governance mechanisms present in governance models worldwide. The functions performed by the boards of directors in subsidiaries controlled by China are similar in structure to those widely disseminated in the Anglo-Saxon Western model but different in practice. They reflect the deep rooting and rigidity of the corporate control logic of the dominant institutions in China. They do not incorporate the service function with the right decision-making knowledge, experience, and information (Huang & Staples, 2018).

Given this, in China, the effectiveness of the council's independence divides scholars' opinions. For example, Meng et al. (2018) and Lew et al. (2018) found a negative effect between the independence of the board and the company's performance in China. They probably attributed this effect to the low level of information in the first years of operation, which will likely prevent them from fulfilling their monitoring and advisory functions. In other words, independent advisors in China are still immature and underdeveloped.

On the other hand, Li et al. (2020) point out that monitoring independent directors is significantly associated with the early identification of the risk of financial difficulties. Board independence also contributes to mitigating the risk of earnings management (Lai & Tam, 2017; Yeung & Lento, 2020), which "refers to purposeful and deliberate actions taken by management with the ultimate goal to alter reported earnings" Kothari et al. (2005). Gong et al. (2020) found that independent directors restrict the tunneling behaviors of controlling shareholders in Chinese companies. When He and Luo (2018) warn that tunneling, among other agency problems, is more pronounced when the board has an even number of members. Shao (2019) found no relationship between the size (or independence) of the board and the performance of the company but that the duality of the CEO reflects negatively on performance; this result was also found by Lew et al. (2018).

Therefore, board independence adds value to state-owned enterprises (SOEs) in both China and India, and the presence of independent directors (I.D.s) on the SOEs board act as performance monitors to protect the interests of minority shareholders (Thenmozhi & Sasidharan, 2020). The findings of Ain et al. (2021) indicate that the presence of women on board improves the monitoring function and reduces agency costs, provided that their participation is effective (not symbolic). Gender diversity is also more effective in SOEs, where agency problems are more pronounced. Additionally, Wang and Sun (2022) found that female audit committee members positively impact CSC disclosures in China.

4.5.4.3 Remuneration Policy

The remuneration of directors used as an incentive mechanism in developed countries is considered an internal corporate governance mechanism. However, in the Chinese structure, remuneration is not seen as an internal corporate governance mechanism (Zhang et al., 2021). Due to the overwhelming domination of state shares, executives of companies listed at the early stage were often paid according to the public service's pay scale. However, the development of stock markets and incentive-based compensation have become increasingly popular for Chinese executives (Firth et al., 2006).

However, in this brief history of China's capital markets, numerous cases have been observed in which executives have been overpaid. Cash compensation dominates stock options in China (Ding et al., 2010; Boateng & Huang, 2017; Cui et al., 2021). That is because, despite the reforms, the government still participates significantly in the listed companies. Thus, to avoid dilution of state ownership, it is not common to design stock options for executives (Hass et al., 2016).

From this perspective, state ownership weakens the remuneration-performance relationship for top managers (Kato & Long, 2006), consequently making managerial promotion dependent on profitability and avoiding layoffs (Chen et al., 2015). In addition, due to the Chinese institutional background being different from that of developed countries, in the view of some scholars, the compensation scheme is not as effective as in Western countries (Jiang & Kim, 2015). However, there is no consensus in the literature in this regard.

In the specific case of SOEs, executives are high-level managers and bureaucrats. Although executive compensation may be lower than non-state companies, differentiated political treatment can be configured as a strong incentive. In addition to increasing executives' income, promotion can also improve management positions, which can be particularly important for their future political careers. In contrast, a rise to a higher position for non-SOE executives will bring more financial benefits but less political privilege. Although the benefits of promotion are different for executives from both classes of companies, they can be equally motivating (Zhang et al., 2021).

4.6 Accounting System and Independent Audit

To converge with IFRS, China launched four main Accounting Regulations (AR), namely, the 1992 AR, the 1998 AR, the 2001 AR, and the 2006 AR (Peng et al., 2008). In late 1992, after the Shanghai and Shenzen stock exchanges opened, China needed to switch to accounting principles generally accepted in market-oriented developed economies. Therefore, the Ministry of Finance (MoF) promulgated the Accounting Standards for Commercial Companies (ASBE) and the General Principles for Business Financing (GPBF) (Ma & Zhang, 2023). However, it still could not be said that China had fully converged on IFRS. Chen et al. (1999) and Ball et al. (2000) report that Chinese GAAP is more aggressive in recognizing profits.

Later, in 1998 and 2001, two other updates to Chinese accounting standards were made. Studies concluded that there were still considerable differences in profits between the 1998 AR and International Accounting Standards and that such differences were reduced with the 2001 AR (Barhamzaid, 2023). Finally, in February 2006, MoF published a set of 38 Accounting Standards that converged with the International Financial Reporting Standards (IFRS). Since then, these rules are the new Chinese Accounting Standards, which came into force on January 1, 2007, being are mandatory for all companies listed in China (Fang et al., 2023).

The evolution of the Chinese capital market over the last 40 years has also impacted the independent auditor's activity. Especially in decentralized capital, the external audit function significantly increases the possibility of raising resources through capital markets (Yeung & Lento, 2020). However, this depends on high-quality external audits (Lisic et al., 2025; Jiang & Kim, 2015). Quality is mainly determined by auditors' professional competence and independence (DeAngelo, 1981). This is because the literature points out that a high-quality, independent audit can reduce the degree of information inequality caused by market imperfections and reduce the opportunistic behavior of corporate managers, consequently increasing the capture of resources by companies (Chen et al., 2017b).

High economic policy uncertainty in China amplifies operational risks and management pressure while driving demand for independent audits (Cheng & Sutunyarak, 2023). However, unlike efficient markets like the United States, where most publicly traded companies are audited by the Big 4, listed companies in China are predominantly audited by local audit firms (Habib et al., 2014; Jiang & Kim, 2015; Fang et al., 2023). Previous research has documented that the presence of independent auditors is positively associated with the manipulation of accounting numbers by Chinese companies due to collusion between auditors and company managers (Chen et al., 2000; Nguyen et al., 2020). Consequently, financial fraud and audit failures have caused the reputation of audit work to decline in China (Peng & Chau, 2023). Hu et al. (2023) found that institutional investors who hold significant stakes in China's listed companies tend to support hiring small, less reputable audit firms to avoid improving the transparency of corporate information. In this sense, the role of institutional investors and independent audits as corporate governance mechanisms must be better understood in less developed capital markets such as China.

On the other hand, studies have identified that the quality of independent auditing in China can positively impact the disclosure of accounting information and voluntary information regarding corporate social responsibility (Zheng & Ren, 2019). Quality auditing also positively impacts investment efficiency (Tiantian, 2021) and corporate liquidity (Peng & Chau, 2023). Furthermore, larger companies and companies with more tangible assets and higher retained earnings are more likely to employ a quality external auditor than older companies and companies that rely more on external financing. Better quality auditing was also found to be associated with lower misreporting practices. However, SOEs are less likely to hire a high-quality auditor (Nguyen et al., 2020). For all the above, investors need to look for quality information and be aware that, at least in China, audited information is not necessarily reliable.

4.7 Final Considerations

The Code of Good Corporate Governance Practices in China differs very little from the governance codes of Anglo-Saxon countries. However, Article 5 of the Chinese governance code states that Chinese Communist Party organizations must be established in all listed companies. This means that the Chinese State must participate in all organizations and be able to influence decisions about their destiny. This fact creates a conflict of interest between the state's and the company's objectives, which may be one of the obstacles to the practice of governance by organizations.

According to the OECD, priority areas of concern in China's Corporate Governance include curbing abusive transactions with related parties, improving board quality, improving shareholder protection, and restricting market abuse. OECD also found it helpful to pay special attention to the critical question of enhancing the effective implementation of governance rules (aspects also very well detailed by empirical literature). In conclusion, the OECD Corporate Governance Committee considered the discussion of China's self-assessment an essential and timely exercise.

Although the Chinese authorities have committed to market-oriented reform of the country's state-owned enterprises since 2013, there are many challenges to be overcome, such as increasing fair competition between companies, opening more strategic and competitive industrial sectors for private sector participation, and improving corporate efficiency and the ability to make profits from Chinese state-owned enterprises. The current wave of state reform has focused on the state's push for consolidation through mergers and acquisitions rather than seeking to improve corporate governance (Yu, 2019).

Regulatory authorities (not only in China but in all emerging markets) should identify the peculiarities of their capital market, both culturally and behaviorally, before transplanting a code of good corporate governance practices. Such an analysis should include the definition of how much the rules should adhere to the shareholders' primacy or be in line with corporate social responsibility. Through monitoring and institutional transformation, opportunistic behaviors and their mechanisms that hinder the proper functioning of the capital market are identified. And only after this evaluation will it be possible to define which governance mechanisms would be more effective.

References

Ain, Q. U., Yuan, X., Javaid, H. M., Usman, M., & Haris, M. (2021). Female directors and agency costs: Evidence from Chinese listed firms. *International Journal of Emerging Markets, 16*(8), 1604–1633. https://doi.org.ez45.periodicos.capes.gov.br/10.1108/IJOEM-10-2019-0818

Ali, A., Qiang, F., & Ashraf, S. (2018). Regional dynamics of ownership structure and their impact on firm performance and firm valuation: A case of Chinese listed companies. *Review of International Business and Strategy, 28*(1), 128–146. https://doi.org/10.1108/RIBS-02-2017-0017

Anderson, H., Chi, J., & Liao, J. (2019). Foreign strategic ownership and minority shareholder protection. *Emerging Markets Review, 39*(March), 34–49. https://doi.org/10.1016/j.ememar.2019.03.005

Ball, R., Robin, A., & Wu, J. S. (2000). Accounting standards, the institutional environment and issuer incentives: Effect on timely loss recognition in China. *Asia-Pacific Journal of Accounting and Economics, 7*(2), 71–96.

Barhamzaid, Z. (2023). The role of accounting regulation on good news recognition and conditional conservatism: Evidence from China's 2006 accounting regulation. *Accounting Research Journal, 36*(1), 92–105. https://doi-org.ez45.periodicos.capes.gov.br/10.1108/ARJ-08-2022-0185

Beltratti, A., Bortolotti, B., & Caccavaio, M. (2012). The stock market reaction to the 2005 split share structure reform in China. *Pacific-Basin Finance Journal, 20*(4), 543–560. https://doi.org/10.1016/j.pacfin.2012.01.004

Boateng, A., & Huang, W. (2017). Multiple large shareholders, excess leverage and tunneling: Evidence from an emerging market. *Corporate Governance: An International Review, 25*(1), 58–74.

Cao, Y., Dong, Y., Lu, Y., & Ma, D. (2020). Does institutional ownership improve firm investment efficiency? *Emerging Markets Finance and Trade, 56*(12), 2772–2792. https://doi.org/10.1080/1540496X.2018.1486705

Carpenter, J. N., Lu, F., & Whitelaw, R. F. (2021). The real value of China's stock market. *Journal of Financial Economics, 139*(3), 679–696. https://doi.org/10.1016/j.jfineco.2020.08.012

Chan, K. H., Lin, K. Z., Mo, P. L. L., & Wong, P. W. (2021). Does IFRS convergence improve earnings informativeness? An analysis from the book-tax tradeoff perspective. *Accounting and Business Research, 53*, 158. https://doi.org/10.1080/00014788.2021.1946764

Chen, X. (2017). Improved corporate governance and Chinese seasoned equity offering announcement effects. *Accounting and Finance, 57*(2), 401–428. https://doi.org/10.1111/acfi.12152

Chen, C. J. P., Gul, F. A., & Su, X. (1999). A comparison of reported earnings under Chinese GAAP vs. IAS: Evidence from the Shanghai Stock Exchange. *Accounting Horizons, 13*(2), 91–111.

Chen, S., Lin, B., Lu, R., & Zhang, T. (2015). Controlling shareholders' incentives and executive pay-for-performance sensitivity: Evidence from the split share structure reform in China. *Journal of International Financial Markets, Institutions and Money, 34*, 147–160, ISSN 1042-4431. https://doi.org/10.1016/j.intfin.2014.10.003

Chen, D., Deakin, S., Siems, M., & Wang, B. (2017a). Law, trust and institutional change in China: Evidence from qualitative fieldwork. *Journal of Corporate Law Studies, 17*(2), 257–290. https://doi.org/10.1080/14735970.2016.1270252

Chen, X. L., Dai, Y. H., & Kong, D. M. (2017b). Effect of international working experience of individual auditors on audit quality: Evidence from China. *Journal of Business Finance & Accounting, 44*, 1073–1108.

Chen, S., Lin, B., Lu, R., & Ma, H. (2018). The disciplinary effects of short sales on controlling shareholders. *Journal of Empirical Finance, 46*(December 2017), 56–76. https://doi.org/10.1016/j.jempfin.2017.12.007

Chen, C. J., Su, X., & Zhao, R. (2000). An emerging market's reaction to initial modified audit opinions: Evidence from the Shanghai Stock Exchange. *Contemporary Accounting Research, 17*(3), 429–455.

Chen, H., Yang, D., Zhang, J. H., & Zhou, H. (2020a). Internal controls, risk management, and cash holdings. *Journal of Corporate Finance, 64*(May), 101695. https://doi.org/10.1016/j.jcorpfin.2020.101695

Chen, J., Cheng, X., Gong, S. X., & Tan, Y. (2020b). Project-level disclosure and investment efficiency: Evidence from China. *Journal of Accounting, Auditing, and Finance*. https://doi.org/10.1177/0148558X20912099

Chen, S., Lin, S., Xiao, J., & Zhang, P. (2020c). Do managers learn from stock prices in emerging markets? Evidence from China. *The European Journal of Finance, 28*, 377. https://doi.org/10.1080/1351847X.2020.1850500

Cheng, M., & Sutunyarak, C. (2023). Impact of economic policy uncertainty on audit fees: Evidence from Chinese listed companies. *Problems and Perspectives in Management, 21*(3), 682–697.

Chizema, A., Jiang, W., Kuo, J. M., & Song, X. (2020). Mutual funds, tunneling, and firm performance: Evidence from China. *Review of Quantitative Finance and Accounting, 55*, 355. https://doi.org/10.1007/s11156-019-00846-z

CSRC Decree No.57. (2008). Notice on Amendment in Regulations for Listed Companies' Cash Dividend, available in: [CSRC Decree No.57] Notice on Amendment in Regulations for Listed Companies' Cash Dividend_CSRC.

CSRC. (2019). *China securities regulatory commission, code of corporate governance for listed companies* (pp. 1–34). http://german.china.org.cn/business/documents/txt/2004-07/09/content_2121138.htm

CSRC. (2020). *China Securities Regulatory Commission Annual Report 2020* (pp 1–165). http://www.csrc.gov.cn/csrc_en/c102063/c1606114/1606114/files/CSRC%20Annual%20Report%202020.pdf

Cui, X., Xu, L., Zhang, H., & Zhang, Y. (2021). Executive compensation and firm performance: Evidence from cross-listed AH-share firms. *International Journal of Finance & Economics, 26*(1), 88–102. https://doi-org.ez45.periodicos.capes.gov.br/10.1002/ijfe.1778

DeAngelo, L. (1981). Auditor size and audit quality. *Journal of Accounting and Economics, 3*(3), 183–199, ISSN 0165-4101. https://www.sciencedirect.com/science/article/pii/0165410181900021. https://doi.org/10.1016/0165-4101(81)90002-1

Deng, X., & Gao, L. (2018). The monitoring of short selling: Evidence from China. *Research in International Business and Finance, 43*(July 2017), 68–78. https://doi.org/10.1016/j.ribaf.2017.07.087

Ding, S., Wu, Z., Li, Y., & Jia, C. (2010). Executive compensation, supervisory board, and China's governance reform: A legal approach perspective. *Review of Quantitative Finance and Accounting, 35*(4), 445–471.

Ding, Y., Xiong, W., & Zhang, J. (2022). Issuance overpricing of China's corporate debt securities. *Journal of Financial Economics, 144*(1), 328–346. https://doi.org/10.1016/j.jfineco.2021.06.010

Duchin, R., Gao, Z., & Shu, H. (2020). The role of government in firm outcomes. *The Review of Financial Studies, 33*(12), 5555–5593. https://doi.org/10.1093/rfs/hhaa005

Fang, X., He, K., Mei, B., & Ye, J. (2023). The role of auditing firms in the implementation of new accounting standards: Evidence from China. *Abacus, 59*, 541–569. https://doi.org.ez45.periodicos.capes.gov.br/10.1111/abac.12256

Firth, M., Fung, P. M. Y., & Rui, O. M. (2006). Corporate performance and CEO compensation in China. *Journal of Corporate Finance, 12*(4), 693–714.

Gan, J., Guo, Y., & Xu, C. (2018). Decentralized privatization and change of control rights in China. *The Review of Financial Studies, 31*(10), 3854–3894. https://doi.org/10.1093/rfs/hhx100

Goetzmann, W. N., & Koll, E. (2005). The history of corporate ownership in China: State patronage, company legislation, and the issue of control. In R. K. Morck (Ed.), *A history of corporate governance around the world: Family business groups to professional managers (issue November)*. University of Chicago Press.

Gong, M., Wang, Y., & Yang, X. (2020). Do independent directors restrain controlling shareholders' tunneling? Evidence from a natural experiment in China. *Economic Modelling*. https://doi.org/10.1016/j.econmod.2020.01.023

Guan, J., Gao, Z., Tan, J., Sun, W., & Shi, F. (2021). Does the mixed-ownership reform work? Influence of board chair on the performance of state-owned enterprises. *Journal of Business Research, 122*(October 2019), 51–59. https://doi.org/10.1016/j.jbusres.2020.08.038

Habib, A., Jiang, H., & Zhou, D. (2014). Audit quality and market pricing of earnings and earnings components in China. *Asian Review of Accounting, 22*(1), 20–34. https://doi.org.ez45.periodicos.capes.gov.br/10.1108/ARA-05-2013-0034

Han, M., Ding, A., & Zhang, H. (2022). Foreign ownership and earnings management. *International Review of Economics & Finance, 80*, 114–133. https://doi.org/10.1016/j.iref.2022.02.074

Hass, L. H., Tarsalewska, M., & Zhan, F. (2016). Equity incentives and corporate fraud in China. *Journal of Business Ethics, 138*(4), 723–742.

He, W., & Kyaw, N. N. A. (2018). Capital structure adjustment behaviors of Chinese listed companies: Evidence from the split share structure reform in China. *Global Finance Journal, 36*(February), 14–22. https://doi.org/10.1016/j.gfj.2018.02.006

He, W., & Luo, J. H. (2018). Agency problems in firms with an even number of directors: Evidence from China. *Journal of Banking and Finance, 93*, 139–150. https://doi.org/10.1016/j.jbankfin.2018.06.006

Hu, H. W., & Sun, P. (2019). What determines the severity of tunneling in China? *Asia Pacific Journal of Management, 36*(1), 161–184. https://doi.org/10.1007/s10490-018-9582-z

Hu, J., Tang, Y., Yin, N., et al. (2023). Institutional investor information competition and accounting information transparency: Implications for financial markets and corporate governance in China. *Journal of the Knowledge Economy, 2023*. https://doi-org.ez45.periodicos.capes.gov.br/10.1007/s13132-023-01482-8

Huang, W. (2017). China's secondary privatization: New evidence on controlling shareholders tunneling. *Applied Economics, 49*(2), 188–201. https://doi.org/10.1080/00036846.2016.1192279

Huang, W. (2019). Government subsidies, dividends, and stock market refinancing of Chinese firms. *Finance Research Letters, 37*, 101345. https://doi.org/10.1016/j.frl.2019.101345

Huang, W., & Sattar, M. (2021). Corporate finance policies, subsidies, and R&D: Evidence from China. *International Journal of Finance & Economics, 26*(3), 3875–3891. https://doi-org.ez45.periodicos.capes.gov.br/10.1002/ijfe.1992

Huang, X., & Staples, W. (2018). Do Chinese corporations take their governance practices abroad? Evidence from Chinese mining subsidiaries in Australia. *Thunderbird International Business Review, 60*(4), 619–632. https://doi.org/10.1002/tie.21918

Huang, W., Ying, T., & Shen, Y. (2018). Executive cash compensation and tax aggressiveness of Chinese firms. *Review of Quantitative Finance and Accounting, 51*(4), 1151–1180. https://doi.org/10.1007/s11156-018-0700-2

Jia, N., Shi, J., & Wang, Y. (2018). Value creation and value capture in governing shareholder relationships: Evidence from a policy experiment in an emerging market. *Strategic Management Journal, 39*(9), 2466–2488. https://doi.org/10.1002/smj.2921

Jia, N., Shi, J., Wang, C., & Wang, Y. (2020). Parasites and paragons: Ownership reform and concentrated interest among minority shareholders. *Journal of Management Studies, 57*(1), 129–162. https://doi.org/10.1111/joms.12537

Jiang, F., & Kim, K. A. (2015). Corporate governance in China: A modern perspective. *Journal of Corporate Finance, 32*, 190–216.

Jones, L., & Zou, Y. (2017). Rethinking the role of state-owned Enterprises in China's rise. *New Political Economy, 22*(6), 743–760. https://doi.org/10.1080/13563467.2017.1321625

Kato, T., & Long, C. (2006). CEO turnover, firm performance, and enterprise reform in China: Evidence from microdata. *Journal of Comparative Economics, 34*(4), 796–817.

Kothari, S. P., Leone, A. J., & Wasley, C. E. (2005). Performance matched discretionary accrual measures. *Journal of Accounting and Economics, 39*(1), 163–197.

Lai, L., & Tam, H. (2017). Corporate governance, ownership structure, and managing earnings to meet critical thresholds among Chinese listed firms. *Review of Quantitative Finance and Accounting, 48*(3), 789–818. https://doi.org/10.1007/s11156-016-0568-y

Lew, Y. K., Yu, J., & Park, J. Y. (2018). The impacts of independent director and CEO duality on performance in the Chinese post-institutional-transition era. *Canadian Journal of Administrative Sciences, 35*(4), 620–634. https://doi.org/10.1002/cjas.1468

Li, M., Liu, C., & Scott, T. (2019). Share pledges and firm value. *Pacific-Basin Finance Journal, 55*(August 2018), 192–205. https://doi.org/10.1016/j.pacfin.2019.04.001

Li, Z., Crook, J., Andreeva, G., & Tang, Y. (2020). Predicting the risk of financial distress using corporate governance measures. *Pacific-Basin Finance Journal, 68*, 101334. https://doi.org/10.1016/j.pacfin.2020.101334

Li, J., Ma, Y., Shi, B., & Yang, Y. (2021). Can the market recognize the value of the corporate governance mechanism of Chinese listed companies? Empirical evidence from COVID-19. *Frontiers in Public Health, 9*.

Lisic, L., Silveri, S., Song, Y., & Wang, K. (2025). Accounting fraud, auditing, and the role of government sanctions in China. *Journal of Business Research, 68*(6), 1186–1195, ISSN 0148-2963. https://www.sciencedirect.com/science/article/pii/S0148296314003567. https://doi.org/10.1016/j.jbusres.2014.11.013

Liu, J., Stambaugh, R. F., & Yuan, Y. (2019). Size and value in China. *Journal of Financial Economics, 134*(1), 48–69. https://doi.org/10.1016/j.jfineco.2019.03.008

Ma, S., & Zhang, W. (2023). How to improve IFRS for intangible assets? A milestone approach. *China Journal of Accounting Research, 16*(1), 100289. https://doi.org/10.1016/j.cjar.2022.100289

Meng, Y., Clements, M. P., & Padgett, C. (2018). Independent directors, information costs, and foreign ownership in Chinese companies. *Journal of International Financial Markets, Institutions, and Money, 53*, 139–157. https://doi.org/10.1016/j.intfin.2017.09.016

Milhaupt, C. J. (2020). The state as owner-China's experience. *Oxford Review of Economic Policy, 36*(2), 362–379. https://doi.org/10.1093/oxrep/graa001

Mutlu, C. C., Van Essen, M., Peng, M. W., Saleh, S. F., & Duran, P. (2018). Corporate governance in China: A meta-analysis. *Journal of Management Studies, 55*(6), 943–979. https://doi.org/10.1111/joms.12331

Nguyen, L. Q. T., Le, D. T., Luu, H. N., Nguyen, A. H., & Hoang, T. G. (2020). The role of audit quality in preventing firm misreporting: Empirical evidence from China. *International Journal of Managerial Finance, 16*(1), 83–100. https://doi.org.ez45.periodicos.capes.gov.br/10.1108/IJMF-04-2019-0122

Ni, X., & Yin, S. (2020). The unintended real effects of short selling in an emerging market. *Journal of Corporate Finance, 64*(May), 101659. https://doi.org/10.1016/j.jcorpfin.2020.101659

OECD. (2011). Corporate governance of listed companies in China: Self-assessment by the China securities regulatory commission. In *OECD-China Policy Dialogue on Corporate Governance*. OECD. https://doi.org/10.1787/9789264119208-en

Pasko, O., et al. (2021). Do convergence to IFRS national standards and corporate governance attributes affect accounting conservatism? Evidence from China. *Scientific Papers of the University of Pardubice, Series D: Faculty of Economics and Administration, 29*(2), 1272. https://doi.org/10.46585/sp29021272

Peng, C., & Chau, K. Y. (2023). Independent audit quality and corporate cash holdings. *Finance Research Letters, 58*(B), 104405. https://doi.org/10.1016/j.frl.2023.104405

Peng, S., Tondkar, R. H., van der Laan Smith, J., & Harless, D. W. (2008). Does convergence of accounting standards lead to the convergence of accounting practices? A study from China. *The International Journal of Accounting, 43*(4), 448–468.

Qin, J., Yang, X., He, Q., & Sun, L. (2020). Litigation risk and cost of capital: Evidence from China. *Pacific-Basin Finance Journal, 68*, 101393. https://doi.org/10.1016/j.pacfin.2020.101393

Schiavini, J. M., Scherer, F. L., & Coronel, D. A. (2012). Understanding guanxi and its influence on international relations. *Contemporary Economics Magazine, 16*(2), 316–332. https://doi.org/10.1590/S1415-98482012000200007

Shahab, Y., & Ye, C. (2018). Corporate social responsibility disclosure and corporate governance: Empirical insights on the neo-institutional framework from China. *International Journal Disclosure Governance, 15*, 87–103. https://doi-org.ez45.periodicos.capes.gov.br/10.1057/s41310-018-0038-y

Shao, L. (2019). Dynamic study of corporate governance structure and firm performance in China: Evidence from 2001-2015. *Chinese Management Studies, 13*(2), 299–317. https://doi.org/10.1108/CMS-08-2017-0217

Song, S., Xu, X., & Yi, Y. (2020). Shareholder voting in China: The role of large shareholders and institutional investors. *Corporate Governance: An International Review, 28*(1), 69–87. https://doi.org/10.1111/corg.12303

Su, K., Wan, R., & Song, V. Y. (2018). Pyramidal structure, risk-taking, and firm value: Evidence from Chinese local SOEs. *The Economics of Transition, 26*(3), 401–427. https://doi.org/10.1111/ecot.12156

Sun, J., Yuan, R., Cao, F., & Wang, B. (2017). Principal–principal agency problems and stock price crash risk: Evidence from the split-share structure reform in China. *Corporate Governance: An International Review, 25*(3), 186–199. https://doi.org/10.1111/corg.12202

Teng, D., Fuller, D. B., & Li, C. (2018). Institutional change and corporate governance diversity in China's SOEs. *Asia Pacific Business Review, 24*(3), 273–293. https://doi.org/10.1080/13602381.2017.1407125

Thenmozhi, M., & Sasidharan, A. (2020). Does board independence enhance the firm value of state-owned enterprises? Evidence from India and China. *European Business Review, 32*(5), 785–800. https://doi-org.ez45.periodicos.capes.gov.br/10.1108/EBR-09-2019-0224

Tiantian, Z. (2021) Research on the relationship among over-investment, audit quality, and corporate risk of listed companies based on big data - Based on the empirical data of listed companies in China. In *E3S Web Conference V 253, 2021 international conference on environmental and engineering management (EEM 2021)*.

Titman, S., Wei, C., & Zhao, B. (2021). Corporate actions and the manipulation of retail investors in China: An analysis of stock splits. *Journal of Financial Economics, 145*, 762. https://doi.org/10.1016/j.jfineco.2021.09.018

Wang, B. (2018). Ownership, institutions, and firm value: Cross-provincial evidence from China. *Research in International Business and Finance, 44*(July 2017), 547–565. https://doi.org/10.1016/j.ribaf.2017.07.125

Wang, J., & Sun, J. (2022). The role of audit committees in social responsibility and environmental disclosures: Evidence from the Chinese energy sector. *International Journal of Disclosure Governance, 19*, 113–128. https://doi-org.ez45.periodicos.capes.gov.br/10.1057/s41310-021-00131-3

Wang, T., Jiao, H., Xu, Z., & Yang, X. (2018). Entrepreneurial finance meets government investment at initial public offering: The role of minority state ownership. *Corporate Governance: An International Review, 26*(2), 97–117. https://doi.org/10.1111/corg.12227

Wang, H., Wu, J., Yang, Y., Li, R., & Liu, Y. (2019). Ownership concentration, identity, and firm performance: Evidence from China's listed firms. *Emerging Markets Finance and Trade, 55*(15), 3653–3666. https://doi.org/10.1080/1540496X.2019.1672042

Wang, H., Luo, T., Tian, G. G., & Yan, H. (2020a). How does bank ownership affect firm investment? Evidence from China. *Journal of Banking and Finance, 113*, 105741. https://doi.org/10.1016/j.jbankfin.2020.105741

Wang, K., Miao, N. N., & Xue, K. K. (2020b). Does the technology background of the party committee secretary affect the firm's innovation efficiency? Evidence from listed state-owned enterprises in China. *Technology Analysis and Strategic Management, 32*(5), 489–502. https://doi.org/10.1080/09537325.2019.1668920

Wang, Q., Xue, X., Yang, D., & Lee, C. K. H. (2020c). Internal control system and mechanism of Chinese listed companies: An empirical study. *Enterprise Information Systems*. https://doi.org/10.1080/17517575.2020.1778094

Weng, C. X.-C. (2017). Inside or outside the corporate law box? Shareholder primacy and corporate social responsibility in China. *European Business Organization Law Review, 18*(1), 155–191.

Xie, X., Shen, W., & Zajac, E. J. (2020). When is a governmental mandate not a mandate? Predicting organizational compliance under Semicoercive conditions. *Journal of Management, XX*(X), 1–29. https://doi.org/10.1177/0149206320948579

Xie, L., Zhang, M., & Zhai, S. (2021). IFRS convergence and international trade: Evidence from China. *Accounting and Business Research, 52*, 838. https://doi.org/10.1080/00014788.2021.1938962

Xu, J., Zhou, M., & Li, H. (2018). The drag effect of coal consumption on economic growth in China from 1953 to 2013. *Resources, Conservation and Recycling, 129*, 326–332.

Yang, D., Jiao, H., & Buckland, R. (2017). The determinants of financial fraud in Chinese firms: Does corporate governance as an institutional innovation matter? *Technological Forecasting and Social Change, 125*(July), 309–320. https://doi.org/10.1016/j.techfore.2017.06.035

Yang, D., Cheng, L., Wang, G., Wang, Y., & Zhang, L. (2020). Investor protection and cost of debt: Evidence from dividend commitment in firm bylaws. *Corporate Governance: An International Review, 28*(5), 294–308. https://doi.org/10.1111/corg.12332

Yeung, W. H., & Lento, C. (2020). Earnings opacity and corporate governance for Chinese listed firms: The role of the board and external auditors. *Asian Review of Accounting, 28*(4), 487–515. https://doi.org/10.1108/ARA-06-2019-0124

Yin, Z., Liu, L., Wang, H., & Wen, F. (2018). Study on the ownership balance and the efficiency of mixed-ownership enterprises from the perspective of heterogeneous shareholders. *PLoS One, 13*(4), 1–15. https://doi.org/10.1371/journal.pone.0194433

Yu, H. (2019). Reform of state-owned Enterprises in China: The Chinese Communist Party strikes Back. *Asian Studies Review, 43*(2), 332–351. https://doi.org/10.1080/10357823.2019.1590313

Yu, H., Nahm, A. Y., & Song, Z. (2020). The power source of Chinese state-owned enterprise leaders, investigation of local core officials, and corporate investment behavior. *Journal of the Asia Pacific Economy, 0*(0), 1–25. https://doi.org/10.1080/13547860.2020.1782039

Yuan, R., Liu, C., Xiao, J. Z., & Sun, J. (2018). The determinants and effects of voluntary adoption of a cumulative voting system: Evidence from China. *Pacific-Basin Finance Journal, 51*(June), 251–266. https://doi.org/10.1016/j.pacfin.2018.07.004

Yugang, C., Yu, L., Shahab, Y., & Yuan, Z. (2019). Do staggered board elections affect firms' financing costs? Evidence from China. *International Journal of Finance and Economics, 2020*, 1–16. https://doi.org/10.1002/ijfe.1897

Zeng, J. S. (2021). Does regulation of defensive tactics with mandatory rules benefit shareholders? Evidence from event studies in China. *International Review of Law and Economics, 66*, 1–13.

Zhang, W. (2018). Six understandings of corporate governance structure in the context of China. *European Journal of Finance, 24*(16), 1375–1387. https://doi.org/10.1080/1351847X.2015.1113194

Zhang, C. M., & Greve, H. R. (2018). Delayed adoption of rules: A relational theory of firm exposure and state cooptation. *Journal of Management, 44*(8), 3336–3363. https://doi.org/10.1177/0149206316673719

Zhang, X., Yang, X., Strange, R., & Zhang, Q. (2017). Informed trading by foreign institutional investors as a constraint on tunneling: Evidence from China. *Corporate Governance: An International Review, 25*(4), 222–235. https://doi.org/10.1111/corg.12206

Zhang, H., Huang, H. J., & Habib, A. (2018). The effect of tournament incentives on financial restatements: Evidence from China. *International Journal of Accounting, 53*(2), 118–135. https://doi.org/10.1016/j.intacc.2018.05.002

Zhang, L., Zhang, H., & Jiang, H. (2021). Tournament incentives, internal promotion, and corporate social responsibility: Evidence from China. *The European Journal of Finance, 28*, 416. https://doi.org/10.1080/1351847X.2021.1937258

Zhang, M., Wu, Y., Tong, L., & e Deng, Y. (2022). Does IFRS convergence promote corporate innovation? Preliminary evidence from China. *Asia-Pacific Journal of Accounting & Economics, 29*(1), 255–274. https://doi.org/10.1080/16081625.2019.1673185

Zheng, P., & Ren, C. (2019). Voluntary CSR disclosure, institutional environment, and independent audit demand. *China Journal of Accounting Research, 12*(4), 357–377. https://doi.org/10.1016/j.cjar.2019.10.002

Zheng, Z. (2022). *State-owned enterprise's ownership reform: A Chinese modernization approach* (1st ed.). Routledge. https://doi.org/10.4324/9781003361404

Zhou, J., & Lan, W. (2018). Investor protection and cross-border acquisitions by Chinese listed firms: The moderating role of institutional shareholders. *International Review of Economics and Finance, 56*(December 2017), 438–450. https://doi.org/10.1016/j.iref.2017.12.003

Chapter 5
Japan

Japanese Corporate Governance

Claudine Pereira Salgado, Eliene Aparecida de Moraes, and Hiroyasu Omura

5.1 Introduction

Historically, both the Commercial Code and the Corporate Law established a healthy corporate governance system for Japanese corporations, with a board of directors and auditors operating functionally; however, before the reform started in 2012, Japanese corporate governance has been criticized for not working well in terms of corporate profitability, for example, a lower return on equity (ROE). What causes this criticism? A significant issue in Japanese corporate governance is that while several effective governance structures have been established for a long time, these structures have not worked well enough to achieve a higher return on equity (ROE) and realize effective use of capital or sustainable growth. One explanation for this is that Japanese corporate governance aims to expand the scale of the company rather than profit growth, which is best for various stakeholders, such as employees, business partners, credit institutions, or customers, rather than shareholders.

Although Japanese corporations face pressure over their corporate governance practices, these pressures affect different groups of companies to a greater or lesser extent, whether they may be unanimously or coordinated. There is a lack of consensus on the weaknesses and strengths of these practices, and it should be emphasized that power and policy restrict the changes caused by these pressures (Aoki &

C. P. Salgado (✉)
Heriot-Watt University, Dubai, United Arab Emirates

E. A. de Moraes
University of Rio Verde, Rio Verde, Brazil

H. Omura
Teikyo Heisei University, Tokyo, Japan
e-mail: h.omura@thu.ac.jp

C. B. Macagnan (ed.), *Corporate Governance in Capital Markets*, CSR, Sustainability, Ethics & Governance,
https://doi.org/10.1007/978-3-031-94751-3_5

Patrick, 1994; Jackson & Miyajima, 2007; Omura, 2020a). Corporate governance standards can be different for companies based in the same country. They can differ in financial and ownership characteristics, board and management characteristics, and employment characteristics and incentives, among other aspects, so governance systems vary from company to company or country to country.

National institutional systems create formal and informal rules for which companies must adapt their governance and ownership structures. Over time, changes in these traditional and legal rules set management decision-making standards. The factors influencing corporate governance can lead to convergence, divergence, or hybridization of corporate governance models (Jerzemowska & Koyama, 2020).

Japan is a non-Western country with one of the largest stock markets in the world. Historically, their companies are not seen by other countries as particularly transparent, have poor protection for minority investors, insider-dominated boards of directors, pyramidal structures, substantial cross-stakes between companies, life-long employment system, and are financed primarily by banks (Aman et al., 2021; Clarke, 2020; Jerzemowska & Koyama, 2020; Koji et al., 2020; La Porta & Lopez-De-Silanes, 1998). All these characteristics affect the corporate governance structure of companies. Japanese companies have a traditional management system that also affects this corporate governance structure, making it different from the corporate governance structure of other countries.

To reach the current governance stage, Japan went through a long journey since the First and Second World Wars, other countries' control of the economy, political and regulatory changes, and governance reforms. To understand this trajectory, this chapter explores what happened to Japanese corporate governance for a long time, why this happened, and what is necessary for better corporate governance in the Japanese context. To meet this objective, it presents the structure of corporate governance, and the Japanese management system based on a systematic review of the theoretical and empirical literature in the Web of Science and Scopus databases.

By conducting the literature review, it was possible to observe that the Japanese Corporate Governance model has relevant and unique characteristics and peculiarities, which include elements of governance and traditional management, encompasses aspects of stakeholder-oriented administration (mainly employees), and incorporates market-oriented governance characteristics, creating a unique type of governance, in which companies can choose the organizational model that best suits their business and culture. Focusing on the structure of the board of directors, it is possible to have a board with official auditors (*Kansayaku* Board), or a board with three committees (3C): remuneration, audit, and appointment, or a mix of the board with the audit and oversight committee.

The chapter is structured as follows: this first section contemplates the introduction. Section 5.2 discusses the structure of Japanese corporate governance. Section 5.3 brings the corporate governance models currently used in Japan and shows why the "Double Codes," Japanese Administration Code, and Corporate Governance Code were introduced. Finally, Sect. 5.4 presents the final considerations, then the references are demonstrated.

5.2 Capital Market Structure in Japan

5.2.1 *Japanese Governance Structure*

The typical Japanese corporate governance system has remained the same since the Commercial Code was established to construct the Japanese corporate system in 1899. However, the Corporate Law was dismembered from the old Commercial Code in 2005. As company owners, shareholders select members of a board of directors at a general meeting and entrust the board of directors with their decision-making authority over the company. The board of directors is responsible for making important decisions while monitoring directors' actions. Theoretically, auditors can monitor directors' actions independently of the board.

The Japanese corporate governance should have been healthy if the company had been managed as the Commercial Code was enacted. According to the code, directors and auditors should have done what they expected. However, Japanese corporate governance began to be criticized for not working well enough to overcome a crisis, especially in an economic crisis after a "bubble burst" at the turn of the century, around 2000. After Japanese stock markets peaked in late 1989, the Japanese economy became negative. In a lower-growth economy, companies struggled with investment in overburdened facilities, too much debt to sustain them, and an excessive workforce.

As the Japanese economic growth was getting, Japan's worst form of corporate management was being negatively criticized while at the same time being admired globally as a "miraculous Japanese success" of recovering from the interruption of World War II. Several critics mentioned that the main reasons for the failure of the Japanese business management system in the "bubble burst" were due to "bad Japanese corporate governance." The failure of a corporate management system does not mean a bad practice of corporate governance because even a company with a typical Japanese management system has been successful in a challenging economic cycle, such as First Retailing Co. (a Uniqlo operating company, a clothing retailer) or Nitori (a manufacturer and distributor of furniture).

Japan's corporate management system should have taken a long time to adjust to the volatile economic environment under severe competition from the world. A malfunction of Japan's corporate governance system should be an alibi for Japan's low-growth economy in the 1990s. The following section will explain how the Japanese business management system closely relates to Japanese corporate governance.

5.2.2 *Japanese Corporate Management and Corporate Governance System*

Japanese managers and directors are typically selected based on their long-term performance and contribution to the company, from senior managers who have worked from recent graduates to division managers throughout their careers.

Corporate managers have competed among their colleagues to occupy better and higher positions in the company hierarchy. The employees' assessment system is built to survive in these competitions. Their performance is evaluated not only based on their performance in the company's earnings or sales but also on the potential management capacity or loyalty to the company.

The entire employee's career spans various business units or a particular specialized business unit based on their potential capability. They have accumulated extensive knowledge and special skills in managing the company or a smaller business unit. These selected managers are some types of representatives of all company employees. Therefore, Japanese corporate managers, such as a board of directors selected after the survival competition, tend to be able to run a business operation in which they have special knowledge to manage.

Because these employees, however, are willing to manage these businesses diligently, they have less opportunity to work for the company efficiently, for example, in terms of practical capital usage for the company's business units. They are not corporate managers because they make strategic, efficient decisions for the company's overall business. Instead, they are experts in a specific business unit where they have been building their professional careers with knowledge for running the business. These managers were selected for their business performance or loyalty to the company, not for corporate management skills such as efficient capital strategy or human resources management.

By the end of the 1980s, most Japanese companies had stable growth above double digits, as their markets for services or products offered grew both in Japan and around the world, especially in the United States or Europe. Currently, Japanese companies are trying to expand their scalability to capture a considerable market share rather than seeking more efficient capital use or greater profitability, as a company's scale expansion needs many jobs or business units and several numbers of selected managers as management positions.

A typical Japanese company is owned by many "stable shareholders" who rarely buy or sell their shares in terms of shareholders. They are primarily banks, insurers, or business partners with some relationship with the company, such as the companies that buy the products or services or provide their products or services to the company. Because Japanese companies are managed efficiently and diligently by representatives of all their employees, they do not like their shareholders to participate in corporate management or influence their company.

Managers ask banks or insurers to make some loans, whether the long-term or short-term loan or for business-related companies, to keep their shares. The goal is for the company to avoid some influence from most of its shareholders and have complete discretion from corporate management. Thus, its shareholders could remain silent in a stable environment for the company, not in a crisis. When the company enters a severe problem, such as a financial crisis, the company could ask financial institutions for support through urgent loans. In some cases, these financial institutions may send a director who used to have a chair on the board of their financial institutions to the troubled company's board and take an initiative role at the company's turn. These influential banks are called "main banks," which, in some cases, can play an essential role in compromising the benefits and losses of various lenders.

Corporate governance is closely related to Japan's traditional corporate management system, especially the company personnel system (employees), which is a valuable tool for Japanese corporate governance. There are several features in the traditional Japanese business management system. One of the essential features of the Japanese personnel system is the life-long employment system. The company recruits several recent graduates directly from a university in a year and instructs them on the at-work training system. They have various work experiences in different business units every two or three years, gradually climbing to a higher hierarchy with change and accumulating business skills while experimenting with multiple positions. Their salary is kept low in their 20 s or 30 s compared to what they did for the company, and as they get a managerial job, the salary gradually increases. At this point, their contribution to the company matches what they have done throughout their career. Before that, their pay was less than what they performed at work.

Management positions are in smaller numbers in a higher hierarchy. However, this compensation system works well enough to select employees based on their performance or ability. The higher the position in the company, the less they are, and this is an efficient tool for selecting appropriate corporate managers among employees for their business skills or loyalty. In some cases, this can accomplish a kind of managerial success process. In this educational process, it is also essential to train new employees to be patriotic and loyal to the company and follow the senior manager's orders, even if it is not rational. Sometimes, employees are taught to get a unique corporate culture to fight competitors with the same mindset as the entire corporation. Based on this career development, most employees work in the same company throughout their business career. The gradual increase in salary can support the employee's life development process, such as getting married, having a home, and raising their children.

Before the Japanese corporate governance reform began in 2013, Japan's corporate governance system was supported by the traditional Japanese corporate management system. Until then, the business of Japan's management system had been building a conventional Japanese corporate governance, and there are three characteristics to this. First, most silent shareholders have never engaged in Japanese corporate governance to monitor or verify what corporate managers perform as directors. Second, corporate managers monitor or demonstrate what they act independently without shareholder involvement. Ultimately, the priority of corporate managers has been the benefit of all employees, not themselves or their shareholders. These characteristics lead us to believe there was no corporate governance in Japan when we defined "corporate governance" as a monitoring or verification device by third parties, such as shareholders, other than corporate directors.

Japanese corporate managers are selected among employees for their long-term contribution to a company, such as their performance or loyalty. They have already experienced many business or core company management units, such as human resources, business strategy planning, or corporate budget planning. Their business skills or management capabilities gradually accumulate for a long business career in the same company. They show skill or management ability by surviving severe competition for a higher corporate hierarchy among employees. They manage the company as selected representatives of all employees. Therefore, the priority for management is how beneficial employees are to the company since corporate managers are considered "up-to-date" employees.

The salaries of these managers are not far beyond those of employees in the United States, United Kingdom, or European Union countries. For this reason, there are fewer agency problems in Japanese companies, as corporate managers manage the company on behalf of an employee and are not seeking better compensation for putting their position in a situation of "conflict of interest" in the company, believing that the company exists for all employees. They have the discipline to run the company for the sake of employees because they come from selected employees, not seeking their benefits or interests. As a result, Japanese corporate governance is run by corporate managers to monitor or verify the company independently. In the next section, we present the main features of the Japanese capital market with a focus on the Tokyo Stock Exchange.

5.2.3 *Japanese Capital Markets*

The Tokyo Stock Exchange (TSE) is the largest stock exchange in Asia and the second largest in the world by market capitalization (USD 5.38 billion). Behind only the U.S. exchanges NYSE and Nasdaq. TSE totaled 3871 companies listed in December/2022 (WFE, 2023). The TSE was established in 1878 under the name *Tokyo Kabushiki Torihikijo*, and in 1943, it joined ten more stock exchanges located in Japanese cities, forming the TSE. However, due to the bombing of Nagasaki, it was closed, and only in 1949 was it reopened (JPX, 2021). Japan Exchange Group (JPX) manages TSE, Asia's largest capital market operator.

Shares traded on the TSE can be divided into three categories or groups. Shares belonging to the first section include companies such as blue chips (these are the most traded shares on the stock exchange, have a higher market value, and tend to have robust operating results and good profit sharing) and large caps (these are mid-capitalization shares, generally between 2 and 10 billion reais in market value/capitalization); the actions of the second section include medium-sized companies, large caps, and mid-caps (These are shares with a low capitalization value and less liquidity, but they are in the process of accelerated expansion.); and the steps gathered in the mother's area include high-growth and emerging companies, including small caps (stocks with low capitalization value and lower liquidity but are in the process of accelerated expansion).

Among the main indexes of the TSE can be listed: (a) the Nikkei 225, which comprises the 225 largest companies in the country and is calculated considering the market value and the volume of trades of the company; (b) Topix, which brings together all companies considered “first section” and calculated according to the capitalization of these companies; and (c) the J30 Index, which is composed of the largest companies in the industrial sector (JPX, 2021). In 2014, JPX also launched the JPX-Nikkei 400, which includes the top 400 companies that meet global investment standards and are based on quantitative factors such as profitability and market value and qualitative factors such as corporate governance and disclosure (JPX, 2021).

In 2020, the TSE’s total amount in negotiations was more than 700 trillion yen (JSDA, 2021). Institutional investors have invested more than 5 trillion yen in securities and more than 200 trillion yen in equity interests in TSE-listed companies. Individual investors add more than 100 million yen of equity interest in these companies, while foreign investors total more than 700 million yen in equity interest on the Tokyo Stock Exchange (JSDA, 2021). In terms of ownership types, institutional investors in 2020 had around 15% share based on market value; foreign investors had approximately 30%; individual investors had about 16%; the government kept around 1%; and financial institutions guaranteed almost 16% share based on market value (JSDA, 2021).

In addition, Japan is among the top ten IPO markets globally (OECD, 2021). Thus, it is relevant to understand the current stage of Japan’s corporate governance system. The Japanese corporate governance system includes regulatory documents that formalize the rules and guidelines companies must follow to execute their activities. To understand these regulatory documents, Sect. 5.2.4 reports on the leading man, primarily national laws and regulations or voluntary adoption, with the “comply or explain” approach impacting the country’s corporate governance system.

5.2.4 National Legislation and Regulation

Japan’s corporate governance reform policy was carried out incrementally due to institutional rigidity and several amendments to the Commercial Code and other corporate laws (Jackson & Miyajima, 2007). One of the primary laws that rule the Japanese system of governance and that serves as the basis for the other regulations is The Companies Act (Act No. 86 of 2005—The Companies Act), which, with a series of rules coupled with it, establishes the guidelines fundamentals principles that companies need to follow, regardless of whether they have publicized capital. These guidelines include the rights and duties of executives, governance bodies, mandatory disclosure of information, and other requirements (FSA, 2005). In addition, Companies Act establishes the obligation for companies to develop basic policies regarding their internal control system.

One of the primary laws that rule the Japanese system of governance and that serves as the basis for the other regulations is The Companies Act (Act No. 86 of 2005—The Companies Act), which, with a series of rules coupled with it, establishes the fundamentals principles that companies need to follow, regardless of whether they have publicized capital. These guidelines include the rights and duties of executives, governance bodies, mandatory disclosure of information, and other requirements (FSA, 2005). Companies Act also establishes that companies should develop basic policies regarding their internal control system.

Another relevant regulation is the Financial Instruments and Exchange Act (Act No. 25 of 1948—the FIEA). It requires listed companies to report issues related to their corporate governance structures, securities, and internal control reports to authorities (FSA, 1948). In addition, the main disclosure requirements on aspects related to corporate governance are broken down in the securities listing regulations published by the TSE (the TSE Regulations). According to the TSE Regulations, the main requirements for listed companies are to carry out corporate governance reports, to elect and disclose the name of at least one "independent office," which is an independent board member or external auditor who is less likely to have a conflict of interest with shareholders and submit a written document regarding the "independent officer."

. There are also some non-regulatory resources with a focus on improving corporate governance quality in the Japanese context. The Stewardship and Corporate Governance Codes were established to meet global governance and corporate management standards. The Codes of Stewardship and Corporate Governance are voluntary adoptions with a "comply or explain" approach; in other words, the company complies with what is in the code or explains why it has not complied.

The Companies Act states that companies must define and formalize internal corporate governance rules, such as the company's governance bodies and the number of directors (FSA, 2005). The Japanese Stewardship Code introduces activism by institutional shareholders, pressuring them to actively participate in their management to improve corporate governance in these companies. The Japan Corporate Governance Code also provides several fundamental principles listed companies must follow to implement an effective governance system. Finally, Japanese companies can voluntarily adopt International Financial Accounting (IFRS) to seek transparency and comparability for their financial reports. However, Japan still has a set of domestic accounting standards that are mandatory for Japanese companies. Section 5.2.4.1 presents the evolutions and changes of corporate legislation as of the Commercial Code of 1899.

5.2.4.1 Corporate Law

The Commercial Code of 1899 was the first national legislation for companies in Japan (it was influenced by English, French, and German law), and before the revision in 1950, directors acted on behalf of companies. Most decided their affairs, and this review incorporated the board of directors to improve management monitoring (Nottage & Kozuka, 2022). The Commercial Code of 1899 introduced key terms such as the general meeting of shareholders (*sokai*), directors (*torishimariyaku*), and statutory auditors (*Kansayaku*). Japanese corporate legislation was changed through monetary and tax policy reforms from the 1990s onward to revitalize the economy and cause its growth and development. The main characteristic of the changes that occurred in the 1990s is that most of them were demanded by businesspeople, having a quick and direct influence on companies' corporate governance (Shishido, 2021). Below is a summary of the changes that impacted the corporate governance system of Japanese companies.

In 1993, there was an introduction to the Commercial Code of provisions dealing with external auditors and the board of corporate auditors, such as extending the contract term for auditors to 2 or 3 years and reducing the rate for share derivatives of shareholders at a fixed price of 8200 yen per share. The company's purchase of shares was prohibited in 1994. Already in 1997, the Commercial Code established that treasury stock options (up to 10%) could be granted pending a resolution of the general meeting specifying name, several shares, transfer price, term of exercise, and conditions of activities. It began to allow state changes to enable the board of directors to carry out repurchases of shares. Still, in 1997, the Tax Code extinguished the prohibition of the formation of holding companies and introduced market value methods for trading operations of financial institutions (FSA, 2021; SESC, 2021; JPX, 2021; TSE, 2021).

In 1998, the Commercial Code reduced the requirements for repurchase and cancellation of shares and allowed the creation of bank-holding companies. In 1999, the Antitrust Act revised business combination regulations through merger and holding of shares; the Commercial Code established the stock exchange system that allowed a parent company to buy the subsidiary through a stock exchange; the Tax Code created an exception to taxation on stock exchanges, and accounting standards reviewed consolidated financial statements procedures (FSA, 2021; SESC, 2021; JPX, 2021; TSE, 2021).

The changes did not stop there. In 2000, the Commercial Code established the stock unfolding system; the Tax Code included prices at market value for financial instruments; accounting standards introduced current prices in financial instrument trading and had rules on retirement benefits and interim financial statements. In 2001, it was created by the Commercial Code, the law of other corporate divisions, and the prohibition of maintenance of treasury shares: The Tax Code promoted the improvement of tax rules on corporate reorganization and the purchase and sale of treasury shares and introduced a consolidated tax system. Accounting standards included standards for pension fund liabilities and introduced market-value accounting for financial products (FSA, 2021; JPX, 2021; SESC, 2021; TSE, 2021). These regulations aim at better accountability and greater transparency.

The Commercial Code of 2002 established the occupational commission system for large companies, and accounting standards introduced market value for crossholdings. In 2003, accounting standards included a reduction in the recoverable value of assets. In 2005, there was a general reform of the Corporate Law. In 2006, the Commercial Code included strengthening shareholders, responsibility, and corporate governance in scope. 2007, the Financial Instruments and Exchange Act, called Japanese SOX, was established and about the North American Sarbanes-Oxley Act. In 2009, a new version of corporate governance principles was implemented for publicly held companies.

In 2013, the Japanese Revitalization Strategy focused on structural reforms and monetary and tax policies. In 2014, as the publications of the revitalization began, the FSA issued the Principles for Responsible Institutional Investors, which became known as the Japanese Code of Administration. In 2015, there were changes in the Companies Act to include international corporate governance recommendations, and the Guidelines for the Prevention of Bribery of Foreign Public Employees were issued. Also, in 2015, the Companies Act began to require Japanese companies to explain the composition of the board if they did not have independent directors or external directors. In 2016, the TSE issued a new listing guide for foreign companies based on the principle of "comply or explain" passed Japan's unfair competition prevention law and published the Principles for Listed Companies dealing with Corporate Malfeasance (means misconduct or illegalities) (FSA, 2021; JPX, 2021; SESC, 2021; TSE, 2021).

The FSA 2017 issued the Audit Firm Governance Code, and in 2018, TSE revised Japan's Corporate Governance Code, seeking sustainable growth and maximizing value in the medium and long term. Also, in 2018, the Tokyo Principles for strengthening the anti-corruption initiatives of the United Nations Global Compact Network in Japan were issued, and TSE revised the Investor Guidelines and Company Engagement. Japan's Corporate Governance Code and the Tokyo Principles for Strengthening Anti-Corruption Initiatives sought to modernize and update management guidelines by fostering transparency and disclosing their governance and anti-corruption practices.

As of April 1, 2018, the Financial Instruments and Exchange Act introduced fair value disclosure rules reinforcing the public disclosure of relevant information. Changes to the Companies Act in Japan entered into force in March 2021, including provisions such as (a) the mandatory appointment of external directors to listed companies represented a step in the development of stricter governance legislation and (b) the obligation to establish remuneration policies for each of its directors if the terms of remuneration for individual directors are not explicitly dealt with in the statutes or the resolutions of shareholders (FSA, 2021; SESC, 2021). In June 2021, the Law for Strengthening Industrial Competitiveness was approved, allowing exclusively virtual assemblies to be held because of the COVID-19 pandemic, which was not permitted by current corporate law that authorized only face-to-face groups (FSA, 2021; SESC, 2021).

5.2.4.2 Accounting System and Japanese Stewardship Code

Regarding accounting standards, countries can adopt International Financial Accounting Standards (IFRS) in the form of "requirement" or "permission." It may be required or permitted for all companies, specific sectors, or companies. In the case of Japan, it is allotted but not needed for domestic publicly traded companies, and IFRS is one of the four financial reporting structures allowed; the others are Japanese GAAP, JMIS–Japan Modified International Standards, and US GAAP (IFRS, 2023). US GAAP are the principles and standards used in the United States, determined by the SEC (Securities and Exchange Commission). Furthermore, IFRS is permitted for foreign listings but is not required or allowed for small- and medium-sized enterprises (IFRS, 2023). JMIS comprises the IFRS issued by the IASB Modification Standards and the Japanese Accounting Standards Board (ASBJ), with two modification standards until 2023, the first issued with standards for accounting for goodwill and the second accounting for other comprehensive results (ASBJ, 2023). Japanese private sector accounting standard-setting body. Central organization within the Financial Accounting Standards Foundation (FASF) in Japan, directly responsible for the development and deliberation of accounting standards and contributions to developing and improving international accounting standards. All accounting standards established by the ASBJ are subject to endorsement by the FSA.

The Business Accounting Council (BAC), in June 2009, issued the report "Opinion on the application of International Financial Reporting Standards (IFRS) in Japan," clarifying that from the year 2010, Japanese companies would be authorized to adopt the IFRS (FSA, 2022) voluntarily. In 2015, approximately 94.5% of listed Japanese companies used Japanese GAAP, 4.8% opted for IFRS, and 0.8% used US GAAP in their financial reports (Gu, 2021). As of July 2020, around 200 companies, mainly large multinationals, have chosen to use IFRS (Aman et al., 2021).

Although Japan's commitment to the convergence of Japanese generally accepted accounting principles (J-GAAP) with IFRS has not yet formally adopted international financial reporting standards, as have other countries such as India, Indonesia, and the United States (Ozu et al., 2018). Historically, from 1996 onward, Japan began to take the first steps toward the adoption of global accounting standards, the so-called "Accounting Big Bang" the review of accounting standards and the issuance of new standards were based on North American practices and IFRS issued by the IASB, for example, Employee Benefits (1998), Recoverability of Assets (2002) and Business Combinations (2003) (Nottage & Kozuka, 2022; Ozu et al., 2018). The Standards Board was established in the Accounting Office of Japan (ASBJ) to facilitate the convergence process, and its mission was to develop standards considering value relevance, reliability, and comparability.

J-GAAP, in any case, was seeking to issue standards of high quality and scope like IFRS; however, ASBJ insisted on maintaining more conservative options; for example, the business combination standard still allowed the amortization of goodwill, and the rules on financial instruments did not allow the option of measuring at fair value (Ozu et al., 2018). In 2005, the ASBJ, together with the IASB, launched a project to achieve convergence between Japanese GAAP and IFRS, with this work being formalized in 2007 as the Tokyo Agreement. In 2008, the European Commission commented that Japanese GAAP was equivalent to the IFRS adopted by the European Union, although there are still differences between the standards (Gu, 2021; Ozu et al., 2018). In 2009, the BAC authorized the voluntary use of IFRS in the consolidated statements of listed companies with financial or commercial activities in other countries, starting from March 31, 2010. In 2013, the BAC extended the option to use IFRS voluntarily for all listed companies. The mandatory adoption of IFRS in the Japanese context should have taken place by 2016, but the schedule was changed, like the SEC's decision in the United States to postpone the adoption of IFRS.

In research conducted by Ozu et al. (2018), promoting a survey of perceptions about the costs and benefits of adopting IFRS, using the opinion of 123 managers from the largest Japanese companies, concluded that managers revealed skepticism regarding the adoption of international standards and almost 70% of respondents indicated their perception that the costs would exceed the benefits of adopting IFRS. The authors highlight that adopting IFRS in Japan continues to be controversial, and interviewees demonstrated high concern about the costs and difficulties of implementing IFRS. The authors further emphasize that as the elimination of the main differences between J-GAAP and IFRS progresses, managers' perceptions of the costs associated with the adoption of IFRS will likely also be moderated.

The Japanese Stewardship Code was adopted in February 2014 and revised in May 2017. The code was drafted as the Principles for Responsible Institutional Investors to promote the sustainable growth of companies through investment and dialogue (FSA, 2014). The Japanese stewardship adopts a system based on principles, not rules; it is not a legally binding regulation, and institutional investors are free to accept it. The Japanese Stewardship Code is not mandatory, assuming the "comply or explain" approach, and has seven principles.

The first, second, and third principles are related to institutional investors having a clear policy on how they fulfill their management responsibilities, how they publicly disclose them, how they manage conflicts of interest, and how they should monitor investee companies so that they can adequately fulfill their management responsibility with guidance for the sustainable growth of companies. The fourth principle states how they should seek a common understanding with the invested companies and work to solve the problems through constructive engagement with the invested companies.

The fifth principle shows institutional investors should have a transparent voting and disclosure policy. The sixth principle deals with how they should periodically inform their management responsibilities, including two voting duties, to their customers and beneficiaries. The seventh principle emphasizes that to contribute positively to the sustainable growth of invested companies, institutional investors must have in-depth knowledge of the invested companies and their business environment and the skills and resources necessary to properly engage with companies and make judgments in fulfilling their management activities.

The Japanese Stewardship Code asks institutional investors to adopt it and notify the FSA of its compliance. As a result, the FSA will publish a listing of the signatory investors (FSA, 2014). In April 2018, there were 227 signatories to the code: 6 trust banks, 162 investment managers (mutual funds and investment advisors), 30 pension funds, 22 insurers, and seven other institutions, including proxy consultants (Goto, 2019).

In practice, the Japanese Stewardship Code's main objective is for asset owners to monitor the management activities of the directors of the investments as if they were direct shareholders. This is simple: Japan's traditional management and governance system comprises directors who monitor and manage the company to benefit employees. Institutional investors can be the solution for more effective monitoring and management focused on greater profitability (ROE). The Japanese Stewardship Code is another relevant mechanism for strengthening the country's corporate and Corporate Governance codes.

Tsukioka (2020) researched the Japanese Management Code's impact on institutional investors' voting behavior. They are finding that the code leads trust banks, insurance companies, pension funds, and signatory foreign shareholders to refrain from lending money to companies and become more likely to vote against the appointment of representative directors and CEOs in less profitable companies and on controversial proposals about voting policies. The research reveals that most major banks and insurance companies accept the code and publish voting policies on their websites. Furthermore, adopting the code makes mutual funds and foreign shareholders less likely to vote against representative director and CEO appointments in companies with higher profitability (Tsukioka, 2020). The results suggest that adopting the Stewardship Code by institutional investors in Japan reinforces corporate governance, improving shareholders' voting behavior when less conflicted. It further indicates that shareholder voting behavior regarding director and CEO appointments reflects shareholder disappointment with management performance. The next section presents the Japanese corporate Governance Code and its evolution in the Japanese context.

5.2.4.3 Japanese Corporate Governance Code

Japan's primary public corporate governance regulators are the Securities and Exchange Surveillance Commission (SESC) and the Financial Services Agency (FSA). SESC is linked to the FSA and its mission through appropriate supervision, ensuring fairness and transparency of the market and protecting investors, contributing to the solid development of capital markets and sustainable economic growth (SESC, 2021). The FSA is responsible for financial regulation to improve national well-being through sustainable corporate and economic growth, seeking a balance between the stability of the financial system and the demonstration of financial intermediation, protection and convenience of the user, and fairness and transparency of the market even in the face of rapid changes in the financial environment, because it is emphasized that "finances are like blood circulating in the human body—an adequate supply of funds improves people's economy and lives" (FSA, 2021).

Together, these bodies, The TSE, the FSA, and the SESC, promote the adoption of more robust corporate governance mechanisms. In March 2004, TSE published the Corporate Governance Principles for Publicly Held Companies that included shareholder rights, disclosure and transparency, and the responsibilities of boards of directors, auditors, and other relevant groups (Jackson & Miyajima, 2007; JPX, 2021).

TSE issued its first Corporate Governance Code on March 5, 2015 (promulgated in June 2015) based on its structure listing requirements with the "comply or explain" approach, emphasizing a mandatory disclosure of annual reports by companies through corporate law. One of the main changes brought by the code was the requirement for the companies listed in Sects. 5.1 and 5.2 of the TSE to have at least two independent members on the supervisory board. The general principles of the Corporate Governance Code are ensuring the rights and equal treatment of majority and minority shareholders, proper operation with stakeholders other than shareholders, ensuring transparency and adequate disclosure of information to the market tab, and listing the responsibilities of the board of directors and dialogue with shareholders.

The Corporate Governance Code was revised in 2018 and 2021. The 2018 revision of the Corporate Governance Code had already incorporated relevant changes, such as a reduction in shares held by crossholdings, the establishment of procedures for the appointment and removal of the establishment of objectives and practices procedures in the compensation system, strengthening the roles of institutional investors, such as corporate pension funds, among others (FSA, 2021; SESC, 2021; TSE, 2021).

Among the changes in the Corporate Governance Code revised in 2021 is the requirement of at least one-third of external directors on the board of directors of listed companies; the dissemination of a matrix of competencies that describes the knowledge, experience, skills, and other relevant factors of each counselor; dissemination of information on climate change and the risks posed by the company's operations, etc. The Corporate Governance Code version 2021 also provides specific guidance, including explanations of key concepts, giving diversity goals, and encouraging disclosure of the diversity status of the company's core members; it provides detailed guidance that includes encouraging the formulation and dissemination of basic policies for sustainability initiatives; offers specific advice on the perspective of protecting minority shareholders in subsidiaries listed; promotes guidance on the establishment of systems that require internal audit departments to report directly to the board of directors and directors, etc. (JPX, 2021).

The Corporate Governance Code issued in June 2021 has the slogan "Seeking sustainable corporate growth and increased corporate value in the medium and long term." It is divided into five sections: (i) Section 1: Securing the Rights and Equal Treatment of Shareholders; (ii) Section 2: Appropriate Cooperation with Stakeholders Other than Shareholders; (ii) Section 3: Ensuring Appropriate Information Disclosure and Transparency; (iv) Section 4: Responsibilities of the Board; and (v) Section 5: Dialogue with Shareholders. Each section presents the general principle dealing with the specific theme of the section, then brings the general principle into specific and supplementary principles. Below, each principle that constitutes each section will be briefly described.

Section 1: Securing the Rights and Equal Treatment of Shareholders, as a general principle, recommends that companies take appropriate measures to fully guarantee the rights of shareholders and develop an environment where shareholders can exercise their rights appropriately and effectively. They must ensure effective equality of treatment of shareholders, paying attention to the issues and concerns of minority and foreign shareholders for the effective exercise of their rights and effective equality of treatment between shareholders. Without adequate cooperation with these stakeholders, it would be difficult for companies to achieve sustainable growth (JCGC, 2022). This general principle is divided into seven specific and complementary principles that address: (a) guaranteeing shareholder rights, including voting rights at the general meeting; (b) exercising shareholder rights at general meetings, providing opportunities for constructive dialogue; (c) explanations of the basic strategy regarding its capital policy; (d) disclosure of cross-holding policies, including policies for reducing cross-holdings; (e) explanations of anti-takeover measures and policies; (f) explanations of capital policy that may harm shareholder interests, such as change of control or significant dilution, including share offerings and acquisitions by management and board; and (g) ensuring that transactions with related parties do not harm the interests of the company or shareholders (JCGC, 2022).

Section 2: Appropriate Cooperation with Stakeholders Other than Shareholders recommends, as a general principle, that companies must fully recognize that their sustainable growth and the creation of business value in the medium- and long-term result from the provision of resources and contributions made by a series of stakeholders. Companies must cooperate adequately with these stakeholders (JCGC, 2022). This principle is divided into six other specific and complementary principles: (i) issuance and maintenance of business principles that will become the basis for creating corporate value in the medium and long term; (ii) development and implementation of a code of conduct for employees; (iii) address sustainability issues, including social and environmental issues; (iv) guarantee diversity, including the active participation of women; (v) establish reporting channels for irregularities, illegal or inappropriate behavior, disclosures or any other serious concerns, without fear of suffering disadvantageous treatment; and (vi) create and disseminate policies to improve human resources to increase investment in pension fund management expertise to ensure that they perform their role as active owners (JCGC, 2022).

Section 3: Ensuring Appropriate Information Disclosure and Transparency addresses the principle that seeks to ensure the disclosure of information appropriately by companies, in compliance with relevant laws and regulations, striving to provide information beyond that required by law. This includes financial and operational information and non-financial information, such as information on business strategies and business, risk, and governance issues (JCGC, 2022). This principle was broken down into two specific and complementary principles: (a) full disclosure, proactively providing information, whether required by law or beyond this requirement, and (b) recognizing the responsibility that external auditors have to shareholders and investors and take appropriate measures to ensure the effective and efficient execution of audits (JCGC, 2022).

Section 4: Responsibilities of the Board generally to bring the board's fulfillment of its functions and responsibilities appropriately, given its fiduciary responsibility and accountability to shareholders (JCGC, 2022). This includes promoting sustainable business growth, increasing business value in the medium and long term, and increasing profit-generating power and capital efficiencies. Such functions and responsibilities must be fulfilled equally and appropriately by the board of directors, regardless of the form of corporate organization—i.e., a company with a *Kansayaku*

Board (in which the Kansayaku and the Kansayaku perform a portion of these functions and responsibilities, the company with Three Committees (Nomination, Audit, and Remuneration), or the company with a Fiscal Board. This general principle is broken down into 14 specific and complementary principles: (1, 2, and 3) functions and responsibilities of the board; (4) roles and responsibilities of the *Kansayaku* and the *Kansayaku* Board; (5) fiduciary duties of directors and actors and *Kansayaku*; (6) business execution and management supervision; (7) roles and responsibilities of independent directors; (8) effective use of independent directors; (9) independence and qualification standards for independent directors; (10) use of an optional approach to the most appropriate organizational structure adopted to improve governance; (11) preconditions for the effectiveness of the Board and the *Kansayaku* Board; (12) active board deliberations; (13) information collection and support structure for directors and *Kansayaku*; and (14) *Kansayaku* director and training.

In the case of Section 4, the emphasis is given to *Kansayaku* and the *Kansayaku* Board can be highlighted. Since their fiduciary responsibilities are to shareholders, they must make decisions from an independent and objective perspective when carrying out their roles and responsibilities. This includes auditing the performance of directors' duties, appointing and dismissing *Kansayaku* and external auditors, and determining auditor remuneration (JCGC, 2022). Companies must provide and organize appropriate training opportunities for each advisor, director, and *Kansayaku*, along with financial support, to stay current as required by their roles and responsibilities. Companies must disclose their training policy to advisors, directors, and *Kansayaku* (JCGC, 2022).

Another aspect to be highlighted in Section 4 is the independence of the directors. Independent directors must adequately represent the views of minority shareholders and other interested parties before the board of directors. Companies listed on the Prime Market of the Japan Stock Exchange must appoint at least one of their directors as independent and at least two independent directors if listed on other markets. The JCGC (2022) recommends that a company listed on Market Prime that believes it needs to appoint most of its directors as independent should do so, considering a wide range of factors such as industry, company size, business characteristics, organizational structure and circumstances that surround the company, and must appoint an enough number of independent directors (JCGC, 2022). Companies that have a controlling shareholder must appoint at least one-third of their directors as independent and who are also independent of the controlling shareholder or establish a special committee composed of independent directors to deliberate and review relevant transactions or actions that conflict with the interests of the controlling shareholder and minority shareholders (JCGC, 2022).

Boards (board of directors and *Kansayaku* board) must establish and disclose independence standards designed to guarantee the effective independence of directors, considering corporate legislation and stock exchange listing rules (JCGC, 2022). Finally, the council and the *Kansayaku* Board must be balanced in knowledge, experience, and skills and must be constituted to achieve diversity, including gender, international and professional experience, age, and appropriate size (JCGC,

2022). Furthermore, at least one advisor with sufficient knowledge of finance and accounting must be included on the *Kansayaku* Board.

Section 5—Dialogue with Shareholders brings as a general principle the need for companies to enter a constructive dialogue with shareholders even outside the general meeting. During this dialogue, directors and advisors must consider shareholders' perspectives, apprehensions, and interests attentively. This requires a clear and comprehensible explanation of corporate policies to garner their support and work toward achieving a balanced comprehension of the positions of shareholders and other interested parties and subsequently implementing appropriate measures (JCGC, 2022). This principle breaks down into two specific and complementary principles: (a) approve and publicize policies for constructive dialogue with shareholders and promote this dialogue with the appointment of a member of management who will be responsible for supervising and ensuring that the dialogue individual or general meetings with investors and other activities take place and (b) establish and disseminate strategies and business plans (JCGC, 2022).

Section 5 speaks directly to the Japanese Administration Code, as through this, institutional investors are encouraged to engage in purposeful dialogue based on in-depth knowledge of investee companies and their business environment. This regular dialogue with shareholders, encouraged by the JCGC, can provide an understanding of strategies and business plans and appropriate decision-making when concerns are useful to companies, strengthening the foundations of management legitimacy and generating collaboration in efforts for sustainable growth.

In Sect. 5.2.5, we demonstrate the primary sources of financing for Japanese companies.

5.2.5 Sources of Funding and Separation Between Property and Control

Financial systems are generally described as bank-based or market-based based on the relative proportion of financing channeled through banks or markets (Iqbal & Mustafa, 2017; Kalara & Zhang, 2018). Financial institutions are bank-based financial systems' primary capital allocation and investment vehicles. In market-based financial systems, a portion of capital and investment are made primarily in the securities market (Iqbal & Mustafa, 2017; Kalara & Zhang, 2018). Notably, although the literature recognizes the distinct characteristics of market-based systems and banks, there is no robust evidence to indicate which method is best for economics (Kalara & Zhang, 2018). What the authors point out is that countries do not grow faster, new companies are not created more efficiently, access to foreign capital is not easier or faster, and companies do not grow faster, whether in the market-based system or the bank-based system, because they also depend on other factors, such as the efficiency of financial, legal institutions and even how stakeholders interact in the decision-making process (Iqbal & Mustafa, 2017; Jackson & Miyajima, 2007).

Until the 1990s, Japanese companies were essentially financed by financial institutions, which provided long-term loans, but in return, had an equity stake in the companies and representation on their boards (Jerzemowska & Koyama, 2020; Morck & Nakamura, 1999; Omura, 2020b; Yafeh, 2000). Since the 1960s, the Japanese economy has experienced stable growth environments and depended on loans from financial institutions due to a lack of capital, known as "bank governance." Banks provided long-term loans to companies that had little capital but, at the same time, maintained stable stakes in these companies with a pro-management attitude. As the largest creditors, banks could influence these companies. When the financial situation becomes negative, banks can monitor them, sending former directors or former employees of the bank to sit on the boards of these companies (Omura, 2020b). The Annual Report on the Japanese Economy and Public Finances of 1961 and 1962 demonstrated that Japanese companies were very dependent on loans from financial institutions because their profits were small, and they used the resources from these loans for capital expenditures (Omura, 2020b).

In the late 1990s, an economic collapse reduced the growth rate to below-trend levels, leaving Japanese companies facing substantial capital expenditures, large debts, and the embarrassment of the lifetime employment system (Omura, 2020a). The 2006 Annual Report on the Japanese Economy and Public Finances demonstrates that companies still depend significantly on the main bank. However, after the bubble burst, banks' ability to take risks decreased significantly (Omura, 2020b). Since then, bank governance has only worked for struggling companies seeking a gradual earnings recovery, and it has been supported by lenient restructuring of labor laws that restricted the workforce and stable and flexible loans from major banks (Omura, 2020b).

Companies currently depend on bank financing and internal control in the Japanese financial system (Clarke, 2020; Miyamoto, 2019). Although recently the distinction between bank-based and market-based systems has become less clear, Japanese companies have traditionally sought financing from banks, so Japan has a traditionally bank-based system in contrast to Anglo-Saxon market-based systems (Iqbal & Mustafa, 2017; Jerzemowska & Koyama, 2020; Kalara & Zhang, 2018; Yafeh, 2000). In research carried out by Kalara and Zhang (2018) to classify the corporate financing system of 28 countries, considering 25 indicators in the period 1995–2016, the authors present results that Japan has the highest level of bank credit to companies than other countries classified as having bank-based financing (e.g., Austria, Germany, Greece, Ireland, Italy, Portugal, Spain, and the Netherlands). The authors also highlight that Japan has more bank credit than the United States and Western European countries. Private credit in Japan remained stable throughout the period and appeared less affected by the crisis than the other countries analyzed. Japan has a low level of securitized loans, second only to Germany; Japan has a developed banking sector, and although the size of the Japanese stock market was reduced during the 2008 crisis, in 2016, it exceeded the pre-crisis level; however, securities remain at a lower level than before the crisis.

The structure of the banking sector is relevant to the functioning of financial intermediation and differs in size and in terms of how internationalized they are. Japan has low asset values in the banking system as a proportion of GDP, along with the United States and Western European countries (Kalara & Zhang, 2018). Focusing on the structure of the banking sector, looking at its concentration measured by the market share of the three largest banks, Japan has a relatively low score compared to European countries, indicating that its financial market has many smaller banks compared to few and larger banks in Europe (Kalara & Zhang, 2018).

Regarding the separation between ownership and control, throughout the Takagawa feudal period (1603–1868), Japanese companies were family-owned or "clan-owned" (Morck & Nakamura, 2007). At that time, family rules and traditions determined aspects of corporate governance (Morck & Nakamura, 2007). For example, it is possible to mention Suzuki, a company where the family had most voting rights. This concentration of ownership indicated that owners had strong incentives to supervise executives and ensure they created wealth for shareholders effectively. With the prohibition of foreign trade, domestic trade enriched several merchant families, and these families often established complicated household rules that governed all aspects of business (Morck & Nakamura, 2007).

The Mistui family is an example; it consisted of 12 founding clans and created rules to maintain control between them; among these, the Mitsui house prohibited the founding clans from withdrawing their ownership shares and prohibited other individuals or branches of the family from obtaining property from actions. Voting power on the Mitsui family council passed to the eldest sons of each founding clan; the youngest sons could be managers, and they even hired competent managers through the adoption of marriage with the Mitsui daughters (Morck & Nakamura, 2007).

Between 1853 and 1854, Edo was bombarded by Americans until the Tokugawa government agreed to open some ports to foreign trade. Edo was renamed from Tokyo in 1868 when the emperor moved from Kyoto to Edo. However, foreign trade remained very limited until the Meiji Restoration. With the advent of industrialization around 1868 (known as the Meiji Restoration), family businesses began to need a much larger volume of capital to keep up with the market's rapid development, so they turned to the capital market. One of the main issues throughout this period of change was the fact that companies wanted to maintain control of their companies, but at the same time, they needed to satisfy their need to raise funds to finance the necessary industrial development. As Morck and Nakamura (2007) contextualize, companies formed a new company (holding) to raise capital for each new venture and organized pyramid groups, in which the family was at the top of these pyramids, controlling the other ventures.

Thus, organizing companies in a pyramid format was a possible solution for families to maintain control of companies. These large family conglomerates, controlled by holding companies, were known as *Zaibatsu* and are like pyramidal groups in other countries (Morck & Nakamura, 2007; Yafeh, 2000). The Meiji government introduced capitalism, and during its radical modernization, Japan adopted a legal system based on German law (Nottage & Kozuka, 2022). In the 1870s, public securities trading began, and in 1878, the Tokyo and Osaka Stock Exchanges were created. The major merchant families issued shares to finance the industrialization of their businesses, and the large pyramidal zaibatsu groups that would dominate the country were formed.

During World War II, Japan nationalized many organizations, subordinating them to the *Kikakuin*, a planning agency created by the 1937 Law to centralize economic planning and administration. *Kikakuin* was created observing various planning methods that the Soviet Union used for its substantial industrialization in the 1930s (Morck & Nakamura, 2007). This required corporate boards to obtain government approval for major business decisions, such as amending articles of incorporation and issuing shares or debt securities (Morck & Nakamura, 2007). The government abolished the rights of councils to establish dividends in 1939 and to appoint managers in 1943, attributing these decisions to *Kikakuin*. After the World War II, Japan began to be governed by the United States military (1945–1952). This allowed the governance model to change over time, becoming more like the American one, where most companies did not have a controlling shareholder. The US-led occupation brought securities regulation, anti-monopoly law, and significant reforms to the Commercial Code based on US laws (Nottage & Kozuka, 2022). General MacArthur abolished the *zaibatsu*.

From then on, companies began to fight to carry out hostile acquisitions of stakes in other companies. The history of Japanese corporate governance was marked by companies' initiatives to try to maintain control and neglect the rights of minority shareholders (Allen & Zhao, 2007). *Keiretsu* systems grew after the end of the US occupation in 1952 and fully developed in the 1960s. *Keiretsu* is the denomination given to a group of companies linked by stable crossholdings between companies. A *Keiretsu* in which a bank plays a central role is called a group of banks *Keirestu* Financial (Iqbal & Mustafa, 2017). The rise of zaibatsu and *keiretsu* organizations was due to several factors, such as economies of scale and scope, contouring of markets and institutions, reputation, benefits from political ties on certain occasions, allowing these institutions to retain governance powers (Morck & Nakamura, 2007). The main objective of zaibatsu and *keiretsu* was to protect the control rights of large families and professional managers, respectively.

The Japanese property system is centered on the idea of corporate networks. Industries seek to maintain even small stakes in each other to add up these stakes and control an economic block collectively. In this context, public shareholders only have access to minority interests. The interests of minority shareholders are not a very relevant aspect of the corporate governance of Japanese companies (Morck & Nakamura, 2007). One of the main network models established by companies in the 1990s was the establishment of relationships with a main bank. This practice underwent significant changes from the 2000s onward, with the occurrence of several reforms in corporate governance systems, resulting in companies starting to keep less cash on hand and starting to pay more to their shareholders (who until then were placed second plan in the old system). Thus, banks that used to be in central positions in companies' networking now have less influence, increasing the importance of management and foreign investor participation (Kato et al., 2017).

5.2.5.1 Ownership Structure of Japanese Companies During and After the 1990s

Until the 1990s, the concentration of ownership interest of Japanese companies was predominantly financial institutions, and they had representatives on the board of directors or sent auditors to those companies to monitor their economic conditions; this management mechanism was known (Iqbal & Mustafa, 2017; Jackson & Miyajima, 2007; Omura, 2020b). Banks financed these companies (Okamoto, 2022) and, at the same time, maintained monitoring within the board; however, after the turn of the century, the shareholding of these institutions gradually reduced (Omura, 2020a).

Significant banks and affiliated groups, known as *Keiretsu*, dominated Japanese companies because of their majority holdings and developed business ties (Iqbal & Mustafa, 2017). These investors are generally stable and build lasting business ties rather than focusing on short-term goals (Titus et al., 2021). *Keiretsu* seeks to strengthen and protect companies from financial difficulties, threats of hostile acquisitions, and exposure to foreign capital markets (usually short-term) in exchange for long-term growth opportunities (Iqbal & Mustafa, 2017; Jackson & Miyajima, 2007; Okamoto, 2022).

Groups include horizontal bank-centric *Keiretsu* or vertical *Keiretsu* structured in standing relationships, such as buyer-supplier in the Japanese auto industry (Jackson & Miyajima, 2007). The *Keiretsu* model even presented data as the largest individual shareholder, usually the central bank, with only 5%. Still, the reciprocal cross-share network represents 20% of the shares and stable shareholders above 40% (Jackson & Miyajima, 2007). These crossholdings have the disadvantage of excluding individual or minority shareholders because the companies involved in cross-participation probably do not exercise their voting rights effectively and may promote them (Okamoto, 2022). Corporate crossholding can be defined as the situation in which two publicly traded companies own shares in each other (Okamoto, 2022). In 1987, cross holdings and stable holdings accounted for between 65% and 70% of shares issued by publicly traded companies in Japan (Okamoto, 2022).

A change in ownership structure bringing a more excellent representation of foreign investors and institutional investors has put new pressure on the boards of Japanese companies to generate shareholder value since, traditionally, these boards are oriented to the interests of stakeholders, especially the interests of employees (Clarke, 2020; Jerzemowska & Koyama, 2020; Koji et al., 2020). According to Iqbal and Mustafa (2017), the rapid change in tax and employment policies and the renewal of incentive schemes by corporate management contributed to the decline of equity interests of affiliated groups and central banks and the increase of market-oriented investors.

In this sense, the percentage of outstanding shares held by banks fell ten percentage points, from 15.1% in 1995 to 4.6% in 2006, considering only the total outstanding shares of companies listed in the first section of the Stock Exchange of Tokyo (Miyajima, 2023). The percentage of shares held by institutional shareholders, especially foreign institutional shareholders, increased rapidly from 10.5% in 1995 to 27.8% in 2006, highlighting that this increase occurred in large-cap companies due to the domestic bias of foreign investors (Miyajima, 2023).

The higher presence of foreign institutional investors, although focusing on large companies in the 2000s (after this decade, domestic and foreign institutional investors influenced more broadly, including mid-caps), may have pressured management to adopt a model of corporate governance aimed at shareholders, with characteristics of the Anglo-American model, which is precisely the model used by other Asian economies (Miyajima, 2023). With the reforms in corporate legislation and the revisions in the Administration Codes and Corporate Governance Code, there was a gradual reduction in cross-shareholdings and intercorporate shareholdings. Intercorporate shareholdings involve significant single blocks of shares from one company to another and are held primarily for strategic reasons such as alliances and joint ventures (Miyajima, 2023). These holdings were reduced on average from 53% in 2010 to 34.7% in 2019, and the probability of selling these shares increased from 3.9% in 2011 to 9.4% in 2019 (Miyajima & Saito, 2019). The reduction in cross-shareholdings was substantial, from 61.8% in 1986 to 31.2% in 2012 (Nottage & Kozuka, 2022).

According to TSE data, foreign investors' shareholding in Japanese companies increased from 7.56% of total investment in 1995 to 30% in 2016 (TSE, 2021). If evolution is outlined, foreign investors held 23.7% of the shares listed on the TSE in terms of market value in 2005; in 1999, they had 14.1%, and in 1992, contained only 6% (Jackson & Miyajima, 2007). Foreign equity interests with a shareholding ratio of 30% or more constitute 9.2% of the companies listed in the TSE in 2020; with a balance between 20% and 30%, the percentage increases to 11.6%; with a ratio between 10% and 20% the percentage practically doubles, moving to 21.7%; and with a proportion below 10%, the rate reaches 57.6% (TSE, 2021). About 38% of Japanese companies currently concentrate their ownership on the three largest shareholders, and 60% focus their requests on the twenty largest shareholders (OECD, 2021). Institutional investors own around 30% of companies listed on the Japan Stock Exchange (OECD, 2021).

The Corporate Governance Code requires disclosure of the existence of controlling shareholders covering parent companies and significant shareholders who hold most voting rights held on their account and the voting rights held by their close relatives or companies in which they hold their majority of voting rights (JPX, 2021). Of the companies listed on the TSE in 2020, 635 (17.3%) have controlling shareholders; of these, 354 (9.6%) have parent companies (TSE, 2021). The concentration of voting rights is critical for companies' corporate governance, as these votes decide on relevant matters, such as determining dividend policies, approving investment projects, appointing executives, remunerating executives, share repurchases, and other strategies necessary for the business (Clarke, 2020).

5.2.5.2 Board of Directors

According to the Japan Corporate Governance Code (JCGC), issued in 2021, due to its fiduciary responsibility and accountability to shareholders, the board of directors must adequately fulfill its functions and duties, which include (1) setting the broad direction of corporate strategy, (2) establish an environment where appropriate risk-taking by top management is supported, and (3) carry out effective oversight of rights and management from an independent and objective standpoint (JCGC, 2022). In Japan, companies can choose one of three forms of organizational structures under the Company Law, revised in 2014: (1) a Company with a Kansayaku Board, (2) a Company with Three Committees— Appointment, Audit, and Remuneration, and (3) a Company with Fiscal Council (JCGC, 2022).

A company with Board *Kansayaku* is a system unique to Japan in which the board of directors assumes certain governance functions, and others are assumed by the *Kansayaku* and the *Kansayaku* Board (board of auditors). Under this system, *Kansayaku* (accountants) audit the performance of directors' duties, and management has investigative powers by law. It must also guarantee the independence and decision-making power of high-level information. To achieve this, at least half of the *Kansayaku*, as appointed by the general meeting of shareholders, must be external, and at least one must be hired full-time (JCGC, 2022). A company with a *Kansayaku* Board can create positions titled "shikkoyakuin" for people to whom the board delegates a certain margin of discretion in business management (JCGC, 2022). The *shikkoyakuin* is not a statutory position.

The Company with Three Committees (*Linkai*) system must have a board of directors, at least one auditor, and three committees: appointment, audit, and remuneration (JCGC, 2022). The three committees are subordinate to the board of directors. The board of directors elects the members of the three committees. According to the Corporate Law, Companies with Three Committees must appoint one or more *shikkoyaku* directors or non-directors by a Board resolution and delegate business management to them (JCGC, 2022). Authorities who make confident business decisions may be delegated to the *shikkoyaku*. The company with the Fiscal Board system (*Kansa–Kantoku Linkai*) has a board of directors and a fiscal board (JCGC, 2022). It must have at least three independent directors, and the general assembly elects the supervisory board members. In a company with a Supervisory Board system, "*shikkoyakuin*" type positions can be created.

The Company with Three Committees and Company with Fiscal Board systems are forms of organizational structure like those practiced in other countries, in which committees are established under the supervision of the board of directors and specific responsibilities are assigned to reinforce monitoring functions (JCGC, 2022). In general terms, the boards of directors of Japanese companies must include advisors with knowledge, experience, and skills, which enable them to fulfill their roles and responsibilities (JCGC, 2022). They must be constituted by observing gender diversity, international and professional experience, the age of its members, and an appropriate size. They should also include advisors with appropriate experience, skills, and necessary finance, accounting, and law knowledge. Specifically, at least one person with sufficient knowledge of finance and accounting must be appointed as a *Kansayaku* (JCGC, 2022).

Insiders traditionally dominate the boards of directors of Japanese companies, that is, directors who have been company employees for several years and have held leadership positions on merit in the so-called lifelong employment (Mielcarz et al., 2021). Lifetime employment systems are jointly institutionalized norms for regular employees, usually men, that emerged with company-based cooperative unions in the early post-war period, and, reflecting strong legal restrictions on dismissals, companies invest in job-specific skills in the company and maintain employees' internal flexibility regarding work roles within the company or related companies (Jackson & Miyajima, 2007). The board of directors is, in part, an extension of the lifelong employment system, in which directors are generally employees of the highest hierarchy within the company rather than loyal representatives of shareholders (Jackson & Miyajima, 2007; Jerzemowska & Koyama, 2020). In this structure, Japanese directors tend to present a low separation between monitoring and management (Endo, 2020; Jackson & Miyajima, 2007; Jerzemowska & Koyama, 2020).

The introduction of independent or external directors has been emphasized so that there is greater effectiveness in the role of monitoring councils and consequently (Fama & Jensen, 1983; Jensen & Meckling, 1976); however, it is unclear how the appointment of independent directors to boards alone will increase the transparency of the company (Aman et al., 2021; Miyamoto, 2019). In a 2019 survey, Arikawa et al. found that boards of directors with a higher proportion of insiders have a more significant influence on the low profitability and market value assessment of Japanese companies and that the presence of independent directors can ensure and promote risk actions that positively impact the performance of companies. The authors conclude that the performance measured through the return on assets and Tobin's Q increased by 0.6% and 0.26%, respectively, when there was an increase of 29% in independent directors (Arikawa et al., 2019).

The board of directors of Japanese companies was historically much more extensive than American companies, and there was no separation between administration and monitoring in terms of function (Miyajima, 2023). The board members and CEOs were employees promoted internally, and self-auditing and the lack of monitoring were natural consequences of this model. However, there is no independence. To make boards of directors more effective, Japanese corporate law, in 2020, allowed companies to opt for a board of directors on the American model, with a committee system. However, there was strong resistance from companies to adopting this model (Miyajima, 2023).

A TSE survey in 2023 shows that independent directors are present in 98.6% (3716 companies) of listed Japanese companies, up 3.0 percentage points from 2022's 95.6%. In 2022, 85.4% of companies will have two or more independent external directors, representing an increase of 6.9 points compared to the previous year, 2021, which was 78.5% (TSE, 2023). The number of listed companies with three or more independent external directors increased considerably by 16.6 points, from 40.5% in 2021 to 57.1% in 2022. The TSE points out as a reason for these increases the fact that a growing number of companies seek to appoint independent external directors with diverse knowledge, experience, and capabilities to ensure diversity among directors and improve discussion within the board of directors (TSE, 2023). Another reason is that the revision of the Corporate Governance Code in 2021 began to require the appointment of at least one-third of independent external directors to the board of directors.

Regarding the appointment of women to executive positions, according to the TSE (2023), in 2013, then Prime Minister Abe Shinzo asked the business community to nominate a woman as one of the members of the board of directors. This resulted in a more than five-fold increase from 630 to 3654 women in 10 years (2012–2022). The Japan Business Federation launched the "Challenge to 30% in 2030 #Here We Go 2030" to increase the number of women on boards. However, despite these trends, the TSE points out that the percentage of women on boards remains below 10% (TSE, 2023).

5.2.6 Information Asymmetry and Opportunism in Japan

Shareholders of Japanese companies are not active in management, leaving the company's management decisions to the directors and shareholders. Directors and advisors are career employees of the company selected from a competition system, their management is focused on employees, prioritizing, for example, growth in scale rather than profitability. In this sense, with shareholders not involved in management, there is no monitoring of the administration carried out by these shareholders, with monitoring being the responsibility of the directors and advisors themselves (Omura, 2020b). Therefore, it is considered that the likelihood of conflict of interest is lower. Thus, there may be the change of a conflict of interest between directors/advisors and other interested parties, such as institutional investors. When the Japanese Administration Code proposes the engagement of institutional investors in management, it encourages third parties to monitor management. It promotes the engagement of shareholders in the company's management routines.

It is also pointed out that there are fewer possible conflicts of interest about management remuneration, as managers are remunerated for being selected employees and not for being specialized professionals hired from a market of management professionals (Omura, 2020b). From this perspective, there is no substantial difference between corporate managers and other employees' compensation. There are few opportunities for conflicting debates between managers and shareholders, as their presence at annual meetings is minimal. Thus, the right to corporate control over decisions is generally made by managers and not by shareholders (Omura, 2020b). Therefore, the costs related to the possibility of conflicts of interest, mainly between owners and CEOs, are relatively low because there are no initiatives by shareholders to take over corporate control or make the mistake of replacing competent corporate managers. These managers use the knowledge acquired and accumulated over years in the company, promoting efficient management (Omura, 2020b).

Institutional investors'presence and activism at annual meetings reduce costs and the possibility of conflict and opportunism because they incorporate ESG assessments into management activities and pay more attention to the demands of other interested parties rather than just shareholders and managers (Omura 2020b). These institutional investors begin to exert the necessary monitoring and pressure on management so that they have better results in terms of profitability. The engagement and activism of institutional investors are exercised by specialized analysts who can collaborate with managers, offering the opportunity to review, change, or create short, medium, and long-term strategies that result in lower costs and less opportunism between principal-agent. Japan's Stewardship Code promotes the engagement of institutional investors. Finally, with the mandatory hiring of external directors, diversification and inclusion of independent members on the board of directors by corporate legislation can increase managers' independence and reduce the possibility of conflicts between owners and managers.

It may occur that Agency Theory approach to corporate governance is not the ideal perspective for the case of Japan. In this sense, another theory, such as the stakeholder theory approach, could be more useful when analyzing the Japanese context. Therefore, as there is no conflict of interest or opportunism between managers and shareholders, in theory, the aim is to incorporate into management the demands of all interested parties, including all types of shareholders.

Regarding information asymmetry and transparency in the disclosure of financial and non-financial information, it is highlighted that companies disclose information to the stock market to help interested parties, including shareholders, investors, and potential investors, stay up to date on performance and the company's equity position (Aman et al., 2021). In a study conducted by Aman et al. (2021) with a sample of 1754 companies listed between 2003 and 2013, it was found that the companies best evaluated by the Nikkei Corporate Governance Assessment System (CGES) make more frequent disclosures when the news are positive (good news). However, these companies are reluctant to disclose adverse information (bad news).

The market for management professionals and the effects of reputation can influence the disclosure decision in companies; however, in Japan, low litigation risks and the expectation of lifetime employment can negatively impact building a reputation for reliable and timely disclosures (Aman et al., 2021; Buchaman, 2007). With the engagement and activism of institutional investors, information about shareholder voting results began to be disclosed, as this data was only disclosed in the general meeting reports. The release of shareholder voting results by institutional investors demonstrates the company's attitudes toward a wide variety of corporate governance issues, such as management compensation, hiring of outside and independent directors, actions taken regarding hostile takeovers, structure of internal and external auditing, etc., which contributes to reducing information asymmetry between managers and other interested parties (Omura, 2020b; Miyajima, 2023). This disclosure includes the qualitative nature of events, financial numbers such as financial performance, and the number of engagement activities by institutional investors. However, the engagement of institutional investors can lead to conflicts between them and the company's managers.

Section 5.3 presents the Japanese corporate management system and the current corporate governance structure, focusing on the board of directors and its committees.

5.3 Corporate Governance System

5.3.1 Corporate Governance Structure in Japanese Companies

The Japanese corporate governance model can be called a pluralistic or hybrid model. It incorporates parts of shareholder-oriented models and retains its traditional stakeholder-oriented model features. Several labels were given to Japanese corporate governance to describe it, such as bank-based or bank-oriented, relationship-oriented, network-oriented governance, insider-based governance, stakeholder-based model, or coordinated corporate governance system (Iqbal & Mustafa, 2017; Jackson & Miyajima, 2007; Kalara & Zhang, 2018; Omura, 2020b).

The hybrid corporate governance model encompasses a mixture of the traditional Japanese management and governance model and the Anglo-American model (Endo, 2020; Jackson & Miyajima, 2007; Jerzemowska & Koyama, 2020). The hybrid Japan model has as its central point the unexpected and diverse forms in which the financial and ownership characteristics and characteristics of the board are combined with the features of the system of lifetime employment and remuneration; for example, the hybrid model, although having market-oriented finances and property does not extinguish the standards of lifetime employment.

The changes in the board of directors are presented as evidence of the hybridization process of Japan's corporate governance system. The organizational structure of a joint stock company in Japan generally consists of shareholders (general assembly), a board of directors, representative director(s), and statutory auditors. The general assembly is the highest body within a company. However, the Companies Law allows for the following three methods of determining the other organizational structure components: (i) since 1890: Company with a *Kansayaku* Board or a Board of Official Reviewers of Accounts; (ii) from 2003: Company with Three Committees (3C)—appointment, audit, and remuneration; and (iii) from 2015: Company with an Audit and Supervision Committee—New Governance System (Jerzemowska & Koyama, 2020; JPX, 2021). The Japanese company can choose and adopt the most appropriate organizational structure to meet its specific needs and can adopt optional approaches when necessary to further improve corporate governance (JPX, 2021).

The *Kansayaku* Board, or board with statutory auditors, is a model in which the statutory auditor must be appointed to supervise the board of directors'activities and cannot be a member. The general assembly must elect the board of directors, consisting of three or more people. In practice, they typically consist of between twenty and thirty members, largely comprised of managers who have been promoted

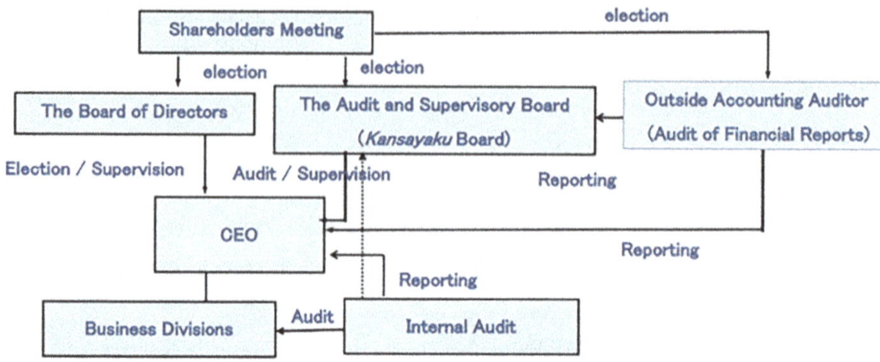

Fig. 5.1 Companies with a Board of Statutory Auditors (*Kansayaku* Board). Source: The Institute of Corporate Governance, Japan—ICGJ (2021)

through the lifetime employment hierarchy system (ICGJ, 2021; Jerzemowska & Koyama, 2020; JPX, 2021; SESC, 2021). Figure 5.1 demonstrates the organizational chart of the *Kansayaku* Board model.

On the board with statutory auditors, or the *Kansayaku* Board, the board of directors is considered a decision-making body, not an executive management monitoring body (JPX, 2021). These companies must have a director or representative manager (CEO) and a senior executive in charge of managing the corporation. The board of directors will appoint him, and he will have the highest authority within the organization (JPX, 2021). However, the representative director is not considered an employee and cannot receive certain benefits granted to employees. The representative director is publicly registered in the official corporate register and must monitor the activities carried out by the board of directors and statutory auditors (JPX, 2021).

In companies with a *Kansayaku* Board, directors assume responsibility for the management and daily operations of the company, sign legal contracts on behalf of the company but are not representatives of shareholders, and monitor the activities of statutory auditors and the board of directors (JPX, 2021). The term of office of directors cannot exceed two years, but they can be reappointed by the Companies Law of 2006. Directors in businesses with a *Kansayaku* board have their performance assessed, and if it is not satisfactory, the advice will not recommend their reappointment. The general meeting must approve the compensation of directors (JPX, 2021; SESC, 2021).

The general meeting may terminate directors at any time. In the case of fixed terms, if they were removed before the deadline without just cause, they can claim damages resulting from the dismissal. Suppose a director violates the law or contractual rule. In that case, he must be responsible for damages to third parties, even if he has acted by a resolution of the general meeting, noting that this provision does not apply to the director who opposes the resolution and notifies the auditors (FSA, 2021; SESC, 2021; TSE, 2021). There is a requirement to appoint at least one external advisor and provide information on compliance with the Japan Corporate Governance Code with the "comply or explain" approach.

Companies that have a Supervisory Board are obliged to appoint an external director and two external statutory auditors who have adequate experience and skills with knowledge in finance, accounting, and law, and one of the statutory auditors must be a specialist in finance and accounting (JPX, 2021; SESC, 2021). *Kansayaku* complements the supervisory function of the board of directors, checking accounting books and other documents and requesting explanations from the director or accounting consultant (Jerzemowska & Koyama, 2020). The *Kansayaku* must examine the documents submitted to the general meeting by the directors or manager and express an opinion on them during the meeting if these documents contain material errors or illegality. The *Kansayaku* must present its objections to the general assembly (JPX, 2021; SESC, 2021).

A separate general meeting of directors with at least one-third of the total votes can appoint or remove *Kansayaku* (JPX, 2021; SESC, 2021). The *Kansayaku* Board comprises auditors, who may be company employees promoted internally with the right to participate in board meetings and receive reports from the board. However, they cannot vote on the decisions of this board (JPX, 2021; SESC, 2021). The Commercial Code states that *Kansayaku* cannot simultaneously serve as a director, manager, and official auditor and that the general meeting must determine their compensation. The company must include at least one full-time *Kansayaku*. The *Kansayaku* Board is responsible for appointing or dismissing auditors and making decisions about audit policies and the type of audit method to be adopted. In 2009, the TSE began requiring at least one Kansayaku on the Kansayaku Board to be independent. The Commercial Code provides that a *Kansayaku* can have a term of office of up to four years and be reappointed.

In 2022, there were 2290 (60.7%) Companies with a *Kansayaku* Board. In 2021, there were 2453 (64.7%) with the *Kansayaku* Board (TSE, 2023). In 2019, the number of companies that adopted the *Kansayaku* Board was 2553 (70.4%) (TSE, 2021). The TSE indicates that the number of companies adopting the company with *Kansayaku* Board model has been decreasing recently and points out, as one of the factors for this reduction and increase in the number of companies adopting the company with Audit and Supervision Committee model, the revision of the Corporate Governance Code in 2021. The number of companies adopting the Kansayaku Board model decreased by 14.6 percentage points between 2017 and 2022.

In practice, the *Kansayaku* Board does not have the power to appoint and remove directors and does not represent the interests of shareholders or employees. There are questions about who oversees the managers because the board of directors appointed them. *Kansayaku* are generally former employees of companies and have difficulties accessing information (Jerzemowska & Koyama, 2020). Furthermore, in 2022, of the companies with a *Kansayaku* Board, 1341 stated that they had introduced a non-statutory executive director system (*shikkoyakuin* system) to promote the separation of supervisory and executive functions (TSE, 2023). And 30.8% (706 companies) mentioned the creation of a committee related to internal control, such as a compliance committee or a risk management committee.

For Companies with a *Kansayaku* Board, creating a Nomination Committee is optional. Regarding the average number of members of the Nomination Committee, in 2022, it was 4.63, with committees with five members representing the highest percentage (31.4%). In these optional nominating committees, 30.8% of members are internal directors, 58.8% are external directors, 1.4% are external experts, and 9% are identified as others, including *Kansayaku*. Companies with a *Kansayaku* Board adopt a system in which companies outside Kansayaku also participate in the Nomination Committee voluntarily to increase the committee‘s independence (TSE, 2023). And in 2022, 59.5% of these Nomination Committees were chaired by an external director.

Regarding the *Kansayaku* Board, in 2022, the average number of members was 3.49 (TSE, 2023). Of these, 70% are external directors. The company may optionally establish a Remuneration Committee. In companies with a *Kansayaku* Board that have established a Remuneration Committee, the average number of members in this committee was 4.56 in 2022, with companies with five members accounting for the highest percentage at 29.7% (TSE, 2023). In 2022, these Remuneration Committees had 31.1% internal directors, 57.4% external directors, 1.5% external experts, and 10% classified as others, including *Kansayaku*. These numbers summarize the context of Japanese companies that use the *Kansayaku* Board company model.

The organizational structure model called *Linkai* comprises three committees (3C). Figure 5.2 shows the organizational chart of the corporate governance model with three committees. Since April 2003, companies have been able to use the committee system that is like that used by listed U.S. companies, and this is an excellent example of the influence of U.S. law on Japanese law and the process of hybridizing corporate governance (Endo, 2020; Jerzemowska & Koyama, 2020; Miyamoto,

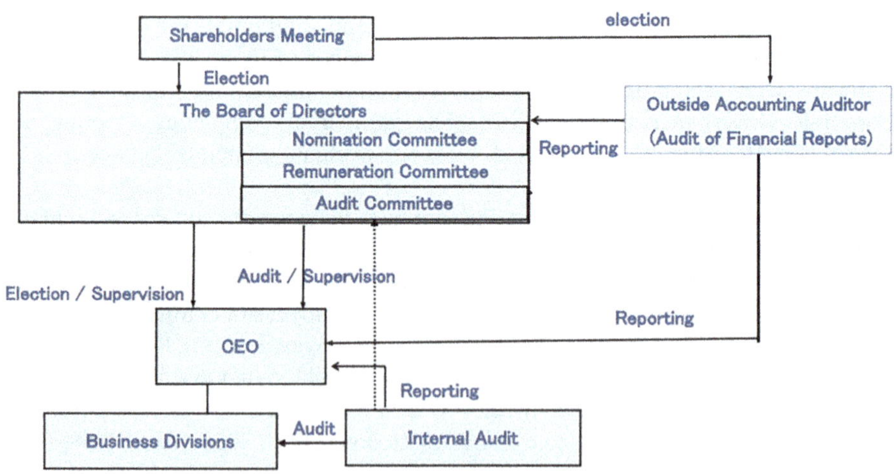

Fig. 5.2 Companies with three committees—3C (*Linkai* Model). Source: The Institute of Corporate Governance, Japan—ICGJ (2021)

2019). A 3C company must have a board of directors and at least one accounting auditor, and the three committees, appointment, audit, and remuneration, are subordinate to the board of directors. The general meeting appoints the directors among candidates selected by the nominating committee, and the elected councilors elect the members of the three committees (JPX, 2021; SESC, 2021).

The Japan Corporate Governance Code recommends the appointment of independent directors. The directors are responsible for establishing and disseminating independence standards, considering the independence criteria established by Japanese law (JPX, 2021). In 3C, the board of directors supervises the executive directors, and the representative directors have a one-year term and can be re-elected (JPX, 2021; SESC, 2021). The managers appointed by the board of directors are the real directors of the company, and these are evaluated for their performance, which, if not satisfactory, can be fired at any time by a board resolution (SESC, 2021).

The audit committee aims to oversee the functions of directors, directors, and accounting advisors, audit the company's financial statements, and determine the content of the proposals for election, dismissal, and refusal of the re-election of accounting auditors presented at a general meeting. It is also your function to monitor and certify the information provided to shareholders, the legal compliance of business operations, and appoint and unblock external auditors submitted to a general meeting (JPX, 2021; SESC, 2021). If you identify irregular, violations, or misconduct, you should immediately report such problems to the board of directors.

The remuneration committee decides on the remuneration of each director or manager, president, and directors, complying with the fixed remuneration policy, and the approval of the general meeting is not required. The appointing committee is responsible for determining the proposals to be submitted to the public meeting regarding the appointment and dismissal of directors and the appointment of directors and chairman. The decisions of these committees may not be rejected by the board of directors, directors, and chairman (JPX, 2021; SESC, 2021).

In 2022, 88 companies adopted the company with three committees model. In 2021, 76 companies adopted this same model, and among the reasons for its adoption are the acceleration of the decision-making process, the strengthening of the business function, and the agility in executing the business with the delegation of authority (TSE, 2021, 2023). There was no significant increase if we compared the periods of 2017 and 2022, which represent 2.1% and 2.3%, respectively, of listed companies that used the company with three committees model (TSE, 2023). A former director might be the chair of one of the committees; there is opposition to appointing external advisors; the CEO typically appoints external advisors, and the CEO serves on the nomination and compensation committees (Jerzemowska & Koyama, 2020). Furthermore, in 2022, of the companies with three committees, 37.5% mentioned having a statutory board system (*shikoyaku* system) (TSE, 2023). And 29.5% (26 companies) mentioned the creation of a committee related to internal control, such as a compliance committee or a risk management committee.

Regarding the Nomination Committee in a Company with three committees, it comprises 24.4% internal directors and 75.6% external directors in 2022 (TSE, 2023). And 63.1% of Nominating Committees were chaired by an external director.

The Audit Committee, in 2022, had an average of 4.06 members per committee. And of these, 80% are external directors. In 2022, the Remuneration Committees had an average number of 3.97 members, with companies with three members representing the largest proportion, 45.5% (TSE, 2023). In 2022, the Remuneration Committees comprised 23.2% internal directors and 76.8% external directors. These numbers summarize the Japanese context about companies that adopt the Company with three Committees model.

The latest model, the *Kansa–Kantoku Linkai* system or company with audit and oversight committee, which became effective in 2015, is seen as a combination of the traditional Japanese style and the North American practice of corporate governance, which would be an intermediate solution between the *Kansayaku* system and the 3C system. Figure 5.3 presents the organizational chart of the model's corporate governance structure with the audit and supervision committee.

A company with an audit and supervisory committees' system is not obliged to set up appointment and remuneration committees and statutory auditors but must have at least three external/independent directors (JPX, 2021; SESC, 2021). The general meeting shall appoint the audit and supervision committee members, who shall be appointed and removed by the general meeting. The term of office of a board member who is a member of the audit and supervision committee shall continue until the end of the ordinary public session of the last fiscal year, closed two years after the election of the board member, while the term of office of the other directors (JPX, 2021; SESC, 2021). Audit and supervisory board members shall be entitled to vote at board meetings.

In addition to the supervisory function, the audit and supervision committee shall ensure the effectiveness of the activities and audit the management results. This committee has a broader audit authority than the statutory auditors in those

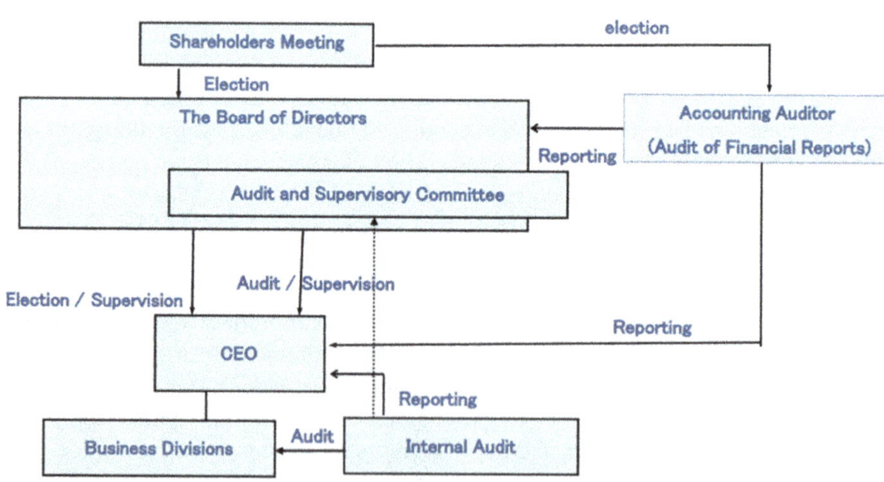

Fig. 5.3 Companies with Audit and Supervision Committee (Model *Kansa - Kantoku Linkai*). Source: The Institute of Corporate Governance, Japan—ICGJ (2021)

companies that adopt them, and their members are authorized to give their opinion on the election, dismissal, and remuneration of directors who are not members of the audit and supervisory board at the general meetings (JPX, 2021; SESC, 2021). The audit and supervisory committee must have a member who is an accounting auditor (JPX, 2021; SESC, 2021). The general meeting shall fix the remuneration of the audit and supervision committee members. The board of directors elects the CEO, and the candidates may not be members of the audit and oversight committee. Directors, executive directors, employees, including managers, the parent company or subsidiaries, and close relatives of company directors and executives are not eligible for external board positions (JPX, 2021; SESC, 2021).

In 2022, 1392 companies adopted the audit and supervision committee system and 1106 companies in 2021 (TSE, 2023). Between 2017 and 2022, there was a significant increase of 14.3 percentage points in companies that started using the Company with Audit and Supervision Committee model, going from 22.6% to 36.9% (TSE, 2023). The TSE considers that this increase was due to the revision of the Corporate Governance Code in 2021. Independent external directors will now be appointed to at least one-third of the board. Listed companies that used the Company with Kansayaku Board model may have changed their organizational structure to the Company with Audit and Supervision Committee model to appoint people who had previously been independent administrators (external auditors) of the company as members of the Audit and Supervision Committee, in compliance with the requirements of the Corporate Governance Code (TSE, 2023). Among the advantages of adopting this model, it increases transparency in management, the ability to obtain support from foreign investors, and the roles of independent directors (TSE, 2021). In practice, the audit and supervisory committee model has weaknesses, such as this committee being chaired by a non-independent director and the members of this supervisory committee not being fully independent (Jerzemowska & Koyama, 2020).

Furthermore, in 2022, of the Companies with an Audit and Supervisory Committee, 766 stated that they had introduced a non-statutory executive director system (*shikkoyakuin* system) to promote the separation of supervisory and executive functions (TSE, 2023). And 32% (445 companies) mentioned the creation of a committee related to internal control, such as a compliance committee or a risk management committee. For Companies with an Audit and Supervision Committee, creating a Nomination Committee is optional. Regarding the average number of members of the Nomination Committee, in 2022, it was 4.48, with committees with five members representing the highest percentage (31.2%). In the optional Nomination Committees, in Companies with an Audit and Supervision Committee, 31.9% of the members are internal directors, 67.1% are external directors, 0.8% are external experts, and 0.3% are classified as others in 2022. And 59.5% of these Nomination Committees are chaired by external directors (TSE, 2023).

The Audit and Supervision Committees in 2022 had an average of 3.49 members per committee. Of these, 80% are external directors. Companies with an Audit and Supervision Committee may voluntarily establish a Remuneration Committee. In 2022, the average number of members who constituted the Remuneration Committee in these companies was 4.46, with companies with three members representing a higher proportion, 30.8% (TSE, 2023). In these committees, 31.7% were internal directors, 67.1% were external directors, 0.8% were external experts, and 0.4% were classified as others. These numbers summarize the corporate governance context for companies that adopt the Company with Audit and Supervision Committee model.

It is noticed that substantial changes are being made in labor relations in Japan because even though employers insisted on the system of lifelong employment and its benefits, there have been changes in the expansion of wage differentials, diversification in wage systems, and changes in working conditions (Clarke, 2020). These changes and resistances contributed to the combination of traditional elements, that is, stakeholders-oriented, with aspects of more market-oriented governance, such as the inclusion of external advisors and foreign equity interests, which resulted in hybrid corporate governance.

5.4 Final Considerations

The change in Japan's corporate governance model throughout the time has been challenging, as traditional practices are required to change, and Japanese culture and beliefs strongly impact social and economic relations. Japanese companies must adopt the corporate governance system that best suits their characteristics and highlight their strengths. Therefore, it is needed to create a hybrid model that includes traditional and new elements and that the change is not radical. As Jerzemowska and Koyama (2020) point out, hybridization reduces conflicts of interest between the state and companies, directors and stakeholders, and foreign and local investors.

Regarding the current state of corporate governance in Japan, one can raise some considerations that are not intended to be final. Various characteristics of traditional corporate governance should be considered, such as the system of lifetime employment through hierarchy and rise to the positions of top managers that influence in a differentiated way opportunistic behavior because the long-term socialization of these employees within a corporate culture that promotes relevant motivational resources, such as a good reputation, can exert control over opportunistic behavior.

Another feature is the unique Japanese audit system in which there are two monitoring mechanisms: one in which the board of directors monitors directors' behavior to verify whether the board's decision is appropriate, and another, in which independent auditors verify the action of directors to consider whether they comply with laws and rules. Furthermore, the fact that shareholders are not engaged in monitoring the actions performed by the board of directors and board of directors is a characteristic that differentiates the corporate governance of countries such as the United States and the United Kingdom.

Some authors are still skeptical of changes in corporate governance mechanisms in Japan and consider that the board's culture and practices remain virtually the same for several companies (Allen et al., 2018; Aman et al., 2021). They point out that a corporate governance model is ready to be used in Japan; however, in fact, it does not work well to conduct everyday corporate trials (Aman et al., 2021; Omura, 2020a).

Another point is that Japanese companies listed on international stock exchanges are forced to adopt corporate governance standards with characteristics distinct from those unique to Japan. For example, Japanese companies listed on the NYSE or NASDAQ will have their corporate governance impacted by the Sarbanes-Oxley Act. Another instance is that, as early as 2007, Jackson and Miyajima claimed that roughly one-third of Japanese listed companies used foreign financing in capital markets. Relationship banks would not disappear but would have a limited role based on explicit and independent contracts. The authors also note that crossholdings were dissolved among companies where bank financing declined.

In addition, adopting the "comply or explain" approach leaves it up to companies to disclose or not items considered relevant, and TSE, investors, and other stakeholders expect timely, complete, and reliable disclosure. Using the "comply or explain" principle leaves corporate governance decisions in charge of companies, allows institutions to smooth out changes in relevant regulations, and maintains old structures, which is the case in Japan. While companies decide on the old or new corporate governance, because the two are allowed legal smoothing, they can comply with or explain non-compliance and follow without more substantial changes and without taking responsibility for real change.

Japan's new Corporate Governance Code (version 2021) presents several elements to promote and encourage sustainability (environmental, social, ethical, etc.) and diversity, as well as to improve the monitoring function of the board of directors; however, it does not provide innovative principles that offer guidance so that they can increase their market values in the medium and long-term that is still an element of Japanese business culture. In conjunction with the Japanese Code of Administration, it also encourages more substantial monitoring through institutional investors.

Furthermore, as Nemoto (2022) argues, research indicates that Japan is unlikely to adopt a shareholder-based corporate governance system identical to that of the US, as the Japanese management model adheres to the traditional customs and values of the stakeholder system, even if it reluctantly adopts some aspects of the shareholder primacy model. The corporate governance model moved toward a hybrid form, maintaining and considering the trajectories of its system. Furthermore, the shareholder primacy model has been questioned and identified as one of the causes of growing environmental degradation, economic inequality and social exclusion, and mistrust and uncertainty. Miyajima (2023) highlights that the COVID-19 pandemic further emphasized the importance of companies adopting objectives beyond the profit and shareholder primacy model.

Finally, this study related to Japanese corporate governance has some limitations. First, the research covered only articles in English, published in the last seven years (2016–2022), in article or review format, so other types of publications were not included. Thus, it is suggested that future research has different types of academic publications. Second, the study was conducted only on the Web of Science and Scopus databases. Even considering they are reliable and useful databases; they may not encompass all articles representing the state of the art.

References

Allen, F., & Zhao, M. (2007). The corporate governance model of Japan: Shareholders are not rulers. *PKU Business Review, 36*(7), 98–102. 10.1.1.672.6775&rep=rep1&type=pdf

Allen, J., Hashimoto, S., & Grow, H. (2018). Japan? Keeping it complicated. In C. Yonts, J. Allen, & M. Zhou (Eds.), *CG watch 2018. Hard decisions. Asia faces tough choices in CG reform* (pp. 207–239). World Scientific Publishing.

Aman, H., Beeckes, W., & Brown, P. (2021). Corporate governance and transparency in Japan. *The International Journal of Accounting, 56*(01), 1–40. https://doi.org/10.1142/s1094406021500037

Aoki, M., & Patrick, H. (1994). *The Japanese Main Bank system: Its relevancy for developing and transforming economies*. Oxford University Press.

Arikawa, Y., Inoue, K., & Saito, T. (2019). Corporate governance, employment, and financial performance of Japanese firms: A cross-country analysis. *SSRN Electronic Journal*, 1–35. https://doi.org/10.2139/ssrn.3312515

ASBJ. (2023). *Accounting standards board of Japan*. Japanese Gaap. https://www.asb.or.jp/en/jp-gaap.html

Buchaman, J. (2007). Japanese corporate governance and the principle of "internalism". *Corporate Governance: An International Review, 15*(1), 27–35. https://doi.org/10.1111/j.1467-8683.2007.00539.x

Clarke, T. (2020). *Corporate governance: A survey* (p. 133). Cambridge University Press. https://doi.org/10.1017/9781108966719

Endo, K. (2020). Corporate governance beyond the shareholder-stakeholder dichotomy: Lessons from Japanese corporations' environmental performance. *Business Strategy and the Environment, 29*(4), 1625–1633. https://doi.org/10.1002/bse.2457

Fama, E. F., & Jensen, M. C. (1983). Separation of ownership and control. *The Journal of Law and Economics, 26*(2), 301–325. https://doi.org/10.1086/467037

FSA. (1948). *Financial services agency. Act n° 25 – The FIEA (Financial Instruments and Exchange Act)*. https://www.fsa.go.jp/

FSA. (2005). *Financial Services Agency. Act n° 86 of July 26 (Companies Act – Part I, Part II, Part III, and Part IV)*. https://www.fsa.go.jp/en/newsletter/weekly2021/427.html

FSA. (2014). *Financial Services Agency. Principles for Responsible Institutional Investors (Japan's Stewardship Code)*. https://www.fsa.go.jp/en/refer/councils/stewardship/20170529.html

FSA. (2021). *Financial services agency*. https://www.fsa.go.jp/en/

FSA. (2022). *Financial services agency*. Business Accounting Council. https://www.fsa.go.jp/en/refer/councils/singie_kigyou/kai2e.html

FSA. (2023). *Financial services agency*. Business Accounting Council. https://www.fsa.go.jp/en/refer/councils/singie_kigyou/kai2e.html

Goto, G. (2019). The logic and limits of stewardship codes: The case of Japan. *Berkeley Business Law Journal*, (2018-E-01), 1–54. https://doi.org/10.2139/ssrn.3311279

Gu, J. (2021). Voluntary IFRS adoption and accounting quality: Evidence from Japan. *Economics Research-Ekonomska Istraživanja, 34*(1), 1985–2012. https://doi.org/10.1080/1331677x.2020.1860793

ICGJ. (2021). *Instituto of corporate governance of Japan*. https://www.icgj.org/en/org.html

IFRS. (2023). *International financial reporting standards. Use of IFRS accounting standards by jurisdiction*. https://www.ifrs.org/use-around-the-world/use-of-ifrs-standards-by-jurisdiction/view-jurisdiction/hong-kong-sar/

Iqbal, M. S., & Mustafa, K. (2017). Ownership structure changes, reforms, and corporate restructuring: Evidence from Japan. *IBA Business Review, 12*(2), 33–64. https://doi.org/10.22495/jgr_v6_i4_p4

Jackson, G., & Miyajima, H. (2007). Introduction: The diversity and change of corporate governance in Japan. In M. Aoki, G. Jackson, & H. Miyajima (Eds.), *Corporate governance in Japan: Institutional change and organizational diversity* (pp. 1–48). Oxford University Press.

JCGC. (2022). *Japan exchange group*. Japan's Corporate Governance Code. https://www.jpx.co.jp/english/equities/listing/cg/index.html

Jensen, M. C., & Meckling, W. H. (1976). Theory of the firm: Managerial behavior, agency costs, and ownership structure. *Journal of Financial Economics, 3*(4), 305–360. https://doi.org/10.1016/0304-405x(76)90026-x

Jerzemowska, M., & Koyama, Y. (2020). The board as an example of Japanese corporate governance system hybridization: An outline of the problem. *Economics and Sociology, 13*(3), 171–202. https://doi.org/10.14254/2071-789x.2020/13

JPX. (2021). *Japan exchange group*. https://www.jpx.co.jp/english/

JSDA. (2021). *Fact Book 2021*. Japan Securities Dealers Association. https://www.jsda.or.jp/en/

Kalara, N., & Zhang, L. (2018). *The changing landscape of firm financing in Europe, the United States, and Japan. CPB discussion paper 383*. CPB Netherlands Bureau for Economic Policy Analysis, pp. 1–48. https://ideas.repec.org/p/cpb/discus/383.html

Kato, K., Li, M., & Skinner, D. J. (2017). Is Japan really a "buy"? The corporate governance, cash holdings and economics performance of Japanese companies. *Journal of Business Finance & Accounting, 44*(3–4), 480–523. https://doi.org/10.1111/jbfa.12235

Koji, K., Adhikary, B. K., & Tram, L. (2020). Corporate governance and firm performance: A comparative analysis between listed family and non-family firms in Japan. *Journal of Risk and Financial Management, 13*(9), 1–20. https://doi.org/10.3390/jrfm13090215

La Porta, R., & Lopez-De-Silanes, F. (1998). Capital markets and legal institutions. In *Beyond the Washington consensus: Institutions matter* (pp. 73–92). https://www.researchgate.net/profile/Rafael-La-Porta/publication/228738060_Capital_markets_and_legal_institutions/links/0a85e52e659a7d1264000000/Capital-markets-and-legal-institutions.pdf

Mielcarz, P., Osiichuk, D., & Pulawska, K. (2021). Increasing shareholder focus the repercussions of the 2015 corporate governance reform in Japan. *Journal of Management and Governance*, 1–31. https://doi.org/10.1007/s10997-021-09619-0

Miyajima, H. (2023). Corporate governance reform, and ownership, and control: Perspective from Japan. *Asian Journal of Political Science, 23*, 1–14. https://doi.org/10.1080/02185377.2022.2159177

Miyajima, H., & Saito, T. (2019). Corporate governance reforms under the Abenomics: The economic consequences of two codes. *SSRN Electronic Journal*, 1–54. https://doi.org/10.2139/ssrn.3684372

Miyamoto, K. (2019). The evolution of the monitoring board in Japan: How the board performs monitoring function in Japanese corporate governance. *Corporate Governance: The International Journal of Business in Society, 19*(5), 999–1014. https://doi.org/10.1108/cg-07-2018-0245

Morck, R., & Nakamura, M. (1999). Banks and corporate control in Japan. *The Journal of Finance, 54*(1), 319–339. https://doi.org/10.1111/0022-1082.00106

Morck, R., & Nakamura, M. (2007). A frog in a well knows nothing of the ocean: A history of corporate ownership in Japan. In *A history of corporate governance around of world* (pp. 367–465). University of Chicago Press.

Nemoto, K. (2022). Revisiting Japan's stakeholder-based system and foreign ownership: IR managers' view of foreign shareholders in corporate governance reform in Japanese companies. *Corporate Governance: The International Journal of Business in Society, 23*(3), pp.534–562.

Nottage, L., & Kozuka, S. (2022). Japan: Corporate governance and gradual transformation. In *Principles of contemporary corporate governance*. Cambridge University Press. https://doi.org/10.33774/coe-2022-nrcqj

OECD. (2021). *Corporate governance Factbook 2021*. Organization for Economic Co-operation and Development. https://www.oecd.org/corporate/corporate-governance-factbook.htm

Okamoto, N. (2022). Financialization in the context of cross-shareholding in Japan: The performative pursuit of better corporate governance. *Journal of Management and Governance*, 1–21. https://doi.org/10.1007/s10997-021-09620-7

Omura, H. (2020a). Stewardship activities and agency problems after Japanese corporate governance reform. *SSRN Electronic Journal*, 1–27. https://doi.org/10.2139/ssrn.3733196

Omura, H. (2020b). What does Japanese corporate governance reform mean? *SSR Electronic Journal*, 1–34. https://doi.org/10.2139/ssrn.3572513

Ozu, C., Nakamura, M., Nagata, K., & Gray, S. J. (2018). Transitioning to IFRS in Japan: Corporate perceptions of costs and benefits. *Australian Accounting Review, 28*(1), 4–13. https://doi.org/10.1111/auar.12168

Panda, B., & Leepsa, N. M. (2017). Agency theory: Review of theory and evidence on problems and perspectives. *Indian Journal of Corporate Governance, 10*(1), 74–95. https://doi.org/10.1177/0974686217701467

SESC. (2021). Securities and Exchange Surveillance Commission. https://www.fsa.go.jp/sesc/english/index.htm

Shishido, Z. (2021). Reform in Japanese corporate law and corporate governance: Current changes in historical perspective. *The American Journal of Comparative Law, 49*(4), 653–677. https://doi.org/10.2307/841053

Titus, V., O'Brien, J. P., & Dixit, J. (2021). Does performance breed slack? Ownership as a contingency to the performance feedback and slack relationship. *Journal of Management*, 1–29. https://doi.org/10.1177/01492063211014263

TSE. (2021). *White paper on corporate governance 2021*. Tokyo Stock Exchange. https://www.jpx.co.jp/english/equities/listing/cg/02.html

TSE. (2023). *White paper on corporate governance 2023*. Tokyo Stock Exchange. https://www.jpx.co.jp/english/equities/listing/cg/02.html

Tsukioka, Y. (2020). The impact of Japan's stewardship code on shareholder voting. *International Review of Economics & Finance, 67*, 148–162. https://doi.org/10.1016/j.iref.2019.12.014

WFE. (2023). *Statistics portal*. World Federation of Exchanges. https://www.world-exchanges.org/our-work/statistics

Williamson, O. E. (1983). Organization form, residual claimants, and corporate control. *The Journal of Law and Economics, 26*(2), 351–366. https://doi.org/10.1086/467039

Yafeh, Y. (2000). Corporate governance in Japan: Past performance and future prospects. *Oxford Review of Economic Policy, 16*(2), 74–84. https://doi.org/10.1093/oxrep/16.2.74

Chapter 6
Russia

Corporate Governance System in Russia

Bruno Teixeira and Tatiana King

6.1 Introduction

Russia is a non-member country of the Organization for Economic Co-operation and Development (OECD), which, in the year 2023, occupied the position of the eleventh largest economy in the world, with a gross domestic product (GDP) of USD 2.02 trillion (OECD, 2024; World Bank, 2024). Historically, Russia remained a closed economy for approximately seven and a half decades, a period that began with the Russian Revolution in 1917 and ended in 1991 with the end of the Soviet Union. The transition from a socialist economy to a market economy started in the following years through successive privatization of state-owned companies (Judge & Naoumova, 2004). However, this has resulted in a capital market characterized primarily by insider-controlled and state-controlled companies (Chernykh, 2008; Grosman et al., 2016). This historical perspective has significantly affected Russia's corporate governance structure and practices over the last 30 years.

A systematic literature review was developed based on articles published in relevant journals on Russian corporate governance. Also, the legislation that regulates the Russian capital market, the corporate governance code published by The Central Bank of the Russian Federation, and other information related to the capital market or corporate governance in Russia were analyzed in the following sources: Word Bank (WB), World Federation of Exchanges (WFE), International Monetary Fund (IMF), Moscow Exchange (MOEX), big four audits, and Russian state bodies.

B. Teixeira (✉)
University of Vale do Taquari, Univates, Lajeado, Brazil

T. King
University of Vaasa, Vaasa, Finland
e-mail: tatiana.king@uwasa.fi

C. B. Macagnan (ed.), *Corporate Governance in Capital Markets*, CSR, Sustainability, Ethics & Governance,
https://doi.org/10.1007/978-3-031-94751-3_6

The results indicate that Russia has sought to improve the structure and practices of corporate governance, particularly with the publication of the corporate governance code and the reformulation of the legislation on corporations. Anglo-Saxon and European traditions inspire such enhancements. However, there are still challenges regarding protecting minority shareholders in terms of enforcement and the participation of women in governance bodies. It is important to highlight that, although this chapter includes data and information following the onset of Russia's second invasion of Ukraine on February 24, 2022, the regulatory context and empirical literature describe corporate governance as it was before the conflict. After this introduction, the chapter continues with Sect. 6.2, which defines corporate governance in Russia. The section is divided into three parts. The first part provides an overview of the Russian stock exchange, its main indices, the leading listed companies, the supervisory and regulatory bodies, and the primary legislation. The second part describes the historical perspective of the privatization process in Russia in the 1990s, which resulted in the current ownership structure. The third part exposes Russian companies' existing corporate governance mechanisms. Finally, part 4 concludes.

6.2 Corporate Governance

Since the beginning of the 1990s, with the end of the Soviet Union and the gradual insertion of a market economy, Russia has sought to improve its corporate governance mechanisms. However, this movement was more important from the beginning of the 2000s through implementing a governance code and revising the legislation on corporations (Johannesson et al., 2012; Alon, 2013). Therefore, this section addresses the main aspects of corporate governance in Russia based on the sources described in the methodology of this article. Thus, this section comprises topics: (a) Capital markets: an overview of the stock exchange and regulatory aspects; (b) The ownership structure of Russian companies; and (c) Corporate governance structure and practices: issues that affect minority shareholders'rights.

6.2.1 Capital Markets: An Overview of the Stock Exchange and Regulatory Aspects

In Russia, trading in shares, bonds, derivatives, currencies, money market instruments, and commodities takes place on its only exchange, the Moscow Exchange (MOEX), founded in 2011 from the union between the Moscow Interbank Currency Exchange (MICEX) and Russian Trading System's (RTS). On February 15, 2013, MOEX carried out its shares' initial public offering (IPO) (MOEX, 2014, 2024). As a result, this exchange is ranked among the 30 leading stock exchanges globally regarding the market value of the shares traded, with the respective sum representing USD 650 billion at the end of 2023 (World Federation of Exchanges, 2024). The historical perspective of MOEX relevance is presented in Graph 6.1 through the percentage ratio between the market value of the shares traded and the Russian GDP between 2011 and 2023.

Graph 6.1 shows that the market value of shares traded on the MOEX has always represented an amount greater than 25% of the Russian GDP. However, this did not occur in 2014 and 2022 due to the wars between Russia and Ukraine, which resulted in sanctions imposed on Russia by the West (Stepanyan et al., 2016; Keleş, 2023). After this period, Russia's GDP did not recover to pre-war levels (before 2013), showing a reduction of approximately 12%. Additionally, the market value of stocks decreased by around 16%. These figures can be seen in Graph 6.2 and support what is shown in Graph 6.1.

Finally, Graph 6.2 shows that although there has been an increase in the value of stocks traded in the Russian capital market after the crisis, this rise has not yet restored the values to the pre-war level of 2013. Russian companies operate in an environment characterized by geopolitical and economic instability. For instance, the sanctions imposed by the United States and the European Union on Russia, arising from geopolitical issues, have limited Russian companies' access to mergers and acquisitions processes, financing, equipment, and technologies (Nurgozhayeva, 2022). Consequently, this diminishes the attractiveness of Russian companies to investors due to the unpredictability of doing business (Ershova et al., 2023; García-Gómez et al., 2023).

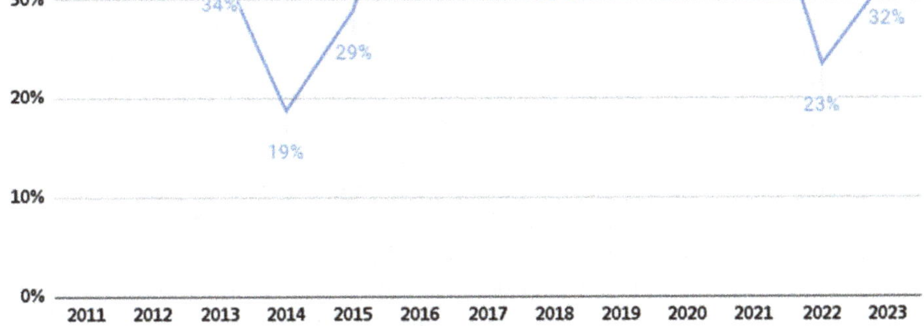

Graph 6.1 Percentage relationship between the market value of shares traded on the MOEX and Russian GDP. Source: Values calculated by the authors based on data from the World Federation of Exchanges (2024) and the World Bank (2024)

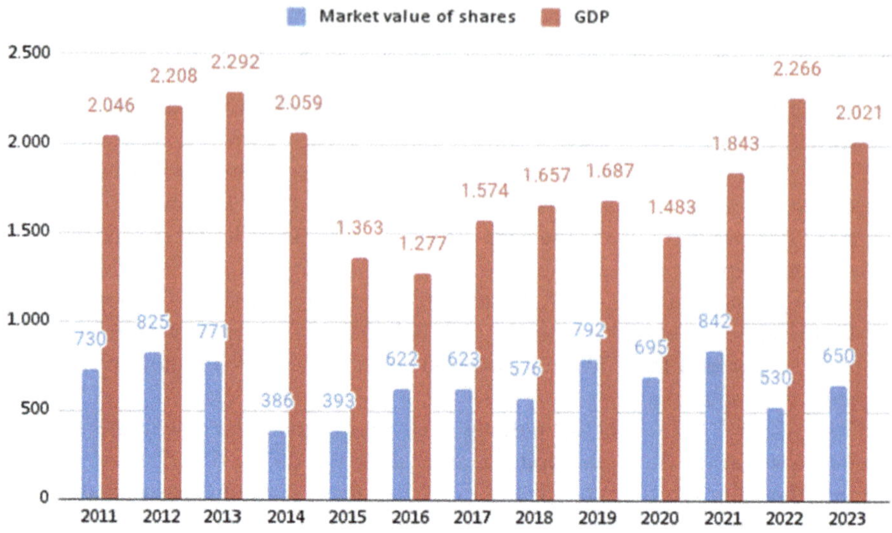

Graph 6.2 Market value of stocks traded on the MOEX and the GDP of Russia (In USD billion). Source: World Federation of Exchanges (2024) and the World Bank (2024)

In December 2023, the MOEX was composed of 828 listed companies. Additionally, as of the mentioned date, the MOEX had 13 stock indices, as shown in Fig. 6.1.

MOEX (2024) categorizes the indices into general thematic equity indices. The indices that make up the general equity indices are the RTS Index (RTSI), the MOEX Russia Index (IMOEX), the Blue-Chip Index (MOEXBC), the SMID Index (MCXSM or RTSSM), the Broad Market Index (MOEXBMI or RUBMI), and the Sectoral Indices, considered the most relevant by MOEX. The RTS Index (RTSI) comprises the 50 most liquid shares of the largest companies on the stock exchange. The main assets traded are concentrated in the energy (45.12%), financial (22.67%), and metals and mining (15.72%) sectors. It was created on September 1, 1995, and is denominated in US Dollars. The MOEX Russia Index (IMOEX) was created on September 22, 1997, and has the same composition as the RTS Index (RTSI). However, the MOEX Russia Index (IMOEX) is measured in the Russian Ruble.

Created on April 23, 2009, the Blue-Chip Index (MOEXBC) comprises the shares of the 15 most liquid companies with the highest market capitalization. The stocks in this index are concentrated in the energy (55.8%), financial (23.86%), and metals and mining (18.49%) sectors. It is expressed in the Russian Ruble. Adopted as of December 17, 2012, the SMID Index (MCXSM or RTSSM) comprises all medium-sized company shares on the stock exchange. The assets of this index are distributed mostly in the sectors of transportation (15.12%), information technologies (15.11%), consumer (13.37%), financials (12.86%), and electric utilities (10.39%). The MCXSM code is used to express the index in Russian Rubles, and the RTSSM code is used to express the index in US Dollars. The Broad Market

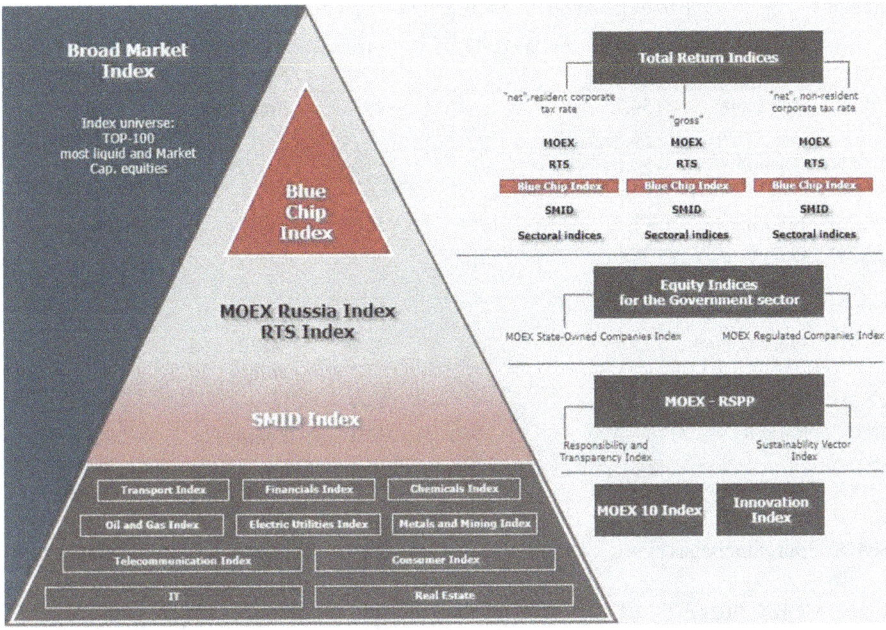

Fig. 6.1 MOEX Stock Index. Source: MOEX (2024)

Index (MOEXBMI or RUBMI) comprises the 100leading stocks on the stock exchange based on liquidity, capitalization, and free float. The assets that stand out are the energy (42.32%), financial (22.44%), and metals and mining (14.93%) sectors. The MOEXBMI code is used to display the Russian Ruble index, and the RUBMI code is used to display the US Dollar index. This index was created on December 30, 2011. The Sectoral Index separates the companies in the Broad Market Index into the following sectoral indices: consumption (MOEXCN), construction (MOEXRE), chemical (MOEXCH), financial (MOEXFN), electric utilities (MOEXEU), metals and mining (MOEXMM), energy (MOEXOG), information technology (MOEXIT), telecommunications (MOEXTL), and transport (MOEXTN). Sector indices are shown in Russian Ruble and US Dollar. This index is calculated since December 30, 2004.

An important aspect to consider is that the most significant stocks in the Russian capital market, which are part of the general equity indices, are concentrated in the following sectors: energy, finance, metals, and mining. These sectors are characterized by state-controlled companies, particularly in the oil and gas segments. Chernykh (2008) reveals that companies in strategic sectors, such as gas, electricity, oil, and telecommunications, were kept mainly under Russian state control during privatization in the 1990s. Also, since 2000, the Russian state has made certain state-owned companies and industry leaders profitable. As a result, it sells minority stakes in these companies to private investors (Grosman et al., 2016). Concurrently, the Russian state resumed expanding its economic participation by acquiring large

Table 6.1 Top 10companies listed on the MOEX (On November 18, 2024)

Code	Companies	Capitalization (USD billions)	Free float	Sector	Ownership
SBER	Sberbank	54.2	48%	Financial	State-owned
ROSN	Rosneft	50.6	11%	Energy	State-owned
LKOH	Lukoil	48.5	55%	Energy	Private
GAZP	Gazprom	30.8	50%	Energy	State-owned
NVTK	Novatek	27.2	21%	Energy	Private
GMKN	Norilsk Nickel	17.5	32%	Metals and mining	Private
YNDX	Yandex NV	13.4	15%	IT	Private
TATN	Tatneft	12.2	32%	Energy	State-owned
CHMF	Severstal	10.1	23%	Metals and mining	Private
SNGS	Surgutneftegas	9.1	25%	Energy	State-owned

Source: MOEX (2024)

private companies, leading to a greater concentration of ownership (Nurgozhayeva, 2022). This context can be seen in Table 6.1, which contains 10 companies that are part of most of the indices that make up the general equity indices.

Table 6.1 shows that among the top 10 companies listed on MOEX, 60% are from the energy sector. Furthermore, 50% are under state control. Among the energy sector companies, 83% are controlled by the Russian state. In 2010, the share of state-controlled Russian companies in the RTS Index (RTSI) was approximately 54.5%, with 89.5% in the financial sector, 66.5% in the oil and gas sector, and 61% in the energy sector. The Russian state's economic expansion accelerated following economic measures adopted to mitigate the effects of the 2008 crisis and the sanctions imposed by the United States and European Union in the 2014 geopolitical crisis (Nurgozhayeva, 2022).

The indices that are part of the thematic equity include the MOEX Russia Total Return Indices (MCFTR), the State-owned Companies Index (MOEX SCI), the Regulated Companies Index (MOEX RCI), the Responsibility and Transparency Index (MRRT), the Sustainability Vector Index (MRSV), the MOEX 10 Index (MOEX10), and the MOEX Innovation Index (MOEXINN). The MOEX Russia Total Return Indices (MCFTR) represent the total return of the stocks that make up each of the following indices: RTS Index (RTSI), MOEX Russia Index (IMOEX), Blue Chip Index (MOEXBC), SMID Index (MCXSM or RTSSM), and Sector Indices. They are calculated by index, separating the results into Russian and non-Russian companies. Their value is expressed in Russian Ruble and began being used on December 30, 2004. Created on December 30, 2011, the State-owned Companies Index (MOEX SCI) comprises companies on the stock exchange whose ownership structure includes the state as a participant. It should be noted that it is shown in the Russian Ruble. The Regulated Companies Index (MOEX RCI) comprises stock exchange companies operating in sectors regulated and supervised by Russian state bodies. It started to be calculated on December 30, 2011 and is expressed in Russian Ruble.

The Responsibility and Transparency Index (MRRT) started to be used on December 30, 2011, comprising equity issuers who fully disclose information on sustainable development and corporate social responsibility. It is expressed in Russian Ruble. Adopted as of December 30, 2011, the Sustainability Vector Index (MRSV) comprises stock company shares that present the best indicators of sustainable development and corporate social responsibility. It is also calculated for Russian issuers only, and its name is Sustainability Russian Companies Vector Index (MRSVR). In addition, MOEX estimates the return of these indices using the MOEX—RSPP Sustainability Vector Total.

The MOEX 10 Index (MOEX10) comprises the 10 most liquid stocks on the exchange, including shares of the companies Aeroflot (AFLT), Gazprom (GAZP), Lukoil (LKOH), Novatek (NVTK), Ozon (OZON), Rosneft (ROSN), Sberbank (SBER), Surgutneftegas (SNGSP), TCS Holding (TCSG), and VTB Bank (VTBR). This index began to be calculated on December 30, 1997, and is expressed in Russian Ruble. The MOEX Innovation Index (MOEXINN) includes shares of companies traded in the investment and innovation markets, such as Artgen Biotech (ABIO), Nauka (NAUK), Nauka-Telecom (NSVZ), and United Aircraft Corporation (UNAC). It started to be calculated on December 29, 2009, and is presented in the Russian Ruble (MOEX, 2024).

The Financial Market Infrastructure Department and the Corporate Affairs Department supervised and regulated the Russian capital market linked to the Central Bank of the Russian Federation. The Financial Market Infrastructure Department was created in 2020 and aims to regulate and supervise financial organizations that operate in the financial market's accounting, trading, settlement, and information infrastructure. The Corporate Affairs Department regulates and oversees issues related to the issuers' compliance with Russian laws and monitors the corporate governance practices of companies listed on the stock exchange (The Central Bank of the Russian Federation, 2021).

Russia is a republic based on civil law (The Constitution of the Russian Federation, 1993; Woodruff, 2004). Therefore, Orazalin et al. (2016) highlight that the performance of supervisory and regulatory bodies in the Russian capital market is based on a set of regulations, mainly those described below:

(a) The Civil Code of the Russian Federation Part One No. 51-FZ of November 30, 1994: The Russian civil code provides that organizations can be constituted as a partnership and a company. It also defines that these organizations have civil rights and obligations when formed. In addition, it limits owners' liability to the commitments of their organizations and vice versa. Finally, it establishes rights (access to accounting information and other documents, receipt of dividends, etc.) and obligations (to carry out the investment following the organization's incorporation documents, maintain the confidentiality of confidential information, etc.) on the part of the partners or shareholders.

(b) Federal Law of December 26, 1995, No. 208-FZ On joint-stock companies: This law regulates the entire operation of public and private companies. Among the main aspects addressed in this law are the following: business combinations, the process of liquidation of companies, types of shares, shareholders' rights, shareholders' agreements, dividend policies, general and extraordinary shareholders' meetings, the board of directors, the executive board, and the required documents.
(c) Federal Law of April 22, 1996, No. 39-FZ On the securities market: The law regulates the relationships established in the issuance and circulation of issued securities, regardless of the type of issuer. It also regulates the activities of professionals participating in the securities market.
(d) Federal Law of March 05, 1999, No. 46-FZ On protecting investors' rights and lawful interests in the securities market: This law aims to ensure the rights and interests of investors and define procedures for the payment of compensation to them arising from damages caused by illegal actions by issuers and other participants in the securities market.

In addition to the laws mentioned above, Federal Law No. 208-FZ On Consolidated Financial Statements, approved at the end of 2011, mandates that companies listed on the MOEX present consolidated financial statements in accordance with international accounting standards (IFRS) as of 2012 (IFRS Foundation, 2024). The adoption of IFRS is seen as a mechanism that enhances corporate governance and is expected to bring multiple benefits, including increased transparency (Alon, 2013). However, accounting in Russia continues to rely on Russian Accounting Standards (RAS) for taxation purposes (Chui et al., 2020). Although RAS is based on IFRS, there are still gaps where certain IFRS standards do not have corresponding RAS equivalents, and some RAS have yet to be fully updated to align with IFRS (Generalova et al., 2024).

As there are two accounting standards, Russian companies can hire the same audit for RAS and IFRS or an audit for RAS and another for IFRS. Russian legislation does not provide for restrictions on hiring auditors to carry out audits of financial statements based on RAS or IFRS. The only requirement is that the auditors are chosen through public selection, and auditors rotate every five years in companies with a minimum state participation of 25% (Chui et al., 2020). However, for other companies, there is no mandatory rotation of auditors (Kamarudin et al., 2022). Federal Law 208-FZ on joint stock companies establishes that the general meeting of shareholders has the prerogative to appoint the company's auditors. On the other hand, the board of directors defines the auditors' fees.

The Federal Law of December 30, 2008, No. 307-FZ On Auditing determines that in Russia, auditing is mandatory for:

- Organizations whose securities are admitted to organized trading.
- Banks, insurance companies, stock exchanges, and investment institutions.
- State and municipal unitary enterprises.

- Companies (except for agricultural cooperatives and unions of these cooperatives) whose annual income for corporate tax purposes for the preceding financial year exceeds RUB 800,000,000 or for which the value of assets on the balance sheet at the end of the year preceding the financial year exceeds RUB 400,000,000;
- Other cases where federal laws require an audit to be conducted.

The Russian Ministry of Finance supervises auditing activities, and quality control and audit certification are the responsibility of the Self-Regulatory Organizations (SROs). In this sense, audit activities are still monitored by the Russian state (Chui et al., 2020).

Since in this section the main aspects of the stock exchange, the supervisory and regulatory bodies, and the legislation governing the Russian capital market were exposed in this section. The following section addresses the predominant role of Russian companies' capital structure on the stock exchange.

6.2.2 The Ownership Structure of Russian Companies

Russian history is characterized by several wars and crises. In 1905, the first Russian revolution took place, with the failed attempt to overthrow the Tsar and transform the autocratic country into a democratic government. In 1914, in the context of the First World War, the Russian economy was devastated. In 1917, Lenin's Bolsheviks took advantage of the weakening of the government and overthrew the corrupt ruling class, forming the Soviet Union. During the Stalin government, between 1929 and 1953, a centralized economic model was adopted, created by a relationship of exchange of favors between government bureaucrats and Soviet managers of companies, resulting, for example, in the falsification of figures relating to the results of companies, against the goals established by the central government. This situation and the Second World War brought down the Russian economy (Judge & Naoumova, 2004). Therefore, informal rules, the exclusion of outsiders, and the withholding of information have become part of the Russian institutional environment (Judge & Naoumova, 2004; Estrin & Prevezer, 2011; Johannesson et al., 2012; Braguinsky & Mityakov, 2015).

During the 1990s, with the end of the Soviet Union, Russia began a process of privatization of companies that, until then, belonged to the state. However, this process occurred by adopting corrupt practices, resulting in companies controlled by well-connected insiders, directors, or controllers with strong influence on the board of directors. In this context, the auction of shares of state-owned companies in the oil and metallurgy sectors, given a guarantee of unpaid loans by the Russian government, was obtained from certain banks, which led to the formation of monopolies of financial-industrial groups. Another relevant aspect is that there are private companies in Russia whose control is difficult to be identified. That occurs as shares can be issued in the name of owners' representatives who hide their identification through offshores (Filatotchev, 1997; Buck et al., 1998; Chernykh, 2008; Demirbas & Yukhanaev, 2011).

Table 6.2 Historical landmarks of state and private participation in Russian companies

Time course	Event
1990–1995	The legislation that allowed the existence of private ownership of companies was established. Thus began the privatization process through free vouchers distributed to all Russian citizens.
1995–2000	In these 5 years, the process of monetary privatization began. The Russian government borrowed from some financial institutions, giving as collateral shares of state-owned companies to extract natural resources. The loans were not repaid, and the shares were auctioned.
2000–2005	Vladimir Putin became president, and the state began to regain company control by purchasing private company assets. As a result, in terms of proportion, the market capitalization of state-owned companies increased from 20% in 2003 to 50% in 2010.
2005–2010	The initial public offering (IPO) of Rosneft, a state-owned oil sector, and VTB, a state-owned financial industry, was held on the London stock Exchange (LSE). In addition, state-controlled assets are consolidated in state-owned companies Rosnanotech and Rostekhnologii.

Source: Kuznetsov and Kuznetsov (1999) and Grosman et al. (2016)

Therefore, Western-style foreign ownership of Russian companies could positively affect the dissemination of Corporate Social Responsibility (CSR) practices. However, foreign ownership of Russian companies between 2012 and 2015 was distributed as follows: 26% in Cyprus or the Virgin Islands, 8% in the United States, Europe, and Canada, and 2% in Bermuda, Cayman Islands, Belize, etc. This context denotes a search for fiscal optimization through offshores, given that a negative relationship exists between foreign ownership of Russian companies and the disclosure of CSR practices (Garanina & Aray, 2021). From the 2000s onward, Russia modified its privatization strategy, strengthening state-owned companies in relevant sectors and selling minority stakes to private investors. In addition, Russia has increased its shareholding in companies through pyramids or golden shares (Grosman et al., 2016). Table 6.2 presents the historical landmarks of state and private participation in Russian companies.

Given the above, the state or private insiders control Russian companies, putting minority shareholders in a weak position (Chernykh, 2008; Pöyry & Maury, 2010). La Porta et al. (2000) state that controlling shareholders can adopt measures that benefit themselves and harm minority shareholders, even causing their expropriation. Among the standards above, in Russia, the following stand out: the creation of shell companies, tax evasion onshore and offshore, non-announcement of the shareholders' meeting, lack of transparency on management decisions and the financial statements, exclusion of the name of shareholder records, etc. (Desai et al., 2007; Markus, 2008; Goncharov & Van Triest, 2014; Nizaeva & Uyar, 2017).

Attention is also drawn to what happened during the 1998 Russian financial crisis. Insiders have divested companies' assets and cash flows in various ways, such as through stock dilution. In addition, they disrespected the interests of creditors and employees through insolvency proceedings that expanded their control over assets.

The poor quality of information generated by accounting facilitated executing these actions (Jesover, 2001; McCarthy & Puffer, 2008). Shleifer and Vishny (1997) also report that insiders of Russian companies threatened to fire employees who owned shares if they did not vote according to their interests.

The weak enforcement, characteristic of the Russian institutional environment and other developing countries, can contribute to the low protection of minority shareholders (Wright et al., 2003; Johannesson et al., 2012; Oliveira et al., 2016; Garanina & Kaikova, 2016). La Porta et al. (2000) point out that, in general, countries that use civil law have weaker protection of minority shareholders compared to countries that use common law. Insufficient protection of minority shareholders can reduce the liquidity of the capital market. In addition, weak enforcement makes it impossible for such shareholders to seek their rights in court when these are disrespected (Shleifer & Vishny, 1997; Li et al., 2012).

An essential aspect is that the 10 largest Russian non-financial companies, in terms of direct investment abroad, have about 30% of the board seats occupied by foreigners (Liuhto, 2017). Furthermore, Garanina and Aray (2021) identified in their study that Russian companies with foreign board members show greater transparency concerning CSR. The authors also emphasize that the international experience of these members, especially from the United States and Europe, helps to create long-term value for shareholders. Besides, the most excellent transparency of CSR is identified in Russian companies listed on stock exchanges in other countries (cross-listing). That may be a way for Russian companies to legitimize themselves in the foreign market.

Given the context, the next section highlights the structure and practices of corporate governance provided for in the regulation's Russian companies, which aim to mitigate the possible agency problems.

6.2.3 Corporate Governance Structure and Practices: Issues Affecting Minority Shareholders' Rights

The Russian corporate governance model is inspired by the Anglo-Saxon and European models (Johannesson et al., 2012; Garanina & Kaikova, 2016). Evidence of this inspiration is described in its joint-stock company law, which states that the general meeting of shareholders is the highest decision-making body for companies and that the board of directors can be made up of one (Anglo-Saxon) or two levels (European). The board is structured on two levels: the management board and the supervisory board (World Bank, 2013; Garanina & Kaikova, 2016). The management board is responsible for the company's current activities and reports directly to the supervisory board and the company's general meeting. On the other hand, the supervisory board has general management aspects as its scope. It reports directly to the company's public meeting (Federal Law of December 26, 1995, No 208-FZ On joint-stock companies).

Regarding the board size, the number of members must be stated in the company's bylaws. However, the Russian corporation law determines some parameters for defining the size of the board, namely, when the company has up to 1000 shareholders with voting rights, the board must not have less than 5 members. If the company has between 5000 and 10,000 shareholders with voting rights, the board must not have fewer than 7 members. Finally, if the company is made up of more than 10,000 shareholders with voting rights, the board must not have fewer than 9 directors (Berezinets et al., 2017). The authors mention that the Russian corporate governance code does not mention the size of the board.

In terms of the composition of the board, the legislation establishes that the participation of executives must be limited to a quarter of the total members and that the Chief Executive Officer (CEO) cannot simultaneously exercise the activity of the chairman of the board (Chairman), that is, duality is not allowed (Iwasaki, 2007; Berezinets et al., 2017). Furthermore, although there is no legal provision, the Russian corporate governance code recommends that a third of the board members be independent (Berezinets et al., 2017; Okhmatovskiy, 2017). In 2011, the Russian government replaced a significant number of state representatives on the boards of state-owned companies with independent members. However, this did not increase the autonomy of SOEs, as lower-level government officials retained their positions on the board. Therefore, they made decisions and voted according to the guidelines of high-ranking government officials (Grosman et al., 2016). In any case, the participation of government-related advisers is higher in Russia than in other emerging countries, such as India and Turkey (Ararat et al., 2021).

The legislation does not present any requirement related to gender equality on board composition. Female participation in the board of directors of Russian companies is associated with a lower turnover of the Chief Executive Officer (CEO), which increases the value of companies, and with greater diligence, resulting from a more significant number of meetings (Kim et al., 2020). However, the proportion of women on boards of Russian companies is still low (Garanina & Kaikova, 2016). Between 1998 and 2014, the women's representation on boards was approximately 12%. Furthermore, the distribution of this participation was as follows: one director in 33% of the companies, two directors in 17% of the companies, and three directors in 7% of the companies. Companies and four or more counselors in only 3% of the companies. Finally, 40% of Russian companies do not have women on their boards of directors (Garanina & Muravyev, 2021).

The corporate governance code recommends the establishment of advisory committees for the board of directors, such as audit, compensation, and appointment committees (The Central Bank of the Russian Federation, 2014). As a result, Russian companies have implemented audit committees. On the other hand, the remuneration and appointment committees have been formed in a single structure, which would not follow the code above's recommendations. Furthermore, an essential feature of the committees formed by Russian companies is the existence of a strategy committee. When implemented, this committee aims to prepare the company's strategy, and the board is responsible for monitoring the defined strategy (Berezinets et al., 2017).

The Russian shareholding system comprises common and preferred shares, with preferences limited to 25% of the company's authorized capital. Common shares allow voting at general shareholders' meetings and participating in company results. On the other hand, preferred shares are usually entitled only to dividends, which can be fixed or on earnings. In addition, certain types of preferred shares may entitle you to vote. The companies' bylaws must provide the rights and types of preferred shares.

Another point to be highlighted about dividends is that the general meeting defines the amount to be paid and cannot be higher than the board of directors recommended. (Federal Law of December 26, 1995, No 208-FZ on joint-stock companies). Therefore, there is no mandatory minimum dividend payment. La Porta et al. (2000) state that the obligation to pay dividends provided by law makes it possible for minority shareholders not to be wholly expropriated and encourages the participation of these shareholders in the capital market. Most members of the board of directors represent the interests of controlling shareholders and do not necessarily decide what is best for the company (World Bank, 2013).

To mitigate the effects of the conflict of interest between controlling and minority shareholders, the Federal Law of December 26, 1995, No. 208-FZ On Joint-Stock Companies, the MOEX, and the Russian Corporate Governance Code have established certain practices to protect minority shareholders. Some of these practices are exemplified below:

- Each share entitles you to one vote.
- Right to participate in general meetings of shareholders in person or remotely (vote on the ballot sent by post or electronic vote).
- Cumulative voting for the election of board members.
- Shareholders who own at least 10% of the shares with voting rights may call an extraordinary general meeting.
- Shareholders with at least 2% of the voting shares may add items to the annual general meeting agenda and nominate candidates for the board of directors.
- A qualified quorum of three-fourth of the shares with voting rights is required to approve transactions whose value exceeds 50% of the company's assets and relevant changes to the bylaws.
- Mandatory approval at the shareholders' meeting of transactions with interested parties whose assets add up to at least 10% of the company's assets.
- Minimum free float of 10%.

On average, the level of implementation of minority shareholder rights in the Russian capital market is equivalent to that of emerging East Asian countries. It is higher than that of Latin American countries. Therefore, there are still corporate governance issues that need to be improved, such as manipulation of values in transactions with related parties, violation of shareholders' right to participate in general meetings, violation of shareholders' rights in corporate reorganization processes, lack of disclosure adequate control structure, among others (IMF, 2000; World Bank, 2013).

In any case, Russia has tried to improve corporate governance practices, and one of the main instruments is the corporate governance code, approved in 2002

(Demidenko & McNutt, 2010). This code was revised and published in 2014 by The Central Bank of the Russian Federation and prepared with support from the Organization for Economic Co-operation and Development (OECD) and the Moscow Exchange (MOEX). Its use is voluntary (Demidenko & McNutt, 2010; Johannesson et al., 2012; Nizaeva & Uyar, 2017). The Russian code is based on the Organization for Economic Co-operation and Development (OECD) governance principles and is divided into seven sections, namely: I. Shareholder rights and equality of conditions for shareholders exercising their rights; II. Board of directors of the company; III. Corporate secretary of the company; IV. The remuneration system is due to members of the board of directors, the executive bodies, and other key company managers; V. Risk management and internal control system; VI. Disclosure of information about the company and its information policy, and VII. Material, corporate actions.

The section titled *Shareholder rights and equality of conditions for shareholders exercising their rights* describes that the company must guarantee equal and fair treatment to its shareholders and the right to participate in the management through actions, opinions, provision of informative materials, voting rights, and participation in the company's profits. Because of this, when defining the value of dividends, transparency must be respected, respecting the limits imposed by law. Furthermore, it is up to the company to guarantee shareholders' equity in the same category and, consequently, to prevent any hierarchy between them. Finally, shareholders must have reliable and efficient means of registering their rights to the shares and the opportunity to dispose of them in a non-onerous manner freely.

The second section, which addresses the *Board of directors of the company*, stipulates that the board of directors are responsible for creating the risk management and internal control system, monitoring actions, appointments, and dismissals of members of the executive body, utilizing the company's development strategy and objectives, setting goals, and evaluating and approving performance indicators, strategies, and business plans related to the areas of operations. Additionally, it determines the policy on compensation for reimbursement of expenses for its directors and discloses information to shareholders. The board of directors are also responsible for including members free from the influence of the company's executive bodies or interested parties, thus following the criterion of independence and enabling the prevention of internal conflicts.

The chair of the board can execute measures that oblige the board to provide information necessary for decision-making. For example, an independent director may be elected as the board's chairperson or coordinate with the other independent directors. Board members must act in ways that benefit the company and shareholders, basing their decisions on information obtained without conflicts and ensuring shareholders' equity. Board meetings and the participation of members are essential to ensure the board's efficiency and that they are held as needed. The board preselects essential issues about the company's business. Evaluating the quality of the work of the board of directors and its committees is crucial to verify that the company's needs were duly met and to identify possible improvements.

The section *Corporate Secretary of the Company* outlines that the corporate secretariat aims to facilitate interaction between shareholders, support the work of the board of directors, and coordinate actions to protect the rights of shareholders. To perform functions in the corporate secretariat, experience, knowledge, good conduct, and independence from executive bodies are essential. In case of a conflict of interest, the members of the corporate secretariat must immediately inform the chairperson of the board of directors.

The fourth section, titled *System of Remuneration Due to Members of the Board of Directors, the Executive Bodies, and Other Key Managers of the Company*, states that the remuneration of the Board of Directors, the Executive Body, and other members is carried out by the policy developed by the remuneration committee and approved by the board of directors. Adequate remuneration leads to motivation and efficiency at work and the retention of qualified professionals. The company must pay attention to higher remuneration levels, especially those that differ from other company employees. The compensation system for directors and management must align with the company's and its shareholders' interests. The remuneration of executive bodies and other managers should be based on their performance and contributions. In the event of early dismissal (golden parachute) of an executive body member or another key manager, it must not exceed twice the fixed part of their annual remuneration.

The *Risk management and internal control system* must be established to ensure that the company achieves its objectives with reasonable security, uses resources rationally, identifies and manages its risks, preserves its assets, ensures the integrity and accuracy of accounting information, and controls compliance with regulations (both internal and external). The board of directors establish and maintain the risk management and internal control system. Also, the company must conduct internal audits to independently and regularly assess the reliability and efficiency of the risk management internal control systems and corporate governance practices. These audits must be done by either an audit department or a third-party company.

The section *Disclosure of information about the company and its information policy* reveals that the company and its activities must follow transparent conduct, enabling the exchange of information with its shareholders and other interested parties. In addition, the company must disclose its governance system and report on compliance with the code's principles. The information disclosed must comply with regulations regarding regularity, consistency, and timeliness, as well as the accessibility, reliability, completeness, and comparability of the disclosed data. The annual report must contain information that enables evaluation of the company's performance results. The company also needs to provide information and documents requested by shareholders, following the principle of accessibility. However, when disclosing information, the company must balance the interests of shareholders with the confidentiality of the information.

Finally, the last section of the corporate governance code, *titled Material Corporate Actions*, describes that actions that may affect the company's share capital and financial position must be undertaken on fair terms and conditions to ensure the rights of shareholders and other interested parties are respected. Relevant transactions must be conducted in the interests of shareholders, ensuring that their rights are not violated. The company can facilitate access to material on corporate actions so that shareholders receive complete information, guaranteeing and protecting their rights. The reasons, conditions, and consequences of this act must be explained whenever information about shares is disclosed. In addition, rules and procedures related to relevant corporate actions carried out by the company must be established in its internal documents.

6.3 Final Considerations

This chapter aimed to describe the main features of Russian corporate governance. For this, the results were segregated into three parts, namely: (a) Capital markets: an overview of the stock exchange and regulatory aspects; (b) The ownership structure of Russian companies; and (c) Corporate governance structure and practices: issues that affect minority shareholders'rights. Regarding the first part, it is possible to emphasize that the market value of companies listed on the Moscow Exchange (MOEX) is relevant to the Russian economy, just as the leading listed companies belong to the energy sector. In regulatory terms, Russia is based on civil law, and the highlight is the Federal Law of December 26, 1995, No 208-FZ, on joint-stock companies. The country sought to convert its accounting standards to IFRS for consolidated financial statements. However, it did not revoke the RAS, which was used for tax purposes, implying the hiring of an independent auditor for two accounting standards.

The second part allows the reflection that minority shareholders still have their rights violated, and the enforcement of laws by judicial means is still insufficient, which makes ex-post mechanisms very fragile. As the World Bank (2013) mentioned, that is a significant challenge that Russian regulators still need to mitigate. Possibly, this fragility stems from the institutional environment arising from the period of the Soviet Union.

Finally, the last part reveals that Russia sought to improve its corporate governance practices, particularly those of an ex-ante nature. However, the corporate governance code, considered one of the milestones in the evolution of Russian corporate governance practices, consists of recommendations that do not have the force of law. Regulating the procedures set out in this document or forcing companies to adopt them could improve the environment for investors. In addition, the code could undergo an update process, including aspects that encourage the participation of women in the companies' governance bodies. Also, it is important to point out that since 2000, there has been an advance in state participation in Russian companies, which, added to the control of private companies, in which it is not possible to identify the real controller, can harm the Russian capital market, considering the deficiencies observed in this article.

It is suggested that other studies be carried out regarding corporate governance in Russia, such as reviews incorporating journals published in different languages, including Russian. Also, it is hoped that this chapter could inspire new empirical research on this topic.

References

Alon, A. (2013). Complexity and dual Institutionality: The case of IFRS adoption in Russia. *Corporate Governance: An International Review, 21*(1), 42–57.

Ararat, M., Claessens, S., & Yurtoglu, B. B. (2021). Corporate governance in emerging markets: A selective review and an agenda for future research. *Emerging Markets Review, 48*, 100767.

Berezinets, I., Ilina, Y., & Cherkasskaya, A. (2017). Board structure, board committees, and corporate performance in Russia. *Managerial Finance, 43*, 1073.

Braguinsky, S., & Mityakov, S. (2015). Foreign corporations and the culture of transparency: Evidence from Russian administrative data. *Journal of Financial Economics, 117*(1), 139–164.

Buck, T., Filatotchev I., & Wright, M. (1998). Agents, stakeholders, and corporate governance in Russian firms. *Journal of Management Studies, 35*(1), 81–104.

Chernykh, L. (2008). Ultimate ownership and control in Russia. *Journal of Financial Economics, 88*(1), 169–192.

Chui, L., Kim, O., & Pike, B. J. (2020). The effect of audit duality on audit quality. *Journal of International Accounting Research, 19*(2), 65–89.

Demidenko, E., & McNutt, P. (2010). The ethics of enterprise risk management as a key component of corporate governance. *International Journal of Social Economics, 37*, 802.

Demirbas, D., & Yukhanaev, A. (2011). Independence of board of directors, employee relation and harmonization of corporate governance: Empirical evidence from Russian listed companies. *Employee Relations, 33*, 444.

Desai, M. A., Dyck, A., & Zingales, L. (2007). Theft and taxes. *Journal of Financial Economics, 84*(3), 591–623.

Ershova, T., Zavertiaeva, M., & Kirpishchikov, D. (2023). The impact of influential shareholders on corporate dividend policy: Evidence from Russia. *Journal of Economic Studies, 50*(4), 821–839.

Estrin, S., & Prevezer, M. (2011). The role of informal institutions in corporate governance: Brazil, Russia, India, and China compared. *Asia Pacific Journal of Management, 28*(1), 41–67.

Federal Law of April 22, 1996, No. 39-FZ On the securities market. Retrieved December 06, 2021, from https://www.cbr.ru/eng/na/

Federal Law of December 05, 2011, No. 208-FZ On Consolidated Financial Statements. Retrieved December 06, 2021, from https://minfin.gov.ru/en/policy_issues/account/

Federal Law of December 26, 1995, No. 208-FZ On joint-stock companies. Retrieved December 06, 2021, from https://www.cbr.ru/eng/na/

Federal Law of December 30, 2008, No. 307-FZ On Auditing. Retrieved December 06, 2021, from https://minfin.gov.ru/en/policy_issues/account/

Federal Law of March 05, 1999, No. 46-FZ On protecting investors' rights and lawful interests in the securities market. Retrieved December 06, 2021, from https://www.cbr.ru/eng/na/

Filatotchev, I. (1997). Privatization and corporate governance in transitional economies. *The World Economy, 20*(4), 497–510.

Garanina, T., & Aray, Y. (2021). Enhancing CSR disclosure through foreign ownership, foreign board members, and cross-listing: Does it work in Russian? *Emerging Markets Review, 46*, 100754.

Garanina, T., & Kaikova, E. (2016). Corporate governance mechanisms and agency costs: Cross-country analysis. *Corporate Governance, 16*, 347.

Garanina, T., & Muravyev, A. (2021). The gender composition of corporate boards and firm performance: Evidence from Russia. *Emerging Markets Review, 48*, 100772.

García-Gómez, C. D., Zavertiaeva, M., & López Iturriaga, F. J. (2023). Do CEO characteristics matter for corporate risk taking? Evidence from Russia. *Corporate Governance: The International Journal of Business in Society*.

Generalova, N. V., Pyatov, M. L., & Sokolov, B. I. (2024). The history of IFRS in Russia in 1991–2021. *Journal of International Accounting Research, 23*, 1–25.

Goncharov, I., & Van Triest, S. (2014). Unintended consequences of changing accounting standards: The case of fair value accounting and mandatory dividends. *Abacus, 50*(3), 341–367.

Grosman, A., Wright, M., & Okhmatovskiy, I. (2016). State control and corporate governance in transition economies: 25 years from 1989. *Corporate Governance, 24*(3), 200–221.

IFRS Foundation. (2024). Retrieved November 20, 2024, from https://www.ifrs.org/use-around-the-world/use-of-ifrs-standards-by-jurisdiction/view-jurisdiction/russia/

International Monetary Fund (IMF). (2000). *Corporate governance in Russia: Is there any chance of improvement?* Retrieved December 09, 2021, from https://www.imf.org/external/pubs/ft/seminar/2000/invest/pdf/vasil2.pdf

Iwasaki, I. (2007). Enterprise reform and corporate governance in Russia: A quantitative survey. *Journal of Economic Surveys, 21*(5), 849–902.

Jesover, F. (2001). Corporate governance in The Russian Federation: The relevance of the OECD principles on shareholder rights and equitable treatment. *Corporate Governance: An International Review, 9*(2), 79–88.

Johannesson, J., Palona, I., Guillen, J. F. S., & Fock, M. (2012). UK, Russia, Kazakhstan, and Cyprus governance compared. *Corporate Governance: The international journal of business in society., 12*, 226.

Judge, W., & Naoumova, I. (2004). Corporate governance in Russia: What model will it follow? *Corporate Governance, 12*, 302.

Kamarudin, K. A., Islam, A., Wan Ismail, W. A., & Jahan, M. A. (2022). The effect of mandatory audit firm rotation and the auditing and reporting standards on the auditor competition and audit fees relationship: Evidence from emerging markets. *International Journal of Auditing, 26*(2), 252–278.

Keleş, E. (2023). Stock market response to the Russia-Ukraine war: Evidence from an emerging market. *Journal of East-West Business, 29*(3), 307–322.

Kim, O., Kuang, Y. F., & Qin, B. (2020). Female representation on boards and CEO performance-induced turnover: Evidence from Russia. *Corporate Governance: An International Review, 28*(3), 235–260.

Kuznetsov, O., & Kuznetsov, A. (1999). The state as a shareholder: Responsibilities and objectives. *Europe-Asia Studies, 51*(3), 433–445.

La Porta, R., Lopez-de-Silanes, F., Shleifer, A., & Vishny, R. W. (2000). Agency problems and dividend policies around the world. *The Journal of Finance, 55*(1), 1–33.

Li, W. X., Chen, C. C. S., & French, J. J. (2012). The relationship between liquidity, corporate governance, and firm valuation: Evidence from Russia. *Emerging Markets Review, 13*(4), 465–477.

Liuhto, K. (2017). Foreign nationals on the boards of directors of Russia's ten largest non-financial companies investing overseas. *Baltic Region, 9*(4), 33–52.

Markus, S. (2008). Corporate governance as political insurance: Firm-level institutional creation in emerging markets and beyond. *Socio-Economic Review, 6*(1), 69–98.

McCarthy, D. J., & Puffer, S. M. (2008). Corporate governance as a foundation for corporate social responsibility in transitioning economies: The Russian experience. *Thunderbird International Business Review, 50*(4), 231–243.

Moscow Exchange. (2014). *Annual report 2014*. Retrieved November 30, 2021, from http://2014.report-moex.com/en/moex/history/

Moscow Exchange. (2024). Retrieved November 19, 2024, from https://www.moex.com/en

Nizaeva, M., & Uyar, A. (2017). Corporate governance codes of Eurasian Economic Union countries: A comparative investigation. *Corporate Governance: The International Journal of Business in Society*.

Nurgozhayeva, R. (2022). Corporate governance in Russian state-owned enterprises: Real or surreal? *Asian Journal of Comparative Law, 17*(1), 24–50.

Okhmatovskiy, I. (2017). Self-regulation of corporate governance in Russian firms: Translating the national standard into internal policies. *Journal of Management & Governance, 21*(2), 499–532.

Oliveira, M. C., Ceglia, D., & Antonio Filho, F. (2016). Analysis of corporate governance disclosure: A study through BRICS countries. *Corporate Governance: The International Journal of Business in Society.*

Orazalin, N., Mahmood, M., & Lee, K. J. (2016). Corporate governance, financial crises and bank performance: Lessons from top Russian banks. *Corporate Governance: The International Journal of Business in Society.*

Organization for Economic Co-operation and Development (OECD). (2024). Retrieved November 19, 2024, from https://www.oecd.org/en.html

Pöyry, S., & Maury, B. (2010). Influential ownership and capital structure. *Managerial and Decision Economics, 31*(5), 311–324.

Shleifer, A., & Vishny, R. W. (1997). A survey of corporate governance. *The Journal of Finance, 52*(2), 737–783.

Stepanyan, A., Roitman, A., Minasyan, G., Ostojic, D., & Epstein, N. P. (2016). The spillover effects of Russia's economic slowdown on neighboring countries. *Spillover Notes, 2016*(003), A001. Retrieved November 30, 2021, from https://www.elibrary.imf.org/view/journals/062/2016/003/article-A001-en.xml

The Central Bank of the Russian Federation. (2014). *Russian code of corporate governance*. Retrieved December 09, 2021, from https://www.oecd.org/daf/ca/RussianCodeofCorporateGovernance2014English.pdf

The Central Bank of the Russian Federation. (2021). Retrieved December 04, 2021, from https://www.cbr.ru/eng/

The Civil Code of the Russian Federation Part One No 51-FZ of November 30 1994. Retrieved December 06, 2021, from https://www.wto.org/english/thewto_e/acc_e/rus_e/wtaccrus58_leg_360.pdf

The Constitution of the Russian Federation. (1993). Retrieved December 06, 2021, from http://www.constitution.ru/en/10003000-02.htm

Woodruff, D. M. (2004). Property rights in context: Privatization's legacy for corporate legality in Poland and Russia. *Studies in Comparative International Development, 38*(4), 82–108.

World Bank. (2013). *Corporate governance in Russia: Report on the observance of standards and codes*. Retrieved December 08, 2021, from https://www.worldbank.org/en/country/russia/publication/rosc

World Bank. (2024). Retrieved November 19, 2024, from https://databank.worldbank.org/

World Federation of Exchanges. (2024). Retrieved November 19, 2024, from https://www.world-exchanges.org/

Wright, M., Filatotchev, I., Buck, T., & Bishop, K. (2003). Is stakeholder corporate governance appropriate in Russia? *Journal of Management and Governance, 7*(3), 263–290.

Chapter 7
Italy

Corporate Governance in Italy: Issues, Systems, Characteristics, and Regulations

Eliene Aparecida de Moraes and Alessandro Zattoni

7.1 Introduction

Several factors have contributed to the debate on corporate governance in recent decades. The shift from bank and private financing to the increasing use of private equity and venture capital, the privatization processes of state-owned companies, the globalization of industries and increasing global competition, the digitization and the emergence of new business models, and some financial scandals (Rizzato et al., 2019; Zattoni, 2019). The corporate governance system must avoid misappropriation and opportunism and promote value creation (Zattoni, 2020). Corporate governance is the system that directs and controls companies (Cadbury Report, 1992). This system comprises internal and external governance mechanisms (Hilb, 2020; Tibiletti et al., 2021). Internal mechanisms encompass, among others, shareholders, boards of directors, managerial incentives, and internal auditors. External mechanisms cover the market for corporate control, corporate law, good governance codes, external auditors, media, stakeholder activism, and governance rating agencies (Hilb, 2020; Parente & Machado Filho, 2020; Zattoni, 2020).

Corporate governance models differ across countries because of the country's institutional characteristics (Clarke, 2020; Kaya, 2020; Roe, 2000). The literature points to some variables as indicative of better governance quality. These indicators are the level of protection for minority investors, a higher shareholding of

E. A. de Moraes (✉)
University of Rio Verde, Rio Verde, Brazil
e-mail: eliene@unirv.edu.br

A. Zattoni
LUISS University, Rome, Italy
e-mail: azattoni@luiss.it

C. B. Macagnan (ed.), *Corporate Governance in Capital Markets*, CSR, Sustainability, Ethics & Governance,
https://doi.org/10.1007/978-3-031-94751-3_7

institutional investors, board independence, and the presence of an audit committee, among others (Clarke, 2020; Goshen & Hamdani, 2015; Moscariello et al., 2019; Omura, 2020; Zattoni, 2020). Investors may be reluctant to invest in public companies unless they have good corporate governance, and so they are protected and confident that they will receive a return on their investment (Aganin & Volpin, 2005; La Porta & Lopez-De-Silanes, 1998; Shleifer & Wolfenzon, 2002). Studies indicate that better legal protection for minority shareholders is related to more developed equity markets, lower concentration of ownership and control, and lower personal benefits arising from shareholder control (Aganin & Volpin, 2005; La Porta et al., 1997, 2000, 2002; Cuomo et al., 2013).

Italy is a European civil law country based on French law (Cebula & Rossi, 2021) with a smaller stock market compared to rich Western countries and traditionally lower protection for minority shareholders and creditors (Balp & Strampelli, 2020; Cuomo et al., 2013; La Porta et al., 1999b). The main features of the Italian corporate governance model are the high concentration of family ownership, the low investor protection, and the use of control mechanisms to widen the divergence between ownership and control (Zattoni, 2019; Aganin & Volpin, 2005). In addition, the director's appointment and board behavior are dominated by large controlling shareholders (Aganin & Volpin, 2005; De Molli & Visani, 2015; La Porta & Lopez-De-Silanes, 1998; Zattoni, 2019).

These characteristics have been stable for decades, but recently, the Italian model of corporate governance has evolved due to external influences and pressures. These influences include the convergence and harmonization of international accounting standards, the corporate governance codes issued by the OECD, the harmonization of European corporate law, and the growing role of institutional investors. They have increased transparency and strengthened the protection of minority investors (Rizzato et al., 2019; Zattoni, 2019).

Given this context and to understand the stage of corporate governance in the Italian context, this chapter describes the evolution of corporate governance in Italy thanks to a systematic review of the literature and governance regulations (e.g., corporate law, corporate governance code). Section 7.2 presents the evolution of the Italian economic system, historical and legal aspects of the Stock Exchange and the Italian Securities Commission, the relevant corporate legislation that impacts companies' corporate governance, and the particularities of adopting international accounting standards. Section 7.3 discusses the corporate governance models allowed for publicly traded companies, funding sources and separation of ownership and control, the types of conflicts of interest and information asymmetry, the activism and rights of minority shareholders, structure and composition of the board of directors, remuneration policies and the external audit system. Finally, final considerations and references are presented.

7.2 Evolution of the Italian Economic System and Corporate Governance Model

Italy has undergone substantial changes in its social institutions since the nineteenth century in different historical aspects, such as the monarchy, fascism, post-war socio-democratic republic, neoliberal republic, and significant changes in economics and politics (Jones & Melis, 2021). From 1882 to 1922, it was a monarchy. Then, between 1922 and 1943, it was under the influence of a totalitarian fascist regime led by Mussolini. Finally, in 1946, a national referendum promoted the birth of the Republic, and in 1948, a new Constitution came into effect (Aganin & Volpin, 2005; Jones & Melis, 2021).

Before the twentieth century, the Italian economic system consisted essentially of rural activities, and the industrialization process was limited to the north of the country, to some industries, mainly mechanical and textile (Melis & Zattoni, 2017). Between 1896 and 1914, there was an intense phase of industrialization promoted by large universal banks like *Banca Commerciale Italiana*, *Banco di Roma*, and *Credito Italiano* (Aganin & Volpin, 2005), financing investments and the growth of companies operating in public services (energy, telecommunications, etc.), steel and mining (Melis & Zattoni, 2017). With the 1929 crisis, banks could not support financing for the development of industrialization as they were affected by the negative consequences of the crisis and collapsed; thus, the state intervened to rescue large companies and banks from bankruptcy. During this period, Italian companies and banks required continued assistance and involvement from the government. To avoid potential negative consequences for the national economy, in 1933, the government created a temporary organization—that is, the Instituto per la Ricostruzione Industriale (IRI)—to acquire and manage the portfolio of companies previously controlled by banks (Aganin & Volpin, 2005).

The *IRI* group constituted a temporary organization that should buy the controlling shares owned by universal banks, restructure and relaunch these companies, and then sell their shares to private shareholders (Zattoni & Cuomo, 2015). The *IRI* group became the controlling shareholder of many Italian companies and banks (Melis & Zattoni, 2017). In 1936, a new banking law was enacted that prohibited the creation of "universal banks" (Lagasio, 2021). Banks could not hold equity interests in non-financial companies to avoid instability in industrial companies that would negatively affect the financial sector (Amatori & Colli, 2000; Lagasio, 2021). As a result, the state became a large shareholder controlling several industrial groups. Beyond the state, entrepreneurial families and cooperatives also played an important role in transforming the Italian economy and promoting industrial growth (Lagasio, 2021).

IRI became a permanent organization in 1937 to combine economic and social purposes (characterizing Italian capitalism as a mixed economy), such as reducing layoffs in underdeveloped areas of the country, until its liquidation in June 2000 (Melis & Zattoni, 2017; Aganin & Volpin, 2005). From the *IRI*, the State began to dominate the national economy through large business groups, controlling several companies that operate in different sectors of the economy and the largest banks in the country, such as *ENI* (*Ente Nazionale Idrocarburi*), *EFIM* (*Ente Partecipazioni and Finaziamento Industrie Manifatturiere*), and *ENEL* (*Ente Nazionale per l'Energia Elettrica*) (Melis & Zattoni, 2017). In addition to the state, some large private groups controlled by wealthy entrepreneurial families also promoted the growth of the Italian economy. Some of these business groups are old and founded between the late nineteenth and early twentieth centuries. Among them, we can mention the Fiat group, belonging to the Agnelli family; the Pirelli group, belonging to the Pirelli family; the *SMI* group—*Societá Metallurgica Italiana*, of the Orlando family; and the *Acciaierie* and Ferriere Lombarde Falck group, from the Falck family (Melis & Zattoni, 2017).

After World War II, Italy became one of the most prosperous countries in the world, with an average annual increase in gross domestic product (GDP) of over 5%. The period between the 1950s and 1960s was called an "economic miracle"—*miracolo economico*—because of the continuous expansion and high growth of the national economy. New families constituted relevant business groups such as Ferrero, Benetton, De Benedetti, and *Fininvest* by Silvio Berlusconi (Melis & Zattoni, 2017). *Mediobanca*, founded in 1946 and formally controlled by some of the largest Italian banks—Banco Commercial, *Credito Italiano*, and *Banco di Roma*—played an important role in the development of corporate governance in the country, as it managed to influence the turnover of CEOs of non-financial companies listed. This was because *Mediobanca* is the "hub" of the main network of cross-participation between the most significant industrial groups in Italy (Melis & Zattoni, 2017).

After the fall of the Berlin Wall in 1989 and the related end of the Cold War due to the collapse of the Soviet Union, Italy faced a significant economic crisis, with the economy in recession, considerable public debt, and the falling Italian currency (Lira) (Jones & Melis, 2021). Under pressure from financial markets and European directives, the Italian government promoted privatizations and liberalizations in the 1990s. Despite several reforms—also concerning corporate governance like the Decree-Law n° 58 of February 24, 1998, or *Testo Único della Finanza (TUF)*, the first good governance code issued by the Italian Stock Exchange in 1999, the revision of the commercial law issued in 2003, and in the Investor, Act issued in 2005 to address governance scandals (Jones & Melis, 2021). The Italian economy could not experience solid and continuous growth (Jones & Melis, 2021).

The global financial crisis hit the country because of the large debt that had accumulated over time. More recently, the global COVID-19 pandemic negatively affected the country's growth (European Commission, 2023). However, as a reaction to this crisis, the European Union (EU) launched the Next Generation EU (NGEU) program, consisting of €750 billion in financial support (i.e., grants and low-interest loans) (European Commission, 2023). Italy received a large amount of financial support (€191.5 billion) thanks to the presentation of the Recovery and Resilience Plan (RRP), which includes investments and consistent reforms. The three main strategic directions of the RRP—that is, digitization and innovation, ecological transition, and social inclusion—are aimed at attenuating the adverse effects of the pandemic crisis, improving the structural conditions of the Italian economy, and favoring Italy's ecological and environmental transition (European Commission, 2023).

According to data from Austin Ratings (2022), Italy achieved real GDP growth in the second quarter of 2022 compared to the first quarter of 2022, 1.1% and 4.7% compared to the second quarter of 2022. 2021. This growth is a victory after a drop in GDP of 8.9% in 2020 (ISTAT, 2022a, 2022b). In 2021, GDP grew by 7.3% compared to 2020 GDP, from €1660.6 billion in 2020 to €1782 billion in 2021 (ISTAT, 2022a, 2022b). Italy ranked ninth among the ten fastest-growing economies in the world in the second quarter of 2022. In October 2020, there were 60,244,639 inhabitants, 51.3% women, and 5.3 million foreigners (ISTAT, 2022a, 2022b). On the same date, there were 23.4 million people employed and 2.6 million unemployed. The female employment rate reaches 50.1%, and the male employment rate reaches 68% (ISTAT, 2022a, 2022b).

Data from 2012 and 2013 show that Italy has about 4.5 million companies. Of these, approximately 837,000 are micro-enterprises responsible for employing more than 23% of Italian workers (3.8 million) (ISTAT, 2022a, 2022b). More than 95% of companies operating in Italy have less than ten employees in an economic context dominated by small- and medium-sized companies. And the Italian economy is also characterized by a high number of self-employed workers, which reaches 5,119,968 (Melis & Zattoni, 2017). Italian companies operate in traditional sectors such as food, wine, textiles, fashion, jewelry, ceramic tiles, machinery, and construction, with few companies operating in the high-tech field on a continental or global scale (Melis & Zattoni, 2017). Finally, the Italian economy is also characterized by a structural division between the north and south, in which more than 50% of companies are in the country's north. Despite investments by the Italian government, the South has a much smaller number of companies and workers. However, the south is still underdeveloped and has a higher unemployment rate than the northern region (Melis & Zattoni, 2017).

7.2.1 Italian Stock Exchange and the Securities and Exchange Commission

The bodies that regulate the capital market in Italy are the Italian Stock Exchange (*Borsa Italiana*) and the Securities and Exchange Commission (*Commissione Nazionale per le Società e la Borsa* or Consob). The Italian Stock Exchange is one of Europe's leading stock exchanges based in Milan. It was founded in 1808 by Èugene de Beauharais, viceroy of the Napoleonic King, under the name *Borsa di Commercio di Milano* (Consob, 2022). In 1873, the Milan Stock Exchange ranked second in trading volume, after only Genoa and before Turin, Florence, Rome, and Naples. Between 1895 and 1907, industrialization contributed to the stock market's growth, going from 27 to 171 listed companies (Aganin & Volpin, 2005). The Italian Stock Exchange operated under public ownership until 1998 when it was privatized.

The stock exchanges have recently undergone profound changes, as traditional sales established as organizations belonging to members or governmental institutions turned into private for-profit companies (OECD, 2021). In addition, many stock exchanges have been consolidated into international groups, such as the Nasdaq OMX Group, responsible for sales in eight jurisdictions, or Euronext, responsible for five jurisdictions (OECD, 2021). As a result, the Italian Stock Exchange merged with the London Stock Exchange through an acquisition in October 2007. Later, in October 2020, the London Stock Exchange Group and the Euronext Group struck a €4.3 billion deal, including the purchase of the Italian Stock Exchange, completed on April 29, 2021 (Consob, 2022; Euronext, 2021).

The Italian Stock Exchange is informally known as *Piazza Affari* (Business Square), in honor of Milan's city square, as its headquarters are in the *Palazzo Mezzanotte* building (HistoryTour, 2021). The Italian Stock Exchange is regulated by the Italian Securities and Exchange Commission (Consob) based in Rome (Consob, 2022). The Italian Stock Exchange plays a vital role in the stock trading of equities and the exchange of ETFs, covered bonds, certificates, and fixed-income instruments. And yet, in managing various equity markets, bond and fixed income markets, ETF markets, and derivatives markets (Euronext, 2021). At the end of September 2022, more than 560 companies were listed on *Borsa Italiana* (Consob, 2022).

The markets managed by the Italian Stock Exchange include equity markets characterized by the highest levels of liquidity in Europe. It encompasses Euronext Milan (EXM), Euronext Growth Milan (EGM), Euronext MIV Milan (MIV), and Euro TLX Equity, segments that focus on liquidity, information transparency, and corporate governance, which are also concerned with small- and medium-sized companies (Consob, 2022; Euronext, 2021). Bond and fixed-income markets include electronic markets, bond trading, and other debt instruments, including equities, structured bonds, guaranteed bonds, mortgages, and government bonds.

Also, a segment designed to offer small- and medium-sized companies quick and easy access to the capital market, trading for covered warrants certificates and certificates jointly referred to as securitized derivatives (Consob, 2022; Euronext, 2021). ETP markets list ETFs, ETCs, ETNS, and open-ended funds and are Europe's leading exchange and counter-exchange markets. Finally, the derivatives market includes one of the largest derivatives markets in Europe, encompassing energy and wheat derivatives trading (Consob, 2022; Euronext, 2021). At the end of 2020, 225 companies were listed on the MTA market—*Mercato Telematico Azionario* with a total market cap of €486 billion. Total market capitalization is distributed among companies belonging to industrial (34%), services (22%), and financial (22%) sectors. The first shareholder owns about 47.6%, and small investors (or the market) own 40% (Consob, 2021). Italy has been among the top 20 jurisdictions in the number of companies launching IPOs of non-financial companies during the last ten years (OECD, 2021).

The Italian Securities Commission (Consob—*Commissione Nazionale per le Società e la Borsa*) is the government authority regulating the Italian securities market, including the Italian Stock Exchange (Consob, 2021). It was instituted in 1974 (Law n° 216, of June 7) by legislation that unified the functions and jurisdictions that until then were part of the Italian Ministry of the Treasury, which was the main power monitoring the securities market (Consob, 2021). A new law introduced in 1983 extended its jurisdiction to protect public savings. In 1985, through Law n° 281 of June 4, it gained legal personality and autonomy. In 1991, it became empowered to audit securities brokerages and monitor the trading of privileged information (Consob, 2021).

Consob's functions include (a) regulating intermediaries' investment services and operations, information obligations of companies listed on regulated markets, and the request for investments from the public; (b) authorization for the functioning of market regulations, publication of prospectuses, centralized management of financial instruments and registration with competent bodies; (c) monitoring of the operations of market management companies, transparency, and orderly conduct of negotiation and transparency and justice in the conduct of intermediaries and financial representatives; (d) penalization of any unfair conduct of the parties mentioned above; and (e) verification of the information provided to the market by entities requesting investments from the public, as well as the information contained in the accounting documents of listed companies (Consob, 2021).

Consob's role is to regulate, authorize, and monitor the Italian financial markets to protect investors and guarantee their efficiency, transparency, and development. It achieves its objectives through regulations and self-regulates its organization and functioning under the control of the prime minister's office (Melis & Zattoni, 2017). Consob's organizational structure includes a central management committee that manages 11 departments and 39 divisions. These include company controls, public bids and ownership structure, monitoring and registration of financial representatives, insider trading, and derivatives markets (Consob, 2021). Consob has offices in Rome and Milan. By March 31 of each year, Consob presents to the Ministry of Economy and Finance a report on the activities carried out, current topics, and the guidelines and strategies of its program (Consob, 2021).

Consob is headed by a collegiate body composed of a president and four members, all appointed by presidential decree by the Prime Minister's proposal. The term of office of the president and members is seven years, and there is no re-election. Consob carries out periodic controls on the quality of the independent audit activity by audit firms, penalizing the audit partners when irregularities are found in their activities (Melis & Zattoni, 2017).

The Italian capital market is still considered underdeveloped and small compared to the capital markets in other developed countries. In 2010, about 300 Italian companies were listed among 4.4 million companies in the country (Zattoni & Cuomo, 2015; Zattoni & Mosca, 2012), and the total market capitalization of the stock exchange represented only 30% of the national GPD. At the end of June 2021, 389 companies were listed; as of September 2022, more than 560 companies were listed on *Borsa Italiana*. The main reasons for the small number of listed companies include the reluctance of entrepreneurs to disclose corporate information to the financial market, share the control with other shareholders, the cost of going public, and the complexity of the listed company regulation (Zattoni & Mosca, 2012).

7.2.2 National Legislation and International Accounting Standards (IFRS)

Aspects of national legal frameworks influence the intensity of agency conflicts among corporate stakeholders. They can also affect internal corporate governance mechanisms to protect minority shareholders and creditors (Kumar & Zattoni, 2016). The principal Italian corporate regulation is the Italian Civil Code, which came into force on March 16, 1942. This code has been amended several times. These corporate regulations are also considered complex laws concerning corporate governance. Italian corporate governance models are also built around soft law, i.e., the Corporate Governance Code by the Italian Corporate Governance Committee, and based on the "comply or explain" approach. The "hard" and "soft" legal mechanisms represent the combination of formal and informal institutions in a country to guide companies and boards of directors in the decision-making process in environments of uncertainty (North, 1990).

7.2.2.1 Corporate Law in Italy

The Civil Code of 1882 regulated corporations and instituted the mandatory constitution of a board of statutory auditors, the Council of Statutory Auditors, to supervise the management of the company on behalf of the shareholders, a unique feature of Italian corporate governance (Zattoni, 2019; Melis & Zattoni, 2017). This code also requires shareholders' approval of an annual report without defining the extent of information disclosure (Aganin & Volpin, 2005). In 1913, stockbrokers were regulated, while banks could not trade on the stock exchange (Aganin & Volpin, 2005).

After this period, there were two relevant revisions: the first in 1942 and the second in 2003. The approval of a new Civil Code in 1942 did not present improvements in corporate governance, i.e., it did not address the consequences of the separation between ownership and control in public companies (De Molli & Visani, 2015). In March 1942, with the institution of the Bankruptcy Law, the main procedures for non-state companies were liquidation or reorganization, while state companies were subject to another process called *liquidazione coatta amministrativa* (Aganin & Volpin, 2005; Repubblica Italiana, 1942b). Furthermore, in 1942, the new Civil Code prohibited multiple voting shares and limited cross-shareholdings between companies (Aganin & Volpin, 2005; Repubblica Italiana, 1942b).

It was only with the reform issued in 1974 that the principle of investor protection was implemented through a series of regulatory innovations, such as the creation of the Securities and Exchange Commission (Consob). The reform also established new cross-participation limits and allowed the issuance of non-voting shares (Consob, 2021; Zattoni, 2019). In 1974, it became mandatory to communicate with Consob within 48 hours of acquiring more than 2% of shares with voting rights. From 1992, this information became a compulsory disclosure to the public (Aganin & Volpin, 2005; Consob, 2021). In 1975, it became mandatory for listed companies to audit their financial statements through independent audit firms (Consob, 2021). In 1979 and 1986, there were changes in the Bankruptcy Act to include special procedures for large companies and simplifying processes for state-owned enterprises (Aganin & Volpin, 2005; Repubblica Italiana, 1942a). In 1983, mutual funds could operate under the supervision of Consob (Aganin & Volpin, 2005).

In 1990, the government enacted the first Law for the Defense of Competition and Market, *Legge* n° 287, of October 10, aiming to protect and guarantee the right of economic initiative, inhibit abuses of dominant business position and concentration (Repubblica Italiana, 1990). In 1991, there was a ban on trading with privileged information, a new regulation for institutional investors, the requirement for consolidated statements for business groups, and the regulation of disclosure requirements by publicly traded companies (Aganin & Volpin, 2005; Zattoni, 2019). In 1992, company acquisitions were regulated, introducing the law for mandatory bidding and editing a rule to protect minority shareholders (Aganin & Volpin, 2005; Zattoni, 2019). Also, in 1992, the reform defined mutual fund information disclosure requirements and accounting standards. In 1993, authorization was issued for the creation of private funds. In 1996, there was a change in the regulation of mutual funds and financial intermediaries (Aganin & Volpin, 2005).

In 1998, there was a reform in corporate law, bringing radical changes with the approval of the *Testo Unico della Finanza (TUF)* to strengthen the protection of savings and minority shareholders. The reform introduced new rules on corporate governance and disclosure, such as (a) strengthening the powers and responsibilities of the board of directors and (b) strengthening the powers of minority shareholders, that is, giving them the right to elect one or two statutory auditors if the board has five members, (c) allowing the withdrawal of members of the shareholders' agreement, syndicate pacts, in the case of a takeover (OPA); etc. The reform significantly strengthened investor protection by raising the anti-director rights index from 1 to 5 (out of 6) (Aganin & Volpin, 2005; Consob, 1998; Ferrarini, 2005; La Porta et al., 1999a; Zattoni, 2019).

The *TUF*, also known as the Draghi Law, has simplified the legal framework for securities offerings, takeover bids, and disclosure obligations of external audit firms and the board of statutory auditors (Melis & Zattoni, 2017). The Draghi Law or Draghi Reform took its name from the chairman of its committee, the Director General of the Ministry of the Treasury, and the MIT-trained economist Mario Draghi (Melis & Zattoni, 2017). The Draghi Law introduced the internal control system for listed companies, with the internal audit function focusing on controls to manage and minimize operational risks (Consob, 1998). *TUF* prohibited managers from opposing acquisitions without shareholder approval. It included a 10% threshold for calling a shareholders' meeting and gave minority shareholders more rights to express their opinions (Consob, 1998). Until the end of 2021, this law underwent more than 70 amendments (Consob, 2021). *TUF* also allowed postal voting to make voting rights easier and less costly for shareholders to increase participation in the general meeting. And finally, it introduced full disclosure of shareholder agreements and a three-year term for such contracts.

In 2001, Legislative Decree n° 23 of June 8 was issued, establishing that organizations were responsible for crimes committed by administrators and employees against the company's interests. The Issuance Regulation, created in 1999 by Consob, aimed to regulate the financial instruments market. Its disclosure to the Italian and foreign public deals with the public offering and sale of financial products, corporate structure, voting rights, protection of minority shareholders, administrative and control bodies, auditing, and privileged information (Consob, 1999). The 1998 reform increased regulatory differences between listed and unlisted companies. As a result, a general reform was carried out in the corporate law in 2003 by Legislative Decrees n° 269, 274, and 350, in force from 2004. The main changes brought about by this reform included: (a) the possibility of issuing shares with different voting rights and dividends; (b) strengthening the protection of minority shareholders and the scope of governance; (c) the introduction of two new administration and control models: (1) the one-tier model and (2) the two-tier model, beyond the traditional model (Consob, 1998; De Molli & Visani, 2015; Zattoni, 2019).

In the traditional model, companies are managed by three distinct corporate bodies: the general assembly (*assemblea degli azionisti*), the board of directors (*consiglio di amministrazione*) and the supervisory board (*collegio sindacale*) (Ghezzi & Malberti, 2008). The Civil Code also provides that in addition to these, an external auditor besides management control may be appointed, considered as complementary and with the same importance from a business and legal perspective (Jouber, 2021). The management control committee performs the function of monitoring management (Ghezzi & Malberti, 2008). The appointment of directors should be made in the general meeting. All directors have the same duties toward the company, with a high degree of responsibility (Datwani et al., 2018). In the one-tier model, the board of directors comprises executive and non-executive directors, and CEO duality is possible (Jouber, 2021). Furthermore, in the one-tier model, the constitution of committees, such as audit, remuneration, ethics, and sustainability, characterizes the council's monist structure (Jouber, 2021).

In the one-tier model, the members of the management control committee are selected from among the members of the board of directors and appointed by the board of directors (Ghezzi & Malberti, 2008). The most striking feature of the one-tier model is the combination of the company's monitoring and management bodies; however, the final decision on the composition of these bodies still rests with the general assembly, as when appointing the members of the board of directors, it is indirectly influencing the final composition of the board of directors and the management control committee (Ghezzi & Malberti, 2008). In this model, members of the board of directors and the management control committee can be removed through a simple general meeting; however, if the decision is taken without cause, the members will have the right to claim compensation (Ghezzi & Malberti, 2008). We can note that dismissing members of the board of directors and the control and management committee is more straightforward than in the traditional and two-tier models, not needing to meet the three conditions: having cause, deliberation by the general assembly, and court approval.

Block and Gerstner (2016) point out the main advantages of adopting the one-tier model: a superior flow of information due to its structure and size, faster decision-making, and better understanding and involvement of the board of directors in the company's business. This model tends to have more meetings at which all members are present. Formal board meetings occur more regularly, allowing for more agile decision-making (Block & Gerstner, 2016). The combination of more frequent meetings with a board of directors that is part of the control and management committee allows for greater integration in the business strategy and decision-making process among its members. However, Block and Gerstner (2016) point out that one of the disadvantages of adopting the one-tier model is that the same members who make the decision are the ones who will monitor it, as the independence of the advisor, in this case, may not be sufficient. To make it neutral, especially in small councils and with close personal relationships.

In the two-tier model, in addition to the powers allocated to the general assembly, the company's day-to-day powers are divided between two mandatory administrative bodies, the board of directors and the supervisory board, organized in a vertical relationship (Jouber, 2021; Datwani et al., 2018). This model generally prevails in civil law countries such as China, Indonesia, Russia, and South Africa (Jouber, 2021; Datwani et al., 2018). The two-tier model is also considered a shareholder-oriented model. However, it allows greater inclusion of stakeholders than the one-tier model (Jouber, 2021; García-Torea et al., 2016). It is noteworthy that the Italian two-tier model, unlike the German two-tier model, did not implement the co-determination system and employee participation in company management (Ghezzi & Malberti, 2008).

Italian legislation does not require representatives of interested parties to be members of the board of directors (Ghezzi & Malberti, 2008). The board of directors comprises executive directors and is appointed by the supervisory board (Jouber, 2021; Ghezzi & Malberti, 2008). The chief executive officer or CEO/CFO may be a member of the board of directors. CEO duality may not occur, and supervisory board members must be non-executive or external directors (Jouber, 2021; Datwani et al., 2018). In the two-tier model, the board of directors manages and represents the company independently, having full responsibility for the usual business, and its powers are limited by law and statutes. The board of directors is jointly responsible for managing the company (Datwani et al., 2018).

In the two-tier model, the supervisory board must have at least three members who appoint, supervise, and advise the board of directors. The members of the supervisory board are appointed by the general meeting of shareholders (Datwani et al., 2018; Ghezzi & Malberti, 2008). The supervisory powers of the supervisory board generally include the supervision and approval of financial statements, management actions and reports, audit matters, and calling extraordinary general meetings when necessary (Datwani et al., 2018). The execution of the work of the supervisory board can be organized through the creation of committees, such as a nomination committee or audit committee. Still, they are scarcer in this type of model (Jouber, 2021). The supervisory board represents the company in all legal matters against the board of directors (Datwani et al., 2018).

Furthermore, in the two-tier model, the general assembly can appoint an external auditor who performs functions like those in the traditional model; however, according to the Civil Code, the function of the external auditor cannot be internalized as in the conventional model (Ghezzi & Malberti, 2008). The board of directors may be removed at any time and may request compensation if they are removed without cause. However, to dismiss the external auditor, the three conditions discussed in the traditional model must be met: that is, there must be just cause, there must be a deliberation by the general assembly, and there must be approval from a court (Ghezzi & Malberti, 2008). Members of the supervisory board can be removed through a simple general meeting without the need for approval by a court, which has been criticized, as the three conditions for dismissal of members of the supervisory board reinforce defensive measures against hostile public offers (Ghezzi & Malberti, 2008).

Block and Gerstner (2016) consider that one of the main advantages of adopting the two-tier model is the independence of the supervisory board members, as they can thus exercise more effective monitoring over the management exercised by others. However, the authors emphasize that this independence, which is relevant for effective monitoring, can result in this member not having access to the information or knowledge necessary to monitor executive actions efficiently. As the authors point out, what can be resolved is a more significant and better flow of information and communication and the participation of members of the board of directors in fiscal council meetings to provide or offer new information.

In 2003, there were changes to the Italian Civil Code, as the control system was perceived as inefficient (De Molli & Visani, 2015; Rizzato et al., 2019). In the following years, some financial scandals, such as *Parmalat, Cirio*, and *Giacomelli,* showed that corporate governance models (e.g., board of directors, audit committees, external auditors) were insufficient to deter fraud and failures (Ferrarini, 2005; Kumar & Zattoni, 2018; Rizzato et al., 2019).

After the Parmalat scandal, the Draghi Law was amended by Legislative Decree n° 262 of December 28, 2005, to the Investor Protection Law—the Savings Law (*Legge sul Risparmio*). The amendments included, among others, provisions for the protection of savings and regulation of financial markets, reinforcing rules on the management and supervisory bodies of companies, requirements on the protection of minorities, the law on foreign companies, provisions on conflict of interests, and financial activities, and rules on external audit (Consob, 1998; Repubblica Italiana, 2005; Rizzato et al., 2019). These changes took effect on January 2, 2006. Specifically, the Savings Act introduced the slate voting system and reserved at least one seat on the board of directors for minority shareholders unrelated to the controlling shareholder (Repubblica Italiana, 2005). It required all listed companies to appoint a director responsible for the reliability of all public information about the company's financial position and performance (*dirigent preposto ala redazione dei documenti contabili societari*) (Repubblica Italiana, 2005).

Furthermore in 2010, Consob regulated related party transactions through Resolution n° 17.221 of June 7, rigorous disclosures on this topic (Consob, 2021). In 2011, the government implemented a quota law requiring representation of at least equal access to administrative and control bodies of companies listed by Law n° 120 of July 12 (Consob, 1998; Repubblica Italiana, 2011). According to the new Law, at least one-third of the directors—one-fifth for the first term—should come from the less represented gender. This prescription should be applied to three consecutive terms. Consob would warn companies that did not comply with this ratio to pay a penalty varying between €100,000 to €1,000,000 (Repubblica Italiana, 2011). The law also states that its provisions apply to companies organized according to the one-tier system of corporate governance (Consob, 1998; Repubblica Italiana, 2011).

In 2019, Law n° 160 of December 27 renewed the mandatory gender equality in the board of directors, requiring a two-fifths gender quota applied in listed companies for six directorships from 2020 (Repubblica Italiana, 2019). These initiatives, implemented from Directive COM (2012) 614 issued by the European Commission, substantially increase the number of women on boards of directors across the European Union. The initiative establishes a minimum of 40% of members of the underrepresented sex among non-executive directors of listed companies (EU, 2012).

The government amended the *TUF* in 2014, enabling companies to change their statutes by granting double voting rights to shareholders and stockholders for at least two years (Consob, 1998). In 2018, Directive 95/2014, issued by the European Union (EU), was adopted, requiring greater disclosure of corporate social responsibility through a non-financial report on social and environmental (Consob, 1998). In May 2019, Law n° 49 amended the *TUF*, making it mandatory to vote on the remuneration policy (the so-called say-on-pay) of directors, the supervisory board, and the board of directors at least every three years or when there is a proposal to amend these remuneration policies by the board of directors (Consob, 1998).

So far, the evolution of corporate law in the Italian context has been presented, considering that they are mandatory rules issued by bodies linked to the government and with the power of law. However, when it comes to corporate governance proposed by codes of best practices, these are voluntary, providing good governance recommendations for companies, discussed in the next section.

7.2.2.2 Italian Corporate Governance Code and International Accounting Standards

Italy's first Corporate Governance Code was issued by the Corporate Governance Committee in 1999 and has been updated eight times (2002, 2006, 2010, 2011, 2014, 2015, 2018, and 2020). The last update was made in 2020 and entered into force in 2022. The Italian Code of Corporate Governance follows a "comply or explain" approach (CCG, 2021) imported from UK corporate governance best practices. The "comply or explain" approach is based on the principle of freedom and responsibility, and the only penalty for non-compliance is the moral persuasion of the stock market (Melis & Zattoni, 2017). The decision not to comply with a recommendation should not be treated as a negative assessment because compliance or not is linked to several factors. For example, the company may not have achieved a framework that allows full adoption of the recommendations, as with newly listed companies or small companies (Melis & Zattoni, 2017).

It should be noted that there is no regulation on the content of the explanations to be disclosed by companies when they fail to comply with corporate governance disclosures. Current and potential investors must judge the adequacy of these explanations. This is in line with EU Directive 2006/46/EC, which requires companies to disclose a corporate governance report in which they declare whether they have complied with the corporate governance code and provide information on its application. The Italian Corporate Governance Code recommends that the company present detailed, specific, and concrete reasons for non-compliance with the best governance practices. Moreover, in the event of non-compliance, it suggests that the company explain how it departed from the recommendation, partially or entirely, how it decided not to comply with it, and when it intends to comply with such recommendation. The Code was inspired by international best practices adapted to the Italian institutional context (CCG, 2021).

The Corporate Governance Committee (CGC) comprises business associations, professional investors, and the Italian Stock Exchange. It promotes good corporate governance in companies listed through the Corporate Governance Code (CCG, 2021). The CGC was constituted in 1999 and chaired by Mr. Stefano Preda, president of Borsa Italiana at the time. The CGC comprised distinguished industrial and financial community representatives and institutional investors (Melis & Zattoni, 2017). This committee has its own rules of composition and functioning, such as the composition of a maximum of 24 members, each with a three-year term, an internal president for coordinating the work, and representing the committee before third parties (CCG, 2021). The committee was established to review the Corporate Governance Code every two years.

The 1999 Corporate Governance Code focused on the gaps left by the Draghi Law, especially in the board of directors' role, structure, and composition (Melis & Zattoni, 2017). It defined the board of directors'role, stressed the importance of appointing independent directors, and highlighted the importance of providing timely and sufficient information. Argued about the need for transparent procedures for the election of directors, described the duties of administrators, specified the president's responsibilities, and encouraged the creation of remuneration and control or audit committees (Melis & Zattoni, 2017). However, this code was criticized mainly for its broad and vague principles and recommendations, not specifying its application, such as the careful self-assessment of directors (Zattoni, 2019). The 1999 code defines corporate governance as the rules by which organizations are managed and controlled, resulting from norms, traditions, and patterns of behavior developed by each legal and economic system. Its main objective is creating shareholder value (CCG, 2021).

The 2002 review expanded the definition of independent directors and the disclosure of private information to third parties, clarifying the responsibilities of the audit and compensation committee and underscoring the importance of internal control (CCG, 2021). This review also reinforced the governance practices of companies controlled by other listed companies. The 2006 review sought to align its content with the evolution of European and national legislation and regulations (CCG, 2021). It is recommended that boards formally assess their size, composition, and performance directors and strengthen internal committees 'roles and design. In addition, the 2006 review introduced the best practices to increase minority shareholders' protection and improve the governance structure and its bodies. The 2006 code shifted from a voluntary approach to a "comply or explain" approach, with companies having to disclose in the corporate governance report whether they comply with the corporate governance code or explain why they do not (CCG, 2021).

In 2010, a review was carried out to include Article 7, which deals with directors' remuneration. In 2011, a new version was issued, proposing simplifying the principles. This review involved four items: (1) the composition of the board, (2) the role and functioning of the council, (3) the organization and attributes of internal committees, and (4) the internal control and risk management system. The review aimed to discriminate the code recommendations between small and large companies, strengthening the board's centrality and rationalizing the directory system (Melis & Zattoni, 2017). In 2014, the recommendations on executive compensation were reviewed. The 2015 review encouraged the board of directors to assess medium and long-term risks (CCG, 2021). In 2015, it was recommended to strengthen the risk management control system to align with international best practices, recent regulations EU Directive 596/2014 on market abuse and EU Directive 36/2013 on prudential supervision and capital requirements and requirements of banks (CCG, 2021). Finally, in the 2015 review, it was suggested that companies should evaluate the opportunity to set up a corporate social responsibility committee (CCG, 2021).

The penultimate review of 2018 invited corporations to adopt diversity criteria for the composition of the board of directors, especially gender, for both the board of directors and the supervisory board. The last revision, from 2020, brings an index of definitions that previous codes did not address, including descriptions of independent and executive directors, CEO, control body, company with controlling shareholder, large company, sustainable success, and senior management (CCG, 2021). This release presents specific recommendations for large companies.

Regarding the role of the board of directors, the 2020 review dismembered the principles by transforming them from two to four, including issues on sustainability and stakeholder management, while the previous version focused on creating shareholder value (CCG, 2021). The recommendations continue to seek flexible applicability. Comments were deleted after the recommendations, so the new version is more summarized, containing 26 pages, while the 2018 version includes 44 pages. This version guides the need for the organization to define a more functional corporate governance model (CCG, 2021). The board of directors shall include at least two independent directors and the chairman. Independent directors must represent at least one-third of the board in large companies with controlling shareholders and at least half of the directors in large companies without controlling shareholders (CCG, 2021).

The 2020 code maintains the diversity criteria for the composition of the administrative and supervisory bodies. At least one-third of the board's members and statutory auditors (the control body) must be members of the less represented gender. In addition, companies should promote equal treatment and opportunities between genders, monitoring its implementation (CCG, 2021). The assessment of the independence of the directors and members of the control body should be disclosed to the market immediately after the designation using a specific notice and, later, in the company's corporate governance report, including the criteria used for carrying out the evaluation. Finally, the 2020 revision deletes the section on shareholder relations.

After several revisions and reforms in corporate law and the Corporate Governance Code, the Italian regulatory and institutional environment is now aligned with the best international corporate governance practices (OECD, 2021; Zattoni, 2019). By 2021, 95% of all companies listed on the MTA—the main stock market of the Italian Stock Exchange—had adopted the provisions of the Corporate Governance Code (Assonime, 2022). These companies represent 99% of the market capitalization of all companies listed on the MTA. There was a slight increase in adopting this code, as in 2013, 93% of companies listed on the MTA adopted the corporate governance standards issued by the CGC.

In 2002, the European Union adopted the IAS Regulation regarding international accounting standards. It required applying international accounting standards to the consolidated financial statements of listed European companies from 2005 onward. It also allows member states to require or permit the preparation of consolidated and unconsolidated financial reports of their non-IFRS listed companies (Di Fabio, 2018). The body issuing Italian accounting standards is the *Organismo Italiano di Contabilitá (OIC)*, established in 2001 (OIC Founders, 2022). Italian companies listed in a regulated market must use the IFRS standards adopted by the European Union in their consolidated financial statements (IFRS, 2022). In addition, the consolidated financial statements of foreign companies listed on the Italian Stock Exchange must comply with IFRS, except for companies whose national standard is equivalent to IFRS (IFRS, 2022). IFRS standards for small and medium-sized companies are not permitted or required in the Italian context, according to information available on the International Accounting Standard Board—IASB (IFRS, 2022).

7.3 Corporate Governance Model Applied in Italy

Corporate governance systems are the cumulative results of regulatory and cultural processes, and it is impossible to implement them in every environment with the expected results. Countries are characterized by multiple optimal situations in which corporate governance practices are accepted and applied to respect certain limits (Khanna et al., 2006; Puchniak, 2007; Salvioni & Gennari, 2016). The Italian corporate governance model belongs to the Latin model along with France, Spain, Belgium, Portugal, and Greece (Melis & Zattoni, 2017). This corporate governance model has two outstanding characteristics: large shareholders and the limited role of the financial market. It differs from the Anglo-American corporate governance model and can be considered a variation of the Japanese-German network model (Melis & Zattoni, 2017). This hybrid corporate governance system allows up to three options: the one-tier, the two-tier, and the traditional model with a board of statutory auditors (OECD, 2021).

The Italian corporate governance model for publicly traded companies encompasses several governance bodies and actors inside and outside the company (see Fig. 7.1). Internal corporate governance bodies include the board of directors, the fiscal council (in the traditional model), and the internal control system. External actors from the private sector play governance roles to protect their interests or analyze and assess the quality of the company's processes and results (Melis & Zattoni, 2017). Furthermore, several public sector actors play a governance role by defining laws and regulations, monitoring the behavior and results of companies, and inspecting and imposing sanctions in cases of misbehavior (Melis & Zattoni, 2017).

The traditional corporate governance model (see Fig. 7.2) has a board of directors (*Consiglio di amministrazione*) and a board of statutory auditors (*Collegio syndicale or Collegio dei sindaci*), both appointed by the general meeting of shareholders (OECD, 2021). The board of directors may delegate management powers to

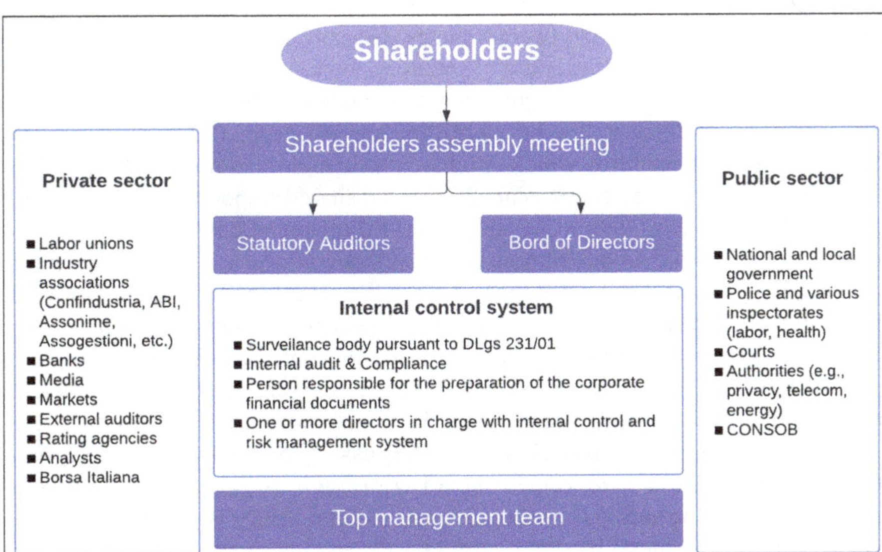

Fig. 7.1 The Italian corporate governance model. Source: A primer on corporate governance (Melis & Zattoni, 2017)

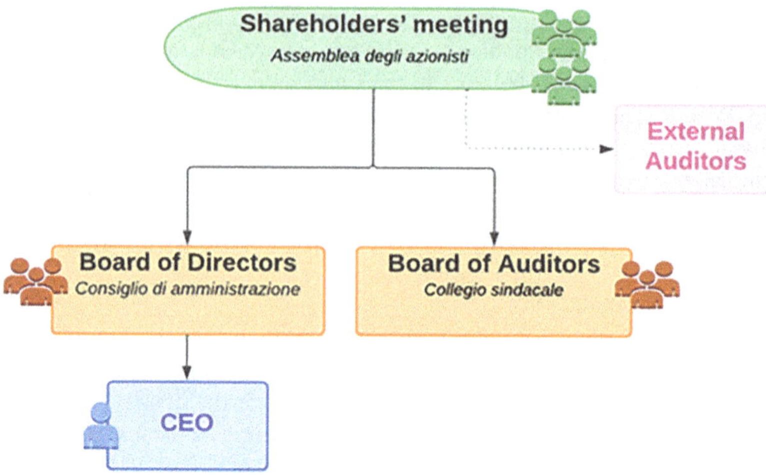

Fig. 7.2 Traditional corporate governance model. Source: Assionime (2022), Ghezzi and Malberti (2008)

executive directors or an executive committee (OECD, 2021). The board of directors performs management and supervision functions, while the board of statutory auditors performs the control and oversight function (Balp & Strampelli, 2020; Lagasio, 2021). The traditional model is the most common board structure in listed and private Italian companies. The board of statutory auditors is considered an internal audit board (OECD, 2021). In this model, managers are re-elected indefinitely unless otherwise provided in the company statute of the organization. And this must have at least three auditors and two alternates (Consob, 1998).

In the traditional model, the board of statutory auditors is responsible for convening the assembly and making the publications provided for by law in cases of omission or unjustified delay by the board of directors (Consob, 1998). The legislator configures the responsibility, which is inherent in the obligations and duties of the fiscal advisor function (Mielcarz et al., 2021), and shared responsibility, which concerns solidarity with the actions or omissions of directors (Consob, 1998). The traditional model's board of directors is assigned strategic and governance tasks like those generally set by Anglo-American boards (Melis & Zattoni, 2017). However, the traditional structure of the Italian board of directors is unique in the supervisory role it assigns to the board of statutory auditors. The board of auditors' main task is to monitor directors' performance in tasks, like the functions performed by independent non-executive directors of Anglo-American companies (Melis & Zattoni, 2017).

The dualistic or two-tier model (see Fig. 7.3) has a supervisory board (*Consiglio di sorveglianza*) and a management board (*Consiglio di gestione*). The general meeting appoints the supervisory board, and the supervisory board nominates the management board unless the statute provides for appointing the board of directors by the general meeting (OECD, 2021). This model is like the German one. The management board has the management function, while the supervisory board has

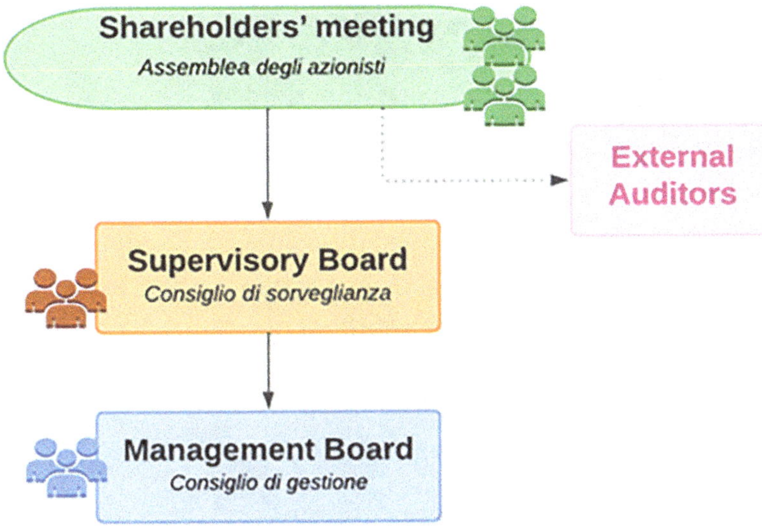

Fig. 7.3 Dualistic or two-tier corporative governance model. Source: Assonime (2022), Ghezzi and Malberti (2008)

supervisory and monitoring positions, including the approval of financial statements and appointing and revocation of the work of managers (Balp & Strampelli, 2020; Lagasio, 2021; Zattoni, 2019). The supervisory board is involved in the most strategic transactions and the company's long-term industrial and financial plans (Melis & Zattoni, 2017). However, unlike the German model, only shareholders elect members of the supervisory board, and there is no representation of employees on the board of directors.

The two-tier model was designed so managers have complete autonomy when the shareholding and its management are actively supervised (Rizzato et al., 2019). At the time of creation, the directors remain in their duties for the period provided in the deed of appointment and for no more than three financial years and may be re-elected indefinitely (Consob, 1998). In the two-tier model, regarding the board of directors' functions, there is a distinction between legal and statutory duties. The legal duties include the execution of all operations necessary for the realization of the company's object, the convening of the meeting, both at the initiative of the board and by requirements of the law, the challenge of nullable resolutions of the shareholders, and the execution of the other duties provided for by law (Consob, 2021). On the other hand, statutory duties, considered additional duties, are those contained in the statute. When the company opts for this model, certain decisions are subject to approval at the general meeting. These decisions include the appointment and removal of members of the supervisory board, the decision on its compensation, deliberation on the responsibility of the supervisory board members, and deliberation on benefit sharing (Consob, 1998).

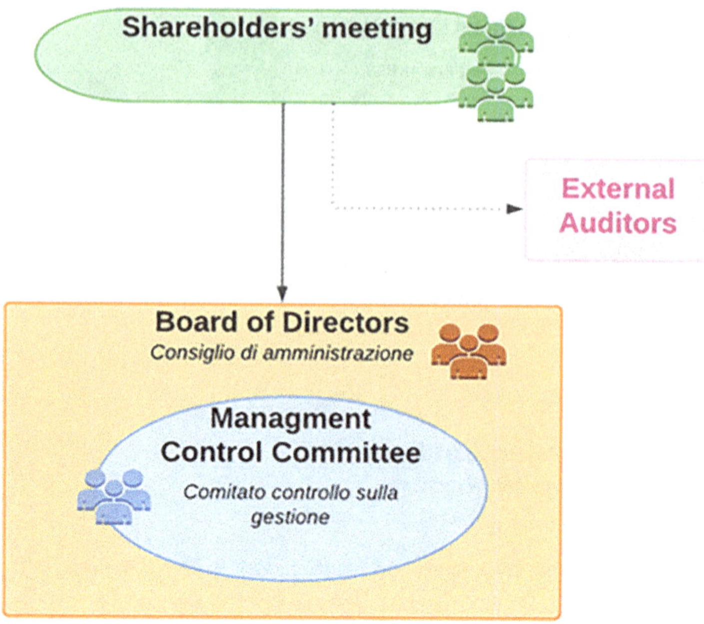

Fig. 7.4 Monistic or one-tier corporate governance model. Source: Assonime (2022), Ghezzi and Malberti (2008)

The monistic or one-tier model (see Fig. 7.4) has a board of directors (*Consiglio di Amministrazione*) and an internal control and audit committee (*Comitato per il controle Interna*) composed of independent directors. The shareholders' assembly appoints the board of directors (Balp & Strampelli, 2020; OECD, 2021). The board of directors may delegate management powers to one or more directors or an executive committee. It is a model like the Anglo-American one, in which the board of directors takes the functions of administration and supervision while the internal audit committee performs the supervision function (Lagasio, 2021; Zattoni, 2019). Without exception, companies that adopt this model must be subject to the accounting control of an auditor registered with the Ministry of Justice. There is also a rigid and necessary division of responsibilities between the board of directors and the internal audit committee.

In the one-tier model, the board of directors is divided into executive and non-executive, independent or non-independent. Non-executive directors are those who do not perform functions related to the management of the company or companies that control or are controlled by it. The difference between independent and non-independent directors lies in the independence requirements in the Italian Civil Code in Article 2399. At least one-third of its members must be independent on the board of directors (Consob, 1998). The internal audit committee should comprise non-executive and independent directors, as Article 2409 of the Italian Civil Code describes. At least one of the members should be a registered auditor of the Ministry of Justice. The audit committee elects its chairman by an absolute majority of votes.

The law does not limit the number of committee members, except for publicly traded companies requiring a minimum of three members. The mandate of the internal audit committee members coincides with that of one of the board of directors' members.

One-tier or two-tier models are rare among Italian-listed companies. In 2020, 220 of the 225 listed companies used the traditional corporate governance model (92.2%), while three companies opted for the one-tier model, and two companies opted for the two-tier model (Consob, 2020). The scenario has not changed since 2014, when 98% of listed companies adopted the traditional model, while three companies opted for the two-tier model (two banks and a football company), and two companies opted for the one-tier model (De Molli & Visani, 2015). The slow shift to alternative models, such as two-tier or one-tier, is believed to be due to the lack of propensity for change typical of the Italian elite. The absence of an autonomous regulatory discipline, the mastery of the traditional model, the lack of knowledge about alternative models, and the natural prudence of shareholders to experiment with new models may explain the limited adoption of alternative models (De Molli & Visani, 2015).

About 20 of the OECD member countries, accounting for about 40% of world GDP, used the one-tier model at the end of 2014 (De Molli & Visani, 2015). Seven OECD countries, representing approximately 16% of world GDP, opted for the two-tier model. Thirteen countries offer flexibility, that is, instead, by giving companies the option of adopting alternative models (De Molli & Visani, 2015). The one-tier and two-tier models are more widespread in the world's leading economies (De Molli & Visani, 2015). In the Italian case, Consob recognizes the need to allow companies to use alternative models enshrined and recognized in advanced economies. This reform was designed also to please institutional investors, who increased between 2010 and 2014 from 12% to 17% of the FTSE Mib. FTSE MIB is the main benchmark of the Italian stock exchange and captures 80% of the national market capitalization. Most institutional investors were American or British, that is, countries traditionally adopting the one-tier model (De Molli & Visani, 2015).

7.3.1 Sources of Funding and Separation Between Ownership and Control

A company's debts, or as it finances itself, influence the degree of compliance with corporate governance, whether with national or international standards (Rizzato et al., 2019). Financial systems differ from one country to another and change over time. Depending on the proportion of financing raised through banks or capital markets, economic systems can be described as based on banks or markets (Iqbal & Mustafa, 2017; Kalara & Zhang, 2018). Financial institutions are the primary vehicles for allocating capital and investment in bank-based financing systems. In contrast, in market-based financing systems, bond markets are the primary vehicle for transferring necessary financing to companies (Kalara & Zhang, 2018). The bank-based or market-based financial systems paradigm provides a valuable tool for comparing economic systems across countries (Kalara & Zhang, 2018).

There is no indication that a bank-based financing system is better than a market-based financing system, as there is no evidence that companies grow faster, countries develop better, or a new company is created more efficiently (Iqbal & Mustafa, 2017; Kalara & Zhang, 2018), using either system. Italy falls within European countries with bank-based financing systems characterized by few listed companies (Kalara & Zhang, 2018; Lepore et al., 2022; Zattoni & Mosca, 2012). The Italian capital market is limited in providing financial resources to companies, so it is considered a bank-oriented financial system. Italian companies prefer to rely on bank loans and bonds (financial debt) and retained earnings than finance their investments through the stock market (Melis & Zattoni, 2017).

Italian companies are almost exclusively medium and small and belong to a few family groups that use bank credit as a primary source of financing (Rizzato et al., 2019; Zattoni, 2019). For example, during the 1990s, around 99.2% of Italian companies had fewer than 100 employees; between 2008 and 2018, micro-enterprises represented 95% of all active enterprises, with approximately 2% and 5% being small and medium-sized enterprises, respectively, less than 1% are considered large enterprises (Lagasio, 2021). After World War II, small- and medium-sized enterprises (SMEs) increased significantly in the context of the Italian economy. A family or an entrepreneur usually controls these SMEs, operating in small industries or market niches left by large companies (Melis & Zattoni, 2017). The Italian economic system is also characterized by many cooperatives like workers' cooperatives, consumer cooperatives, and social or consortium cooperatives, among others. Cooperatives operate in various businesses, such as services, agriculture, retail, manufacturing, construction, etc. There are about 80,000 cooperatives employing 1.3 million workers, and this number has been favored by cultural, political, and tax incentives (Melis & Zattoni, 2017).

The separation between ownership and control is one of the substantial differences between countries' corporate governance systems (Lambert, 2021). Depending on the ownership and control structure, they differ into external systems, characterized by an expansive scattered property, and internal systems, described by a concentrated property (Salvioni & Gennari, 2016). The external system's corporate governance model favors the maximization of short-term profits, being shareholder-oriented corporate governance (Berle & Means, 1984; Friedman, 1970; Jensen & Meckling, 1976; Salvioni & Gennari, 2016). In the internal system (insider), the high concentration of ownership and control of management by the majority shareholders generates corporate governance oriented to creating value over time (Salvioni & Gennari, 2016).

The ownership structure of Italian companies is characterized as a substantial holder of a block of shares that a family usually represents, and recently, there has been an increase in the number of institutional investors, both domestic and foreign (Rizzato et al., 2019). Italy presents a limited development of the stock market, in which control is carried out by a few groups and with a limited number of investments (Rizzato et al., 2019). In addition, the state has a strong presence in the economy; from this perspective, the trend is the inefficiency of control and credit acquisition (Rizzato et al., 2019). Despite recent regulatory reforms and privatization processes, concentrated and family ownership remained stable (Zattoni & Cuomo, 2015). According to the Milan Chamber of Commerce with the Regional Institute for Policy Support of Lombardy (PoliS-Lombardia), in 2019, Italy had 1,220,301 joint share companies, 755,103 private partnership companies, 3,029,956 companies with unique owners, and 132,318 companies classified as others in their legal form (Camara Di Commercio Milano, 2020; PoliS-Lombardia., 2020).

Listed Italian companies have a high ownership concentration level. Most companies are controlled by a single shareholder or a group formed by a limited number of shareholders (Strampelli, 2020). As a result, Italy displays companies with more concentrated ownership than countries such as France, Germany, and Spain (OECD, 2021). In 2021, 57% of listed companies had concentrated ownership, and of these, 86% had one or more controllers; a family-controlled 73% of them; the state or local administration controlled 15%; and 12% were controlled by other agents, mainly financial companies (Assonime, 2022).

Listed and unlisted family businesses represented approximately 90% of Italian companies in 2019 and tiny, small, and medium-sized companies with simplified governance models and high ownership concentration (Nigri & Di Stefano, 2021). A family business can be defined as a company in which all the venture capital is held by a family or a small number of families, in which all family members work in the company, or, although management is outsourced and is decisively conditioned by the family(s) owner(s) (Casson, 1999; Chrisman et al., 2005; Zellweger et al., 2010). Family businesses in 2019 accounted for almost 64% of the Italian stock market and 25.6% of the total capitalization; companies owned by the state and other local authorities accounted for 17.5% of the Italian stock market (Consob, 2020).

Pyramidal groups are one of the main mechanisms of enhancement mechanisms (CEMs) in Italy. The pyramidal group is usually controlled by a person or family, situated at the top, and by means of vertical or horizontal holdings in listed or unlisted companies, each member owns shares in subsequent companies, gradually descending the pyramid, that is, the controlling shareholder oversees several companies through the separation existing between a controlling shareholder and a non-controlling shareholder (Briamonte et al., 2017). CEMs are corporate governance devices that allow controlling shareholders to increase their decision-making power to the potential detriment of minority shareholders, whose votes become ineffective (Melis & Zattoni, 2017; Intrisano, 2012). Through this system, a shareholder, or a group of shareholders, controls one or more companies with limited capital investment, maximized by creating several vertical levels (Briamonte et al., 2017; Melis & Zattoni, 2017).

To better understand this mechanism, imagine a holding A that owns 51% of shares in company B, which in turn owns 51% of shares in company C. The shareholder or group that controls holding A can also control company C, even if its shareholding in Company C is equal to zero, since company B is the controlling shareholder of C, withholding A having indirect control over company C. This three-level pyramid allows the holding shareholder or group of controlling shareholders to control the company at the bottom with only 12.5% of its cash flow rights (Melis & Zattoni, 2017). Shareholders use other mechanisms to increase control of Italian companies, such as cross-shareholdings, preferred (non-voting) shares, voting rights ceilings, shareholder agreements, and dual-class or multiple-vote claims (Intrisano, 2012; Zattoni & Cuomo, 2015).

At the end of 2019, companies belonging to pyramidal groups, or the vertical part of a mixed group, represented 12.8%, while in 2018, they were 15.5%, representing 33.8% and 41.4% of the total market value, respectively (Consob, 2020). According to data from Consob, the proportion of listed Italian companies that do not belong to any group of companies in 2019 was 84.2%, representing 64.9% of the market capitalization value, the highest value ever recorded. As for preferred shares, which are shares with limited voting rights (or even no votes), Italian companies have traditionally used two types of shares with limited voting rights: (1) preferred shares (*azioni previlegiate*) which allow shareholders to vote in extraordinary meetings; (2) savings shares (*azioni di risparmio*) that do not give the right to vote, except at general meetings whose agenda directly affects their interests as shareholders, for example, approving mergers, conversions of savings shares into ordinary shares, but receive a more significant dividend (Melis & Zattoni, 2017). Italian law establishes that limited or non-voting shares cannot represent more than 50% of the share capital. This type of CEM was prevalent in Italy until the 1990s. Consob reported that around 10% of listed Italian companies used preferred shares at the end of 2015. A considerable reduction compared to 32% in 1998 and 37% in 1992.

Shareholder agreements are specially organized at the holding level to stabilize the controlling shareholder's controlling position. Shareholder agreements between Italian companies have remained stable over the last decade, with more than 60% of listed companies having shareholder agreements at the end of 2015 (Consob, 2016). The CEM called the voting rights ceiling, prohibits shareholders from voting above a specific limit, regardless of the number of shares they hold. In Italy, for example, Snam Rete Gas and Terna, companies in which the State is the main shareholder, have established voting ceilings of 15% for Snam Rete Gas and 5% for Terna of all outstanding votes (Melis & Zattoni, 2017). There are also priority shares, which are CEMs called "Golden shares," that grant their holders specific decision-making powers or veto rights, regardless of their shareholding. In the most prominent private Italian companies, for example, ENEL (Utility), UNI (Oil and Gas), Finmeccanica (Industrial), Telecom Italia (Telecommunications), the Italian government has special rights, such as vetoing decisions to dissolve the firm, spin-off, transfer of headquarters and amendment of these special rights in the articles of association (Melis & Zattoni, 2017). The government also is entitled to appoint a member to the board of directors of these companies without consulting the shareholders.

Cross-holdings, or reciprocal holdings, are CEMs in which company A holds an equity interest in company B, which in turn holds an equity interest in company A. Cross-ownership can also be circular; for example, when company A has shares in company B, company B has shares in company C, and company C has shares in company A. Cross-holdings are the least used CEM in Italy, as the Draghi Law suspends voting rights when a listed company holds 5% of the voting shares of another listed company; the latter cannot exercise the voting rights inherent to claims that exceed 5% of the voting rights of the former and must sell its shares.

Dual-class shares are CEMs that have been reduced since their introduction in 1974 through Law No. 216. In 1999, 27.78% of listed companies owned dual-class shares; in 2007, this percentage dropped to 10.76% (Intrisano, 2012). As for shareholder agreements, a CEM is also widely used in Italy; in 1999, 75 contracts were signed by 73 companies (27.04% of listed companies). In 2007, 130 shareholder agreements were signed in 96 companies (27.91% of listed companies), showing no significant change in shareholder agreements (Intrisano, 2012). Regarding CEMs called loyalty shares or multiple voting shares, in 2021, about a third of companies adopted these mechanisms. Small and large companies use loyalty or multiple voting shares: 32% and 34%, respectively (Assonime, 2022). These CEMs are used more in family businesses and newly listed companies.

One of the substantial changes in the ownership structure of listed companies worldwide has been the increase in institutional ownership. Institutional investors represent the largest category of investors at the aggregate global level, holding 43% of the world market capitalization, 11% owned by private companies, 10% owned by public sector companies, and 9% individually owned (OECD, 2021). According to Consob, the leading Italian institutional investors are regarded as investment funds, banks, and insurance companies subject to obligations to provide information according to the rules of this body, and their holdings cannot exceed 10% (Consob, 2020).

Institutional investors' properties in listed Italian companies represented 29.4% of the stock market in 2019, and foreign institutional investors opted for more diversified investments in size and sector, while domestic institutional investors opted for smaller companies (Consob, 2020; Zattoni, 2019). Institutional investors owned an average of 7.6% of listed companies in 2018, which represented 26.8% of the market capitalization of the Italian Stock Exchange; domestic institutional investors participated in 13 companies, while foreign institutional investors held shares in 51 companies (Consob, 2020). However, the increase in institutional ownership is not enough to stimulate their more active participation in the company's governance, and the Italian context demonstrates that regulatory factors also contributed to the engagement of institutional shareholders, such as the increase in voting and participation in assemblies (Balp & Strampelli, 2020).

Traditionally, Italian corporate governance is characterized by the presence of a shareholder at the top of large listed companies; there is a strong separation between banks and industrial companies; there is substantial state intervention in the national economy; there is a lack of an asset market of corporate control, and the presence of passive institutional investors, describing a system of weak managers, holders of solid blocks and unprotected minority shareholders (Zattoni & Cuomo, 2015). In summary, most Italian companies, whether listed or not, are under the influence of a large shareholder, which is usually a family, and the State and local public administrations continue to hold essential stakes in some large, listed companies and are not quoted (Melis & Zattoni, 2017; Zattoni, 2009).

7.3.2 Asymmetry of Information and Type of Opportunism

In Italian companies, some controllers or blockholders hold most shares with greater voting power, making decisions for their benefit. Minority owners hold a much smaller proportion of the company's shares (Kaya, 2020; Moscariello et al., 2019; Panda & Leepsa, 2017). This type of opportunism problem prevails in countries or companies where few people or families hold the equity stake in their hands and minority shareholders have difficulty protecting their interests or wealth (Kaya, 2020; Moscariello et al., 2019; Panda & Leepsa, 2017).

A typical example of this type of corporate governance in the Italian context is the company Parmalat, founded in 1961, one of the largest companies in the country in the food sector, with 139 factories worldwide and around 36,000 employees. The company has recently acquired stakes in TV, football, and tourism. Parmalat has a complex pyramid structure; Mr. Calisto Tanzi held more than 50% of the company's shares and was the CEO and chairman of the board of directors (Kaya, 2020; Melis & Zattoni, 2017). Four members of the Tanzi family held executive and non-executive positions on the company's board of directors. Parmalat has become the eighth-largest industrial group in Italy, accounting for 0.8% of the national GDP, and has 6000 dairy farms that depend on the company (Kaya, 2020). In 2003, he announced debts he could not pay, involvement in forgery and document fraud, declared bankruptcy, and Calisto Tanzi was arrested.

Several corporate governance failures led to Parmalat's bankruptcy. Although it was not a unique event, we can mention that there were no independent directors, the chairperson of the board and CEO of the company was Mr. Tanzi, and the positions were not separate. Mr. Tanzi was the controlling shareholder, demonstrating a conflict between the controlling shareholder who makes the decisions, and the minority shareholders. Minority shareholders had no voice (Kaya, 2020).

Allowing minority shareholders to have representatives on the board of directors can represent a relevant system to mitigate principal-principal conflict and reduce agency costs. Representatives of minority shareholders can perform essential functions in monitoring transactions with related parties and management behavior, reducing the risk of fraud and misappropriation of values in favor of controlling shareholders, and controlling activities to maximize the company's value (Moscariello et al., 2019; Panda & Leepsa, 2017). However, board members appointed by minority shareholders can create friction within the board, threatening its collegiality and weakening its monitoring function (Moscariello et al., 2019). Minority shareholders have the right to appoint at least one member of the board of directors of listed Italian companies through slate voting (Consob, 1998), strengthening the protection of minority shareholders' rights.

As pyramidal groups are characteristic in the Italian context, the type of conflict of interest generated by these pyramidal groups differs from the principal-principal type of conflict. This type of conflict can refer to the incompatibility between the owner and the power of control over those who can stimulate opportunistic behavior to extract their benefits at the expense of minority shareholders. For example, when government members can satisfy private benefits through earnings management, managers opt for lower gains to limit the tax burden (Briamonte et al., 2017). Using a sample of 97 groups, of which 16 were pyramidal, and 81 were not, between 2003 and 2007, Briamonte et al. (2017) reveal that empirical evidence suggests that, in the presence of a pyramidal structure, there may be a greater tendency toward earnings management. The pyramid structure can favor controlling shareholders by expropriating minority shareholders. This result reinforces the fact that majority and minority shareholders conflict in Italian companies that are part of pyramidal groups.

Furthermore, decisions on transactions with related parties are among the most relevant choices to reduce agency costs generated by the principal-principal conflict, as they are associated with the potential of controlling shareholders for self-negotiation (Balp & Strampelli, 2020). Article 2391 of the Italian Civil Code regulates transactions with related parties in Italy. This gives Consob the authority to establish standards to ensure that these transactions are transparent, presented in the board's annual report and the financial statements, and comply with procedural requirements. Article 154 of the *TUF* also addresses the issue, requiring that the board's interim report to the semi-annual financial statements include information on related party transactions.

Regulation n° 17221, issued by Consob in 2010, requires the board to adopt a specified internal procedure to ensure transparency, substantial and procedural fairness in transactions with related parties, and public disclosure of material transactions. The Regulations also provide that the board can approve transactions with associated parties only if a committee of independent directors issues a favorable opinion. However, the board can agree to the transaction even with a negative view of the committee of independent directors if, and only if, a shareholders' meeting is called, and most unrelated shareholders approve the transaction.

7.3.3 Activism and Rights of Minority Shareholders

Investor protection, in other words, how healthy country laws protect foreign investors, helps to explain differences between countries, such as ownership and concentration of control in publicly traded companies, dividend policies, and companies' access to external investors (Melis & Zattoni, 2017). These laws represent a set of mechanisms that protect foreign investors or minority shareholders from expropriation by insiders (La Porta et al., 2000). In the last two decades, Italian corporate law has given more "voice" to minority shareholders seeking to protect their interests.

Thus, minority shareholders, more specifically institutional investors, became more active, putting pressure on Italian policymakers and influencing corporate decisions to avoid expropriation by the controlling shareholder (Belcredi et al., 2014; Melis & Zattoni, 2017).

One way to increase the protection of minority shareholders is to include them in corporate management (Kaya, 2020). Minority shareholders who hold up to 5% of the shares have the right to request a general meeting and set the agenda by Articles 2367 and 2325 of the Civil Code and Article 125 of the Draghi Law. Other rights granted to Italian minority shareholders are described in Table 7.1. The minimum shareholding for requesting a general meeting is 5%, and to include items on the agenda, a shareholding of 0.1–2.5% (OECD, 2021). Another vital right of minority shareholder is appointing at least one member to the board of directors of listed Italian companies through slate voting (Consob, 1998).

One of Italy's most peculiar forms of shareholder activism is the presentation and voting on "minority slates" in corporate elections (Melis & Zattoni, 2017). The slate voting system applies to the election of members of the board of directors and the supervisory board, as provided for in Article 148 of the Draghi Law. According to information on the Consob website, 51% of listed Italian companies had at least one director appointed by minority shareholders in 2019 (Consob, 2020, 2022). In the slate voting system, directors must be appointed based on the proposal of minority shareholders of alternative candidates, and at least one director must be elected

Table 7.1 Rights of Italian minority shareholders

Description of law	Bound	Legal source
Request meeting advance for a maximum of five days if they are not informed of the plan	Limit of at least 1/3 of the general share capital	Article 2374 of the Civil Code
Right to veto any waiver or legal action agreement against directors	Limit of at least 5% of share capital	Article 2393 of the Civil Code
Right to sue directors.	Limit of at least 2.5% of the share capital or less if written in the statute	Article 2393 of the Civil Code
Right to challenge a resolution of the general meeting	Limit of at least 0.1% of voting shares	Article 2377 of the Civil Code
Right to register a relationship in the tax to report any "reasoned suspicion" about severe irregularities in the company's management.	Limit of at least 5% of general social capital	Article 2409 of the Civil Code
Right to lodge complaints with the fiscal council regarding the company's management.	Limit at least 5% of general social capital or any shareholder.	Articles 2409 and 2388 of the Civil Code
Right to request the addition of one or more items on the agenda or submit new motions for resolutions on things that are already on the schedule (ten days from the date of call)	Limit of at least 2.5% of the share capital issued	Article 125-ter of the consolidated finance act (TUF)
Right to propose a list of candidates for council elections, vote by plate.	Limit decided by Consob	Consob

Source: Consob (2022)

from the minority slate (Melis & Zattoni, 2017; Balp & Strampelli, 2020). The director elected by the slate proposed by the minority shareholders has no connection with the controlling shareholder. In this sense, Consob recommended that minority shareholders who present candidate slates disclose any significant relationship between the candidates and the controlling shareholder (Melis & Zattoni, 2017).

The only way a minority shareholder who presents a slate of candidates cannot nominate any of its representatives to the board is when more than one slate of candidates is offered by different minority shareholders (Melis & Zattoni, 2017). In this case, the director is selected from the list of minority shareholders who obtain the highest votes. *TUF* has established that a slate of candidates can only be presented by shareholders, individually or jointly, who own several shares exceeding a participation limit. This limit, which cannot exceed 4.5% of the capital stock, is established for each company listed by Consob based on specific criteria, such as market capitalization, the percentage of shares owned by the controlling shareholder, and the percentage of floating shares. Listed companies cannot set a higher limit than that indicated by Consob but may set a lower limit in their bylaws. This way, minority shareholders gain adequate voting power (Melis & Zattoni, 2017).

The slate or list voting system was introduced in 1998 for statutory audit board elections. 2005, after the Parmalat financial scandal, the slate voting system was extended to the board of directors (Balp & Strampelli, 2020). To promote the participation and engagement of minority shareholders, proxy voting and proxy solicitation systems were deregulated and simplified in 2010 (Consob, 1998). In a study carried out with non-financial companies listed from 2007 to 2012, Moscariello et al. (2019) found that the majority of minority shareholders who present a list of candidates for the board are institutional investors (62.2%) and private companies (29.25%). The authors also found that a higher proportion of independent directors appointed by minority shareholders leads to more excellent value for the company. In contrast, a more substantial proportion of independent directors appointed by the controlling shareholder does not impact company value.

In 2019, around 50% of listed companies reported having at least one director representing minority shareholders (in 2018, it was 44%). Listed companies had 190 minority directors in 2019 and 172 in 2018. The number of directors representing minority shareholders varies according to the company's size: 2.4 directors in the FTSE Mib, 1.7 counselors at mid-cap, and 1.2 directors in Small Cap in 2019. That same year, the number of statutory auditors representing minority shareholders reached 56% of listed companies (Assonime, 2020). There was a 4.24% increase in statutory auditors representing minority shareholders in listed companies from 2018 (118) to 2019 (123). Comparing the number of statutory auditors representing minority shareholders in 2015 and 2019, the increase is even more significant, at 21.78%.

It is worth noting that minority shareholders are more likely to engage in activism and nominate candidates if the expected benefit of this activity is high, in other words, when they fear the risk of expropriation by the controlling shareholder (Melis & Zattoni, 2017).

7.3.4 Board of Directors

The board of directors is a central body in the corporate governance structure of a company, functioning as a value protection mechanism against agency costs, monitoring administrators, and preventing them from opportunistic behavior (Clarke, 2020; Forbes & Milliken, 1999; Moscariello et al., 2019; Salvioni & Gennari, 2016). The effectiveness of the board's monitoring function can be improved by increasing the number of independent directors, as they can perform their duties without collusion with administrators (Fama & Jensen, 1983; Mirone et al., 2021). At a minimum, the board of directors must have an independent director by the Italian Corporate Governance Code (OECD, 2021). The code provides for a maximum term of office of eight to ten years for independent directors (OECD, 2021). Companies in an integrated group controlled by another listed company (pyramid) must have a majority board of independent directors as a listing requirement. In addition, independent directors cannot serve on the parent company's board of directors (Consob, 2022). The Italian code does not explicitly recommend separating the chairman of the board of directors and CEO positions. Moreover, the concentration of jobs requires the appointment of a lead independent director (LID) (CCG, 2021).

Italy has gradually imposed gender quotas on the board of directors to allow time for cultural change. The law established in 2011, applicable to listed companies, required a minimum of 20% of board seats for each gender, with the first appointment starting in August 2012 and a minimum of 33% for the second term (OECD, 2021). In 2019, another law increased the minimum threshold from 33% to 40% in 2020 and extended its application to six successive terms of appointments to the board, that is, 18 years (OECD, 2021). These initiatives culminated in an increase in female representation on the boards of Italian companies from 3% in 2009 to 36.5% in 2019 (OECD, 2021). Approximately three-quarters of women are independent directors in Italian companies (Consob, 2020).

In Italy, the board of directors traditionally has the role of "stamp" decisions outside the board. These decisions are made by the executive committee or in private meetings of controlling shareholders (Melis & Zattoni, 2017). Currently, the boards of directors of Italian companies have a more balanced composition, with the presence of executive and non-executive directors and independent directors. There is also a balance in terms of diversity of demographic and professional backgrounds (Melis & Zattoni, 2017).

The average size of the board of directors of listed Italian companies is ten directors. However, this number varies significantly with the company size (from 8.6 for small companies to 12.5 for large companies) (Assonime, 2021). Companies in the financial sector have an average of 13 directors, and companies in the non-financial sector have an average of 9.5 directors (Assonime, 2021). A size considered balanced, noting that small boards tend to be easier to convene, require fewer leadership efforts, have better communication, and have a more relaxed and informal culture that can lead to faster decisions (Melis & Zattoni, 2017; La Rosa et al., 2021). On the other hand, larger councils can provide critical resources in terms of competence and experience (La Rosa et al., 2021); neo-institutional and stakeholder theories hold that larger boards are representative of diverse interests (Hillman & Keim, 2001); under the resource dependence theory view, the large boards have better information and knowledge and bring different points of view on the company's problems (Beji et al., 2021).

As for the profile of the members of the boards of directors of listed Italian companies, on average, 26% are executives, 27% are non-executive and non-independent, and 47% are independent (Assonime, 2021). Independent directors represent, on average, more than half of the board members of large companies (56%). The average participation of independent directors is 6% lower in companies with a concentrated corporate structure (Assonime, 2021). In 2020, 93% of listed companies met the Italian Corporate Governance Code recommendations on the board's composition, ensuring the presence of executives, non-executives, and at least one-third of independent directors (Assonime, 2021).

At the end of 2021, the directors were, on average, 57 years old; women counselors are, on average, five years younger than men (Assonime, 2021). Statutory auditors are, on average, 56 years old. The term of office of directors in years is 6.6 and is strongly influenced by their role; that is, executives have an average time of office of 11.1 years, practically twice the middle term of office of non-executives, which is 5.2 years (Assonime, 2021). Independent directors have an average office time of 4.1 years. Councilors have a shorter average tenure of 4.6 years. Among CEOs, women have a shorter average tenure than men, 11.2 and 10.2 years, respectively, noting that they are also underrepresented (Assonime, 2021). And the middle term of statutory auditors in 2021 was five years.

In 2021, among the 523 executive directors, 231 (44%) were identified as Chief Executive Officers (CEO) (Assonime, 2021). Of these 523, 73 executive directors are also employed as general managers. According to Assonime (2021), considering the delegation of powers within the board, in 2021, four different management models were identified: (1) a pure CEO, in which all delegated powers are entrusted to an individual administrator, is very most frequent, representing 83% of all models; (2) multiple CEOs, representing 8%; (3) CEO with an executive committee, representing 6%; and (4) only one commission, representing 3%. Models with multiple CEOs, CEOs with the executive committee, and only one committee are more frequent in large companies with a controlling shareholder. The appointment of a general manager who is not a member of the board of directors is less and less frequent, occurring in 30% of the 94 companies with at least one general manager in the year 2021 (Assonime, 2021).

Among the 219 chairpersons of the board of directors in 2021, 62% are executive directors, 32% are non-executive directors, and only 6% are independent (Assonime, 2022). In 49% of cases, the board of directors' chairman was also the company's

CEO. This duality of roles is frequent in companies with concentrated ownership, reaching 35% against 22% in less concentrated companies. The appointment of a LID is recommended when there is a significant concentration of positions, such as when the chairman of the board of directors is also the company's CEO or a controlling shareholder. The underlying logic is that the CEO should run the company. In contrast, a different person—the chairperson or controlling shareholder—should run the board of directors to facilitate board effectiveness (Melis & Zattoni, 2017). An LID was appointed in 97 companies, or 44% of companies listed with dual roles in 2021 (Assonime, 2022).

The board of directors may create committees according to the Italian Corporate Governance Code. When created, the members of these committees are generally appointed by the board of directors among its directors. In 2021, 153 companies (70%) established a nominating committee. A compensation, control, and risk committee was set up in 94% of the listed companies. They noted that the control and risk committee must have at least one member with financial and accounting knowledge. There was an increase in remuneration committees over the period, and in 2008, 80% of the companies established one; in 2015, 90% of companies had one. There was also an evolution in the percentage of companies that constituted a control and risk committee; in 2009, it was 65%, and in 2013, it was 90%. The presidency of the remuneration committees and the control and risk committees were occupied by 52% and 61%, respectively, by women, with a particular gender balance. In the nominating committee, women represent 44% of the members, and generally, their presidency is occupied by men (61%) (Assonime, 2021).

The average number of meetings held by the board of directors in 2021 was 11.7, a slight increase compared to 10.2 in 2014. The average annual frequency of meetings in 2021 was higher among larger companies (13.4) and companies in the financial sector (19.3). The board of statutory auditors and the supervisory board met on average 15.3 times in 2021 (Assonime, 2021). Most listed companies (80%) assessed the board of directors in 2021. Listed companies that did not carry out the assessment (20%) provide justifications for not complying with the review, referring to the company's characteristics, such as the size or composition of the board (Assonime, 2021).

Finally, there was a disclosure of board interlocking in 45% of listed companies in 2021, and of this percentage, 90% occurred in the financial sector, and 70% occurred in large companies (Assonime, 2021). In 2021, 95% of board members or statutory auditors across companies disclosed information on board interlocking. This year, the number of board interlocking was 2.06, demonstrating that the interlocking of directors decreased over time, as it was 2.54 in 2014 and 3.26 in 2011 (Assonime, 2021). The board interlocking of only listed companies is 1.15, with a total of 82 members of control bodies in the year 2021. Of these, 53 (65%) are women. Board interlocking has been decreasing, as, in 2015, 60% of listed companies declared they had at least one interconnected director on their board.

7.3.5 Remuneration of Directors and Statutory Auditors: Policies and Practices

The design of the board of directors' compensation must be based on clear, comprehensive, and varied performance criteria, considering, where relevant, corporate and social responsibility (OECD, 2021). The disclosure of the remuneration policy is mandatory, both the total amount and the individual amount (OECD, 2021). The recommendations of the Italian Corporate Governance Code, since its first edition in 1999, were developed to provide specific guidance on the structure of remuneration policies (Assonime, 2021). The objective is to promote the compatibility of remuneration policies with the company's long-term strategic purposes and improve its transparency for investors.

According to the European Commission's 2004 and 2009 Guidelines, from 2010 onward, companies were required to publish an annual remuneration report at least 21 days before the general meeting (Melis & Zattoni, 2017). Article 123 of the *TUF* (amended by Legislative Decree n° 49 of May 2019) made a preliminary vote on the company's compensation policy mandatory. There is a vote every three years on the executive compensation plan, the so-called "say on pay." This occurs whenever the board of directors proposes any change to the remuneration policy that is last approved by the shareholders. Companies can only award fees to executives based on the most recent remuneration policy approved by shareholders (Balp & Strampelli, 2020). In this sense, the "say on pay" is a mechanism in which the remuneration policy defined by the shareholder council is subject to shareholder approval, which was only advisory until 2019 and is now binding (Assonime, 2021).

The binding character of the "say on pay" came from the need to align the provisions on the remuneration policy of listed companies with the conditions already in force for banks and insurance companies in Italy. It has been expanded to include compensation of board members or statutory auditors, general managers, the board of directors, and executives with strategic responsibilities (Balp & Strampelli, 2020). This rule is a valuable tool, as the votes strengthen the monitoring of the minority investor, who can vote against or withhold voting against the remuneration, demonstrating that some shareholders do not support the board and make their disagreement public (Balp & Strampelli, 2020).

To support companies with the challenges posed by these changes, the 2020 Italian Corporate Governance Code reinforced the need to properly align remuneration policies with the company's sustainable success (Assonime, 2021). In more detail, it is recommended that the variable remuneration component be predominantly oriented toward the long term and, if possible, associated with non-financial parameters. Virtually all compensation policies provide for a mixed compensation package for executive directors. In 2021, 89% of listed companies disclosed the existence of a variable component in the remuneration of executive directors (Assonime, 2021). The companies that did not assign a variable part (11%) are primarily companies with concentrated ownership, in which about half of the CEOs are also significant company shareholders (Assonime, 2021). Of the remuneration policies that provide variable remuneration, 97% set a limit to the maximum possible amount. Assonime (2021) points out that the relative weight of the fixed and variable components of directors' compensation is not standardized and often lacks adequate details.

Less than half of the companies provide detailed information on the time horizon of the incentives, which allows for assessing the relative weight of the short-term and the long-term if the targets of the incentive plans are reached (Assonime, 2021). In 2021, fixed compensation represented 42% of total compensation, 27% represented short-term fixed compensation, and 31% expressed long-term compensation. The relative weight of the variable components varies according to the size of the companies. The FTSE MIB has greater importance in the long term (38% on average), and Small Caps have a greater weight in the short term (31% on average). Regarding the performance targets of variable compensation, in 2021, 99% of listed companies disclosed that their targets are linked to parameters based on accounting (Assonime, 2021). Other performance goals, such as strategic or ESG (environmental, social, and corporate governance), are used in about two-thirds of cases. Equity-based compensation plans are adopted by 57% of listed companies, most often by large companies (88%) and companies in the financial sector (80%).

As for the remuneration of the board of directors, in 2021, the payment of non-executive directors was significantly lower and more stable than that of executives and differed according to the function performed (Assonime, 2021). Executive presidents received an average of €281,600, independent directors received an average of €61,100, and the other members received €74,600. The difference in remuneration between independent and non-executive directors is linked to the differentiated role these categories play in the company (Assonime, 2021). Independent directors receive additional fees (€19,000 on average; 31% of their total compensation) for being members of one or more boards of directors' committees. On the other hand, non-executive directors receive bonuses (€20,000 on average; 30% of their total remuneration) for services rendered to the company and its subsidiaries.

Independent directors' compensation is affected by the size of the company. In 2021, these advisors earned in medium and large companies, respectively, two or three times more than in small companies (€33,000 in Small Caps; €63,000 in Mid-Caps, and €106,000 in FTSE Mib companies) (Assonime, 2021). Gender is a factor that impacts director compensation. In 2021, independent women directors received 10% less payment than male directors. Larger companies pay women less (−9% in mid-cap and −6% in FTSE Mib), while small companies, on average, pay women more than men (+3% in small cap) (Assonime, 2021). Finally, in 2021, statutory auditors received an average remuneration of €46,000. The payment of statutory auditors varies according to the company size; FTS MIB companies pay €87,000, about 2.9 times the average remuneration in Small Caps (Assonime, 2021). And the fixed component of statutory auditors' remuneration represents 83% of total compensation.

7.3.6 External Audit System

The external auditor's professional opinion on the financial statements' substantial reliability is essential in ensuring corporate information's transparency. In Italy, the external audit firm is appointed by the general meeting, considering the opinion of the board of statutory auditors (Melis & Zattoni, 2017). The development of external auditing in Italy began with Law n° 1966, on November 23, 1939, which disciplined audit firms and voluntary auditing in authorized firms. However, the natural development of external audit activity only occurred in the mid-1970s.

In 1975, Presidential Decree n° 136 was published, establishing the registry of auditing companies authorized to perform auditing functions. These functions included regular bookkeeping control, effective matching of financial statements to records, compliance with standards, certification, and balance sheet assurance. The services also had an opinion on the price of shares about proposed capital increases through contributions, stating the equity of the exchange ratios of shares on mergers and the exercise of the functions assigned to statutory auditors in the event of a capital increase through contributions in kind. In addition, it established mandatory audits for the financial statements of listed companies with the issuance of certification or opinion (Repubblica Italiana, 1975). This standard also introduced the compulsory rotation of auditing firms for publicly listed companies, with a maximum term of office of three years, rehiring for two more periods equal to three years, and then a period of leave of five years. And it did not impose the rotation of the auditing firm's partner.

In 1981, ASSIREVI (Association of Main Auditing Firms in Italy) issued Resolution n° 2. In that report, they mentioned compliance with the principles and any deviations, thus emphasizing the relevance of accounting principles in practice. In 1982, Consob issued Resolution n° 1079, indicating the accounting principles for listed and external auditing companies as a reference for preparing and certifying financial statements. In 1992, Legislative Decree n° 88 amended or replaced articles of Presidential Decree n° 136/1975, highlighting two-way audits, that is, the function of auditor could be assumed either by individual people endowed with professional competence registered in the Ministry of Justice, as by auditing firms, also written (Repubblica Italiana, 1992). In the late 1990s, external audits underwent a substantial regulatory overhaul with the Draghi Law of 1998 issuance. This law distinguished the role of the board of statutory auditors from that of external auditors. It replaces the term certification with professional judgment, which it admits is more appropriate to the nature of the external auditor's statement, which must be expressed in a separate report. In addition, article 156 now provides four different types of auditor judgments: (i) qualified judgment, (ii) judgment with conclusions, (iii) judgment, and (iv) inability to express an opinion (Miles et al., 2021).

The 1998 and 2003 corporate law reforms included companies subject to external audit, unlisted companies that listed companies'control, and even some private limited liability companies (Cameran et al., 2015a, 2015b). These reforms substantially increased the number of companies required to perform external audits. The market for external audit firms has also grown, even if it is still small compared to countries such as the US and the UK (Melis & Zattoni, 2017). Legislative Decree 58 of 1998 re-established that the hiring of the audit firm should last three years, with the possibility of renewal for two more periods of three years. However, this standard did not refer to the period of leave, which caused several problems of interpretation (Cameran et al., 2015b). Consob stated that the removal for rehiring the auditing firm would be three years.

In 2005, Law n° 262 reinforced the legal framework for external auditing through mandatory rotation, duration of attributions, causes of auditor incompatibility, the definition of the network of companies belonging to the same group, the responsibility of the auditing company, and the extension of Consob's powers (Repubblica Italiana, 2005). It required a six-year term for external audit firms, renewable once with a three-year leave period. For the first time, it included a rule on audit partner rotation, whereby audit partners had to be changed every six years, with a three-year leave period. Furthermore, it required the leading external audit firm to assume responsibility for the actions of other audit firms that worked as subcontractors (Repubblica Italiana, 2005). In 2006, Legislative Decree 303 limited the maximum period for hiring the audit firm to nine consecutive years and fixed a period of leave of three years.

In 2010, Legislative Decree n° 39 was edited, resulting from the reception of Directive 2006/43/CEE, constituting a new Consolidated Auditing Law. The decree replaced the previous expressions "accounting control" and "audit" with the term "legal audit." Auditing companies must be registered with Consob and responsible for inspecting their practical independence, technical suitability, and how the accounting audit is carried out. The auditor, an individual, must meet the integrity requirements established by Consob, have completed an internship, and perform and pass an aptitude test for knowledge of Italian legislation. In the case of auditing companies, most of their board of directors'members must be authorized to audit in a member state of the European Union, and those responsible for the audit must be individuals registered with Consob.

Article 10 of Legislative Decree 39/2010 makes the auditor's independence mandatory. Furthermore, it provides that auditors are jointly and severally liable to the managers of the audit firm for damage caused to the company, its partners, and third parties who have contracted the audit. For non-compliance with their duties, this responsibility extends to the auditors and employees who carried out the audit activities (Repubblica Italiana, 2010). In 2016, Legislative Decree n° 135 amended Legislative Decree n° 39/2010 and included Directives 537/2014/EU and 2014/56/EU. The ways of continuing auditor education, ethical standards and professional secrecy, auditor independence, and standardization of processes and the audit report were reviewed. The decree defined the term of office for the audit firm in nine financial years and the partners' time as seven financial years, and for rehiring, a period of at least four years must have elapsed from the end of the previous contract (Repubblica Italiana, 2016).

According to the Italian legislation on external audit, it is possible to notice the relevance given to the independence of the external auditor with the use of mechanisms such as the rotation of auditors since 1975; however, in the literature on the independence of the external auditor, there is no consensus on its relevance for audit quality, for example, in a literature review of studies carried out in environments of voluntary adoption of external auditor rotations, Lennox (2014) concludes that a longer term does not seem to impair audit quality; however, there is no evidence that a more extended period of external audit can improve audit quality (Lennox, 2014).

The question of the external auditor's independence is relevant because the auditor's independence increases the possibility that generally accepted accounting principles prepare the accounting and financial statements. Investors are more likely to trust financial statements if the auditor is independent, as increased independence is closely linked to audit quality (Cameran et al., 2015b; Melis & Zattoni, 2017). Auditor independence aims to ensure that the accounting and financial statements are reliable and improve the efficiency of capital markets (Heralth & Pradier, 2018). Auditor independence involves two aspects: objectivity, that is, the auditor's ability to suppress biases and integrity, in other words, the auditor's willingness to express an opinion that truthfully represents the assessment of what was discovered during the audit process (Melis & Zattoni, 2017). A long-term relationship between the auditor and the client can generate connections and excessive familiarity with the client's management and undermine the objectivity and integrity of the external auditor (Ewelt-Knauer et al., 2013; Heralth & Pradier, 2018).

Mandatory audit rotation is a possible solution to avoid threats to auditor independence and audit quality (Ewelt-Knauer et al., 2013). Rotation may apply to the audit firm or the partner of the audit firm (Cameran et al., 2015b). Italy is one of the few countries where the two types of rotation (partner and audit firm) coexist (Cameran et al., 2015b). Research on mandatory audit firm rotation is incipient and does not provide solid and consistent evidence linking mandatory firm rotation to greater independence and improved audit quality (Ewelt-Knauer et al., 2013; Cameran et al., 2015b). However, it should be noted that such research reports that audit quality tends to be lower in the first three terms of office, suggesting that the audit firm needs at least three years to obtain adequate knowledge and experience about the new audited company (Ewelt-Knauer et al., 2013; Cameran et al. 2015a, 2015b).

In empirical research carried out by Cameran et al. (2015a) with 275 Italian companies audited by the Big 4, the results indicated that the mandatory rotation of the audit firm causes a decline in the average quality of audited earnings in the initial three years after the process about subsequent years of audit mandate. Moreover, a 36% increase in auditors' work provisions in the first three years compared to the following years. The authors highlighted that the audit market in Italy is small and that if this result is observed in countries with a larger audit market, the adverse effects of audit rotation maybe even more significant, such as in the USA. The results also reveal that the audit fees for the last term of office are, on average, 7% higher than in other years, which can hide opportunistic prices; the costs of incoming auditors are, on average, 16% lower.

According to Melis and Zattoni (2017), the market for external audit firms is highly concentrated in Italy in terms of the number of clients and turnover. An oligopoly of auditing firms is dominated by the so-called Big Four (Ernest Young, KPMG, Deloitte, and PricewaterhouseCoopers). In 2015, Consob reported that these auditing firms held 86% of the market in terms of the number of listed companies audited. Cameran et al. (2015b) point out that the audit firms' rotation alone does not increase competition in the audit market. This percentage is not so different from other countries; in a study with 17 countries, Choi et al. (2017) revealed that the average rate of listed companies audited by the Big Four is 90.2%.

Finally, regarding the internal control of Italian companies, the *Borsa Italiana* Code of Self-Discipline recommends that an internal audit committee be set up, with advisory and propositional functions to the board of directors on internal controls, such as the monitoring of the company's internal and external control mechanisms.

7.4 Final Considerations

This chapter aims to describe the evolution of corporate governance in Italy based on a systematic review of the literature and national regulations (e.g., the Code of Corporate Governance and Corporate Law). The development of Italian corporate law was presented from the Civil Code of 1882 until the issuance of Law n° 49 of 2019, which amended the Consolidated Law on Finance. The evolution of the Corporate Governance Code was also analyzed from its first edition in 1999 until its last revision in 2020, which entered into force on January 1, 2021.

Data were presented regarding the last years (2018–2021) of the ownership and control structure of the Listed Italian companies and the three corporate governance models that can be adopted by companies voluntarily, the traditional model, and the alternative models, dualistic or two-tier and monistic or one-tier. The corporate governance model in Italy is characterized as a hybrid. Corporate governance in the Italian environment may be described as follows:

1. There has been a large evolution of corporate governance practices and rules in the last decades. Corporate law has been amended several times to strengthen investors' protection and to align the corporate governance of listed companies with international best practices. The same is true for the corporate governance code that has been revised to strengthen its principles and recommendations.
2. Despite the improvement of practices and regulations, the high concentration of ownership and the use of control-enhancing mechanisms do not exclude the risk of misappropriation for minority shareholders.
3. Corporate control is mostly in the hands of a few wealthy entrepreneurial families or the state (directly or through *Cassa Depositi e Prestiti—CDP*), whose main strategic objectives may not overlap with minority investors' ones.

4. Using alternative models (i.e., one tier or two tiers) is still embryonic, as they represent less than 2% of the listed companies. The lack of knowledge about alternative models and the prudence in experimenting with new models push almost all companies to adopt the traditional model.
5. The "comply or explain" approach allows companies to decide whether to comply with the requirements of the Corporate Governance Code or to explain the reasons for their deviance. This may help companies to adopt practices that better fit their specific characteristics, but it may also lead to non-substantial changes or delay the adoption of new practices.
6. Over time, several mechanisms to protect minority investors have been introduced. Among them is the slate voting for directors' election and promoting institutional investors' engagement.

Globalization in the financial market promotes the standardization of countries' corporate governance systems. However, that standardization will not occur (especially in the short term) because corporate governance systems result from institutional (e.g., regulatory or cultural) forces that do not change quickly. For example, in Italy, even after regulatory reforms aimed at creating a more favorable environment for institutional investors and minority shareholders' activism, the high concentration of equity ownership and the slow development of foreign institutional investors did not necessarily increase the effectiveness of internal and external controls.

This literature review has some limitations. First, the research covered only articles that dealt with English and Italian subjects in business, management, and accounting between 2006 and 2022. Thus, we suggest that future studies consider a larger number or a different publication type. Second, the basis for this research was the year of journal publication, and it may take a few years before the article is published.

References

Aganin, A., & Volpin, P. (2005). The history of corporate ownership in Italy. In R. K. Morck (Ed.), *A history of corporate governance around the world: Family business groups to professional managers* (pp. 325–365). University of Chicago Press.

Amatori, F., & Colli, A. (2000). Corporate governance: The Italian story. *Quaderno di Ricera dell'Istituto di Storia Economica, 1*(May), 1–63.

Assonime. (2020). *La Corporate Governance in Italia: autodisciplina, remunerazioni e comply-or-explain (anno 2020).* https://www.assonime.it/_layouts/15/Assonime.CustomAction/GetPdfToUrl.aspx?PathPdf=https://www.assonime.it/attivita-editoriale/studi/Documents/Note%20Studi%203_2021%20def.pdf

Assonime. (2021). *Corporate governance in Italy: The implementation of the Italian corporate governance code (year 2021).* https://www.assonime.it/_layouts/15/Assonime.CustomAction/GetPdfToUrl.aspx?PathPdf=https://www.assonime.it/attivita-editoriale/studi/Documents/Note%20e%20Studi%204-2022.pdf

Assonime. (2022). *L'Associazone fra le società italiane per azione.* https://www.assonime.it/Pagine/Home.aspx

Austin Ratings. (2022). *Ratings*. https://www.austin.com.br/Ratings-Todos.html

Balp, G., & Strampelli, G. (2020). Empowering institutional investors in concentrated ownership contexts: The case do Italy. *South Carolina Journal of International Law and Business, 17*(1), 1–64.

Beji, R., Yousfi, O., Loukil, N., & Omri, A. (2021). Board diversity and corporate social responsibility: Empirical evidence from France. *Journal of Business Ethics, 173*(1), 133–155. https://doi.org/10.1007/s10551-020-04522-4

Belcredi, M., Bozzi, S., Ciavarella, A., & Novembre, V. (2014). Say-on-pay in a context of concentrated ownership. Evidence from Italy. *SSRN Electronic Journal*. https://doi.org/10.2139/ssrn.2403886

Berle, A. A., & Means, G. C. (1984). *A Moderna Sociedade Anônima e a Propriedade Privada* (D. d. A. Azevedo, Trans.). Abril Cultural.

Block, D., & Gerstner, A.-M. (2016). One-tier vs. two-tier board structure: A comparison between the United States and Germany comparative corporate governance and financial. *Regulation, 1*, 1–70. https://scholarship.law.upenn.edu/cgi/viewcontent.cgi?article=1001&context=fisch_2016

Briamonte, M. F., Addeo, F., Fiano, F., & Sorrentino, M. (2017). The effect of pyramidal structures on earnings management: Evidence from Italian listed companies. *Corporate Ownership and Control, 14*(3), 64–73. https://doi.org/10.22495/cocv14i3art7

Cadbury Report. (1992). Report with code of best practice. In *The committee on the financial aspects of corporate governance and Gee and Co. Ltd.* (Vol. Cadbury Report, p. 90). Burgess Science Press.

Camera di Commercio Milano Monza Brianza Lodi. (2020). *Camera di commercio Milano Monza Brianza Lodi*. https://www.milomb.camcom.it/

Cameran, M., Francis, J. R., Marra, A., & Pittinicchio, A. (2015a). Are there adverse consequences of mandatory auditor rotation? Evidence from the Italian experience. *Auditing: A Journal of Practice & Theory, 34*(1), 1–24. https://doi.org/10.2308/ajpt-50663

Cameran, M., Negri, G., & Petticnicchio, A. K. (2015b). The audit mandatory rotation rule: The state of the art. *Journal of Financial Perspectives, 3*(2), 1–33. https://ssrn.com/abstract=3083484

Casson, M. (1999). The economics of the family firm. *Scandinavian Economic History Review, 47*(1), 10. https://doi.org/10.1080/03585522.1999.10419802

Cebula, R. J., & Rossi, F. (2021). Religiosity and corporate risk-taking: Evidence from Italy. *Journal of Economics and Finance, 45*(4), 751–763. https://doi.org/10.1007/s12197-021-09543-x

Choi, J.-H., Kim, J.-B., Lee, Y., & Sunwoo, H.-Y. (2017). Audit market concentration and audit fees. In *An international investigation Hawai'i accounting research conference (HARC)*. Shidler College of Business.

Chrisman, J. J., Chua, J. H., & Sharma, P. (2005). Trends and directions in the development of a strategic management theory of the family firm. *Entrepreneurship Theory and Practice, 29*(5), 555–575. https://doi.org/10.1111/j.1540-6520.2005.00098.x

Clarke, T. (2020). *Corporate governance: A survey*. Cambridge University Press. https://doi.org/10.1017/9781108966719

Comitato per la corporate governance. (2021). *Comitato per la Corporate Governance*. Borsa Italiana. https://www.borsaitaliana.it/comitato-corporate-governance/homepage/homepage.htm

Consob. (1998). *Testo Unico della Finanza (TUF)*. Repubblica Italiana. Febbraio. https://www.consob.it/documents/46180/46181/dlgs58_1998.pdf/e15d5dd6-7914-4e9f-959f-2f3b88400f88

Consob. (1999). *Regolamento Emittenti Adottato con Delibera n. 11971 del 14 maggio 1999*. Repubblica Italiana. Maggio. http://www.consob.it/main/regolamentazione/tuf/tuf.html?queryid=main.regolamentazione.tuf&resultmethod=tuf&search=1&amp%0Asymblink=/main/regolamentazione/tuf/index.html%0Apapers3://publication/uuid/7B865505-5F92-458C-A001-9D958E2D11C9

Consob. (2020). *Report on corporate governance of Italian listed companies - 2020 [statistics and analysis]*. T. E. Roma.

Consob. (2021). *Commissione Nazionale per le Società e la Borsa*. https://www.consob.it/web/consob/home

Consob. (2022). Borsa Italiana. (Euronext). https://www.borsaitaliana.it

Cuomo, F., Zattoni, A., & Valentini, G. (2013). The effects of legal reforms on the ownership structure of listed companies. *Industrial and Corporate Change, 22*(2), 427–458. https://doi.org/10.1093/icc/dts015

Datwani, M., Dochi, J., Goo, S. H., & Seidenfuss, K.-U. (2018). One-tier, two-tier and hybrid board structures in Hong Kong, Germany, and Japan: A governance perspective. *The Company Lawyer, 39*(10), 345–348. https://www.researchgate.net/publication/353356551_

De Molli, V., & Visani, M. (2015). *I vantaggi del modello monistico. Il Sole 24 Ore*. I vantaggi del modello monistico - Il Sole 24 ORE.

Di Fabio, C. (2018). Voluntary application of IFRS by unlisted companies: Evidence from the Italian context. *International Journal of Disclosure and Governance, 15*(2), 73–86. https://doi.org/10.1057/s41310-018-0037-z

EU. (2012). *COM (2012) 614 final 2012/0299 (COD). In Diretiva do Parlamento Europeu e do Conselho* (p. 31). European Union: Comissão Europeia.

Euronext. (2021). *Euronext Group*. https://www.euronext.com/en

European Commission. (2023). *Italy's recovery and resilience plan*. https://commission.europa.eu/business-economy-euro/economic-recovery/recovery-and-resilience-facility/country-pages/italys-recovery-and-resilience-plan_en

Ewelt-Knauer, C., Gold, A., & Pott, C. (2013). Mandatory audit firm rotation: A review of stakeholder perspectives and prior research. *Accounting in Europe, 10*(1), 27–41. https://doi.org/10.1080/17449480.2013.772717

Fama, E. F., & Jensen, M. C. (1983). Agency problems and residual claims. *The Journal of Law and Economics, 26*(2), 327–349. https://doi.org/10.1086/467038

Ferrarini, G. (2005, March). *Corporate governance changes in the 20th century: A view from Italy*. ECGI – Law Working Paper n° 29/2005, Available at SSRN https://ssrn.com/abstract=695762

Forbes, D. P., & Milliken, F. J. (1999). Cognition and corporate governance: Understanding boards of directors as strategic decision-making groups. *Academy of Management Review, 24*(3), 489–505. https://doi.org/10.4324/9780203888711

Friedman, M. (1970). The social responsibility of business is to increase its profits. *The New York Times Magazine*, 31–35. https://doi.org/10.1007/978-3-540-70818-6_14

García-Torea, N., Fernandez-Feijoo Souto, B., & de la Cuesta, M. (2016). Board of Directors Effectiveness and the stakeholder perspective of corporate governance: Do effective boards promote the interests of shareholders and stakeholders? *BRQ Business Research Quarterly, 19*(4), 246–260. https://doi.org/10.1016/j.brq.2016.06.001

Ghezzi, F., & Malberti, C. (2008). The two-tier model and the one-tier model of corporate governance in the Italian reform of corporate law. *European Company and Financial Law Review, 5*(1), 1–47. https://doi.org/10.1515/ecfr.5.1.1

Goshen, Z., & Hamdani, A. (2015). Majority control and minority protection. In J. N. Gordon & W.-G. Ringe (Eds.), *The Oxford handbook of corporate law and governance* (pp. 1–28). Oxford University Press. https://doi.org/10.5860/choice.50-5912

Heralth, S. K., & Pradier, T. (2018). A literature review on auditor independence. *The Business and Management Review, 9*(3), 1–6. https://cberuk.com/cdn/conference_proceedings/2019-07-14-10-55-01-AM.pdf

Hilb, M. (2020). Toward artificial governance? The role of artificial intelligence in shaping the future of corporate governance. *Journal of Management and Governance, 24*(4), 851–870. https://doi.org/10.1007/s10997-020-09519-9

Hillman, A. J., & Keim, G. D. (2001). Shareholder value, stakeholder management, and social issues: What's the bottom line? *Strategic Management Journal, 22*, 125–139. https://doi.org/10.1002/1097-0266(200101)22:2<125::AID-SMJ150>3.0.CO;2-H

HistoryTour, B. I. (2021). *200 Anni di Borsa Italiana*. History Tour Borsa Italiana. https://web.archive.org/web/20110722035921/http://www.historytour.it/default.php?idp=s&ids=10

IFRS. (2022). *International accounting standards board*. IFRS Foundation. https://www.ifrs.org

Intrisano, C. (2012). Control-enhancing mechanisms in Italian companies. *China-USA Business Review, 11*(3), 328–358. https://ssrn.com/abstract=2418352

Iqbal, M. S., & Mustafa, K. (2017). Ownership structure changes, reforms and corporate restructuring: Evidence from Japan. *IBA Business Review, 12*(2), 33–64. https://doi.org/10.22495/jgr_v6_i4_p4

ISTAT. (2022a). *Istituto Nazionale di Statistica*. https:// www.istat.it/en/

ISTAT. (2022b). *Annual report 2021: The state of the nation*. https://www.istat.it/it/files/2021/09/Annual-Report-2021_Summary_EN.pdf

Jensen, M. C., & Meckling, W. H. (1976). Theory of the firm: Managerial behavior, agency costs and ownership structure. *Journal of Financial Economics, 3*(4), 305–360. https://doi.org/10.1016/0304-405x(76)90026-x

Jones, M. J., & Melis, A. (2021). The continuity of the Board of Statutory Auditors across social, economic and political institutional changes. *European Accounting Review, 30*(2), 349–380. https://doi.org/10.1080/09638180.2020.1761850

Jouber, H. (2021). Is the effect of board diversity on CSR diverse? New insights from one-tier vs two-tier corporate board models. *Corporate Governance: The International Journal of Business in Society, 21*(1), 23–61. https://doi.org/10.1108/cg-07-2020-0277

Kalara, N., & Zhang, L. (2018). *The changing landscape of firm financing in Europe, the United States and Japan*. CPB Discussion Paper, CPB Netherlands Bureau for Economic Policy Analysis.

Kaya, M. K. (2020). Notion of protection of minority shareholders: Theoretical framework. *İstanbul Medeniyet Üniversitesi Hukuk Fakültesi Dergisi, 5*(9), 195–219.

Khanna, T., Kogan, J., & Palepu, K. (2006). Globalization and similarities in corporate governance: A cross-country analysis. *Review of Economics and Statistics, 88*(1), 69–90. https://doi.org/10.1162/rest.2006.88.1.69

Kumar, P., & Zattoni, A. (2016). Institutional environment and corporate governance. *Corporate Governance: An International Review, 24*(2), 82–84. https://doi.org/10.1111/corg.12160

Kumar, P., & Zattoni, A. (2018). Ownership structure, corporate governance, and institutional environment: Going beyond managerial opportunism and the principal-agent framework. *Corporate Governance: An International Review, 26*(2), 82–83. https://doi.org/10.1111/corg.12232

La Porta, R., & Lopez-De-Silanes, F. (1998). Capital markets and legal institutions. In *Beyond the Washington consensus: Institutions matter* (pp. 73–92). World Bank.

La Porta, R., Lopez-De-Silanes, F., Shleifer, A., & Vishny, R. W. (1997). Legal determinants of external finance. *The Journal of Finance, 52*(3), 1131–1150. https://doi.org/10.1111/j.1540-6261.1997.tb02727.x

La Porta, R., Lopez-De-Silanes, F., & Shleifer, A. (1999a). Corporate ownership around the world. *The Journal of Finance, 54*(2), 471–517. https://doi.org/10.1111/0022-1082.00115

La Porta, R., Lopez-De-Silanes, F., Shleifer, A., & Vishny, R. (1999b, December). *Investor protection: Origins, consequences, and reform*. (NBER Working Paper n° w7428, Available at SSRN https://ssrn.com/abstract=227587.

La Porta, R., Lopez-De-Silanes, F., Shleifer, A., & Vishny, R. (2000). Investor protection and corporate governance. *Journal of Financial Economics, 58*(1–2), 3–27. https://doi.org/10.1016/s0304-405x(00)00065-9

La Porta, R., Lopez-De-Silanes, F., Shleifer, A., & Vishny, R. (2002). Investor protection and corporate valuation. *The Journal of Finance, 57*(3), 1147–1170. https://doi.org/10.1111/1540-6261.00457

La Rosa, F., Paternostro, S., & Bernini, F. (2021). Corporate and regional governance antecedents of the legality rating of private Italian companies. *Journal of Management and Governance*. https://doi.org/10.1007/s10997-021-09612-7

Lagasio, V. (2021). Corporate governance, ownership, and performance: A closer look at the Italian case. *Corporate Ownership and Control, 19*(1), 8–16. https://doi.org/10.22495/cocv19i1art1

Lambert, D. (2021). Disciplinary power in corporate governance: A Foucauldian analysis of the emergence and development of proxy advisors. *Accounting History, 26*(3), 409–433. https://doi.org/10.1177/1032373220986232

Lennox, C. (2014). Auditor tenure and rotation. In *The Routledge companion to auditing* (Vol. 1, pp. 89–106). https://prod.marshall.usc.edu/sites/default/files/clennox/intellcont/Book%20chapter-1.pdf

Lepore, L., Landriani, L., Pisano, S., D'Amore, G., & Pozzoli, S. (2022). Corporate governance in the digital age: The role of social media and board independence in CSR disclosure. Evidence from Italian listed companies. *Journal of Management and Governance.* https://doi.org/10.1007/s10997-021-09617-2

Melis, A., & Zattoni, A. (2017). *A primer on corporate governance: Italy* (1st ed.). Business Expert Press, LLC.

Mielcarz, P., Osiichuk, D., & Puławska, K. (2021). Increasing shareholder focus: The repercussions of the 2015 corporate governance reform in Japan. *Journal of Management and Governance, 2021*, 1–31. https://doi.org/10.1007/s10997-021-09619-0

Miles, J. R., Anders, C., Kivlighan, D. M., III, Platt, A., & a. B. (2021). Cultural ruptures: Addressing microaggressions in group therapy. *Group Dynamics: Theory, Research, and Practice, 25*(1), 74–88. https://doi.org/10.1037/gdn0000149

Mirone, F., Sancetta, G., Sardanelli, D., & Mele, S. (2021). How independent directors affect firms' performance and sustainability: An analysis of Italian firms. *Corporate Governance and Organizational Behavior Review, 5*(2), 72–81. https://doi.org/10.22495/cgobrv5i2p7

Moscariello, N., Pizzo, M., Govorun, D., & Kostyuk, A. (2019). Independent minority directors and firm value in a principal–principal agency setting: Evidence from Italy. *Journal of Management and Governance, 23*(1), 165–194. https://doi.org/10.1007/s10997-018-9421-0

Nigri, G., & Di Stefano, R. (2021). Family business in Italy: A humanistic transition of assets and values from one generation to the next. *Humanistic Management Journal, 6*(1), 57–76. https://doi.org/10.1007/s41463-020-00085-8

North, D. C. (1990). *Institutions, institutional change and economic performance*. Cambridge University Press.

OECD. (2021). *OECD corporate governance Factbook.* https://www.oecd.org/corporate/corporate-governance-factbook.htm

OIC Founders. (2022). Organismo Italiano di Contabilità. https://www.fondazioneoic.eu/?lang=en

Omura, H. (2020). Stewardship activities and agency problems after Japanese corporate governance reform. *SSRN Electronic Journal, 1-27.* https://doi.org/10.2139/ssrn.3733196

Panda, B., & Leepsa, N. M. (2017). Agency theory: Review of theory and evidence on problems and perspectives. *Indian Journal of Corporate Governance, 10*(1), 74–95. https://doi.org/10.1177/0974686217701467

Parente, T. C., & Machado Filho, C. A. P. (2020). Conselhos de Administração no Brasil: Revisão da literatura e agenda de pesquisa. *Revista de Administração Mackenzie, 21*(6), 1–35. https://doi.org/10.1590/1678-6971/eRAMD200066

PoliS-Lombardia. (2020). *Instituto Regional de Apoio às Políticas da Lombardia.* PoliS-Lombardia. https://www.polis.lombardia.it/wps/portal/site/polis

Puchniak, D. W. (2007). The Japanization of American corporate governance? Evidence of the never-ending history for corporate law. *Asian-Pacific Law & Policy Journal, 9*(1), 1–64. https://ssrn.com/abstract=2256489

Repubblica Italiana. (1942a). *Codigo Civile*. Presidenza del consiglio dei ministri. https://www.normattiva.it/uri-res/N2Ls?urn:nir:stato:legge:1990-10-10;287!vig=

Repubblica Italiana. (1942b). Regio Decreto, 16 marzo 1942, n. 267. Italy. lla Legge Vigente/Presidenza del consiglio dei ministri. Available in.: https://www.normattiva.it/uri-res/N2Ls?urn:nir:stato:regio.decreto:1942-03-16;267!vig=.

Repubblica Italiana. (1975). *Decreto del Presidente della Repubblica n° 136, 31 marzo 1975*. Presidenza del consiglio dei ministri. Marzo. https://www.normattiva.it/uri-res/N2Ls?urn:nir:presidente.repubblica:decreto:1975-03-31;136

Repubblica Italiana. (1990). *Legge n. 287, 10 ottobre 1990*. Presidenza del consiglio dei ministri. Ottobre. https://www.normattiva.it/uri-res/N2Ls?urn:nir:stato:legge:1990-10-10;287!vig=

Repubblica Italiana. (1992). *Decreto Legislativo n° 88, 27 gennaio, 1992*. Presidenza del consiglio dei ministri. gennaio. https://www.normattiva.it/atto/caricaDettaglioAtto?atto.dataPubblicazioneGazzetta=1992-02-14&atto.codiceRedazionale=092G0134&atto.articolo.numero=0&atto.articolo.sottoArticolo=1&atto.articolo.sottoArticolo1=10&qId=d2bf66f9-b4eb-4247-ae1e-e139d3de7865&tabID=0.671322688488859&title=lbl.dettaglioAtto

Repubblica Italiana. (2005). *Legge n° 262, 28 dicembre, 2005*. Normativa II Portale Della Legge Viggente. Dicembre. https://www.normattiva.it/atto/caricaDettaglioAtto?atto.dataPubblicazioneGazzetta=2005-12-28&atto.codiceRedazionale=005G0295&atto.articolo.numero=0&atto.articolo.sottoArticolo=1&atto.articolo.sottoArticolo1=10&qId=e03d276d-5d9b-4402-8fba-262391f83efb&tabID=0.671322688488859&title=lbl.dettaglioAtto

Repubblica Italiana. (2010). *Decreto Legislativo n° 39, 27 gennaio 2010*. Normativa II Portale Della Legge Viggente. Gennaio. https://www.normattiva.it/atto/caricaDettaglioAtto?atto.dataPubblicazioneGazzetta=2010-03-23&atto.codiceRedazionale=010G0057&atto.articolo.numero=0&atto.articolo.sottoArticolo=1&atto.articolo.sottoArticolo1=10&qId=10025e4d-8660-49ab-9c80-2cb983e4f663&tabID=0.671322688488859&title=lbl.dettaglioAtto

Repubblica Italiana. (2011). *Legge n° 120, 12 luglio 2011*. Presidenza del consiglio dei ministri. luglio. https://www.normattiva.it/uri-res/N2Ls?urn:nir:stato:legge:2011-07-12;120!vig=

Repubblica Italiana. (2016). *Decreto Legislativo n° 135, 17 luglio, 2016*. Normativa II Portale Della Legge Viggente. Luglio. https://www.normattiva.it/atto/caricaDettaglioAtto?atto.dataPubblicazioneGazzetta=2016-07-21&atto.codiceRedazionale=16G00151&atto.articolo.numero=0&atto.articolo.sottoArticolo=1&atto.articolo.sottoArticolo1=10&qId=bdb13d8a-3a11-4545-ad3d-d3aa4cb94586&tabID=0.671322688488859&title=lbl.dettaglioAtto

Repubblica Italiana. (2019). *Legge n° 160, 27 dicembre 2019*. Presidenza del consiglio dei ministri. Dicembre. https://www.normattiva.it/atto/caricaDettaglioAtto?atto.dataPubblicazioneGazzetta=2019-12-30&atto.codiceRedazionale=19G00165&atto.articolo.numero=0&atto.articolo.sottoArticolo=1&atto.articolo.sottoArticolo1=10&qId=530ef136-9d4d-45bc-9e35-fc1e89a2fd30&tabI

Rizzato, F., Busso, D., Devalle, A., & Zerbetto, A. (2019). Corporate governance system in Italy: Compliance and quality. *Corporate Ownership and Control, 16*(1–1), 217–133. https://doi.org/10.22495/cocv16i1c1art9

Roe, M. J. (2000). Political preconditions to separating ownership from corporate control. *Stanford Law Review, 53*, 539–608. https://doi.org/10.2139/ssrn.165143

Salvioni, D. M., & Gennari, F. (2016). Corporate governance, ownership, and sustainability. *Corporate Ownership and Control, 13*(2CONT3), 604–612. https://doi.org/10.22495/cocv13i2c3p9

Shleifer, A., & Wolfenzon, D. (2002). Investor protection and equity markets. *Journal of Financial Economics, 66*(1), 3–27. https://doi.org/10.1016/s0304-405x(02)00149-6

Strampelli, G. (2020). Institutional investor stewardship in Italian corporate governance. *SSRN Electronic Journal, 2020*, 1–30. https://doi.org/10.2139/ssrn.3626288

Tibiletti, V., Marchini, P. L., Furlotti, K., & Medioli, A. (2021). Does corporate governance matter in corporate social responsibility disclosure? Evidence from Italy in the "era of sustainability". *Corporate Social Responsibility and Environmental Management, 28*(2), 896–907. https://doi.org/10.1002/csr.2097

Zattoni, A. (2009). Corporate governance in Italy: The structural conflict of interests between majority and minority shareholders. In F. J. Lopez Iturriaga (Ed.), *Codes of good governance around the world*. Nova Science Publishers.

Zattoni, A. (2019). The evolution of corporate governance in Italy: Formal convergence or path-dependence? *Corporate Governance and Research & Development Studies, 1*, 13–35. https://doi.org/10.3280/cgrds1-2019oa8799

Zattoni, A. (2020). *Corporate governance – How to design good companies*. Bocconi University Press.

Zattoni, A., & Cuomo, F. (2015). Institutional change and ownership patterns in Italy. In M. Goranova & L. V. Ryan (Eds.), *Shareholder empowerment* (1st ed., pp. 267–296). Palgrave Macmillan. https://doi.org/10.1057/9781137373939_12

Zattoni, A., & Mosca, C. (2012). Corporate governance and initial public offerings in Italy. In A. Zattoni & W. Judge (Eds.), *Corporate governance and initial public offerings: An international perspective* (pp. 210–237). Cambridge University Press.

Zellweger, T. M., Eddleston, K. A., & Kellermanns, F. W. (2010). Exploring the concept of families: Introducing family firm identity. *Journal of Family Business Strategy, 1*(1), 54–63. https://doi.org/10.1016/j.jfbs.2009.12.003

Chapter 8
Australia

Corporate Governance in Australia: Issues, Systems, Characteristics, Regulations, and Opportunities

Luis Felipe Orsatto, Rafael Vaz Palmeira, and Sardar M. N. Islam

8.1 Introduction

Australia is the largest country in Oceania. In March 2023, it had a population of 26,473,055 inhabitants. Its GDP per capita in 2022 was USD 70,011.00, with a total GDP, also in 2022 of about USD 1820 trillion. An active member of the Organization for Economic Co-operation and Development (OECD) since 1971, its currency is the Australian Dollar (AUD), and it is considered a developed country, being the fifth country with the highest Human Development Index (HDI) in the world (HDI = 0.951) (Australian Bureau of Statistics, 2023; Organization for Economic Co-operation and Development, 2023; The World Bank, 2023; United Nations, 2023).

Although it is not as competitive as the USA and the UK, Australia has one of the most developed equity markets in the Asia-Pacific region. Such size and regional competitiveness might improve managers' freedom of action, leading them to pursue their interests (Dignam, 2007; Gray et al., 2007; Shan et al., 2019).

The work *The Modern Corporation and Private Property* by Berle and Means (1932) highlighted the discussion of the separation between property rights and company control. Berle and Means (1932) reflect on ownership logic in this study. The owner, or shareholders, no longer exercise control over the company's destiny

L. F. Orsatto (✉)
State University of Western Paraná, Cascavel, Brazil
e-mail: luis.orsatto@unioeste.br

R. V. Palmeira
University of Salamanca, Salamanca, Spain
e-mail: rafaelvaz@usal.es

S. M. N. Islam
Victoria University, Melbourne, VIC, Australia
e-mail: sardar.islam@vu.edu.au

C. B. Macagnan (ed.), *Corporate Governance in Capital Markets*, CSR, Sustainability, Ethics & Governance,
https://doi.org/10.1007/978-3-031-94751-3_8

but delegates it to a group responsible for managing the entity. The authors point out that this can create a divergence between the owners' interests and those who control the company. Berle and Means (1932) also highlight the powers of those who control the company. These powers are the power over the shareholding of shares, the power over the distribution of profits on the shares, and the power to change the original contractual rights of the shareholders. In short, it is possible to observe a specific concern with the role of the shareholder of a corporation. According to Berle and Means (1932), the interests of the shareholders are relegated to the desire of the group that controls the entity, leaving those only with the expectation that the controlling group exercises the management of the company, seeking to maximize dividends.

Jensen and Meckling (1976) developed a firm's ownership structure theory by looking at the agency, property rights, and finance theories. In this study, the authors focus on the behavioral implications and the analysis of agency costs caused by contractual agreements between the company's owners and managers. Thus, to monitor and to minimize the risks related to the agent's activities, the owners incur costs, which are understood as agency costs, and it is unlikely that, in a relationship between principal and agent, such cost is zero (Jensen & Meckling, 1976). Thus, based on concepts of separation between ownership and control and ownership structure, this chapter aims to understand corporate governance characteristics in Australia, especially in companies listed on the Australian Securities Exchange (ASX), the central stock exchange in this country. For ASX, corporate governance is the responsibilities, rules, relationships, systems, and processes by which companies exercise and manage authority (ASX, 2019).

The Australian stock market, strongly focused on the natural resources sector, is characterized by good governance standards (Nguyen et al., 2018). However, it was not always like that. In 2001, Australia witnessed a series of corporate meltdowns in various sectors, including the bankruptcy of large corporations such as mining companies Centaur and Pasminco, HIH Insurance, telecommunications company One Tel, and Ansett Airlines. The loss from the bankruptcy of these and other companies in this period was more than USD 13 billion, with a loss of at least 20,000 jobs. Before this crisis, huge performance bonuses were paid to Australian companies' CEOs, with public opinion questioning the validity of this pay-for-performance model for executives. The information asymmetry related to the remuneration between principal and agent was considered responsible for the governance failure and the Australian corporate control market's impaired functioning in this period. In this way, the disclosure of the remuneration of directors and executives became a relevant issue in Australia from the first decade of the twenty-first century, driven by the pressure exerted by institutional investors as a reaction to governance failures (Gray et al., 2007; Mees & Smith, 2019; O'Sullivan et al., 2008; Riaz et al., 2013; Robins, 2006).

Looking at Australia from an international perspective, this country has been one of the key jurisdictions for corporate governance reform, providing a unique environment to assess the impact of corporate governance mechanisms. This uniqueness can be explained by Australia following the Anglo-American corporate governance system, with Australian companies having similar board structures and mechanisms to the US and UK boards. Furthermore, in the Australian market, banks do not play an active role as company shareholders, as in countries like Germany and Japan. At the same time, compared to the US and UK, corporate control of the Australian market is much less active as a corrective mechanism against management entrenchment and corporate bankruptcy. Another striking aspect is that most large Australian corporations are highly unionized, in which such unions actively monitor management. Differences also concern the competitive environment, company size, ownership structure, audit regulation, and shareholder activism. These characteristics make the duty of internal governance mechanisms, such as independent boards and management incentives, possibly more important in Australia than in these other countries. As highlighted earlier, such characteristics make the Australian stock market a unique object for research on corporate governance mechanisms (Al Farooque et al., 2021; Mees & Smith, 2019; Monem, 2013; Nguyen et al., 2016; Pham et al., 2012; Shan et al., 2019).

Previous studies on governance in Australia have some limitations, as they were limited to just one point of view on this topic. Moreover, those studies did not cover all the aspects discussed in this chapter, individually exploring subjects such as the Australian capital market, shareholding system, or dividend policy in Australian companies. The difference in this chapter is that it analyzes the governance system in Australia as a whole and all its peculiarities. Thus, we hope to contribute to the discussion since this country has unique characteristics that differ from other countries: the significant presence of unions, the Anglo-American governance model, and a low presence of banks as shareholders.

This chapter presents the following structure: Australian capital markets; Shareholding system, dividend policy, minority shareholder rights, and ownership structure of companies listed on the ASX; Australian corporate law and regulation; Australian accounting system; Audit of companies listed on the ASX; Governance codes used in Australia; and Governance structure of companies listed on the ASX. Finally, the final considerations are presented.

8.2 Capital Market

In 1987, due to the merger of several existing state stock exchanges, the *Australian Stock Exchange* (ASX) was created, Australia's first national stock exchange. The Australian Securities Exchange (ASX), the current Australian stock exchange, emerged after the merger of the Australian Stock Exchange and the Sydney Futures Exchange in July 2006. In December 2022, ASX, considered the leading stock exchange in Australia, had 2135 equity-issuing companies, with a market value of AUD 2.463 trillion, making it the 16th largest stock exchange globally by market value. Of all the companies listed, 1977 are domestic, and 158 are foreign. ASX offers integrated listing, trading, clearing, settlement, technical information, technology, data, and post-trade services. Figure 8.1 shows the evolution of ASX Market

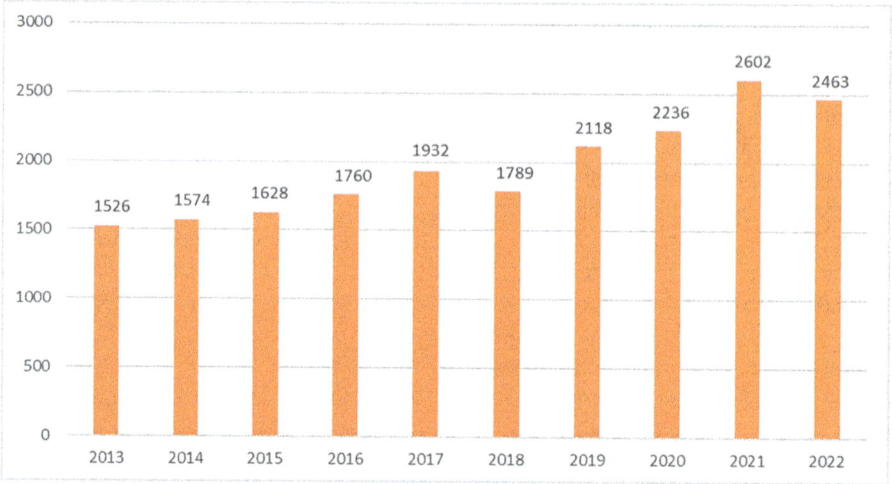

Fig. 8.1 ASX Market Capitalization 2013–2022 (in USD billion). Source: World Federation of Exchanges (2022)

Capitalization between 2013 and 2022 (ASX, 2023; Mees & Smith, 2019; Rashid & Islam, 2014; World Federation of Exchanges, 2022).

ASX follows S&P Dow Jones's GICS® industry ranking methodology, and its 2135 listed companies are divided into 11 industry sectors (ASX, 2023): The energy sector is divided into oil and gas drilling, equipment and services manufacturing companies, oil, gas, or fuel exploration, production, refining, storage, and transportation. This sector is responsible for 6.6% of Australia-listed firms. The largest company in this sector is Woodside Petroleum Ltd., with a market value of AUD 68.14 billion in October 2023.

The Materials sector is divided into metal manufacturing and processing, mining, chemical, building materials, containers, packaging, and paper industries. It represents approximately 34.43% of Australia's listed firms, with the most relevant company in this sector being the BHP Group Limited, with a market value of AUD 227.28 billion in October 2023.

The Industrial sector, which comprises capital goods industries, companies providing services to the capital goods industries, and transport companies such as airlines, road, rail, maritime, and transport infrastructure companies, is responsible for 7.47% of the listed firms. The most valuable company in this sector is the Transurban Group, which is focused on mobility and had a market value of AUD 38.99 billion in October 2023.

The consumer discretionary comprises retail companies, consumer service providers (hotels, restaurants, and leisure businesses), consumer durables industries (textiles, apparel, and luxury goods), and automotive components. This sector represents 5.52% of Australian listed firms, and the highest market value in this sector belongs to Wesfarmers Limited, with AUD 60.08 billion in October 2023.

The consumer staples sector comprises the food, beverage, and tobacco industries, the household and personal products industries (personal hygiene items, vitamins, and supplements), and the retail and distribution companies of food and medicines. Woolworths Group Limited is the largest company in this sector, with a market value of AUD 46.15 billion in October 2023.

The healthcare sector includes companies producing and selling medical equipment and supplies in the pharmaceutical and biotechnology industries. The company with the highest market capitalization in this sector, with AUD 115.08 billion in October 2023, is CSL Limited.

The financial sector comprises companies providing various financial services (such as asset management, personal finance, and mortgage finance), insurance companies, and banks. The largest company in this sector is the Commonwealth Bank of Australia, with a market value of AUD 170.29 billion in October 2023, and the sector represents almost 20% of Australian listed firms.

The information technology sector is divided into three primary industries: software development companies, internet service providers, and data processing; hardware manufacturing industries; and semiconductor industries and their equipment. The largest company in this sector is Wisetech Global Limited, with a market value of AUD 21.50 billion in October 2023.

The communication services sector comprises the media and entertainment industry and provides mobile telecommunications services. Telstra Limited has the highest market capitalization in this sector, with AUD 44.94 billion in October 2023.

The utilities sector comprises companies generating, supplying, and distributing electricity, gas, water, and sewage. Origin Energy Limited has the highest market value in this sector, with AUD 15.95 billion in October 2023.

The real estate sector is divided into real estate investment funds and companies providing real estate development, sales, and management services. Goodman Group is the largest company in this sector, with a market value of AUD 42.65 billion in October 2023.

In the same sense, Fig. 8.2 shows the division into sectors of the companies listed on the ASX in October 2023. Among these companies, 34.43% are from the Materials sector, 19.85% from Financials, 7.69% from the health care sector, 7.65% from the Information technology sector, 7.47% from Industrials, 6.6% from the Energy sector, 5.52% from the Consumer Discretionary sector, 3.46% from Consumer staples, 3.18% from Communication Services, 3.03 from Real estate and finally 1.12% from companies in the Utility sector (ASX, 2023).

The Australian financial system has two regulatory bodies: the Australian Securities and Investment Commission (ASIC) and the Australian Prudential Regulatory Authority (APRA). The APRA is an independent statutory authority that oversees banking, insurance, and retirement institutions. It promotes the stability of the financial system in Australia, playing a significant role in regularizing financial institutions and maintaining capital adequacy requirements in those organizations. In the meantime, it is healthy to understand that the Australian financial system is governed by the Reserve Bank of Australia, the Australian central bank. This entity conducts Australia's monetary policy, issuing the Australian Dollar, managing

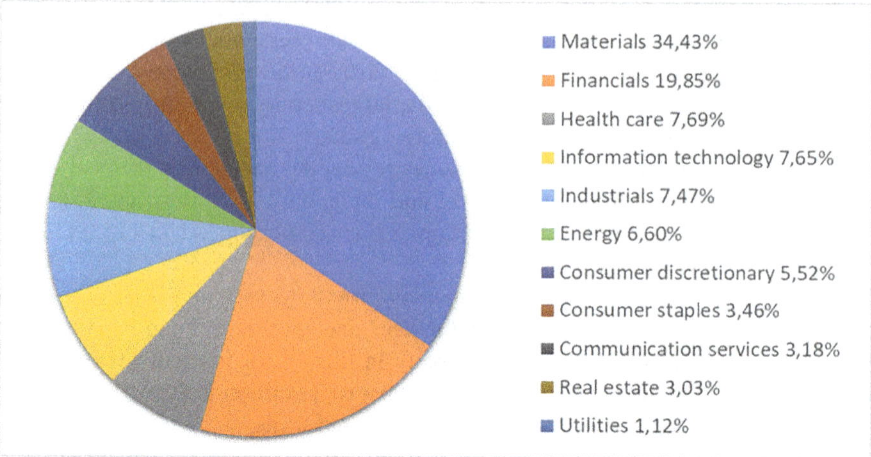

Fig. 8.2 Sectors of the companies listed on the ASX. Source: ASX (2023)

Australia's gold and foreign currency reserves, and providing banking and registry services to various Australian government agencies and several central banks and institutions (Australian Prudential Regulatory Authority, 2021; Rashid & Islam, 2014; Reserve Bank of Australia, 2021).

On the other hand, the Australian Securities and Investment Commission (ASIC) is the Australian capital market's control and regulation body, playing an essential role in protecting shareholder rights. ASIC was created by the Australian Securities and Investments Commission Act (ASIC Act) in 2001. Since then, several tasks have been under its scope, such as:

(a) maintaining, facilitating, and improving the financial market's performance and the entities that comprise it; promoting investors' participation safely.
(b) administering the law effectively and with minimal procedural requirements.
(c) make publicly available information about companies and other bodies (Australian Securities and Investment Commission, 2021; OECD, 2021; Rashid & Islam, 2014).

The vision of ASIC is to establish a fair, strong, and efficient financial market. To achieve this, ASIC uses a range of regulatory tools to deliver positive consumer and investor outcomes, address misconduct, and stimulate the innovative development of the financial system. ASIC regulates financial services and consumer credit activities, licenses and supervises financial services providers, and ensures compliance with established standards. It also oversees the activities of authorized financial markets operating in Australia. In administering and enforcing various laws, including the ASIC Act and the Corporations Act, ASIC has the power to register financial services providers, maintain publicly accessible registers, grant financial service and credit licenses, intervene to ban illegal products, create legislative rules to ensure financial market integrity and seek civil penalties against violators. ASIC's powers are designed to protect consumers from misconduct and harm related to financial products and services (Australian Securities and Investment Commission, 2021).

8.3 Shareholder System, Dividend Policy, Minority Shareholders' Rights, and Ownership Structure

If a company wishes to make an initial public offering and be admitted to the Australian Securities Exchange (ASX), it must meet specific requirements such as (ASX, 2021a). It must have a minimum number of shareholders of 300 unaffiliated investors, with an investment of AUD 2000.00 each. It also reports the free float must be 20%. Besides, the aggregate profit of at least AUD 1 million from continuing operations in the last three years more consolidated profit of at least AUD 500,000.00 from continuing operations in the previous 12 months, or at least AUD 4 million in net tangible assets, or market capitalization of at least AUD 15 million.

Three different shares are traded on the Australian Securities Exchange (ASX): ordinary, preference, and partly paid shares. Each type of stock has its characteristics, which directly affect how investors allocate their resources. Most of the shares traded on the ASX are ordinary shares, whose main feature is the granting of the right to vote at the company's general meeting and to participate in any dividends or distribution of assets in a possible liquidation of the company, always in proportion to the number of shares that the ordinary shareholder owns. However, this share does not grant special rights to receive dividends (ASX, 2021b, 2014b; OECD, 2021).

Another type of share trading on the ASX is preference shares, which give the holder priority over ordinary shareholders in paying dividends or the company's liquidation. It is also important to point out that there are different rights and characteristics even among the preference shares. Generally, holding preference shares has voting rights restricted to circumstances or resolutions. Nevertheless, these rights will depend on the terms of the shares. Some examples of cases in which holders of preference shares are entitled to vote (ASX, 2021b, 2014b; OECD, 2023):

- Proposals for reducing the entity's share capital.
- Resolutions to approve share repurchase terms.
- Proposals that affect the rights inherent to the preferred share.
- Proposal for the sale of all the company's assets and undertakings.
- Property liquidation proposal.

Finally, partly paid or contributed shares are traded on the ASX. These shares are issued without the company demanding the full-issue price payment. For this to occur, a future date or date is defined in which the company will have the right to redeem all or part of the special issue price, and the shareholder at the time of the purchase option is obliged to pay the purchase option. As a rule, a holder of a partly paid share has the same voting rights and the same rights to receive dividends as a holder of ordinary shares. However, such rights will be proportional to the amount paid for the share (ASX, 2021b, 2014b; OECD, 2023).

The literature review shows that corporate governance mechanisms such as board size, independence, and audit quality can significantly influence Australian companies' dividend payment decisions. This positive relationship implies that board and institutional investors can use dividend payments to mitigate conflict of interest issues in Australian companies (Al Farooque et al., 2021; Cotter & Silvester, 2003; Setia-Atmaja et al., 2009).

As for the rights of minority shareholders, it can be admitted that the regulatory authorities effectively protect such holders of shares, providing solid legal protection for predominantly minority shareholders. Also, in this sense, the presence of financial institutions as shareholders block tends to reduce the risks for minority shareholders, as they have greater power to pressure managers so that cash flows are not diverted, and capital is used more efficiently. Optimized to maximize shareholder wealth (Al Farooque et al., 2021; Pham et al., 2012; Rashid & Islam, 2014).

Along with Finland, Iceland, the United Kingdom, and the United States, Australia makes up the countries where the capital market has the lowest concentration of ownership, measured as the combined share of the three largest shareholders. In these five jurisdictions, less than 20% of companies maintain ownership concentration above 50% of share capital among the three largest holders of shares. In Australia, only 19% of companies do the three largest shareholders own more than 50% of the shares. Furthermore, the average share of the 20 largest shareholders of companies listed on the ASX is around 50%, while this proportion of ownership concentration in the US and UK stock exchanges exceeds 60% (OECD, 2021).

Studies on the Australian capital market corroborate the assertion that shareholding is dispersed, classifying the ownership structure as following the Anglo-Saxon "outsider" system. However, such research also demonstrates that this ownership structure presents blocks of ownership concentration despite this context of dispersed shareholding. The proportion of shares held by institutional investors in Australia tends to be somewhat lower than in other common law jurisdictions such as the US and UK (Dignam, 2007; Monem, 2013; Pham et al., 2012; Rashid & Islam, 2014; Shan et al., 2019).

Still, concerning institutional investors, the ownership structure of companies listed on the Australian Stock Exchange reflects the influence and importance of pension funds (retirement plans) co-sponsored by unions, which hold more than 10% of all the votes of listed companies on ASX. Australian pension funds face fewer conflicts of interest than other institutional investors. They have considerable influence in monitoring management activities, playing an essential role in corporate governance mechanisms in the companies where they own shares (Mees & Smith, 2019; Pham et al., 2012).

8.4 Legislation and Corporate Regulation

From the 1980s to the early twenty-first century, significant corporate governance issues triggered a general reform in the Australian corporate regulatory framework. One of the turning points was the institution, in 2003, of a corporate responsibility index, known as CRI, financed by the Australian government. However, regulatory initiatives originated in 1938 in the province of Victoria. As a result, for the first time, companies based in Australia must disclose the remuneration in brackets of all executives with income above AUD 100,000.00. Over the years, Australian corporate law has been improved, with particular attention to improving the disclosure of the remuneration of executives of companies in this country (Dignam, 2007; Kemp, 2011; Mees & Smith, 2019; Riaz et al., 2013).

In the 1980s, specifically in 1986, a set of disclosure rules was enacted through Clauses 24 and 28, Annex 7 of the Company Codes for the Province of New South Wales. According to this legislation, companies must disclose compensation information, identifying the highest-paid directors and five executives individually. However, this strict disclosure regime was short-lived and faced intense criticism from business organizations, being replaced in 1987. Still, in 1987, through amendment No. 206 of the Company Regulation, the listed companies were requested to disclose the total annual compensation of executives earning more than AUD 100,000.00. In addition, directors' remuneration should be disclosed in the range of AUD 10,000.00, with no need to identify the executives (Riaz et al., 2013).

Another legislative initiative regarding disclosure was the Company Law Review Act (CLR Act) of 1998. This act introduced Section 300(A), which required listed companies to disclose three aspects of director and executive compensation: (a) the broad policy regarding the nature of emoluments and the number of directors and executives company seniors; (b) a discussion of the link between the company's remuneration policy and its performance; and (c) details of the compensation of each director and the company's five highest-paid executives. However, this initiative was thwarted due to intense criticism from business organizations, leading to various short-lived disclosure regimes. The substantial confusion surrounding the interpretation of "fees" led to criticism. Such criticism forced the Australian Securities and Investments Commission (ASIC) to issue an Interim Practice Note, PN68, in November 1998 to clarify some terms of the CLR Act (Clarkson et al., 2006; Riaz, 2016; Riaz et al., 2013).

Despite this, the big event that changed corporate governance paradigms in Australia took place in the first half of 2001, before the famous Enron case in the United States, with a series of corporate collapses in various sectors, including corruption scandals, governance, and bankruptcy of large companies, with the loss of around 20,000 jobs. Three examples of defaults can explain what happened in this period: One Tel's bankruptcy, Harris Scarfe, and HIH Insurance—in the case of One Tel's telecommunications company, a good part of the problems consisted of administrative and managerial ineptitude, with a flawed billing system that made the company unable to collect all its revenues.

At the same time, relevant financial information was withheld from the board of directors, and the company eventually collapsed with around AUD 2.4 billion in debt and losses. The case of retailer Harris Scarfe was somehow different, nevertheless equally severe. The company went into voluntary liquidation after six years of disclosing inflated asset values, among other accounting irregularities, in its reports without the board of directors and external auditors realizing something was wrong. Thus, the *Chief* Financial Officer (CFO) was sentenced to imprisonment for six years after pleading guilty to corruption charges (Gray et al., 2007; O'Sullivan et al., 2008; Robins, 2006).

The case of HIH Insurance, then the second-largest insurer in Australia, is considered the most significant corporate scandal in that country, as it affected many consumer policyholders. This scandal resulted in enormous public unrest and generated discomfort in the Australian government, which created a commission to investigate and identify the causes that resulted in losses amounting to AUD 5.3 billion for the company. A legal inquiry was instituted and lasted more than 18 months. It was concluded that the leading cause of the collapse of HIH was the recurrent failure to set aside enough money to pay the claims of insured consumers.

During the court proceedings, it became clear that both the auditing firm Arthur Andersen LLP (responsible for the firm's external audit) and the Australian Prudential Regulatory Authority (APRA) ignored a July 1998 document that revealed that HIH had, for several years, under-reserved amounts related to the payment of indemnities. Coincidentally or not, there was an independent director on the audit committee in none of these three highlighted companies (One Tel, Harris Scarfe, and HIH Insurance) (Gray et al., 2007; Robins, 2006).

Robins (2006) documents that after the cases of scandals and corporate collapses, the legislation on corporate governance in Australia was revised, which resulted in some movements that changed the landscape of governance in this country, such as the creation of a corporate governance council (CGC) to strengthen the disclosure requirements of the top 500 listed companies. The rules governing the disclosure of reports remained the responsibility of the ASX, but supervision and monitoring for the ASIC. The "Group of 100" also introduced a code of conduct, representing the CFOs of the top 100 ASX-listed companies. Additionally, the Australian Securities and Investment Commission (ASIC) and the Australian Prudential Regulatory Authority (APRA) reviewed the performance and responsibility of regulatory authorities in the corporate sector.

Furthermore, the enactment of a corporate law economic reform law, the Corporate Law Economic Reform Program Act, known as CLERP 9, took effect on July 1, 2004, and amended some provisions of the Corporations Act of 2001, strengthening the financial reporting framework. Still, on CLERP 9, the Australian government devoted attention to ensuring that the legislation was supported by industry and the public and was designed both in response to calls to reduce excessive executive pay in Australian corporations and restore public confidence. CLERP 9 was intended to help shareholders and other capital market operators price the risk associated with a particular agent, facilitating decision-making on future company transactions. In addition, this law promoted greater responsibility and transparency of information and data by clearly and timely disclosing the remuneration of company administrators and managers (Banks et al., 2009; Kemp, 2011; Mees & Smith, 2019; Riaz et al., 2013).

It is worth noting that, until today, a regulation considered to be hybrid is in force as a result of the enactment of CLERP 9, under the responsibility of the Australian government and the Principles of Good Practices of Corporate Governance and Recommendations of Best Practices, conceived by Corporate Governance Council (CGC), linked to the then Australian Stock Exchange. While CLERP 9 forced companies to disclose information on the compensation of directors and executives, ASX, through good governance practices, pressured listed entities to implement the best existing governance tools, especially concerning the compensation of directors and executives. Thus, CLERP 9 and the ASX Principles of Good Governance Practice were introduced relatively quickly in response to the crashes in Australia and are credited as two distinct forms of regulation that complement each other to provide a hybrid regulatory framework in this country (OECD, 2021; Riaz, 2016).

8.5 Accounting and Auditing System

The Australian Accounting Standards Board (AASB) is the government body that develops and standardizes accounting norms and standards for Australian entities according to the international standards set by the International Financial Reporting Standards (IFRS). Although Australia has adopted IFRS standards since January 1, 2005, the convergence with international standards, organized by the then International Accounting Standards Committee (IASC), occurred in 1996 (International Financial Reporting Standards, 2017).

The AASB's mission is to create and uphold high-quality financial reporting standards that encompass all sectors of the Australian economy and play a part in shaping global financial reporting standards. The primary objectives of the AASB regarding standard-setting are as follows:

(a) To release Australian adaptations of documents from the International Accounting Standards Board.
(b) Formulate standards that ensure the uniform treatment of similar transactions.
(c) To play a substantial role in shaping the evolution of International Financial Reporting Standards.
(d) Pinpoint areas that necessitate fundamental reassessment and introduce standards to address those areas.
(e) To advocate for the worldwide uniform application and interpretation of accounting standards. (Australian Accounting Standards Board, 2023).

The Australian Accounting Standards have two requirements for accounting reporting: "Level 1—Australian Accounting Standards" and "Level 2—Australian Accounting Standards—Reduced Disclosure Requirements." All IFRS standards are incorporated into Level 1 of the Australian Accounting Standards, with the addition of information on the applicability of each standard in the Australian environment. Level 2 comprises the exact requirements as Level 1 regarding recognition, measurement, and presentation, but disclosure requirements are substantially reduced. The Australian government and state, territorial, and local governments, and all for-profit entities that are required by law to be publicly accountable (among them ASX-listed publicly traded companies, pension funds, and financial entities) must follow Level 1 requirements, that is, they meet all standards established by IFRS. On the other hand, public sector entities other than the Australian government and state, territorial, and local governments, as well as private, not-for-profit entities, and private for-profit entities that are not listed on the ASX, may meet both the Levels 1 and 2 Australian Accounting Standards requirements (International Financial Reporting Standards, 2017).

Another important organization is the Financial Reporting Council (FRC), which is responsible for supervising the effectiveness of Australia's financial reporting framework. In this sense, the primary responsibilities encompass overseeing the processes of setting accounting and auditing standards for both public and private sectors, offering strategic counsel regarding the quality of audits carried out by Australian auditors, and furnishing advice to the Minister on relevant issues that impact Australia's financial reporting framework (Financial Reporting Council, 2023).

Under the Australian Securities and Investments Commission Act 2001, the FRC's objectives require accounting standards to provide information that is not only easily understandable but also relevant and reliable for assessing performance, financial position, financing, and investment. The FRC also oversees auditing standards, which should offer comprehensive guidance to Australian auditors in forming opinions on financial report compliance with the Corporations Act and require the preparation of auditor reports that are reliable and understandable to financial report users (Financial Reporting Council, 2023).

As for auditing standards, the Auditing and Assurance Standards Board (AUASB), an independent and non-corporate Commonwealth entity of the Australian government, is responsible for developing, issuing, and maintaining auditing and assurance standards. In this sense, the AUASB, with legally enforceable standards for audits and reviews as mandated by the Corporations Act 2001, collaborates with other standards setters and aims to enhance stakeholder confidence in Australia's economy and capital markets (Auditing and Assurance Standards Board, 2023).

The annual financial statements and remuneration reports in ASX-listed companies are subject to external audits conducted by Australian auditing standards and certified auditors. In addition, the entity's external auditor audits and reviews the half-yearly financial statements. However, the annual report of the board of directors is not normally audited or reviewed by an external auditor, who merely reads the report to determine whether there are any material inconsistencies with the financial statements he has audited. Thus, the external audit report typically includes an express qualification that the auditor's opinion covers the financial statements only and that the auditor does not express an audit opinion or any form of assurance conclusion on the other information in the report (ASX, 2020, 2022).

As for internal audit, ASX-listed companies can choose from establishing an internal audit and describing its structure and role, altern https://meet.google.com/zdd-fspn-vyhative arrangements to achieve an equivalent outcome to an internal audit or adopting the recommendations and explaining its logic to the market under the "if not, why not" approach.

The internal audit option is the most widely adopted by ASX-listed entities, and they must report on internal audit recommendations for all financial years. Companies choosing the alternative arrangement or explaining option "b" or "c" should ensure that the costs of other options for internal audit do not outweigh the potential benefits and that they are comfortable with the risks arising from not implementing an internal audit (ASX, 2014a).

Regarding the audit committee, the ASX determines that listed companies that are part of the S&P All Ordinaries Index or the S&P/ASX 300 must have an audit committee and follow specific recommendations regarding this committee. The audit committee must have at least three non-executive and independent members. It must also be chaired by an independent director who is not the chairman of the board of directors. Finally, the audit committee should disclose the committee's charter, the qualifications of its members, and the number of times the committee has met throughout the reporting period (ASX, 2020).

8.6 Governance Code and Governance Structure

Since the early 1990s, different associations in Australia have tried to publish governance codes for best practices. However, these entities could not unite the conflicting interests in consolidating and developing a code of good governance practices. Intending to facilitate the development of a self-regulatory framework, the Australian government supported the then-Australian Stock Exchange in developing a self-regulatory framework. Thus, the Australian Securities Exchange (ASX) governance code, known as Corporate Governance Principles and Recommendations, was first released in 2003, the second in 2007, the third in 2014, and the fourth in 2019. In 2002, the Australian Stock Exchange established the Corporate Governance Council (CGC). One of the objectives of this council was to develop agreed corporate governance requirements and show best practice recommendations for Australian entities. The CGC developed 28 recommendations based on ten principles of good corporate governance, which have become ASX's governance code. This council has 19 participating entities, bringing together business groups, shareholders, and economic sectors. They are part of the CGC: Association of Superannuation Funds of Australia Limited; ASX Limited; Australasian Investor Relations Association; Australian Council of Superannuation Investors; Australian Institute of Company Directors; Australian Institute of Superannuation Trustees; Australian Shareholders' Association; Business Council of Australia; Chartered

Accountants Australia and New Zealand; CPA Australia Ltd.; Financial Services Council; Financial Services Institute of Australasia; Governance Institute of Australia; Group of 100; Institute of Internal Auditors—Australia; Institute of Public Accountants; Law Council of Australia; Property Council of Australia; and Stockbrokers and Financial Advisors Association Limited (ASX, 2019, Gibson & O'Donovan, 2007; Gray et al., 2007; Riaz, 2016; OECD, 2023).

The approach to the principles and recommendations of the ASX governance code is "apply or explain" ("comply or explain" or "if not, why not"), which ensures that listed companies can consider that a code recommendation is not appropriate to its circumstances. Of course, the company has the right not to do so, explaining its reasons. In the second edition of the Corporate Governance Principles and Recommendations 2007, eight core principles were established, updated in the third and fourth editions. Table 8.1 presents the principles in the fourth edition of the ASX governance code (ASX, 2019; Nguyen et al., 2018).

As highlighted in Table 8.1, the fourth edition of the ASX governance code introduces critical principles to enhance corporate governance practices. These principles encompass delineating roles and responsibilities for effective management and supervision, structuring boards appropriately with skilled and committed members, fostering a culture of ethical and lawful behavior, ensuring the integrity of corporate reports, promoting timely and balanced disclosure, respecting bondholders' rights,

Table 8.1 ASX governance principles

	Principle	Comment
1	Establish solid foundations for management and supervision	The roles and responsibilities of a company's board and management must be delineated, and their performance must be regularly reviewed.
2	Structure the board to be effective and add value.	The board of directors of a listed entity must be of an appropriate size. In addition, its members must have the skills, commitment, and knowledge of the entity and its industry to fulfill its functions and effectively add value.
3	Instill a culture of acting legally, ethically, and responsibly.	A listed entity must continually instill and reinforce an organization-wide culture of lawfully acting ethically and responsibly.
4	Design the integrity of corporate reports.	Processes must be in place to verify the integrity of the corporate reports.
5	Disclose in a timely and balanced manner.	In a timely and balanced manner, the company must disclose all matters expected to have material effects on the price of its securities.
6	Respect for the rights of bondholders	A listed entity must provide its security holders with appropriate information and resources to exercise their rights effectively.
7	Recognize and manage risk.	A solid risk management framework must be established, and the effectiveness of this framework must be periodically reviewed.
8	Pay fairly and responsibly.	The remuneration of directors and executives must be sufficient to attract and retain high-quality directors and executives, aligning their interests with creating value for bondholders.

Source: ASX (2019)

establishing robust risk management frameworks, and offering fair and responsible remuneration to align interests with value creation for bondholders. These guidelines emphasize transparency, ethics, and effective governance in ASX-listed entities. In addition to these principles, the ASX governance code presents 35 specific general application recommendations designed to affect these principles and three additional recommendations that apply only in limited cases (ASX, 2019).

One of these recommendations is Recommendation 1.1, which expresses that a listed company should have and disclose a board charter outlining the respective roles and responsibilities of its board and management, along with matters reserved for the board and those delegated to management. The board's responsibilities include leadership, defining the entity's purpose, appointing key personnel, and overseeing the entity's performance, risk management, and governance practices. The senior executive team implements objectives and provides the board with the necessary information. The board charter should also define the chairperson's role, the company's policy for seeking independent professional advice, and board composition and succession considerations. The division of functions should be regularly reviewed for relevance (ASX, 2019). The ASX governance code also recommends that listed companies establish a remuneration committee consisting of at least three members, most of whom are independent directors chaired by an independent director. The company should also disclose committee-related information. In addition, the code advises separate disclosure of remuneration policies for non-executive directors and executive directors/senior executives, including dismissals and adjustments in cases of misconduct. For entities with equity-based remuneration schemes, there should be a policy addressing participant transactions that limit economic risk, and this policy should be disclosed (ASX, 2019).

More recently, Cooke et al. (2024) related the ASX CGC recommendations to three key concerns of directors regarding corporate governance: relationship, risk, and remuneration. In this context, the relationship relates to principles 1, 2, and 6, as the authors describe challenges to delegate and separate board and management responsibilities.

Furthermore, Cooke et al. (2024) relates risk to principles 3, 4, 5, and 7. Principle 3, which recommends instilling a culture of acting legally and ethically, is reflected in the necessity of enforcing a code of conduct. Principle 4, which regards designing the integrity of corporate reports, is often related to the consistency and rigor necessary to approve reports relevant to shareholders. The authors also highlight the need to look back to risk events. It could also relate to principle 5 (disclose in a timely and balanced manner), in which the directors' time and effort spent in disclosure content approval is worth notice. and 7, in which both the conduct of conduct and the directors' view of management risks as a critical component of their role.

Finally, Cooke et al. (2024) highlights the directors' concerns regarding remuneration (principle 8), in which they express the need to hire consultants to conform to executive structure and remuneration according to averages.

The governance structure of companies listed on the ASX follows the Anglo-American governance structure model, as presented in Fig. 8.3. The main body of this structure is the board of directors, whose main objective is the development and

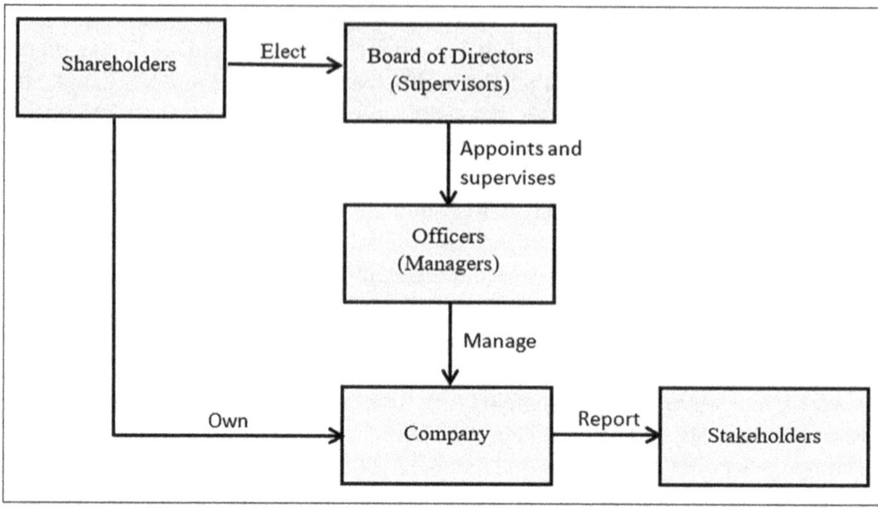

Fig. 8.3 Anglo-American Governance Structure Model. Source: Fernando (2012) and Mostepaniuk (2017)

final approval of the management of the corporate strategy and the company's performance objectives and monitoring the executive management. One of the principles of good corporate governance of the Australian Stock Exchange about the board of directors is that it should be structured to add value to the company. The recommendation is that independent directors should form most of the board of directors. The Australian Securities Exchange (ASX) defines in its governance code that a director is independent when free from any business or other relationship with the company that could interfere with exercising his free and independent judgment. The ASX also recommends that listed companies regularly assess and disclose the independence of each director following this definition (ASX, 2019; Chen et al., 2009; Clarke, 2007; Huang et al., 2020).

In the Anglo-American governance structure model, as shown in Fig. 8.3, shareholders hold the company's ownership and exercise their right to elect the board of directors. This board is responsible for appointing and overseeing the executives responsible for efficiently managing the company while ensuring the required information is provided to all stakeholders (Clarke, 2007; Fernando, 2012; Mostepaniuk, 2017).

In companies listed on the ASX, it is recommended but not mandatory that the Chief Executive Officer (CEO) and the chairman of the board of directors are not the same people. It is recommended that the same person does not simultaneously perform the functions of CEO and chairman of the board of directors in each company. Unlike American companies, this duality of roles is not very common in large companies listed in Australia, which is more observed in small companies than in large companies. Thus, most Australian companies listed on the ASX have separate leadership structures, and most have independent directors on their boards (ASX, 2019; Kiel & Nicholson, 2003; Monem, 2013; Nguyen et al., 2018; OECD, 2023).

Recommendation 2.5 in the ASX governance code emphasizes the need to appoint an independent director as the chairman of a listed company, specifically to prevent the chairman from also assuming the CEO role. This separation of roles promotes an open and constructive board culture, enabling diverse viewpoints. Separation of management and control is essential for effective governance. If the chairman is not independent, the entity should consider appointing an independent director as deputy chair or a "senior independent director" to handle conflicts. Even if the chairperson is independent, a deputy chair or senior independent director can help evaluate the chairperson's performance and provide a separate communication channel for security holders, especially regarding chair-related matters. This recommendation recognizes the demanding role of the chairman and emphasizes the importance of avoiding positions that could interfere with work (ASX, 2019).

As per the number of directors, the ASX recommends that the board be of sufficient size so that business requirements can be met and changes in the board's composition and its committees can be managed without undue interruptions. However, it should not be so big as it is difficult to drive. Some studies of companies listed on the ASX have found that the average size of the board is around 5.2 directors. Other studies have observed a certain negative effect of board size on the performance of Australian companies, concluding that companies with a large board have significantly lower market values (ASX, 2019; Monem, 2013; Nguyen et al., 2016; Petrovic-Lazarevic, 2010; Rashid & Islam, 2014).

Another point to highlight is women's representation on boards of companies listed on the Australian Stock Exchange. In this country, in addition to the recommendation of disclosing the gender composition of the boards present in the ASX corporate governance code, the Workplace Gender Equality Act, the 2012 Gender Equality in the Workplace Act, requires private sector companies with 100 or more employees to file annual records with the state gender equality agency. As a result, the presence of women on the boards of directors of ASX's 200 largest companies in 2019 was 31.2%, up from 8% in 2010 (Mees & Smith, 2019; OECD, 2023). Additionally, Ahmed and Hussain (2024) highlight the relevance of board gender diversity by showing a negative relation between such diversity and cash holding, suggesting that more diverse boards lead to less available cash for discretional use and, consequently, fewer agency problems.

As for the other bodies of the governance structure of Australian companies, the ASX governance code indicates that entities listed among the 300 largest on the stock exchange must have a remuneration committee composed of at least three members, the majority of which are independent. To analyze the remuneration of directors and executives, ensuring that financial incentives for executives encourage them to seek the entity's growth and success, but without rewarding conduct contrary to the entity's values to which they belong (ASX, 2019; Riaz, 2016).

The audit committee is mandatory for companies that comprise the index of the 500 largest companies listed on the ASX. Also composed of at least three members, most of whom are independent, it has the objective of overseeing the process of preparing corporate reports efficiently and effectively. The risk committee should monitor management's performance against the entity's risk management framework. Finally, the nominating committee primarily aims to make recommendations to the board concerning the board of directors' succession planning (ASX, 2019).

8.7 Final Considerations

This chapter aimed to understand the scenario of corporate governance in Australia, especially the capital market in this country, materialized in the Australian Securities Exchange (ASX), the Australian stock exchange. In 1987, the Australian Stock Exchange (ASX) was established through the merger of state stock exchanges, evolving into the Australian Securities Exchange (ASX) in 2006. As of October 2021, ASX hosted 2108 companies with a total market value of AUD 2.531 trillion, ranking 16th globally. Sector-wise, ASX employs the S&P Dow Jones GICS® industry classification system. When comparing Australia's GDP and the market value of shares traded on the ASX, it was observed that the stock exchange is a relatively small part of the Australian economy.

In the Australian Securities Exchange (ASX) context, stringent admission criteria are in place, including the necessity of 300 unaffiliated investors with individual investments of AUD 2000.00, a 20% free float, and specific financial performance benchmarks. The ASX offers a variety of shares: ordinary, preference, and partly paid shares, each endowed with unique attributes and privileges. Corporate governance mechanisms, such as board composition and audit quality, wield significant influence over dividend policies in Australia, serving as a countermeasure to conflicts of interest. Regulatory authorities exhibit efficacy in safeguarding minority shareholder rights, particularly those held by financial institutions. At the same time, the capital market displays low ownership concentration, with less than 20% of companies witnessing over 50% ownership held by their top three shareholders. This ownership structure aligns with the "outsider" system but retains pockets of concentration, with institutional investors, notably pension funds, playing a pivotal role in overseeing management and bolstering corporate governance.

From the 1980s to the early twenty-first century, Australia embarked on a transformative journey in corporate governance instigated by pressing issues within the corporate regulatory framework. The corporate governance landscape in Australia was forever altered in the early 2000s, preceding the Enron scandal in the United States. Corporate collapses, including One Tel, Harris Scarfe, and HIH Insurance, drew attention to concerns about governance and corruption. Such concerns spurred legislative reforms, encompassing the creation of the Corporate Governance Council (CGC), formulating codes of conduct, reviewing regulatory authorities, and enacting the Corporate Law Economic Reform Program Act (CLERP 9) in 2004. CLERP 9 aimed to enhance transparency, particularly in executive remuneration disclosure, forming a hybrid regulatory framework alongside the ASX Principles of Good

Governance Practice, which underpin Australia's robust corporate governance landscape.

The Australian Accounting Standards Board (AASB) oversees accounting standards aligned with International Financial Reporting Standards (IFRS). IFRS adoption began in 2005 after convergence efforts since 1996. Australian Accounting Standards comprise "Level 1" (complete IFRS standards with Australian context) for government, for-profit, and publicly accountable entities, including ASX-listed firms, and "Level 2" (reduced disclosure) for others. ASX-listed companies audit annual financial statements and remuneration reports externally. Half-yearly statements undergo similar audits, but the board's annual report gets a limited review. Internal audit options include establishment or alternatives, with explanations for non-compliance. Audit committees in major indices must have at least three non-executive, independent members chaired by an independent director. Disclosure requirements ensure transparency, fostering Australia's robust accounting and auditing framework.

The Australian government supported the Australian Securities Exchange (ASX) in creating the Corporate Governance Principles and Recommendations to facilitate self-regulation. Introduced in 2003 and updated subsequently, this code consists of 8 core principles and 35 general application recommendations. ASX-listed companies follow an "apply or explain" approach, allowing flexibility with a requirement for explanations for non-compliance. Governance structures in these firms emphasize independent directors, often separate CEO and chairperson roles, and maintain a balanced board size. Increased female board participation is driven by ASX code and legislative requirements. Critical committees, including remuneration, audit, risk, and nominating committees, play vital roles in corporate governance for ASX-listed entities. The audit committee is mandatory for the top 500 ASX-listed companies, focusing on independence and efficient corporate reporting. Risk and nominating committees handle risk management and succession planning, contributing to Australia's robust corporate governance framework.

References

Ahmed, A., & Hussain, A. (2024). Board gender diversity and corporate cash holdings: Evidence from Australia. *International Journal of Acounting & Information Management, 32*(4), 622–650. https://doi.org/10.1108/IJAIM-10-2023-0256

Al Farooque, O., Hamid, A., & Sun, L. (2021). Does corporate governance have a say on dividends in Australian listed companies? *Australasian Accounting, Business and Finance Journal, 15*(4), 47–75. https://doi.org/10.14453/aabfj.v15i4.4

Auditing and Assurance Standards Board. (2023). *About AUASB*. Retrieved October 18, 2023, from https://auasb.gov.au/about-auasb/

Australian Accounting Standards Board. (2023). *General FAQs*. Retrieved October 18, 2023, from https://aasb.gov.au/research-resources/general-faqs/

Australian Bureau of Statistics. (2023). *Australian statistics*. Retrieved October 12, 2023, from https://www.abs.gov.au/

Australian Prudential Regulatory Authority. (2021). *About us*. Retrieved November 30, 2021, from https://www.apra.gov.au/about-us

Australian Securities and Investment Commission. (2021). *Our role*. Retrieved November 30, 2021, from https://asic.gov.au/about-asic/what-we-do/our-role/

Australian Securities Exchange. (2014a). *A guide to meeting your obligations under ASX CGC Recommendation 7.3*. Retrieved July 20, 2022, from https://www.asx.com.au/documents/asx-compliance/guide-to-reporting-under-asx-cgc-recommendation-7-3.pdf

Australian Securities Exchange. (2014b). *Chapter 6: Securities*. Retrieved November 30, 2021, from https://www2.asx.com.au/about/regulation/rules-guidance-notes-and-waivers/asx-listing-rules-guidance-notes-and-waivers

Australian Securities Exchange. (2019). *Corporate Governance Principles and Recommendations (4)*. Retrieved November 10, 2021, from https://www.asx.com.au/documents/regulation/cgc-principles-and-recommendations-fourth-edn.pdf

Australian Securities Exchange. (2020). *ASX Listing Rules: Guidance note 9*. Retrieved July 20, 2022, from https://www.asx.com.au/documents/rules/guidance-note-9.pdf

Australian Securities Exchange. (2021a). *Listing requirements*. Retrieved November 30, 2021, from https://www2.asx.com.au/listings/how-to-list/listing-requirements

Australian Securities Exchange. (2021b). *Types of shares*. Retrieved November 30, 2021, from https://www2.asx.com.au/investors/learn-about-our-investment-solutions/shares/types-of-shares

Australian Securities Exchange. (2022). *Chapter 19: Interpretation and definitions*. Retrieved July 20, 2022, from https://www.asx.com.au/documents/chapter19.pdf

Australian Securities Exchange. (2023). *Datasphere*. Retrieved October 12, 2023, from https://www.asxdatasphere.com.au/s/

Banks, G., Fitzgerald, R., & Fels, A. (2009). *Executive remuneration in Australia*. Productivity Commission Inquiry Report. Retrieved December 8, 2021, from https://www.pc.gov.au/inquiries/completed/executive-remuneration/report

Berle, A., & Means, G. (1932). *The modern corporation and private property*. Macmillan.

Chen, R., Dyball, M., & Wright, S. (2009). The link between board composition and corporate diversification in Australian corporations. *Corporate Governance: An International Review, 17*(2), 208–223. https://doi.org/10.1111/j.1467-8683.2009.00734.x

Clarke, T. (2007). *International corporate governance*. Routledge.

Clarkson, P., Van Bueren, A. L., & Walker, J. (2006). Chief executive officer remuneration disclosure quality: Corporate responses to an evolving disclosure environment. *Accounting and Finance, 46*(5), 771–796. https://doi.org/10.1111/j.1467-629x.2006.00197.x

Cooke, S., Sheridan, A., Perry, M., Marimuthu, S. B., & Conway, M. L. (2024). Relationships, risks, and remuneration: Australian directors "doing" corporate governance. *Corporate Governance*. https://doi.org/10.1108/CG-11-2023-0476

Cotter, J., & Silvester, M. (2003). Board and monitoring committee independence. *Abacus, 39*(2), 211. https://doi.org/10.1111/1467-6281.00127

Dignam, A. (2007). Transplanting UK takeover culture: The EU takeovers directive and the Australian experience. *International Journal of Disclosure and Governance, 4*(3), 148–166. https://doi.org/10.1057/palgrave.jdg.2050056

Fernando, A. C. (2012). *Business ethics and corporate governance* (2nd ed.). Pearson Education.

Financial Reporting Council. (2023). *About the FRC*. Retrieved October 18, 2023, from https://frc.gov.au/about-frc

Gibson, K., & O'Donovan, G. (2007). Corporate governance and environmental reporting: An Australian study. *Corporate Governance: An International Review, 15*(5), 944–956. https://doi.org/10.1111/j.1467-8683.2007.00615.x

Gray, S. J., Kang, H., & Cheng, M. (2007). Corporate governance and board composition: Diversity and independence of Australian boards. *Corporate Governance: An International Review, 15*(2), 194–207.

Huang, P., Lu, Y., & Wee, M. (2020). Corporate governance analysts and firm value: Australian evidence. *Pacific-Basin Finance Journal, 63*(July), 101430. https://doi.org/10.1016/j.pacfin.2020.101430

International Financial Reporting Standards. (2017). *IFRS standards - Application around the world: Australia*. Retrieved December 8, 2021, from https://www.ifrs.org/use-around-the-world/use-of-ifrs-standards-by-jurisdiction/view-jurisdiction/australia/

Jensen, M. C., & Meckling, W. H. (1976). Theory of the firm: Managerial behavior, agency costs, and ownership structure. *Journal of Financial Economics, 3*(4), 305–360. https://doi.org/10.2139/ssrn.94043

Kemp, S. (2011). Corporate governance and corporate social responsibility: Lessons from the land of OZ. *Journal of Management and Governance, 15*(4), 539–556. https://doi.org/10.1007/s10997-010-9133-6

Kiel, G. C., & Nicholson, G. J. (2003). Board composition and corporate performance: How the Australian experience informs contrasting theories of corporate governance. *Corporate Governance: An International Review, 11*(3), 189–205. https://doi.org/10.1111/1467-8683.00318

Mees, B., & Smith, S. A. (2019). Corporate governance reform in Australia: A new institutional approach. *British Journal of Management, 30*(1), 75–89. https://doi.org/10.1111/1467-8551.12298

Monem, R. M. (2013). Determinants of board structure: Evidence from Australia. *Journal of Contemporary Accounting and Economics, 9*(1), 33–49. https://doi.org/10.1016/j.jcae.2013.01.001

Mostepaniuk, A. (2017). Corporate governance. In O. L. Emeagwali (Ed.), *Corporate governance and strategic decision making*. IntechOpen.

Nguyen, P., Rahman, N., Tong, A., & Zhao, R. (2016). Board size and firm value: Evidence from Australia. *Journal of Management and Governance, 20*(4), 851–873. https://doi.org/10.1007/s10997-015-9324-2

Nguyen, P., Rahman, N., & Zhao, R. (2018). CEO characteristics and firm valuation: A quantile regression analysis. *Journal of Management and Governance, 22*(1), 133–151. https://doi.org/10.1007/s10997-017-9383-7

O'Sullivan, M., Percy, M., & Stewart, J. (2008). Australian evidence on corporate governance attributes and their association with forward-looking information in the annual report. *Journal of Management and Governance, 12*(1), 5–35. https://doi.org/10.1007/s10997-007-9039-0

Organization for Economic Co-operation and Development. (2021). *OECD Corporate Governance Factbook 2021*. Retrieved November 10, 2021, from https://www.oecd.org/corporate/corporategovernance-factbook.htm

Organization for Economic Co-operation and Development. (2023). *Country profile of Australia*. Retrieved October 12, 2023, from https://data.oecd.org/australia.htm

Petrovic-Lazarevic, S. (2010). Good corporate citizenship in the Australian construction industry. *Corporate Governance: The International Journal of Business in Society, 10*(2), 115–128. https://doi.org/10.1108/14720701011035648

Pham, P. K., Suchard, J.-A., & Zein, J. (2012). Corporate governance and the cost of capital: Evidence from Australian companies. *Journal of Applied Corporate Finance, 24*(3), 84–93. https://doi.org/10.1111/j.1745-6622.2012.00392.x

Rashid, K., & Islam, S. M. N. (2014). Corporate governance, firm performance, and complementarities in a developed market: A study of the Australian case for the period 2000-2003. *International Journal of Disclosure and Governance, 11*(3), 255–283. https://doi.org/10.1057/jdg.2013.19

Reserve Bank of Australia. (2021). *Our role*. Retrieved November 30, 2021, from https://www.rba.gov.au/about-rba/our-role.html

Riaz, Z. (2016). A hybrid of state regulation and self-regulation for remuneration governance in Australia in. *Corporate Governance: The International Journal of Business in Society, 16*(3), 1–31.

Riaz, Z., Ray, S., Ray, P. K., & Kirkbride, J. (2013). Collibration as an alternative regulatory approach to governance: A contextual analysis of Australia. *International Journal of Disclosure and Governance, 10*(3), 246–260. https://doi.org/10.1057/jdg.2013.1

Robins, F. (2006). Corporate governance after Sarbanes-Oxley: An Australian perspective. *Corporate Governance: The International Journal of Business in Society, 6*(1), 34–48. https://doi.org/10.1108/14720700610649445

Setia-Atmaja, L., Tanewski, G. A., & Skully, M. (2009). The role of dividends, debt, and board structure in the governance of family-controlled firms. *Journal of Business Finance and Accounting, 36*(7–8), 863–898. https://doi.org/10.1111/j.1468-5957.2009.02151.x

Shan, Y. G., Troshani, I., & Tarca, A. (2019). Managerial ownership, audit firm size, and audit fees: Australian evidence. *Journal of International Accounting, Auditing, and Taxation, 35*, 18–36. https://doi.org/10.1016/j.intacaudtax.2019.05.002

The World Bank. (2023). *Australia*. Retrieved October 12, 2023, from https://data.world bank.org/country/Australia

United Nations. (2023). *Latest human development index ranking*. Retrieved October 12, 2023, from http://hdr.undp.org/en/content/latest-human-development-index-ranking

World Federation of Exchanges. (2022). *2022 Annual statistics guide*. Retrieved October 12, 2023, from https://www.world-exchanges.org/our-work/articles/2022-annual-statistics-guide

Chapter 9
India

Corporate Governance in India: Significant Advances Made and Ways Forward

Bruno Teixeira, Ana Flavia Albuquerque Ventura, Arti Chandani, Mohit Pathak, and Prashant Ubarhande

9.1 Introduction

India is a non-member country of the Organization for Economic Co-operation and Development (OECD, 2022). In 2024, India ranked fifth largest economy in the world, with a gross domestic product (GDP) of USD 3.55 trillion (World Bank, 2024). Historically, from British colonization in 1858 to independence in 1947, India's economy was predominantly agrarian, with its industries and resources exploited to benefit imperial interests. Post-independence, inspired by socialist ideals and influenced by the planned economies of the Soviet Union, India adopted a mixed economy model (Joshi, 2017). The state took on a central role, implementing five-year plans to steer development. The focus was on self-reliance, with heavy industries and infrastructure prioritized under state control. Import substitution and

B. Teixeira (✉)
University of Vale do Taquari, Univates, Lajeado, Brazil

A. F. A. Ventura
Federal University of Rio Grande do Sul, Porto Alegre, Brazil
e-mail: flavia.ventura@ufrgs.br

A. Chandani
Jaipuria Institute of Management, Lucknow, Lucknow, India
e-mail: arti.chandani@jaipuria.ac.in

M. Pathak
International Management Institute – Kolkata, Kolkata, India
e-mail: m.pathak@imi-k.edu.in

P. Ubarhande
Symbiosis Skills and Professional University, Pune, India
e-mail: prashant.ubarhande@scdl.net

C. B. Macagnan (ed.), *Corporate Governance in Capital Markets*, CSR, Sustainability, Ethics & Governance,
https://doi.org/10.1007/978-3-031-94751-3_9

protective tariffs were introduced to shield domestic industries from foreign competition, reflecting the broader goal of reducing dependence on external economies. This inward-looking strategy was guided by the belief that protectionism would nurture India's nascent industries and protect its economy from the vulnerabilities of external markets. However, this approach also led to inefficiencies and limited growth.

To address persistent developmental needs, the government began nationalization initiatives in the mid-twentieth century. The government nationalized the insurance industry in 1956, creating the Life Insurance Corporation (LIC) to mobilize savings for development. In 1969, under Prime Minister Indira Gandhi's leadership, 14 major banks were nationalized to ensure that credit flowed to underserved sectors like agriculture and small businesses. These measures increased financial inclusion and strengthened state control over key economic pillars, but they also resulted in bureaucratic inefficiencies (Dutta & Vashisth, 2023).

In the 1990s, India transitioned from a closed economy to a market economy through reforms inspired by the Anglo-Saxon system, including the sale of stakes in state-owned companies, with the economic reforms of 1991, led by Prime Minister P.V. Narasimha Rao and Finance Minister Dr. Manmohan Singh, marking a turning point toward liberalization, privatization, and globalization (La Porta et al., 1998; Mohanty & Mishra, 2021; Pareek & Sahu, 2022).

This historical context led to the formation of a capital market where most companies are controlled by large family business groups or the state (Dash, 2012; Arora & Singh, 2020; Pareek & Sahu, 2022). It also influenced the corporate governance practices adopted in India over the last three decades (Guha et al., 2019; Mohanty & Mishra, 2021). Therefore, the purpose of this chapter was to describe the main characteristics of Indian corporate governance. This purpose is relevant given that the book organized by Randall Mork and Lloyd Steier (2005), which addressed corporate governance in India, was published more than 15 years ago. Moreover, significant reforms on this subject have occurred since then.

The literature review shows that India has improved its corporate governance structure and practices, especially with the Companies Act 2013 and the amendments to Clause 49 of the Equity Listing Agreement, in 2014 (Nagar & Sen, 2016). However, there are still challenges regarding the protection of minority shareholders in terms of enforcement and in the absence of restrictions for the chief executive officer (CEO) to be able to exercise, at the same time, the activity of the chairman of the board (chairman). Furthermore, the participation of women on the board of directors has been used for the appointment of women from the owning families of large Indian business groups (Arora, 2021). Following this introduction, Sect. 9.2 provides an overview of capital markets and regulatory frameworks. Section 9.3 discusses corporate governance and concludes with the final section.

9.2 Overview of Capital Markets and Regulatory Frameworks

Capital markets play a crucial role in mobilizing resources for economic growth by facilitating the exchange of capital between investors and businesses. In India, the capital markets have undergone significant evolution, shaped by historical developments, regulatory interventions, and changing ownership structures. The economic liberalization of the 1990s marked a major turning point, ending the licensing regime and the gradual insertion of a market economy, India has sought to improve its corporate governance. This movement had significant advances with the Companies Act of 2013 and reformulated Clause 49 of the Equity Listing Agreement in 2014 which strengthened transparency and accountability in corporate practices (Nagar & Sen, 2016).

9.2.1 Capital Market

9.2.1.1 Bombay Stock Exchange (BSE)

India has two stock exchanges, namely the Bombay Stock Exchange (BSE) and the National Stock Exchange (NSE) (Mayur & Saravanan, 2017). BSE is Asia's first and Fastest Stock Exchange in the world with a speed of 6 microseconds and one of India's leading exchange groups, founded in 1875. As of 2013, it has established a partnership with Standard & Poor's Dow Jones Indices (S&PDJI) through the joint venture Asia Index Private Limited (AIPL). This partnership aims to provide a set of indices for local and foreign investors to participate in the South Asian capital market (S&PDJI, 2022). As of June 2024, 5210 entities are listed on BSE (2024). Concerning importance, Graph 9.1 demonstrates the relationship between the total market value of shares traded on the BSE and India's gross domestic product (GDP) between 2010 and 2022.

Graph 9.1 shows that the total market value of stocks traded on the BSE has consistently been above 60% of India's GDP, except in 2011. These numbers became more significant as the Indian economy grew by approximately 104% between 2010 and 2022. Graph 9.2 reveals the total market value of shares traded on BSE and India's GDP in trillions of dollars.

As can be seen in Graph 9.2, the total market value of shares traded on the BSE reached its lowest value in 2011 (USD 1.01 trillion) and its highest value in 2021 (USD 3.57 trillion). The performance of 2011 stems from the European debt crisis (Al-ahdal & Hashim, 2021). Another notable point is that immediately after the COVID-19 pandemic, the market value of shares traded on the BSE and India's GDP showed significant growth. The Indian economy was the second-fastest growing in 2022 (7.2%) among the G20 countries, and it is expected to end the year 2023 as the fastest-growing (S&P Global, 2023). The growth was driven by economic

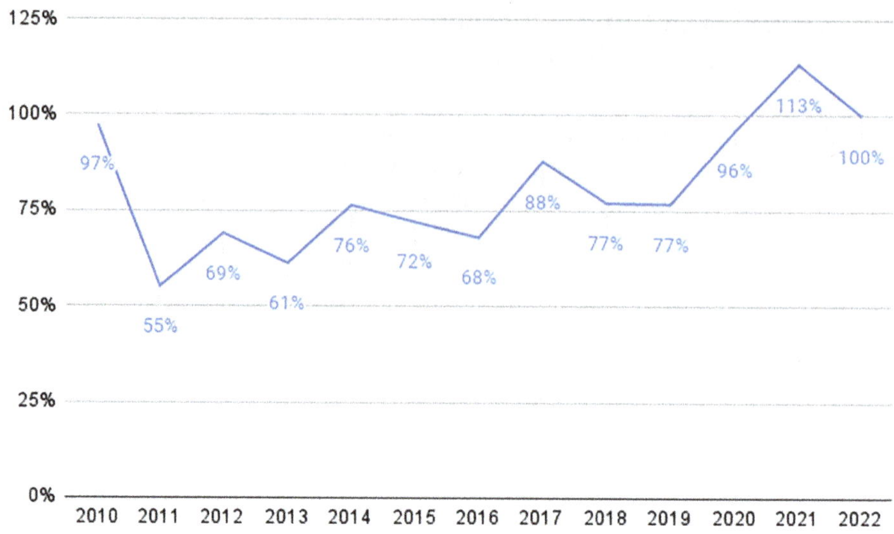

Graph 9.1 Total market value of shares traded on BSE about India's GDP. Source: Values calculated by the author based on data from the BSE (2024), the World Bank (2024), and the World Federation of Exchanges (2024)

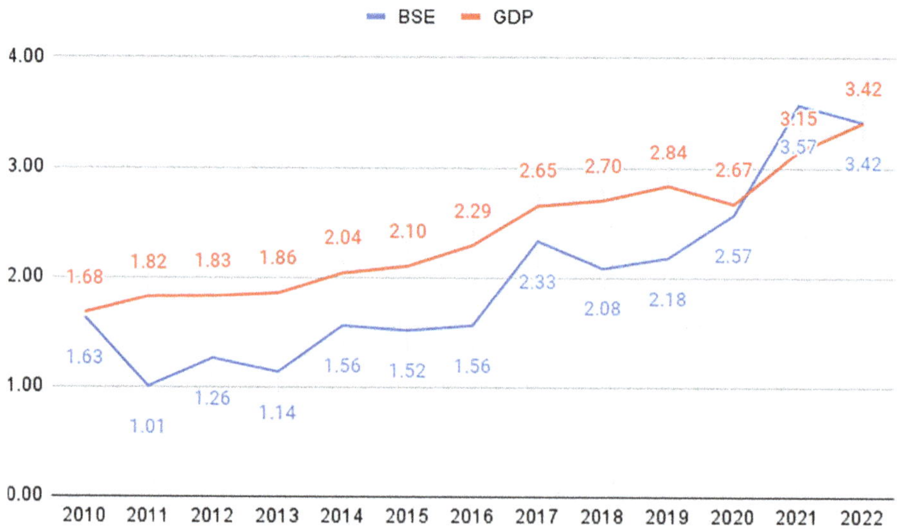

Graph 9.2 Total market value of shares traded on BSE and India's GDP (in USD trillion). Source: BSE (2024), World Bank (2024), and World Federation of Exchanges (2024)

reforms, investments in infrastructure and technology, financial inclusion of the population, and an increase in the exports of products and services with higher added value (World Bank, 2023; Deloitte, 2024).

AIPL classifies BSE stock indices into seven categories, namely Market Cap/Broad (22 indices), Sector & Industry (20 indices), Thematic (10 indices), Strategy (16 indices), Sustainability (03 indices), and Volatility (03 indices) (AIPL, 2024). On January 29, 2024, the top 5 indices of the BSE, in terms of value, were: S&P BSE SENSEX (71,941.57), S&P BSE SENSEX Next 50 (66,716.52), S&P BSE CAPITAL GOODS (58,116.38), S&P BSE SME IPO (57,066.76), and S&P BSE BANKEX (51,467.89) (BSE, 2024). The S&P BSE SENSEX (SENSEX) index was launched on January 1, 1986. This index comprises the 30 most significant, most liquid, and financially sound companies in the Indian economy listed on the BSE. It is expressed in both the Indian Rupee and the US Dollar. Reflected in the Indian Rupee and US Dollar, the S&P BSE Sensex Next 50 measures the performance of the 50 largest and most liquid component stocks of the S&P BSE LargeMidCap, excluding the constituent stocks of the S&P BSE SENSEX. It was launched on February 27, 2017. The S&P BSE CAPITAL GOODS index comprises companies listed on the BSE that are part of the S&P BSE 500 index and belong to the capital goods sector. It was launched on August 9, 1999, and its values are disclosed in Indian Rupee and US Dollar. It is made up of 27 companies. Launched on December 14, 2012, the S&P BSE SME IPO Index measures the performance of stocks of small and medium-sized enterprises after the completion of the initial public offering (IPO) process. It is denominated in both US dollars and Indian rupee. The S&P BSE BANKEX index comprises the shares of companies listed on the BSE that are part of the S&P BSE 500 index and classified as banks. It is expressed in the Indian Rupee and US Dollar. It was launched on June 23, 2003. This index contains ten companies (AIPL, 2024).

Upon analyzing the companies that make up the S&P BSE SENSEX index, it is possible to identify that 65% of the market value of the traded shares are concentrated in the financial, information technology, and oil and gas sectors (BSE, 2024). Graph 9.3 clearly illustrates this information.

Graph 9.3 shows that the financial sector has the highest percentage share in the market value of the stocks that are part of the S&P BSE SENSEX index, with a portion of 36.6%, followed by the information technology sector, with 15.8%. The Indian financial sector is dominated by banks. In addition, most banking business is carried out by banks under state control (Mayur & Saravanan, 2017; Schipke et al., 2023). Regarding the information technology sector, India has services with competitive advantages that lead it to dominate international expansion, along with engineering and healthcare services (Zattoni et al., 2009). The information technology sector accounted for 60% of India's service exports, together with business process outsourcing (BPO) services, in the year 2022 (EY, 2023).

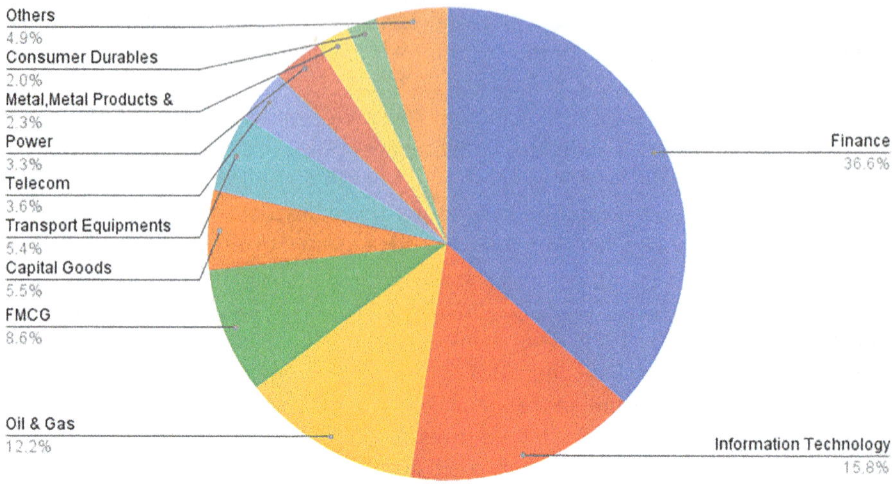

Graph 9.3 Sectoral percentage share in the market value of companies in the S&P BSE SENSEX index. Source: BSE (2024)

9.2.1.2 National Stock Exchange (NSE)

The NSE was established in 1992 and started its operations as a stock exchange in 1994 (NSE, 2024). In 2022, it was India's only stock exchange member of the World Federation of Exchanges (WFE), with a total of 2168 listed companies, which had a market value of USD 3.39 trillion, making it one of the 10 major stock exchanges in the world (WFE, 2024). Regarding its importance, Graph 9.4 presents the relationship between the total market value of shares traded on the NSE and India's GDP in 2010 and 2022.

According to Graph 9.4, the market value of shares traded on the NSE was less than 60% of India's GDP only in the year 2011, as was also the case with the BSE. However, it is essential to note that for most of the period between 2010 and 2022, the total market value of shares traded on the BSE was higher than that of shares traded on the NSE, as shown in Graph 9.5.

Graph 9.5 reveals that the total market value of shares traded on the NSE reached its minimum value in 2011, at USD 0.99 trillion, and its maximum value in 2021, at USD 3.55 trillion. The only period in which the market value of shares traded on the NSE was higher than that of shares traded on the BSE was in the year 2017. However, it should be noted that between 2010 and 2022 the average number of companies listed on the BSE (5429 companies) was higher than the average number of companies listed on the NSE (1834) (BSE, 2024; WFE, 2024). This may influence the financial differences presented so far between the two Indian stock exchanges.

The NSE is composed of 73 indices segregated into Broad Market (18 indices), Sectoral (15 indices), Strategy (19 indices), Thematic (14 indices), and Fixed Income (7 indices). The primary benchmark index of the NSE is the NIFTY 50, as

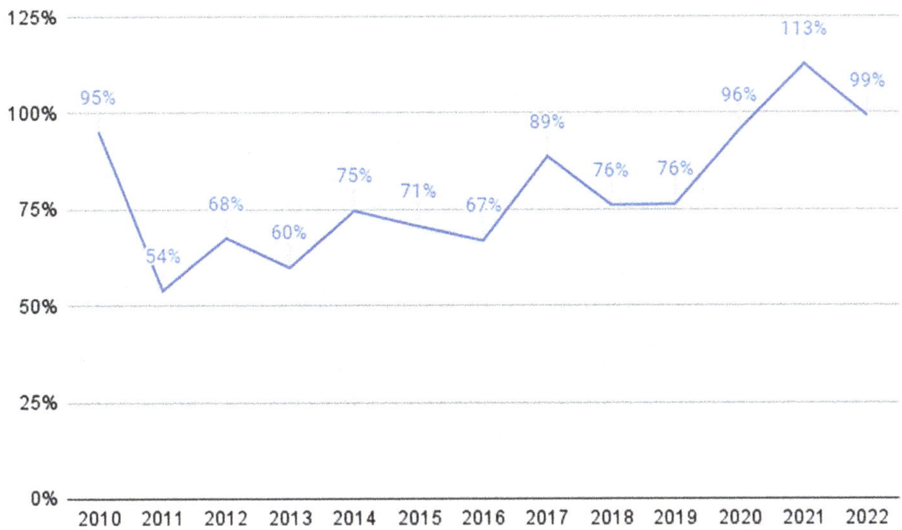

Graph 9.4 Total market value of shares traded on the NSE about India's GDP. Source: Values calculated by the author based on data from the World Bank (2024) and the WFE (2024)

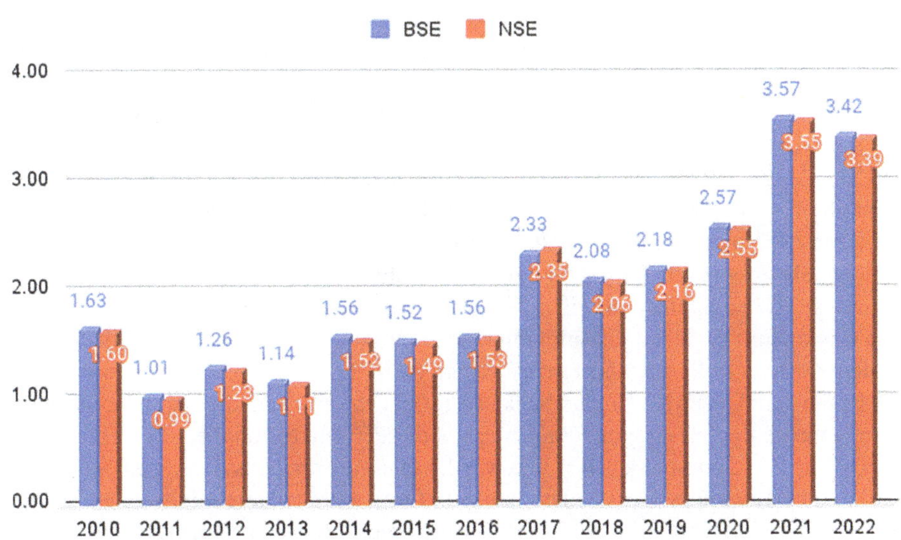

Graph 9.5 Total market value of shares traded on the BSE and NSE (in USD trillion). Source: BSE (2024) and WFE (2024)

it measures the performance of the 50 largest and most liquid companies listed on the NSE. It was launched on April 22, 1996 (Kathiravan et al., 2017; NSE, 2024). Graph 9.6 displays the percentage share of each sector in the market value of the stocks that make up the NIFTY 50.

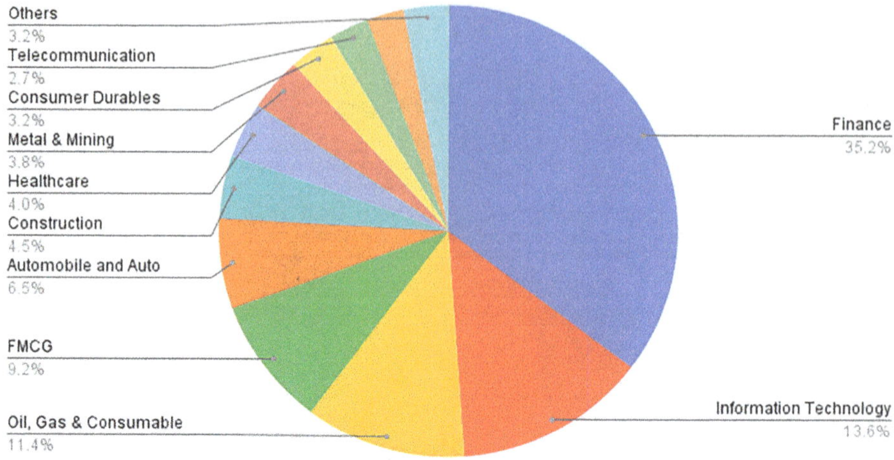

Graph 9.6 Sectoral percentage share in the market value of companies in the NIFTY 50 index. Source: NSE (2024)

Just as with the S&P BSE SENSEX index, the financial sector holds the largest share in the market value of the stocks that are part of the NIFTY 50 index, with 35.2%. In second position is the information technology sector, with 13.6%. These data underscore the predominance of the financial and information technology sectors in the Indian capital market.

When analyzing the NSE indices from a value perspective, on January 31, 2024, the top 5 indices were NIFTY NEXT 50 (55,299.25), NIFTY FMCG (55,071.40), NIFTY MIDCAP150 MOMENTUM 50 (52,673.45), NIFTY MIDCAP 100 (48,568.60), and NIFTY ALPHA 50 (47,075.20). The NIFTY NEXT 50 index was launched on November 4, 1996. It represents the 50 companies listed on the NSE, which make up the NIFTY 100 index, after excluding the companies of the NIFTY 50 index. The companies in this index are predominantly classified in the financial services sector (19.53%), fast-moving consumer goods sector (12.16%), metals and mining sector (11.91%), and energy sector (9.14%). Launched on September 22, 1999, the NIFTY FMCG index seeks to reflect the performance and behavior of companies in the fast-moving consumer goods sector listed on the NSE. This index is made up of 15 companies. It is noteworthy that they are considered fast consumer goods, non-durable products, mass consumption, and available on the shelves. The NIFTY MIDCAP150 MOMENTUM 50 index measures the performance of the top 50 companies that are part of the Nifty Midcap 150 index.

The selection of these companies is based on a normalized momentum index. It was launched on August 16, 2020. It is primarily composed of companies from the financial services sector (26.89%), capital goods sector (19.94%), and healthcare sector (19.68%). Launched on July 18, 2005, the NIFTY MIDCAP 100 is primarily composed of companies from the financial services sector (18.04%), capital goods sector (10.76%), and healthcare sector (10.09%). This index aims to capture the behavior of the top 100 mid-cap companies listed on the NSE. The NIFTY ALPHA 50 index measures the performance of the 50 stocks that showed the highest Alphas in the last year. The NIFTY ALPHA 50 was launched on November 19, 2012. The stocks in this index predominantly belong to the following sectors: information technology (28.53%), financial services (16.02%), and energy (10.28%) (NSE, 2024).

9.2.2 *Regulatory Framework*

The Indian capital market is supervised and regulated by the Securities and Exchange Board of India (SEBI), linked to the Department of Economic Affairs (DEA) of the Ministry of Finance (MoF). It was established as a statutory body in 1992 to protect securities investors and the development of the Indian capital market (SEBI, 2022; DEA, 2022; MF, 2022). Securities and Exchange Board of India was formulated on the lines of the Securities Exchange Commission of the USA. The main role of SEBI is to act as a regulator of the capital markets and its constituents. These powers were initially with the central government ministries like Law, Finance, and Company Affairs. These powers are now given to SEBI, and it has become the sole regulator of the Capital Markets. Another Indian state body responsible for regulating India's corporate sector is the Ministry of Corporate Affairs (MCA). This ministry is also responsible for supervising class entities, namely: the Institute of Chartered Accountants of India (ICAI), the Institute of Company Secretaries of India (ICSI), and the Institute of Cost Accountants of India (ICAI) (MCA, 2022).

In regulatory terms, India adopted the common-law system under its English colonization (La Porta et al., 1998; Lattemann et al., 2009). La Porta et al. (2000) point out that, in general, countries that use civil law have weaker protection of minority shareholders compared to countries that use the common-law system. Corporate governance specifies the relationship among various primary participants such as shareholders, directors, and managers in determining the directions and performance of corporations. Because insiders have an inherent informational advantage over outside stakeholders, it is required that the governance systems empower independent parties to monitor their behavior and reports. Indian legal and regulatory system plays a crucial role in creating an effective corporate governance mechanism in a country, development of stock exchanges, and economic growth. The regulatory bodies in India have advocated comprehensive and rigorous corporate governance reforms that emphasize the importance of the credibility and integrity of the listed companies, the responsibilities of minority shareholders, and the necessity for information disclosure (MCA, 2022; SEBI, 2022). The regulatory framework of corporate governance consists of:

9.2.2.1 Companies Act, 2013

The Companies Act consolidates the legislation on companies. It establishes the differentiation between public and private companies. It regulates the business combination process, initial public offering, governance, disclosure, and auditing of companies' accounting and liquidation information. This act provides for public companies to list their securities in stock exchanges of a permissible foreign jurisdiction. It also facilitates the central government to require a class of unlisted companies to prepare a financial report on a periodical basis.

9.2.2.2 The Limited Liability Partnership Act, 2008

For capital market purposes, the main point of this law is the aspect that limits the partner's liability to his participation in the legal entity with limited liability. Therefore, when formed, this legal entity has civil rights and obligations, which do not depend on the composition of the partners. In addition, the referred law defines how the entry and exit of the partners of these legal entities, the payment of their capital stock, the registration, disclosure, and auditing of their accounting information, the conversion of other forms of companies to a limited liability legal entity and the liquidation and dissolution of this type of company.

9.2.2.3 Depositories Act 1996 (as Amended by the International Financial Services Centers Authority Act, 2019 Web October 1, 2020)

This law is intended to regulate the activity of securities depositaries. Therefore, it determines how a company is authorized to act as a depositary and the rights and obligations of depositaries, participants, issuers, and beneficiaries of securities. It also reinforces SEBI's power in monitoring the capital market.

9.2.2.4 Securities and Exchange Board of India Act, 1992 (as Amended by the Finance Act, 2021 [13 of 2021] Web April 1, 2021)

The primary role of this law in creating SEBI is to develop and regulate the securities market, protecting the interests of investors. The law establishes the location of SEBI's headquarters, the composition and duration of the term of office of its members, the process of dismissal of its members, the function and powers of said body-wide Section 11 (SEBI, 2021), and so on. This act was introduced to prevent undesirable transactions in the securities market by regulating the entities and businesses involved in stock exchange affairs. As per this act, every recognized stock exchange has to furnish the central government with a copy of the annual report containing all the particulars as may be prescribed in the act to protect the interest of shareholders.

9.2.2.5 Securities Contracts (Regulation) Act, 1956 (as Amended by the Finance Act, 2021 [13 of 2021] Web April 1, 2021)

The law aims to regulate transactions involving securities, avoiding undesirable operations. Among the regulations are the following matters: recognition and withdrawal of recognition of stock exchanges by the central government, the statute of stock exchanges, the rights and obligations of stock exchanges, the power of the central government, and SEBI over exchanges of values, penalties, and processes.

A particularity that draws attention is that India has not yet required that the accounting practices of companies listed on its stock exchanges be carried out following the International Financial Reporting Standards (IFRS) issued by the International Account Standard Board (IASB). However, accounting standards issued by the Institute of Chartered Accountants of India (ICAI) are substantially converged with IFRS (IFRS Foundation, 2022; Nepal & Deb, 2024). According to section 133 of the Companies Act, 2013, ICAI is responsible for issuing technical and professional accounting standards. This body is linked to the Ministry of Corporate Affairs (IFRS Foundation, 2022; MCA, 2022).

Considering that the main aspects of the stock exchanges, the supervisory and regulatory bodies, and the legislation governing the Indian capital market were exposed in this section. The next section addresses the predominance of Indian companies' capital structure on their stock exchanges.

9.2.2.6 Accounting Standards

As per the provisions of Clause 49 of the Equity Listing Agreement, which is related to corporate governance, the company should implement prescribed accounting standards in letter and spirit in the preparation of financial statements taking into consideration the interest of all stakeholders and should also ensure that the annual audit is conducted as per provisions. In the last few years, Indian companies voluntarily accepted international accounting standards though they are not legally binding on them. They have voluntarily gone for greater disclosures and more transparent governance practices than are mandated by law.

9.2.2.7 Codes and Guidelines

Official Codes and Guidelines play a significant role in corporate governance through certain official guidelines such as Voluntary Guidelines, Guidelines on Corporate Governance for Central Public Sector Enterprises, Enhanced Disclosure and Investor Protection Guidelines, and National Code on Corporate Governance. Private codes and guidelines include the Confederation of Indian Industry (CII) Code on Corporate Governance which plays a superintendent role in the Indian securities market.

9.3 Corporate Governance

In India, corporate governance has evolved significantly over the years, shaped by both domestic needs and global influences. The rise of public companies and increasing investor awareness have highlighted the importance of transparency, accountability, and ethical conduct in business practices. To address these challenges, India has implemented various regulatory frameworks, such as the Companies Act of 2013 and the guidelines issued by the SEBI, to improve the standards of corporate governance. These frameworks emphasize the role of the board of directors, shareholder rights, and financial disclosures to ensure that companies operate in the best interests of all stakeholders. As India's corporate sector continues to grow and globalize, the focus on robust corporate governance remains critical in fostering investor confidence, sustainable business practices, and long-term economic growth.

The Companies Act of 1956 was a significant early milestone, establishing the legal framework for company formation, management, and shareholder protection. However, the absence of clear guidelines on transparency, board accountability, and financial disclosures led to widespread inefficiencies and concerns about corporate governance.

In 1998, the Confederation of Indian Industry (CII) took a significant step toward improving corporate governance in India by releasing the report "Desirable Corporate Governance: A Code", The code was a voluntary guideline aimed at encouraging companies to adopt higher standards of transparency, accountability, and ethical business practices. It focuses on improving the role of boards of directors, promoting independent auditing, and ensuring greater disclosure of financial information.

In 1999, the Committee on Corporate Governance, chaired by Kumar Mangalam Birla, was constituted by the SEBI in response to growing concerns over the state of corporate governance in India. Its key recommendations laid the foundation for Clause 49 of the Listing Agreement, which set specific norms for listed companies. The major recommendations included the majority of independent directors on the board, the establishment of independent audit committees, the separation of the role of CEO and chairman, and the adoption of a formal code of conduct for directors.

In 2001, the Standing Committee on International Financial Standards and Codes constituted the Advisory Group on Corporate Governance, chaired by Dr. R. H. Patil, was established in 2001 by the Ministry of Corporate Affairs (MCA) to further strengthen corporate governance standards in India, following the growing concerns about corporate scandals and the need for greater transparency in corporate practices. The recommendations covered the responsibilities of the board of directors, accountability to shareholders/stakeholders, criteria for selection of independent members of the board, size, and composition of the board, appointment of committees of the board such as audit committee, nomination committee, remuneration committee and investment committee, disclosure and transparency of information and data, and the role of shareholders in a company.

In April 2001, the Consultative Group of Directors of Banks and Financial Institutions was set up by the Reserve Bank of India (RBI) to examine and recommend improvements to the corporate governance practices for banks and financial institutions in India. The report aimed to promote more effective governance and reduce the risk of corporate mismanagement and financial scandals. The recommendations from the report contributed to the formulation of subsequent regulatory frameworks and have been instrumental in shaping corporate governance standards in Indian banks and financial institutions.

In 2002, the Naresh Chandra Committee was constituted by the Ministry of Corporate Affairs (MCA) to address critical issues related to corporate governance and corporate auditing practices in India. In the wake of high-profile corporate scandals like Enron and WorldCom in the United States, and emerging concerns about governance and audit failures in India, the Committee was tasked with recommending reforms to enhance transparency, accountability, and integrity in corporate governance. The key recommendations focused on the independence of auditors, accountability board, financial disclosures, and regulatory oversight.

In 2003, to review the existing code of corporate governance arose from two perspectives, to evaluate the adequacy of the existing practices, and to further improve the existing practices SEBI constituted a Committee on Corporate Governance under the Chairmanship of Shri N. R. Narayana Murthy, Chairman and Chief Mentor of Infosys Technologies Limited. The key recommendations focused on disclosure of contingent liabilities, CEO/CFO certification, composition & duties of the audit committee, related party transactions, risk management, proceeds from initial public offering, remuneration of non-executive directors, nominee directors, and whistle-blower policies.

In 2004, The J.J. Irani Committee was constituted by the Government of India. The committee aimed to simplify company law, promote transparency, and facilitate ease of doing business while ensuring robust corporate governance. The committee provided recommendations that focused on the minimum number of independent directors on the boards of larger companies, training, and certification programs for directors to enhance their understanding of governance practices, rights of minority shareholders, and introduction of risk management frameworks as part of corporate governance.

In 2017, the Uday Kotak Committee, was formed by the Securities and Exchange Board of India (SEBI) and was tasked with improving corporate governance standards in India. The recommendations focused on strengthening board independence, improving disclosures, and protecting the interests of minority shareholders while ensuring that governance frameworks remain practical and effective. The committee recommended that at least 50% of the board members of listed companies should be non-executive directors. In cases where the chairperson is a promoter or related to the promoter, at least two-thirds of the board should consist of independent directors. Independent directors should not serve on more than eight listed entities. A mandatory separation of the roles of chairperson and CEO/MD in listed companies. The committee recommended having at least one independent woman director on the boards of listed companies to enhance diversity and inclusivity.

9.3.1 *Ownership Structure and Minority Shareholders*

It is essential to revisit the history of India to understand the current context of the ownership structure of companies listed on Indian stock exchanges. Thus, it is noteworthy that for centuries India had its business activities dominated by ethnic and sectarian groups (Morck & Steier, 2005; Damaraju & Makhija, 2018). Part of this historical perspective is described in Table 9.1.

According to Table 9.1, the ownership structure of companies listed on Indian stock exchanges is concentrated in large family business groups and the Indian government (Shleifer & Vishny, 1997; Dash, 2012; Kumar & Singh, 2013; Arora & Singh, 2020; Pareek & Sahu, 2022). The OECD data indicate that, between 2001 and 2018, the share of promoters in all companies listed on the stock exchanges of India was approximately 50%, in terms of the number of shares. This means that half of the shares of the companies that make up the Indian capital market are in the hands of promoters. Furthermore, there has been a steady increase in the number of companies where promoters hold more than 50% of the share capital. These

Table 9.1 Historical perspective of the participation of ethnic and sectarian groups in the ownership structure of Indian business groups

Period	Event
1858–1947	When India was a British colony called the British Raj, the Tata family (Parsi priestly origin) controlled India's most influential business group for the last 60 years. The group had contracts with the imperial government and protection from imperial tariffs.
1947–1956	After India's independence, the Tata family lost its neutrality benefits on this issue. As a result, the Birla family became the second-largest Indian business group in 1969. In addition, this family financed Mohandas Gandhi and the Congress party significantly.
1956–1991	The first Prime Minister Jawaharlal Nehru led India toward socialism through a set of regulations and inspections consisting of the following instruments: (a) Industrial Policy Resolution (1956); (b) Monopolies and Restrictive Trade Practices (MRTP, 1969), (c) Industrial Licensing Policy (1970); and (d) Foreign Exchange Regulation Act (1973). Therefore, companies had to seek a series of regulatory authorizations before starting a new operation or even increasing production capacity. This period became known as the "License Raj" or licensing regime. Attention is drawn to the fact that the owners of large family business groups, known as promoters, found it easy to get the license because of their relationships with bureaucrats. Another important point related to this period is that state-owned companies started to have exclusivity, or dominance, in sectors that demand high volumes of capital.
After 1991	In 1991, India started opening its economy and ended up with the License Raj. That allowed other large companies to emerge, especially in the information technology and e-commerce sectors. However, companies linked to large family business groups remained predominant in its economy. In addition, the Indian government sold part of its shares in state-owned companies, retaining control.

Source: Morck and Steier (2005), Gollakota and Gupta (2006), Singh and Gaur (2009), Damaraju and Makhija (2018), Mohanty and Mishra (2021), and Pareek and Sahu (2022)

numbers become more pronounced when the same analysis is conducted on the Top 500 companies with the highest market value in India (OECD, 2020).

Such concentration allows the interests of minority shareholders to be harmed, as they can be expropriated through mechanisms that transfer their wealth to controlling shareholders (La Porta et al., 2000). As an example of these mechanisms, the following can be cited: pyramidal corporate structures, complex corporate arrangements using cross-shareholdings and private funds, and disclosure only of mandatory information (Singh & Gaur, 2009; Jackling & Johl, 2009; Sriram, 2020). In addition, during the License Raj period, promoters from the same family launched several unrelated ventures with minimal resources. The rest of the capital was obtained through public offerings or financial institutions, especially from government banks. In this way, the family started to control the interests of several companies (Gollakota & Gupta, 2006; Guha et al., 2019). Akerlof (1970) points out that this context may have limited investments in the Indian industrial sector. In the case of companies under government control, the problem lies in the increase in privileges or non-salary gains of managers, such as unnecessary travel (Singh & Gaur, 2009).

Added to the above scenario, India has weak enforcement and rules for protecting minority shareholders' rights, even using the common-law system (La Porta et al., 2000; Nagar & Sen, 2016; Fahad & Busru, 2021). Since most businesses in India are family-owned, ensuring the independence of the board and safeguarding the rights of minority shareholders presents a significant challenge. Weak enforcement is characteristic of emerging countries and discourages minority shareholders from seeking their rights in court when they are not respected, reducing capital market liquidity (Shleifer & Vishny, 1997; Oliveira et al., 2016).

Various provisions in the Companies Act, 2013, SEBI regulations, and judicial precedents are designed to protect minority shareholders and ensure fair treatment. These safeguards help safeguard their interests and provide avenues for addressing grievances related to oppression or mismanagement. Under Sections 241–242 of the Companies Act, minority shareholders can approach the National Company Law Tribunal (NCLT) if they believe the company's affairs are being conducted in an oppressive or prejudicial manner. SEBI's Listing Obligations and Disclosure Requirements (LODR) mandate timely and transparent disclosures for listed companies, ensuring greater corporate accountability. Additionally, the LODR regulations require that certain Related-Party Transactions (RPTs) be approved by a majority of disinterested shareholders, thus protecting minority interests from being overridden by promoters or major shareholders. The SEBI Takeover Code (2011) further ensures that minority shareholders have an exit option during substantial acquisitions or takeovers, providing them with a fair price. Furthermore, Section 245 of the Companies Act, 2013, allows minority shareholders to initiate class action suits against the company or its auditors for fraudulent practices or mismanagement. If fraud or mismanagement is suspected, Section 213 of the Companies Act enables minority shareholders to request an investigation by applying with the NCLT. Lastly, Section 151 of the Companies Act allows small shareholders (owning shares worth up to INR 20,000) to collectively elect a director to represent their interests on the board of a listed company.

9.3.2 Corporate Governance Structure and Practices

India has adopted the Anglo-Saxon model of corporate governance (Oliveira et al., 2016; Guha et al., 2019; Kanojia & Bhatia, 2021; Pahi & Yadav, 2021). Therefore, the board of directors is of only one level and reports directly to the company's general meeting, which is the body responsible for its appointment. In terms of size, the board of directors of Indian companies must have a minimum of 3 members and a maximum of 15 members. There should be at least one women director on the board (Companies Act, 2013). The board of directors must contain at least one-third of the independent members. In addition, if a company can elect more than 15 members to the board of directors. In addition to the Companies Act 2013, Indian companies must observe Clause 49 of the Equity Listing Agreement, updated in 2014, regarding the composition of the board of directors, which establishes that at least 50% of the directors must be non-executive.

If the chairman of the board of directors is a non-executive director, then at least one-third of the directors should be independent directors but if the chairman of the board of directors is an executive director, then at least 50% of the directors should be independent directors.

The code entitled Integrity and Transparency in Governance and Responsible Code of Conduct (The CII Code) of the Confederation of Indian Industry (CII) recommends that, in addition to the aspects already mentioned regarding gender diversity, the board of directors is composed of at least one independent member with knowledge of the sector in which the company operates. Female representation on the board of directors of Indian companies rose from 5% in 2012 to approximately 14% in 2017. This increase resulted from a maneuver by the companies, which involved appointing a woman from a promoter's family to the board of directors. In response to this situation, as of 2017, SEBI required that all companies should have at least one independent director. As per SEBI, LODR (Listing Obligation and Disclosure Requirement) regulation 2015 states that the top 500 listed companies (based on market capitalization) should have at least one independent woman director from April 1, 2019, and for the top 1000 listed companies the applicable date is April 1, 2020. However, many companies did not comply with this regulation (Arora, 2021). There were penalties imposed on these companies as per section 172 of the Companies Act, 2013.

The Companies Act 2013 made it mandatory for Indian companies to have an audit committee to advise the board of directors. The committee is obliged to evaluate investments made by Indian companies in their subsidiaries, based in India or abroad, not listed on the stock exchange, as well as other remittances of funds (loans, donations, etc.) above 100 Crore Rupees (equivalent to USD 12.9 million on June 2, 2022) or that represent an amount greater than 10% of the subsidiary's assets, whichever is lower. In addition to this obligation, the audit committee is responsible for appointing, compensating, and evaluating the independent auditors, examining the financial statements, assessing risk management systems and internal controls, approving related party transactions, and so on. This committee must be composed of at least three directors, most of whom are independent directors. The chairperson of the audit committee should be an independent director. Finally, the audit committee must meet at least five times a year (Companies Act, 2013; Al-ahdal & Hashim, 2021; Deloitte, 2022). Shrivastav (2022) identified in his study that the characteristics of the audit committee, such as size, independence, and frequency of meetings, positively impact the value of companies, measured by Tobin's Q. In addition, the size of the audit committee has a positive and significant impact on ROE. On the other hand, the number of audit committee meetings has a negative effect on ROE.

Another mandatory committee for Indian companies is the Nomination and Remuneration Committee (Mishra & Mohanty, 2014). Its responsibility is to identify people qualified to assume higher positions in the company. According to established criteria, the nomination and remuneration committee recommends to the board of directors the appointment or dismissal of directors, evaluate directors' performance, select directors' compensation, key management personnel, and other employees. The nomination and Remuneration committee shall consist of at least three non-executive directors, and 50% of the members must be independent directors. The committee should meet at least once a year. If the chief executive officer (CEO) is on the nomination and Remuneration committee, he or she cannot chair it (Companies Act, 2013; Deloitte, 2022).

The Indian stock system is made up of common and preferred shares. The common shares give the right to vote proportional to the participation in the company's paid-in capital stock and dividends. Preferred shares provide a preferential right to receive dividends in the form of a fixed amount or fixed percentage, which may be exempt or subject to income tax and reimbursement. It should be noted that the amount to be paid as dividends is defined by the general meeting and cannot exceed that recommended by the board of directors. Furthermore, the board of directors may pay interim dividends to shareholders if justified by the company's profit (Companies Act 2013). Rajput and Jhunjhunwala (2019) identified that Indian family-controlled companies pay fewer dividends and keep more cash on hand for expropriation. This effect is smaller when there is a higher proportion of independent members on the board of directors and when the board of directors is larger.

As a way of minimizing possible opportunism and conflicts of interest arising from the separation between control and ownership, India has promoted several changes in its legislation aimed at strengthening corporate governance practices in companies. The main ones are the Companies Act 2013 and SEBI's Clause 49 Listing Agreement (Nagar & Sen, 2016). These changes originated from reports produced by the Bajaj Committees (1996), Kumar Mangalam Birla Committee (2000), Naresh Chandra Committee (2002), Narayanan Murthy Committee (2003), and Irani Committee (2005), which SEBI instituted (Jackling & Johl, 2009; Zattoni et al., 2009; Mishra & Mohanty, 2014; Mohanty & Mishra, 2021). The following are examples of some of the corporate governance practices established:

- Provision of independent directors in the composition of the board of directors.
- Institution of the audit committee, the nomination and remuneration committee, and the stakeholder relations committee.

- The performance evaluation process of the board of directors, executive officers, and auditors.
- Rotation of independent auditors every five years.
- Statement of responsibility by the CEO and CFO on the financial statements, internal controls, and compliance structure of the companies in the annual report.
- Minimum free float of 25% for all companies.

In addition to the above-mentioned practices, the Confederation of Indian Industry (CII) developed a code of voluntary adherence to corporate governance practices (Chahal & Kumari, 2013; Oliveira et al., 2016). The code is divided into 15 sections, namely: (1) Integrity, Ethics, and Governance, (2) Responsible Governance and Citizenship, (3) Role of Board, (4) Balancing Interests of Stakeholders, (5) Independent Directors and Women Directors, (6) Safe Harbors for Independent Directors, (7) Risk Management, (8) Succession Planning, (9) Role of the Audit Committee, (10) Improving audit quality (11) Disclosure and Transparency related issues, (12) Vigil Mechanism, (13) Stakeholder, Vendor, and Customer Governance, (14) Investor Activism, and (15) MSMEs and Start-ups.

The section titled *Integrity, Ethics, and Governance* highlights that the integrity of organizational processes is significantly influenced by the leadership, culture, and values of the company. It also reveals that the effectiveness of the board of directors depends on the right leadership, whose commitment to high ethical standards is essential. Therefore, it emphasizes the importance of the tone at the top. The absence of such an ethical level can compromise governance processes and compliance programs.

The section *Responsible Governance and Citizenship* reinforces the need for organizations to formally commit to ESG principles, aiming for responsible corporate citizenship. Furthermore, companies must be transparent and ethical by implementing policies capable of mitigating corruption, money laundering, market manipulation (insider trading), etc. The board of directors and executives need to understand that business competitiveness, corporate governance, and corporate citizenship must be correlated.

The third section, titled *Role of a High-Performing Board*, reveals that for a board of directors to be effective, it is necessary to align organizational strategy and develop the relevant capabilities of board members. The board of directors carries out the supervisory and management activities of the company. However, these activities must be conducted in a balanced manner. Another aspect addressed is the need to measure the board's performance through goals and deadlines. Finally, the section highlights the importance of the board developing skills related to digital technology and innovation, to complement their traditional skills in finance, legal, and industry.

The section *Balancing Interests of Stakeholders* describes the importance of balancing the interests of stakeholders in a company. This involves the need for board members and executives to disclose potential conflicts of interest to avoid personal enrichment. Furthermore, the section emphasizes the importance of clear policies to ensure that transactions with related parties are in the interest of the corporation and its stakeholders. The need to establish confidential policies within the group and to protect confidential information is also highlighted. Conflicts of interest go beyond financial interests and should be addressed through disclosures based on conflict-of-interest principles. The section reveals that transparency and collective discussion of these issues at the board level can help maintain the trust of investors and stakeholders.

The section *Independent Directors and Women Directors* describes the importance of independence and gender diversity on a company's board of directors. It emphasizes that the independence of each board member should be evaluated based on the context of the individual's position and the ability to raise issues and suggestions constructively, aiming at the collective success of the board. It also mentions that diversity, especially gender diversity, enriches perspectives within the board, contributing to more comprehensive and inclusive decisions. Furthermore, it envisions that the selection of independent directors should be meticulous, considering the relevant experience and the specifics of the organization, whether it's a start-up or a company established in the market. These professionals must be able to devote sufficient time to the organization's matters and have the freedom to question the relevant managers and shareholders when necessary. The corporation, in turn, should support the critical role of these directors by promoting open and challenging discussions during board meetings. Continuous dialogue between the chairman and the independent directors is essential to foster a healthy and responsible governance environment.

The *Safe Harbors for Independent Directors*. This section discusses the growing concern about the liability and reputation of independent directors in listed companies. Such concern stems from the fact that many processes related to irregularities in corporations end up involving all directors, regardless of each one's involvement in the irregularities. This has led to a shortage of qualified independent directors, driven by the fear of legal implications associated with their roles. The solution proposed in this section involves the implementation of clear "safe harbors", that is, safeguards, that protect independent directors, ensuring that proceedings against them are initiated only when there is preliminary evidence of their involvement in the irregularities, and not automatically. This measure aims to attract talent to company boards, emphasizing the importance of protecting these professionals and addressing minor infractions through alternatives to criminal prosecution. The section also mentions the need to decriminalize business laws and introduce transparent resolution mechanisms for minor offenses, to facilitate the business environment and promote corporate integrity and transparency.

The seventh section, whose title is *Risk Management*, states that given the global economic uncertainties, it is important for the board of directors to implement a policy of risk identification and management. One way of implementing this type of policy is through the establishment of a risk management committee. In addition, aspects involving information technology should be considered in the risk identification and management process, due to cyber-crimes. The committee should also take care of the identification and mutation of various financial risks to which the company is exposed.

The sections *Succession Planning* and *Role of the Audit Committee* address that the board of directors plays a key role in the executive and board members' succession process. Therefore, it is advisable to establish a nominations and remunerations committee to proactively act in succession planning of top managerial people such as the chairman, executive director, and managing director. Regarding the audit committee, the section highlights the importance of financial statements for investors. In this regard, to ensure the preparation and publication of quality financial statements, the audit committee must observe the following principles: (a) appropriate composition and dynamics of the committee; (b) an updated charter with clearly defined responsibilities; c) a risk-based approach to setting the committee's agenda; (d) understanding of current and emerging issues; (e) clear expectations regarding the communication of issues to the board; and (f) proactive and engaged supervision beyond the meeting room. Finally, the audit committee should pay special attention to potential risks related to the tone at the top, culture, and incentives.

The sections *Improving audit quality and enhancing the accountability of third parties who play a fiduciary role* and *Disclosure and Transparency related issues* highlight that improving audit quality is an important focus area. This is due to increased legal and compliance risks because of significant distortions in financial statements and a global effort in law enforcement. Therefore, it is crucial that the governance and management of corporations effectively collaborate with the work of auditors, especially regarding access to documents, reports, key personnel of the organization, and so on. Another key point of these sections is the need for corporations to have a responsible information disclosure policy, especially when the information can impact stock prices and when the corporation is listed in multiple jurisdictions. This section also focuses on the establishment of social media policy concerning sharing information of price-sensitive information.

The 12th section, titled *Vigil Mechanism*, describes that whistleblower mechanisms play a crucial role in corporate governance. It is recommended that boards create and integrate clear and robust principles, ensuring that complaints are received, analyzed transparently, and addressed in a manner proportional to their severity. Furthermore, it is important to have periodic updates on the status of the complaints received, ensuring that the conclusions of investigations are conducted fairly and proportionally.

The sections *Stakeholder, Vendor, and Customer Governance* and *Investor Activism* highlight that in the realm of corporate governance and regarding the relationship with stakeholders, it is crucial to adopt a non-political alignment stance, ensuring the demonstration of high ethical standards. It is vital to manage conflicts of interest with transparency and responsibility, in addition to ensuring that the segregation of duties is approved and monitored strictly at regular intervals. Principles of good governance should be extended to the immediate and important stakeholders such as creditors, customers, bankers, and employees. Concerning investor activism, it is advisable to seek a balance between granting management the necessary flexibility to implement their programs and establishing effective awareness channels with stakeholders. Such measures aim to encourage shareholders to express their opinions and exercise their voting rights actively on all relevant matters, thereby promoting a more inclusive and participative corporate governance.

Finally, the last section *MSMEs and Start-ups* emphasizes the importance of start-ups and micro, small, and medium-sized enterprises for economic growth, innovation, job creation, and foreign direct investment, among others. However, the boards of such corporations should not focus solely on economic and financial growth metrics. They should also adopt good governance practices, as these contribute to better access to financing, reduced dependence on promoters, effective organizational structures, and a higher likelihood of the company's long-term survival.

Although not mandatory, the Confederation of Indian Industry (CII), corporate governance code has significant alignment with the Companies Act 2013 and the amendments made in 2014 to Clause 49 of the Listing Agreement of SEBI. In addition, it is noteworthy that it seeks to lead Indian companies to observe ESG principles, which are highlighted in the current context. This topic sought to describe the relevant issues regarding Indian corporate governance observed in the bases that supported this chapter. The final considerations constitute the following section.

9.4 Conclusions

India has improved its corporate governance practices, primarily those of an *ex-ante* nature. However, the rights of minority shareholders are still violated, and the enforcement of laws through judicial means remains insufficient, making the *ex-post* mechanisms weak. This represents a significant challenge that still needs to be addressed by Indian regulatory bodies (Nagar & Sen, 2016; Fahad & Busru, 2021). This vulnerability possibly stems from the institutional environment established during the British colonization period and extended into the License Raj era.

The regulatory reforms stemming from the Companies Act of 2013 and Clause 49 of the Listing Agreement, 2014 of SEBI, considered milestones in the evolution of corporate governance practices in India, have resulted in obligations for companies regarding the inclusion of non-executive and independent members on the board of directors, the participation of women on the board, the establishment of audit, nomination and remuneration, and stakeholder relationship committees, as well as the performance evaluation of advisors, directors, and auditors. However, the inclusion of women on the board has been used to increase the influence of promoters' families within companies, and it is still allowed for the CEO to concurrently hold the position of board chairman (Arora, 2021; Kanojia & Gupta, 2022). An interesting point is that the governance manual, published by the Confederation of Indian Industry (CII), addresses aspects related to environmental, social, and corporate governance (ESG). Although the manual is voluntarily adopted, it may indicate a path for future regulations in the Indian capital market.

The present study put forth the corporate governance in India and various regulations and legislations governing the capital market including the NSE and BSE. In India, SEBI is the regulatory body that ensures that the NSE and BSE adhere to the various rules and regulations with an overall objective of protecting the investor's interest. Finally, it is emphasized that the objective of this chapter is to provide an overview of corporate governance practices in India and the same is achieved. It is suggested that other studies be carried out regarding corporate governance in India, such as, for example, reviews that incorporate journals published in other languages. Also, it is hoped that this chapter will be an inspiration for developing new empirical research on this topic.

References

Akerlof, G. A. (1970). The market for "lemons": Quality uncertainty and the market mechanism. *Quarterly Journal of Economics, 84*(3), 488–500.

Al-ahdal, W. M., & Hashim, H. A. (2021). Impact of audit committee characteristics and external audit quality on firm performance: Evidence from India. *Corporate Governance: The International Journal of Business in Society.*

Arora, A. (2021). Gender diversity in the boardroom and its impact on firm performance. *Journal of Management and Governance*, 1–21.

Arora, N., & Singh, B. (2020). Corporate governance and underpricing of small and medium enterprises IPOs in India. *Corporate Governance: The International Journal of Business in Society.*

Asia Index Private Limited (2024). Retrieved January 29, 2024, from https://www.asiaindex.co.in/

Bombay Stock Exchange. (2024). Retrieved January 29, 2024, from https://www.bseindia.com/index.html

Chahal, H., & Kumari, A. (2013). Examining talent management using CG as a proxy measure: A case study of state Bank of India. *Corporate Governance: The International Journal of Business in Society.*

Companies Act 2013. Retrieved May 31, 2022, from https://www.mca.gov.in/content/mca/global/en/acts-rules/companies-act/companies-act-2013.html

Damaraju, N. L., & Makhija, A. K. (2018). The role of social proximity in professional CEO appointments: Evidence from caste/religion-based hiring of CEOs in India. *Strategic Management Journal, 39*(7), 2051–2074.

Dash, A. K. (2012). Media impact on corporate governance in India: A research agenda. *Corporate Governance: The International Journal of Business in Society.*

Deloitte. (2022). Retrieved June 2, 2022, from https://www2.deloitte.com/in/en/pages/risk/articles/governance-101.html

Deloitte. (2024, January 28). *India economic outlook*. Retrieved January 28, 2024, from https://www2.deloitte.com/us/en/insights/economy/asia-pacific/india-economic-outlook.html

Department of Economic Affairs. (2022). Retrieved May 18, 2022, from https://dea.gov.in/

Dutta, D., & Vashisth, G. (2023). Nationalization regime: A comparative study. *International Journal of Law Management & Humanities., 6*(2), 2134.

EY Insights. (2023, January). *How India is emerging as the world's technology and services hub*. Retrieved January 30, 2024, from https://www.ey.com/en_in/india-at-100/how-india-is-emerging-as-the-world-s-technology-and-services-hub

Fahad, P., & Busru, S. A. (2021). CSR disclosure and firm performance: Evidence from an emerging market. *Corporate Governance: The International Journal of Business in Society.*

Gollakota, K., & Gupta, V. (2006). History, ownership forms and corporate governance in India. *Journal of Management History, 12*(2), 185–198.

Guha, SK, Samanta, N., Majumdar, A., Singh, M., & Bharadwaj, A. (2019). Evolution of corporate governance in India and its impact on the growth of the financial market: An empirical analysis (1995-2014). *Corporate Governance: The International Journal of business in Society.*

IFRS Foundation. (2022). Retrieved May 22, 2022, from https://www.ifrs.org/use-around-the-world/use-of-ifrs-standards-by-jurisdiction/view-jurisdiction/india/

Jackling, B., & Johl, S. (2009). Board structure and firm performance: Evidence from India's top companies. *Corporate Governance: An International Review, 17*(4), 492–509.

Joshi, A. (2017). Impact of political economy on economic strategy making in India (1947–1991). *Strategic Analysis, 41*(3), 236–256.

Kanojia, S., & Bhatia, B. S. (2021). Corporate governance and dividend policy of the US and Indian companies. *Journal of Management and Governance*, 1–35.

Kanojia, S., & Gupta, S. (2022). Bankruptcy in Indian context: Perspectives from corporate governance. *Journal of Management and Governance*, 1–41.

Kathiravan, C., Selvam, M., Venkateswar, S., Lingaraja, K., & Oli, S. M. (2017). Effect of temperature on stock market indices: A study on BSE and NSE in India. *International Journal of Economic Research.*

Kumar, N., & Singh, J. P. (2013). Effect of board size and promoter ownership on firm value: Some empirical findings from India. *Corporate Governance: The International Journal of Business in Society.*

La Porta, R., Lopez-de-Silanes, F., Shleifer, A., & Vishny, R. W. (1998). Law and finance. *Journal of Political Economy, 106*(6), 1113–1155.

La Porta, R., Lopez-de-Silanes, F., Shleifer, A., & Vishny, R. W. (2000). Agency problems and dividend policies around the world. *The Journal of Finance, 55*(1), 1–33.

Lattemann, C., Fetscherin, M., Alon, I., Li, S., & Schneider, A. M. (2009). CSR communication intensity in Chinese and Indian multinational companies. *Corporate Governance: An International Review, 17*(4), 426–442.

Mayur, M., & Saravanan, P. (2017). Performance implications of board size, composition, and activity: Empirical evidence from the Indian banking sector. *Corporate Governance: The International Journal of Business in Society.*

Ministry of Corporate Affairs. (2022). Retrieved May 22, 2022, from https://www.mca.gov.in/content/mca/global/en/home.html

Ministry of Finance. (2022). Retrieved May 18, 2022, from https://finmin.nic.in/

Mishra, S., & Mohanty, P. (2014). Corporate governance as a value driver for firm performance: Evidence from India. *Corporate Governance, 14*, 265.

Mohanty, P., & Mishra, S. (2021). A comparative study of corporate governance practices of Indian firms affiliated to business groups and industries. *Corporate Governance: The International Journal of Business in Society.*

Mork, R., & Steier, L. (2005). The global history of corporate governance: An introduction. In *A history of corporate governance around the world: Family business groups to professional managers* (pp. 1–64). University of Chicago Press.

Nagar, N., & Sen, K. (2016). How does regulation affect the relation between family control and reported cash flows? Comparative evidence from India and the United States. *Corporate Governance: An International Review, 24*(5), 490–508.

National Stock Exchange. (2024). Retrieved January 31, 2024, from https://www.nseindia.com/

Nepal, M., & Deb, R. (2024). Do IFRS convergence affects firm performance? Picturing Indian-listed manufacturing firms. *Rajagiri Management Journal, 18*(1), 82–94.

OECD. (2020). *Ownership structure of listed companies in India.* Retrieved February 1, 2024, from https://www.oecd.org/corporate/ownership-structure-listed-companies-india.pdf

OECD. (2022). Retrieved June 4, 2022, from https://www.oecd.org/about/members-and-partners/

Oliveira, M. C., Ceglia, D., & Antonio Filho, F. (2016). Analysis of corporate governance disclosure: A study through BRICS countries. *Corporate Governance: The international Journal of Business in Society.*

Pahi, D., & Yadav, I. S. (2021). Product market competition, agency cost, and dividend payouts: New evidence from emerging market. *Journal of Management and Governance*, 1–32.

Pareek, R., & Sahu, T. N. (2022). How far the ownership structure is relevant for CSR performance? An empirical investigation. *Corporate Governance: The International Journal of Business in Society.*

Rajput, M., & Jhunjhunwala, S. (2019). Corporate governance and payout policy: Evidence from India. *Corporate Governance: The International Journal of Business in Society.*

S&P Global. (2023, December 23). *India seizes crown of fastest growing G20 economy*. Retrieved January 28, 2024, from https://www.spglobal.com/marketintelligence/en/mi/research-analysis/india-seizes-crown-of-fastest-growing-g20-economy-dec23.html

Schipke, A., Turunen, J., Choueiri, N., & Gulde, A. M. (Eds.). (2023). *India's financial system*. International Monetary Fund. Retrieved Jan 30, 2024, from https://doi.org/10.5089/9798400223525.071

Securities and Exchange Board of India. (2021). Retrieved December 5, 2024, from https://www.sebi.gov.in/legal/acts/apr-2021/securities-contracts-regulation-act-1956-as-amended-by-the-finance-act-2021-13-of-2021-w-e-f-april-1-2021-_49750.html

Securities and Exchange Board of India. (2022). Retrieved May 18, 2022, from https://www.sebi.gov.in/index.html

Shleifer, A., & Vishny, R. W. (1997). A survey of corporate governance. *The Journal of Finance, 52*(2), 737–783.

Shrivastav, S. M. (2022). Corporate governance, audit committee characteristics and firm performance: Evidence from India. *IUP Journal of Corporate Governance, 21*(1).

Singh, D. A., & Gaur, A. S. (2009). Business group affiliation, firm governance, and firm performance: Evidence from China and India. *Corporate Governance: An International Review, 17*(4), 411–425.

Sriram, M. (2020). Do firm specific characteristics and industry classification corroborate voluntary disclosure of financial ratios: An empirical investigation of S&P CNX 500 companies. *Journal of Management and Governance, 24*(2), 431–448.

Standard & Poor's Dow Jones Indices. (2022). Retrieved May 14, 2022, from https://www.spglobal.com/spdji/en/regional-exposure/asia-pacific/#indices

World Bank. (2023, October 3). *India's growth to remain resilient despite global challenges*. Retrieved January 29, 2024, from https://www.worldbank.org/en/news/press-release/2023/10/03/india-s-growth-to-remain-resilient-despite-global-challenges

World Bank. (2024). Retrieved January 26, 2024, from https://data.worldbank.org/indicator/NY.GDP.MKTP.CD

World Federation of Exchanges. (2024).Retrieved January 26, 2024, from https://www.world-exchanges.org/

Zattoni, A., Pedersen, T., & Kumar, V. (2009). The performance of group-affiliated firms during institutional transition: A longitudinal study of Indian firms. *Corporate Governance: An International Review, 17*(4), 510–523.

Chapter 10
Spain

Corporate Governance in Spain

Maicon Manoel Benin, Clea Beatriz Macagnan, and Rafael Vaz Palmeira

10.1 Introduction

Governance is crucial in fostering a transparent, responsible, and trustworthy corporate environment in the relationship between the company, its shareholders, and the market. OECD (2016) argues that to promote long-term investment, institutionalizing corporate governance is vital to encourage long-term investment, financial stability, and the integrity of business relations. One of its best-known objectives is to help the company mitigate information asymmetry, opportunism, and conflicts of interest, which characterize the relationships between control and ownership when separated (Jensen & Meckling, 1976). In this context, we understand corporate governance as the set of mechanisms that address behaviors potentially detrimental to the corporation's and its stakeholders' economic results.

The study of specific markets can be relevant to understanding why some practices are adopted or avoided and why the results of such adoption or avoidance change according to the environment. Leblanc et al. (2012) highlights the European Commission's efforts to examine essential aspects of Corporate Governance and clarify the application and its criteria. In the EU Directive as regards disclosure of non-financial and diversity information by certain large undertakings and groups

M. M. Benin (✉)
Pontifical Catholic University of Rio Grande do Sul, Porto Alegre, Brazil
e-mail: maicon.benin@pucrs.br

C. B. Macagnan
Federal University of Paraíba, João Pessoa, Paraiba, Brazil

R. V. Palmeira
University of Salamanca, Salamanca, Spain
e-mail: rafaelvaz@usal.es

C. B. Macagnan (ed.), *Corporate Governance in Capital Markets*, CSR, Sustainability, Ethics & Governance,
https://doi.org/10.1007/978-3-031-94751-3_10

(Directive 2014/95/EU), the European Parliament argues the importance of non-financial and diversity information disclosure to pursue long-term profitability, social justice, and environmental protection. Such regulation proposal causes the adaptation of EU members' legislation as the French law through ordinance 07/18/2017 and decree 08/09/2017 (Gillet-Monjarret, 2022) or the Spanish Law 11/2018 of December 28, the latter considered by Anguiano-Santos and Rodríguez-Entrena (2024) one of the strictest in Europe Union. This specific chapter aims to review the components of the corporate governance structure in Spain.

According to the Spanish Institute of Family Firms, Spain relies heavily on family firms, representing more than 80% of companies and most of the employment and gross domestic product. Consequently, the Spanish market is characterized by a high concentration of capital in non-institutional shareholder groups, as highlighted by Gutierrez and Surroca (2014). In this regard, Galve-Górriz and Hernández-Trasobares (2015) argue that capital concentration on family firms can protect shareholders against weak regulation. Additionally, Gutierrez and Surroca (2014) find the Spanish minority shareholder protection regulation to be weak compared to the UK and the US.

Therefore, this chapter provides a literature review on corporate governance in Spain, considering regulations adopted in the country and articles published in some of the leading scientific journals. The chapter comprises this first section addressing the introduction. Section two discusses the Spanish stock market and the corporate governance structure. Finally, section three offers the final considerations and references.

10.2 Spanish Corporate Law and Stock Market

Spain is a southern European country with approximately 48.6 million inhabitants (*Instituto Nacional de Estadística*, 2024), and reached, in 2022, a gross domestic product (GDP) of about 1.4 trillion US Dollars (World Bank, 2023). The country is a member of the European Union, and its currency is the Euro. It is also a member of the Organization for Economic Co-operation and Development (OECD) (International Monetary Fund, 2021; OECD, 2021). In December 2023, the value of companies listed on the Spanish Stock Exchanges was about 1.2 trillion Euros (*Bolsas y Mercados Españoles*, 2024) as shown in Fig. 10.1.

10.2.1 Spanish Capital Market Development

The Spanish capital market officially began on September 10, 1831, with the creation of the Madrid Stock Exchange, which is still the largest stock exchange in Spain today. Initially, listed companies were limited to banks, railroads, and steel mills. Over time, the market took shape and began to expand with the creation of the

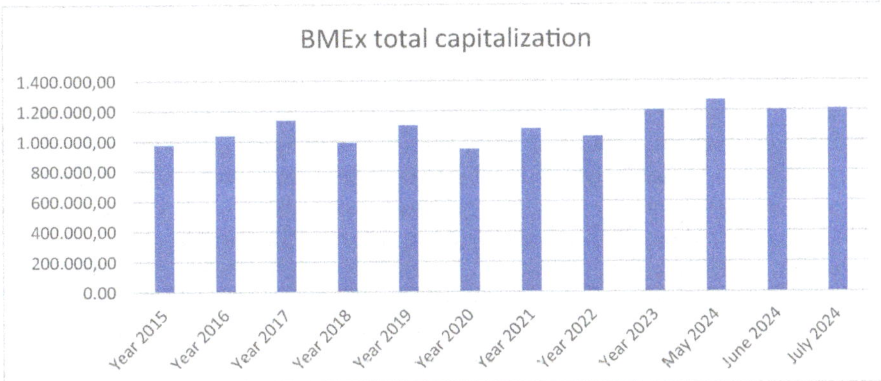

Fig. 10.1 BMEx total capitalization—2015–2024. *Source*: Values calculated by the authors based on data from the BME (2024)

Bilbao Stock Exchange in 1890, the Barcelona Stock Exchange in 1915, and the Valencia Stock Exchange in 1980. In 1988, Spain became part of the European Monetary System. Spain also became part of the Schengen Agreement in 1991, which progressively eliminated border controls between EU members. Spain has also been a member of the European Monetary Union (EMU) since 1999, which implies standard monetary policy and fiscal rules and economic policy coordination among EMU members.

The technological innovation of the Spanish market allowed its unification under the BME umbrella. In this sense, Spanish marked created an electronic trading platform (SIBE) in 1995, which was updated in 2001 as another significant milestone occurred with the creation of *Bolsas y Mercados Españoles* (BME) Spanish Exchanges, the group responsible for operating all the stock markets and financial systems in Spain. Since 2001, the Spanish capital market has been unified through SIBE, which guarantees the interconnection between the four Spanish exchanges, functioning as a single market (Madrid Stock Exchange, 2023; Bolsas y Mercados Españoles, 2023; Royal Legislative Decree 1/2010).

This entire market is supervised and inspected by the CNMV, which works primarily to ensure transparency, correct pricing, and investor protection in the Spanish capital market. All information received is publicized, valuing the security of all transactions in the market. In addition to advising the Spanish Government on matters related to the capital market, the CNMV participates in international institutions such as the International Organization of Securities Commissions (IOSCO) and the European Securities and Markets Authority (ESMA). Regarding Corporate Governance in Spanish, the CNMV actively contributed to issuing the Good Governance Code of *Olivencia* in 1998. Especially with the *Código Unificado de Buen Gobierno de las Cotizadas*, created in 2006, the code adhered to the mechanisms recommended for good Corporate Governance and had its most recent review in 2020 (CNMV, 2020). The Spanish capital market ended 2022 with 1498 listed companies, of which 1472 are national domestic and 27 are foreign (World Bank,

2023). About the categories, 121 are in the Continuous Market, 9 in other companies listed for floor trading, 19 in the LATIBEX, and 1349 in the BME Growth (Bolsas y Mercados Españoles, 2023).

The continuous market-listed companies are part of the Spanish Stock Exchange (BME), where the most significant companies are. This market is on an order-based model, a single e-wallet, and a trading system based on price-time priority. In addition to shares, subscription bonuses, certificates, and exchange-traded funds (ETFs) are traded. Furthermore, another segment destined only for Latin American companies is the LATIBEX, created in 1999 for the international market of Latin American bonds. The Spanish Stock Exchange (SIBE) electronic system quotes securities in euros, and companies provide the market with the same information as the supervisory institutions of their respective home markets. The main indexes of BME and their capitalization are depicted in Fig. 10.2.

Another segment is BME Growth, which focuses on small capitalization companies that want to expand, with regulation tailored to their needs and costs and adapted to their characteristics. Under this premise, companies benefit from the advantages of a market: funding, visibility, liquidity, and valuations. In addition to expanding companies, other types of collective investment institutions are also listed on the Alternative Stock Market in differentiated segments, such as Variable Capital Investment Societies (SICAVs or *Sociedades de Inversión de Capital Variable*), Real Estate Investment Companies (SOCIMIs or *Sociedades Anónimas Cotizadas de Inversión en el Mercado Inmobiliario*), Capital Entities Risk (ECRs or *Entidades de Capital riesgo*) and Free Investment Companies (SIL or *Sociedades de inversión Libre*). Finally, the companies listed for floor trading trades through an electronic system. Previously, the extinct so-called "System of Corros" was the traditional floor trading with traders physically present. However, with the

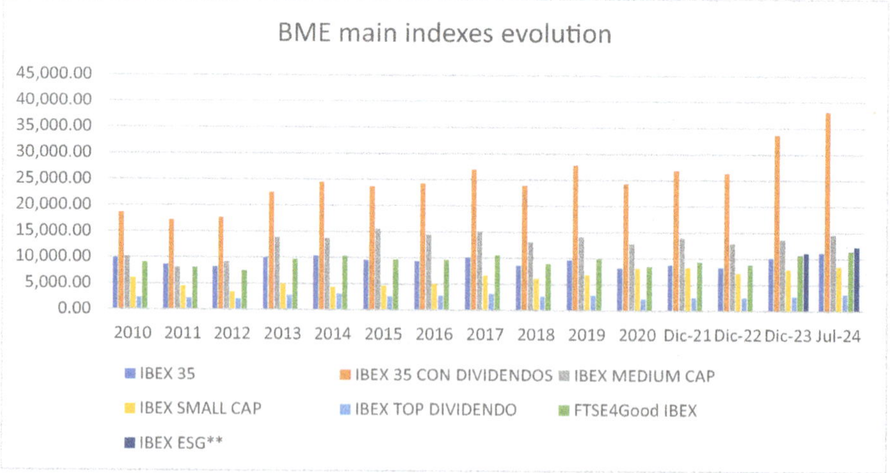

Fig. 10.2 BME main indexes evolution—2010–2024. *Source*: Values calculated by the authors based on data from the BME (2024)

advancement of technology and integrated systems, an online trading system was implemented and is hegemonic.

As for the dividend policy, there is no specific rule regarding the percentage of dividends that must be distributed by the companies, overseeing the statutory provisions of each one. However, according to Royal Legislative Decree 1/2010 (2010), Article 95 defines that when there is a Preferred-share dividend, the dividend value must be informed if it is not already defined in the company's bylaws; other shares (ordinary) will not receive the dividend before the dividend value for preferred shares has not been paid. Besides, bylaws must define the consequences of not paying the agreed value. In Article 99, non-voting shares have the right to the minimum annual dividends (fixed or variable).

If there are insufficient distributable profits, the unpaid part of the minimum dividend must be paid in the following five years. Until the unpaid value is not satisfied, the preferred shares will have the same rights as ordinary ones and retain economic benefits. Once all statutory reserves have been assigned, dividends are distributed proportionally to the paid-in capital. The company's dividend agreement must determine the payment term, which cannot exceed 12 months. A governance structure based on good practices can be significant for this market to function while respecting the objectives of companies and investors.

10.2.2 Spanish Corporate Law Development

Spain has a legal system based on civil law, specifically French civil law. As Spain became part of the European Monetary System in 1988, it simultaneously enacted Law 24/1988, called the Securities Market Law, reformed by the Royal Legislative Decree 1/2010, which has been continuously revised as per Law 25/2011 of August 1, which incorporates EU directive 2007/36/CE, the Royal Legislative Decree 9/2012 of March 16 which establishes urgent measures for the protection of insolvent mortgagors; the Law 1/2012 of June 22; the Royal Legislative Decree 1/2012 of June 22; the Law 14/2013, of September 27; Royal Legislative Decree 4/2015, by Law 2/2021 of March 29, Law 18/2022 of September 28, and by Law 6/2023 of March 17. This regulation has a financial aspect and is fundamentally governed by the principle of transparency, aiming to ensure the proper functioning of markets and the protection of investors. The economic aspect of listed companies is regulated by the Royal Legislative Decree 1/2010 and its modifications, which specifically focus on the corporate economic elements of listed companies (Royal Legislative Decree 1/2010, 2010; Madrid Stock Exchange, 2023). The financial aspect is regulated by law 6/2023, which substitutes the Royal Decree 4/2015, which, in turn, redraws Law 24/1988.

The stock market law in Spain aims to give greater coherence to the capital market ordering in the country, and its development shows an outstanding commitment to adapting to Spanish stock market development. It seeks to strengthen this market in a European-unified market. Chronologically, Law 24/1988 develops the necessary framework for the Spanish capital market development, providing the basis for creating the National Securities Market Commission (CNMV). The enactment of the law definitively transformed the country's capital market. In 1989, the continuous stock market began to operate, experiencing significant growth.

In addition, based on Law 24/1988, in 1989, the National Securities Market Commission (CNMV) was recognized as the supervisory body of the Spanish capital market and responsible for market transparency and efficient price formation. The legal framework expanded from Law 24/1988 by a series of updates that converged to the redraw text published under the Royal legislative decree 4/2015 of October 23, including Law 41/1999. The Law 44/2002 which regulated audit committees for publicly traded companies. Law 26/2003 modifies Law 24/1988 and Royal Legislative Decree 1564/1988 of December 22. Finally, the Law 6/2023 of March 17 establishes a new framework for the capital market in Spain.

10.2.2.1 Spanish Companies' Capital Market Pre-requisites

Funding sources for small and medium-sized businesses in Spain were historically limited to banks (Deeg & Perez, 2000). This context often ended up hindering the development of these societies. The Alternative Stock Market expanded funding possibilities. The listed companies' indexes are the IBEX 35, composed of the 35 listed companies with the highest liquidity and market value. The companies that make up this index are from different sectors and subsectors of the economy; however, they are all classified in the continuous market category.

The minimum requirement to register the company on the Spanish capital market is to have all its capital paid and not be subject to any statutory provision prohibiting its trading. In addition, the minimum share capital must be EUR 1,202,025.00, not counting holdings equal to or greater than 25%. Furthermore, the company needs to have a market value of at least 6,000,000.00 euros, a minimum of 25% of shares available to the public (free float), and sufficient disclosure of information to the public (Bolsas y Mercados Españoles, 2023).

According to the *Guía para salir a la bolsa* (IPOs Guide) developed by Bolsa y Mercados Españoles (2023), the preliminary steps include a detailed economic, financial, and legal study (due diligence). Then, the bylaws must reflect the newly listed company status: corporate governance, shareholders' rights to information and voting, and creating a corporate website, for example. Afterward, documents of the legal regime are analyzed, and an independent auditor audits the financial statements and delivers a prospectus containing information about the issuer and the security. Finally, after approval by the CNMV, the prospectus must be made public, and only then will the public offer for sale (IPO) be carried out. After completing all the procedures and meeting the requirements, the CNMV forwards the authorization for BME to end the listing process, which will take place within 4 to 6 months.

Regarding this listing process, two points stand out: (1) exclusion of participation equal to or greater than 25% of the minimum capital required and (2) minimum 25% free float requirement. The first point may indicate an attempt to combat ownership concentration, while the second points to a considered low level of shares available to the public, contributing to this concentration. There seems to be an attempt to balance this situation (Gutierrez & Surroca, 2014; Galve-Górriz & Hernández-Trasobares, 2015). It is also worth noting an essential finding of the study by Mejía (2021), in which the evidence points to a strong influence of the institutional environment on the content of decisions made by regulatory agencies. The study concludes that Spanish regulatory agencies have a higher rate of appeal decisions (21%) than the United Kingdom (9%).

For a more profound understanding of the functioning of the Spanish capital market, it is necessary to know the characteristics of the capital structure and the functioning of the country's shareholding system. Thus, the next section of this chapter addresses this system's main classifications and features.

10.3 Spanish Market Capital Structure, Shareholding System, and Dividend Policy

According to Galve-Górriz and Hernández-Trasobares (2015), the level of development of the institutional structure influences the concentration of ownership, promoting higher dispersion of capital. Observing some aspects of the Spanish institutional environment is essential to better understanding its capital structure and the characteristics of its shareholding system. The capital structure of organizations directly impacts the problem of asymmetry, opportunism, and the emergence of conflict of interest, as managers can make decisions freely if the owner acts passively.

Institutional environments with better dispersion of capital are prone to higher asymmetry, opportunism, and the emergence of conflict of interest between managers and owners, given the difficulty of owners monitoring the company's managers. However, capital concentration can raise problems of asymmetry, opportunism, and the emergence of conflict of interest between controlling and minority shareholders (Jensen & Meckling, 1976). This opportunism risk is related to the possibility that the majority shareholder chooses the manager with whom they will have direct contact, be able to guide decisions, and access the company's information, mitigating the possibility of opportunism and conflict of interest.

According to La Porta et al. (1997), the French civil law system adopted by Spain does not provide legal protection for investors as the common law. This configuration is usually related to the concentration of ownership, mainly in domestic groups, combined with weak corporate control, and this seems to be the case for the Spanish market. In Spain, large groups of shareholders and the tendency toward the lack of independence of the boards of directors end up culminating in the takeover of minority shareholders, the possibility of introducing entrenchment mechanisms by managers, and the lack of transparency (Ruiz-Mallorquí & Santana-Martín, 2009; Gutierrez & Surroca, 2014).

Additionally, the Spanish market is characterized by a significant presence of family firms (Otero González et al., 2024). According to the Family Firms Institute (2024), family firms represent more than 80% of Spanish companies and are responsible for nearly 60% of the labor force and the country's GDP. It is worth considering that family businesses are characterized by higher ownership concentration, as highlighted by Galve-Górriz and Hernández-Trasobares (2015). Besides, Denis and McConnell (2003) and Galve-Górriz and Hernández-Trasobares (2015) suggest that ownership concentration in family groups can protect shareholders under weak legal protection. Regarding family "firms" performance, Isakov and Weisskopf (2014) found that family firms with high ownership concentration (more than 80%) have similar performance to non-family firms with lower valuation, explained by the authors as a potential agency conflict, while moderated owned benefit from both higher performance and valuation.

The Spanish business segment has always had a capital structure with substantial participation in the banking sector. In carrying out its functions as a supplier and creditor in the market, it actively participates as the main controlling shareholder of various businesses. However, this context has gradually changed into a hybrid scenario, where domestic shareholders have become the protagonists regarding market control (Ruiz-Mallorquí & Santana-Martín, 2009). Still, in the Spanish context, Delgado-García et al. (2010) analyzed Spanish companies from 2000 to 2007. They found a negative relationship between the concentration of capital, typical of the Spanish environment, and their reputation. In addition, Garbe and Garcia-Cestona (2012) found the relationship between ownership structure and human resources strategy in Spanish firms.

Another issue that deserves a more in-depth analysis involves the results of companies that underwent privatization processes between 1985 and 2003. The evidence does not indicate a significant improvement in profitability and efficiency after privatization (Cabeza-García & Gómez Ansón, 2007). However, there seemed to be a decrease in these companies' capital concentration when comparing the pre- and post-privatization periods. Regarding the classes of shares traded, the Spanish stock exchange system is divided into ordinary shares, preferred shares, non-voting shares, and redeemable shares.

When the share is classified as ordinary, each share will be entitled to one vote at the shareholders' meeting. In other words, one ordinary share corresponds to one vote for all deliberations included in the meeting agenda. Consequently, the power to influence the company will be limited to the number of shares owned, even though the shares have guaranteed the right to vote. The owner of common shares will not have preferences in the company's dividend payments. The company's preference for paying dividends is the first right of owners of another type of share, which has a preference: preferred shareholder.

The preferred shareholder owns preferred stock. This kind of share is developed for those who prefer receiving dividends over voting rights. Unlike ordinary shares, the ownership of preferred shares usually does not give voting rights. However, this characteristic may vary in other countries, depending on the institutions that regulate the respective capital market. Although Spanish regulation does not define a minimum dividend payout, the bylaws must establish the amount paid to preferred shares, the consequences of non-payment of part or all the preferential dividends, and the rights of holders of privileged shares.

Similarly, there are the non-voting shares. These shares are issued only with the right to receive a minimum dividend; in situations of liquidation of the company, these shareholders have a preference over common shareholders in reimbursing their shares. Furthermore, if non-compliance with the minimum dividend payment by the company is not met, the shareholders acquire the right to vote. Another option is redeemable shares, whose redemption, total or partial purchase by the issuer or third parties, is fixed within the term or released at the shareholder's option, depending on the issuance conditions (Guide to Business in Spain, 2023).

As for the dividend policy, there is no specific rule regarding the percentage of dividends that must be distributed by the companies, overseeing the statutory provisions of each one. However, according to Royal Legislative Decree 1/2010 (2010), dividends can only be distributed when the legal reserve reaches 20% of the share capital; in the case of new capital, 10% of the profit will be allocated to the legal reserve until it gets the required percentage. Once all statutory reserves have been assigned, dividends are distributed proportionally to the paid-in capital. The company's dividend agreement must determine the payment term, which cannot exceed 12 months. A governance structure based on good practices can be significant for this market to function while respecting the objectives of companies and investors.

Besides the continuous market, BME has a specific segment that focuses on small capitalization companies that want to expand, with regulations tailored to their needs and costs, and adapted to their characteristics, called BME Growth. Under this premise, companies benefit from the advantages of a market: funding, visibility, liquidity, and valuations. This segment is relevant to the Spanish market because of the concentration of small and medium companies. More than 99% of Spanish companies are classified as SMEs, responsible for more than 80% of the labor and 65% of Spanish GDP, according to BME-Growth (2024).

In addition to expanding companies, collective investment institutions are listed in differentiated segments on the Alternative Stock Market. There is a need to define Collective investment institutions specifically, as Spanish legislation defines two significant groups of such institutions. The funds (*fondos*) are institutions that do not have a juridical form. Funds are managed by Investment Service Firms (ESI or *Empresas de Servicios de inversión*), and its investors do not have voting rights regarding the institution's investment strategy. Due to that, such funds must formally develop formal documents to explain and register the investment strategy in CNMV.

The second major group is the investment societies (SI or *Sociedades de inversión*). Those collective investment institutions must be registered as a public limited company (*Sociedad Anónima*). Having a juridical form and identity, it can self-manage and assign part of its value to its management. Another difference from the funds is that the investors in investment societies are considered shareholders and have the right to vote regarding their management and investment strategy. As a public limited company, it must follow the Royal Legislative Decree 1564/1988 of

September 22 regarding public limited companies and the Royal Legislative Decree 1/2010 of July 2 regarding Capital Markets and their updates. Besides, it must follow Law 35/2003 of November 4 regarding Collective Investment Institutions. Before starting the approach related to the Spanish corporate governance structure, it is essential to understand how the accounting and audit systems function.

10.4 Accounting and Audit System

The Spanish market Adopts and enforces the International Financial Reporting Standards (IFRS), or international accounting standards. Such standards are mandatory for all companies after publishing a new General Accounting Plan (PGC) in 2007 (Royal Decree 1514/2007 of November 16). Besides, the country also published an adaptation applicable to small and medium-sized companies on Royal Decree 1515/2007 of November 16). The rules were enacted for information processed on January 1, 2008 (Ortiz-Martínez et al., 2019; IFRS, 2021).

The Spanish General Accounting Plan is regulated by the *Instituto de Contabilidad y Auditoria de Cuentas* (ICAC), an autonomous body created in 1988 under Law 19/1988 of July 12. The plan follows a basic conceptual framework, where the key elements to understand and interpret the rest of its content are defined; in this way, we highlight some relevant points.

The company's annual accounts include the balance sheet, profit and loss statement, cash-flow statement, and annual report. Annual accounts must be displayed to be useful for users' decision-making. They must represent the actual image of the company's assets, financial situation, and results. Moreover, the information must be relevant, faithful, complete, transparent, and comparable. Related to this, CNMV and BME require companies listed on the Spanish stock exchange to periodically disclose, in a transparent and standardized manner, their financial information, as follows:

- Annually: the company's individual and consolidated financial statements, management report, and audit report for each year ended.
- Semi-annual: the financial statements with information like the annual ones. Term of 60 days from the end of each semester.
- Quarterly: results and relevant information. Term of up to 45 days from the end of the quarter.

The annual statements must comprise accounts of assets, liabilities, equity, income, and expenses. The business management is deemed to remain in business for the foreseeable future, recording their transactions considering the generating events of operations and following the uniformity about the criteria adopted to register the operations. These accounting records must be verified and expressed in a way that represents the economic and financial reality of the organization, valuing prudence, and the relevance of information. In addition, companies must publicly communicate any financial or legal event that may have a material impact on their equity, corporate, operational, or economic structure. In this sense, Amat and Zanotti (2018) argue that good accounting and financial practices contribute to improving governance.

The Spanish audit system has its operating rules described in the Royal Legislative Decree 1/2010 of July 2, regarding Capital Companies, in its fourth chapter, specifically in articles 263 to 271. All organizations operating in the Spanish capital market are required to undergo an annual external audit, except those that, for two consecutive years, meet at least two of the following requirements: the total assets do not exceed 2,850,000.00 euros; the net value of the turnover does not exceed 5,700,000.00 euros; the average number of employees during the year does not exceed 50. This possibility is lost if organizations do not fulfill two of these requirements for two consecutive years (Law 14/2013 of September 27 that changes the Royal Legislative Decree 1/2010 of July 2).

The law establishes that it is up to the general meeting to appoint individuals or legal entities to conduct the audit; this choice must be made by the end of the current year. The initial period cannot be less than three or more than ten years, counted from the start date of the first year of the audit. If the general meeting does not fulfill this attribution before the audit of the first fiscal year, any director or partner may request the CMNV to appoint the auditors. In addition, auditors cannot receive any benefit or value from society other than that intended for their legal remuneration based on clear criteria.

Regarding the specific regulation on the exercise of audit activities in Spain, Law 22/2015 (2015) was approved, which adapted Spanish internal legislation to the European standard 2014/56/EU issued by the European Parliament. The main objective of the standard is to strengthen audit independence, improve its quality, and reinforce confidence in the organizations' economic and financial information. The Spanish standard follows international and auditing standards adopted by the European Union Commission.

According to Law 22/2015 (2015), which regulates auditing and was incorporated into the text of the Royal Decree 1/2010 of July 2, the maximum duration of audit contracts must be nine years. However, the replacement of the main auditors must occur in periods not exceeding five years, with an interval of three years being necessary for these same auditors to re-audit the organization. Regarding the search for audit independence, the auditor must not have provided, for example, accounting, internal audit, and legal services to the audited organization or its related parties in the previous year to which the audited financial statements refer. In addition, there must be a fee cap to mitigate conflicts of interest.

Auditors must analyze whether the annual accounts faithfully represent the companies' equity, financial, and economic situation, issuing a clear and detailed opinion on the results of their work within one month. Therefore, it is the role of the company's audit committee to provide the necessary information, annually monitor the internal audit work and communicate with the external auditors and the board of directors. The Spanish Code of Good Governance (CNMV, 2020) mentions that the audit committee supervises the preparation process and ensures the companies' financial and non-financial information integrity.

The following section describes aspects related to the composition and functioning of the audit committee and other discussions related to the corporate governance structure of Spanish companies.

10.5 Corporate Governance Structure

In Spain, boards of directors have a tradition of being dominated by foreign directors, with low independence of their members. To reform this operating structure of the boards of directors, in 1998, the CNMV approved the "Olivencia Code of Good Governance." The code's main recommendation was the inclusion of independent directors on the boards of directors, aiming to protect the interests of floating capital (Pucheta-Martínez & Fuentes, 2007; Gutierrez & Surroca, 2014). In 2006, the CNMV developed and first published the "Unified Code of Good Governance for Public Limited Companies" to expand and further develop the country's governance structure. Therefore, Spain's current corporate governance structure must be evaluated by considering two levels: the mandatory regulations resulting from Spanish corporate laws and regulations and the voluntary recommendations in the Code of Good Governance.

This "Unified Code of Good Governance for Public Limited Companies" is advisory; consequently, it is altered to exclude recommendations that achieve regulation status. Due to its nature, it has suffered several updates during the almost two decades of existence. The most recent revision occurred in 2020. However, this code's voluntary recommendations are based on the principle of compliance or explanation. Either the company complies with the recommendations or explains why it has not adhered to them, primarily aimed at publicly traded companies.

However, when applicable, it can be used by any company. Given the voluntary nature of the recommendations contained in the Spanish Good Governance Code, it is up to shareholders, investors, and the market in general to analyze and evaluate the information disclosed and the explanations provided by companies, and the CNMV is not responsible for using the degree of compliance as a criterion in its deliberations. This situation is without prejudice to the monitoring powers and other competencies regarding CNMV.

The code contains important recommendations, such as compliance with the one-share, one-vote rule. The bylaws must not limit the votes of the same shareholder or make it difficult to take control by acquiring shares in the market. When the company is under the control of another organization, it must inform them of the respective activities developed with the related parties and the mechanisms adopted to resolve possible conflicts of interest.

Companies should inform them of changes that have occurred and the reasons for not following any recommendations. During the annual meeting, the chairman must verbally inform shareholders about the most relevant facts of the company's corporate governance, supplementing the written information circulated in the annual report. In this way, companies should define and promote a policy for communication and contact with shareholders and institutional investors through the media, social networks, and other channels.

Companies must value transparency and facilitate the exercise of rights by shareholders on equal terms, including the disclosure of voluntary reports with transparency and on time for the shareholders. In addition, the company should make public on its website, permanently, the requirements and procedures that it will accept to prove the ownership of the shares, the right to attend the general meeting of shareholders, and the exercise or delegation of the right to vote.

The board of directors must be directly responsible for monitoring the company's management to achieve corporate objectives by treating all shareholders equally and expressing when they consider that any decision does not serve social interests. It must be an adequate size to support its efficient operation, the participation of all directors, and agility in decision-making. It must have at least half of independent directors (5–15 members recommended), and the number of female directors should account for at least 40% of the board of directors' members before the end of 2022.

The directors will dedicate sufficient time to effectively developing their functions, getting to know the company's business and the governance norms it governs, and participating in the orientation and updating programs that organize the company. Proprietary directors should resign when the shareholders they represent dispose of their ownership interest in its entirety. If such shareholders reduce their stakes, thereby losing some of their entitlement to proprietary directors, the latter number should be reduced accordingly.

Another critical point is that the board of directors should not delegate powers to issue shares or convertible securities without pre-emptive subscription rights for an amount exceeding 20% of capital at the time of such delegation. The audit committee should ensure that the financial statements presented to the board agree with the accounting norms. In cases where the auditors include any qualification in their report, the audit committee chairperson should clearly explain their opinion regarding the scope and content at the general meeting.

Companies must establish rules that oblige directors to disclose any circumstances that may damage the name or reputation of the organization, related or not to their role in the company, and to present their resignation, if applicable, and the advice of any criminal charges brought against them and the progress of any subsequent trial. Furthermore, the board of directors must not propose the dismissal of independent directors before the end of the statutory term, except when there is cause, upon proposal by the nominating committee.

The board shall meet as frequently as necessary to carry out its responsibilities effectively, establishing committees as needed. The president is primarily responsible for the functioning and must adopt an action plan and assess and correct deficiencies detected about the board's operational efficiency, functioning, and composition of the committees; diversity of the board, and competence of the members; the performance of the chairman of the board, and the company's chief executive. When there is an executive committee, it must be composed of at least two non-executive members, at least one of whom must be independent. The recommendation is to separate the roles of the CEO and chairman.

The compensation for executives and directors must be adequate and transparent. The remuneration of the board of directors will be adequate to attract and retain directors with the desired profile and reward the dedication, qualification, and responsibility required by the position, but without compromising the independent judgment of the non-executive directors, to promote the achievement of the society, incorporating precise mechanisms to avoid excessive risk-taking and the reward of unfavorable results. The code recommends disclosing total amounts but not in detail, compromising information transparency. In this regard, Sánchez-Marín et al. (2022) examined the influence of governance mechanisms on excessive executive remuneration, comparing companies in the United Kingdom and Spain. The results indicated that Spanish companies present higher excessive remunerations, mainly due to the lower effectiveness of the shareholding structure and the board of directors.

Regarding the audit committee, the members should be appointed based on their knowledge and experience in accounting, auditing, and risk management. The company's standards must reinforce the qualification requirement, independence, and scope of action. Moreover, a company must maintain a risk control and management function under the responsibility of an internal unit or department, directly supervised by the audit committee or, where appropriate, by another specific board committee.

It is also highlighted that the company must define an appropriate environmental and social sustainability policy as a non-delegable board power and report its development, application, and results transparently and in detail. The findings of Gutiérrez-Ponce et al. (2022) indicate that companies in the IBEX35 index need to improve the transparency and robustness of this information, making it more accessible and in compliance with Environment, Social, and Governance (ESG) parameters.

Although the code of good corporate governance practices in Spain was first published in 2006, in his study, Turnbull (1995) highlighted the Mondragón region as the birthplace of companies with controls that reinforced the idea of Corporate Governance as a determining factor. Some points of the Spanish good governance code are worth highlighting in building a sustainable competitive advantage, with empirical evidence from the studies analyzed in this review. The study by Cortijo-Gallego and Yezegel (2008) investigated the North American Law Sarbanes-Oxley's impacts on corporate governance practices in Spain. The results indicate significant efforts to increase disclosure and improve governance mechanisms. The publication of the Spanish Code of good corporate governance practices can be considered an action in this sense.

Regarding the Spanish efforts to improve governance mechanisms, we can compare the study by Gutierrez and Surroca (2014), which highlighted that Spain had weaker corporate control, a high concentration of capital, and low transparency compared with the United Kingdom and the United States. The more recent study by Anguiano-Santos and Rodríguez-Entrena (2024) states that the Spanish adaptation of the EU directive 2014/95/ EU regarding non-financial disclosure is one of the strictest in Europe.

According to Gutierrez and Surroca (2014) evidence, there was still much to be developed on corporate governance. However, one must not analyze a regulation without considering its environment, and as highlighted by Otero-Lastres in Ramil (2019), regulations always follow society. It is vital to adapt the regulation to society fast enough to minimize the gap between common practice and its regulation. In this sense, the proliferation of Spanish regulations regarding the capital market is evidence of the effort to adapt to the common practice. Besides, the specific aspects of the Spanish market must be considered. In this context, the regulation must follow the actual characteristics of the Spanish Market, with more than 80% of its companies defined as family firms, which doubles the proportion estimated by Faccio and Lang (2002) for continental Europe (44.29%).

A recommendation to solve a situation evidenced by empirical data is that by the end of 2022, the board of directors should be occupied by a minimum of 40% women. The Cabo et al. (2011) study indicated fewer women in management positions. In addition, it identified that the occurrence of women increases the probability that other women will occupy the same jobs, suggesting a vector of this transformation. According to the last Corporate Governance Reports of issuers of securities admitted to trading on regulated markets (CNMV, 2022), there were 31.9% of women on Spanish Boards. IBEX35 companies showed 37.6% of women on the board of directors in 2022, compared to 27% in 2019.

Hernández-Madrigal et al. (2012) analyzed the Spanish Code of Good Governance's influence on the disclosure of risk-related information. The results indicated an improvement in the quality and quantity of this information. Along the same lines, evidence points to the association between national characteristics of culture, religion, and political functioning with the strength of accounting controls (Kleinman et al., 2019). These results reinforce the already-mentioned influence of the institutional environment on the adoption and the unfolding of the regulations issued.

Regarding the emphasis on transparency-related recommendations, Baraibar-Diez et al.'s research (2016) analyzed 24 European codes of good governance to identify how transparency is addressed. The results indicate that countries with a French civil law legal system, such as Spain, have the worst focus index on transparency-related aspects. This result aligns with what Ramírez and Tejada (2018) found when analyzing the importance of stakeholders from Spanish universities regarding the transparency of Corporate Governance practices. It also aligns with the concentration of family firms, considering Denis and McConnell (2003) and Galve-Górriz and Hernández-Trasobares (2015) argument that family firm groups are a defense mechanism against weak shareholder protection legislation.

Other code points worth mentioning are about executive compensation; the code recommends the disclosure of total amounts but not in detail, which jeopardizes the transparency of information; there is only a mild recommendation related to environmental prevention and social assistance policies, except in the cases concerning the participation of women in the board of directors, there are no clear recommendations regarding effective ways for companies to guarantee diversity in the boards and committees; there is no clear position regarding the cases of CEO duality. Finally, regarding the relationship with some empirical evidence, although with the distinction of periods and themes, it seems coherent to recognize that the Spanish code of good governance practices still needs improvement. Moreover, as discussed throughout the text, some institutional issues specific to Spain and countries that also share civil law must be structured adequately, especially regarding protecting minority shareholders and information transparency.

10.6 Final Considerations

The Spanish stock market was regulated by Law 24/1988 and is supervised by the CNMV. The operation of the stock exchanges is the responsibility of BME, being carried out in a unified manner. The main index is the IBEX35, composed of the 35 highest-value companies, and the share classes are divided into ordinary, preferential, non-voting, and redeemable shares. To operate, companies listed on the Spanish stock exchange must periodically calculate and publish accounting information by IFRS standards, have an internal audit committee, and undergo periodic external audits, according to the rules established in Law 24/1988 and Law 22/2015. The most recent version of the Spanish Code of Good Governance Practices was published in 2020 by the CNMV and follows standards established by other international codes of good governance, such as the OECD code.

Our objective was to analyze the regulations and voluntary initiatives adopted in the Spanish capital market and discuss their content based on empirical data from scientific articles published in some of the main journals. The discussions are mainly based on evidence of a market with a high concentration of capital, a low level of transparency, and weak protection for minority shareholders. In addition, the rules' content often suggests the occurrence of these situations, and empirical evidence supports this.

The institutional feature, based on the legal framework of French civil law, is an aspect that seems to significantly contribute to the quality of corporate governance of firms listed on the Spanish market; however, it does not act alone. The period of use of the Spanish code of good governance practices is still short, and research such as the present one aims to contribute to understanding the actual state of the applicable norms and their empirical adherences. Understanding the market of a country like Spain can even serve as evidence so that other countries with similar characteristics can have a foothold.

We do not intend to exhaust the discussion but bring a broad, grounded review of relevant aspects of Spanish Corporate Governance. We recommend carrying out future studies to deepen specific aspects of the Spanish business environment and analyze the impacts caused by the Spanish Governance Code.

References

Amat, O., & Zanotti, C. (2018). Buen Gobierno en materia contable y financiera. *Revista de Contabilidad y Dirección, 25*(2), 35–52.

Anguiano-Santos, C., & Rodríguez-Entrena, M. (2024). Sustainability reporting in focus: Analyzing Spanish transposition of the non-financial reporting European directive in the Agri-food sector. *Agricultural and Food Economics, 12*, 10. https://doi.org/10.1186/s40100-024-00303-z

Baraibar-Diez, E., Odriozola, M. D., & Sánchez, J. L. F. (2016). Transparency through European corporate governance codes. *International Journal of Disclosure and Governance, 13*(3), 244–261. https://doi.org/10.1057/jdg.2015.17

Bolsa de Madrid. (2023). Retrieved October 27, 2023, from https://www.bolsamadrid.es/esp/aspx/Portada/Portada.aspx

Bolsas Y Mercados Españoles. (2023). *A guide to listing on the stock market*. Retrieved June 6, 2024, from https://www.bolsasymercados.es/bme-exchange/docs/docsSubidos/Listing/Guide-How-to-list-BME-Exchange.pdf

Bolsas Y Mercados Españoles. (2024). *Market report 2023*. Retrieved June 6, 2024, from https://www.bolsasymercados.es/docs/infmercado/2023/ing/Market-Report-BME-2023.pdf

Cabeza-García, L., & Gómez Ansón, S. (2007). Governance and performance of Spanish privatized firms. *Corporate Governance: An International Review, 15*(4), 503–519. https://doi.org/10.1111/j.1467-8683.2007.00584.x

CNMV. (2020). *Código unificado de buen gobierno de las sociedades cotizadas*. https://www.cnmv.es/DocPortal/Publicaciones/CodigoGov/CBG_2020.pdf

CNMV. (2022). *Corporate governance reports of issuers of securities admitted to trading on regulated markets*. https://www.cnmv.es/DocPortal/Publicaciones/Informes/IAGC_2022.pdf

Cortijo-Gallego, V., & Yezegel, A. (2008). Contagion effect of the Sarbanes–Oxley Act: Evidence from Spain. *International Journal of Disclosure and Governance, 5*(2), 140–152. https://doi.org/10.1057/jdg.2008.6

Deeg, R., & Perez, S. (2000). International capital mobility and domestic institutions: Corporate finance and governance in four European cases. *Governance, 13*(2), 119–153. https://doi.org/10.1111/0952-1895.00126

Delgado-García, J. B., De Quevedo-Puente, E., & De La Fuente-Sabaté, J. M. (2010). The impact of ownership structure on corporate reputation: Evidence from Spain. *Corporate Governance: An International Review, 18*(6), 540–556. https://doi.org/10.1111/j.1467-8683.2010.00818.x

Denis, K., & McConnell, J. (2003). International corporate governance. *Journal of Financial and Quantitative Analysis, 38*(1), 1–36. https://doi.org/10.2307/4126762

de Cabo, R. M., Gimeno, R., & Escot, L. (2011). Disentangling discrimination on Spanish boards of directors. *Corporate Governance: An International Review, 19*(1), 77–95. https://doi.org/10.1111/j.1467-8683.2010.00837.x

Directive 2014/95/EU of the European Parliament as regards disclosure of non-financial and diversity information by certain large undertakings and groups. https://eur-lex.europa.eu/legal-content/EN/TXT/?uri=CELEX:32014L0095

Faccio, M., & Lang, L. (2002). The ultimate ownership of Western European corporations. *Journal of Financial Economics, 65*(3), 365–395. https://doi.org/10.1016/S0304-405X(02)00146-0

Family Firms Institute. (2024). *Cifras de la empresa familiar en España*. https://www.iefamiliar.com/la-empresa-familiar/cifras/#:~:text=Se%20estima%20que%201%2C1,el%20total%20de%20las%20empresas

Fundo Monetário Internacional. (2021). Retrieved November 16, 2021, from https://www.imf.org/en/Countries/ESP

Galve-Górriz, C., & Hernández-Trasobares, A. (2015). Institutional framework, concentration of ownership, and results of large family corporations in Latin America and Spain. *Corporate Governance., 15*(4), 409–426. https://doi.org/10.1108/CG-12-2014-0144

Garbe, J. N., & Garcia-Cestona, M. (2012). Ownership structure and human resources strategy: The case of Spanish manufacturing firms. *Academy of Management Proceedings, 2012*(1), 15042. https://doi.org/10.5465/AMBPP.2012.242

Gillet-Monjarret, C. (2022). Promoting sustainability assurance mission in the European Directive regulatory context. *Journal of Applied Accounting Research, 23*(1), 184–206. https://doi.org/10.1108/JAAR-04-2021-0085

Guide to Business in Spain 2023. (2023). https://www.guidetobusinessinspain.com/wp-content/uploads/2023/09/ANNEX-1_Guidetobusinessinspain-2023_INVESTINSPAIN.pdf

Gutierrez, I., & Surroca, J. (2014). Revisiting corporate governance through the lens of the Spanish evidence. *Journal of Management & Governance, 18*(4), 989–1017. https://doi.org/10.1007/s10997-012-9250-5

Gutiérrez-Ponce, H., Chamizo-González, J., & Arimany-Serrat, N. (2022). Disclosure of environmental, social, and corporate governance information by Spanish companies: A compliance analysis. *Sustainability, 14*(6), 3254. https://doi.org/10.3390/su14063254

Hernández-Madrigal, M., Blanco-Dopico, M. I., & Aibar-Guzmán, B. (2012). The influence of mandatory requirements on risk disclosure practices in Spain. *International Journal of Disclosure and Governance, 9*(1), 78–99. https://doi.org/10.1057/jdg.2011.22

International Financial Reporting Standards. (2021). https://www.ifrs.org/use-around-the-world/use-of-ifrs-standards-by-jurisdiction/view-jurisdiction/spain/

Instituto Nacional de Estadística. (2024). Annual Population Sensus. Retrieved July, 16, 25, from https://www.ine.es/dyngs/Prensa/en/CENSO2024.htm

Isakov, D., & Weisskopf, J. P. (2014). Are founding families special blockholders? An investigation of controlling shareholder influence on firm performance. *Journal of Banking and Finance, 41*, 1–16. https://doi.org/10.1016/j.jbankfin.2013.12.012

Jensen, M. C., & Meckling, W. H. (1976). Theory of the firm: Managerial behavior, agency costs, and ownership structure. *Journal of Financial Economics, 3*(4), 305–360. https://doi.org/10.1007/978-94-009-9257-3_8

Kleinman, G., Lin, B. B., & Bloch, R. (2019). Accounting enforcement in a national context: An international study. *International Journal of Disclosure and Governance, 16*(1), 47–67. https://doi.org/10.1057/s41310-019-00056-y

La Porta, R., Shleifer, A., Vishny, R. W., & Lopez-de-Silanes, F. (1997). Legal determinants of external finance. *Journal of Finance, 52*, 1131–1150. https://doi.org/10.1111/j.1540-6261.1997.tb02727.x

Leblanc, R., Bankes, J., Kam, A. F., Fraser, J. R., Gryglewicz, P., Hill, C., et al. (2012). General commentary on European Union corporate governance proposals. *International Journal of Disclosure and Governance, 9*(1), 1–35.

Ley 1/2012 de 22 de junio de 2012. *Ley de simplificación de las obligaciones de información y documentación de fusiones y escisiones de sociedades de capital*. https://www.boe.es/buscar/act.php?id=BOE-A-2012-8406

Ley 11/2018 de 28 de diciembre de la que se modifica el Código de Comercio, el texto refundido de la Ley de Sociedades de Capital aprobado por el Real Decreto Legislativo 1/2010, de 2 de julio, y la Ley 22/2015. https://www.boe.es/buscar/doc.php?id=BOE-A-2018-17989

Ley 14/2013 de 27 de septiembre de apoyo a los emprendedores y su internacionalización. https://www.boe.es/buscar/act.php?id=BOE-A-2013-10074

Ley 18/2022 de 28 de septiembre. de creación y crecimiento de empresas. https://www.boe.es/buscar/act.php?id=BOE-A-2022-15818

Ley 19/1988 de 12 de julio de 1988. Ley de Auditoría de Cuentas. https://www.boe.es/buscar/act.php?id=BOE-A-1988-.

Ley 2/2021 de 29 de marzo de medidas urgentes de prevención, contención y coordinación para hacer frente a la crisis sanitaria ocasionada por el COVID-19. https://www.boe.es/buscar/act.php?id=BOE-A-2021-4908

Ley 22/2015 de 20 de julio de 2015. *Ley de Auditoría de Cuentas*. Retrieved July 20, 2022, from https://www.boe.es/buscar/act.php?id=BOE-A-2015-8147

Ley 24/1988 de 28 de julio de 1988. Ley de Mercados españoles. Retrieved November, 10, 2021, from https://www.boe.es/buscar/act.php?id=BOE-A-1988-18764

Ley 25/2011 de 1 de agosto de reforma parcial de la Ley de Sociedades de Capital y de incorporación de la Directiva 2007/36/CE. https://www.boe.es/buscar/doc.php?id=BOE-A-2011-13240

Ley 44/2002 de 22 de noviembre, de Medidas de Reforma del Sistema Financiero. https://www.boe.es/buscar/act.php?id=BOE-A-2002-22807

Ley 6/2023 de 17 de marzo, de los Mercados de Valores y de los Servicios de Inversión. https://www.boe.es/buscar/act.php?id=BOE-A-2023-7053

Mejía, L. E. (2021). Judicial review of regulatory decisions: Decoding the contents of appeals against agencies in Spain and the United Kingdom. *Regulation & Governance, 15*(3), 760–784.

OECD. (2016). *Princípios de governo das Sociedades do G20 e da OCDE*. https://www.oecd-ilibrary.org/docserver/9789264259195-pt.pdf?expires=1718893517&id=id&accname=guest&checksum=B24B477EFFD0A8BBD5D03C3104C871B1

OECD. (2021). Retrieved November 18, 2021, from https://www.oecd.org/

Ortiz-Martínez, E., Antón-Renart, M., & Marín-Hernández, S. (2019). La reforma contable en España: un análisis desde la perspectiva del tiempo y grado de conocimiento de los profesionales. *Revista Brasileira de Gestão de Negócios, 21*, 365–386. https://doi.org/10.7819/rbgn.v21i2.3979

Otero González, L., Querentes Hermida, R. E., Durán Santomil, P., & López Penabad, C. (2024). Evaluation of the performance of Spanish family businesses portfolios. *Journal of Family Business Management*. https://doi.org/10.1108/JFBM-02-2024-0036

Pucheta-Martínez, M. C., & de Fuentes, C. (2007). The impact of audit committee characteristics on the enhancement of the quality of financial reporting: An empirical study in the Spanish context. *Corporate Governance: An International Review, 15*(6), 1394–1412. https://doi.org/10.1111/j.1467-8683.2007.00653.x

Ramil, A. (2019, June 4). *El derecho siempre va detrás de la sociedad, debe adaptarse a la realidad en que se vive*. La Opinión, Coruña. https://www.laopinioncoruna.es/sociedad/2019/06/04/derecho-detras-sociedad-debe-adaptarse-23767216.html

Ramírez, Y., & Tejada, Á. (2018). Corporate governance of universities: Improving transparency and accountability. *International Journal of Disclosure and Governance, 15*(1), 29–39. https://doi.org/10.1057/s41310-018-0034-2

Real decreto 1514/2007 de 16 de noviembre de 2007. *aprueba el Plan General de Contabilidad*. Retrieved September 18, 2022, from https://www.boe.es/buscar/act.php?id=BOE-A-2007-19884

Real decreto 1515/2007 de 16 de noviembre de 2007. aprueba el Plan General de Contabilidad de Pequeñas y Medianas Empresas y los criterios contables específicos para microempresas. Retrieved September 18, 2022, from https://www.boe.es/buscar/act.php?id=BOE-A-2007-19966

Real decreto legislativo 1/2010 de 02 de julio de 2010. aprueba el texto refundido de la Ley de Sociedades de Capital. Retrieved November 17, 2021, from https://www.boe.es/buscar/act.php?id=BOE-A-2010-10544

Real decreto legislativo 1564/1988 de 22 de diciembre, por el que se aprueba el texto refundido de la Ley de Sociedades Anónimas. https://www.boe.es/buscar/doc.php?id=BOE-A-1989-30361

Real decreto legislativo 4/2015, de 23 de octubre, por el que se aprueba el texto refundido de la Ley del Mercado de Valores. https://www.boe.es/buscar/act.php?id=BOE-A-2015-11435

Real decreto-ley 9/2012 de 16 de marzo. de simplificación de las obligaciones de información y documentación de fusiones y escisiones de sociedades de capital. https://www.boe.es/buscar/doc.php?id=BOE-A-2012-3812

Ruiz-Mallorquí, M. V., & Santana-Martín, D. J. (2009). Ultimate institutional owner and takeover defenses in the controlling versus minority shareholders context. *Corporate Governance: An International Review, 17*(2), 238–254. https://doi.org/10.1111/j.1467-8683.2009.00735.x

Sánchez-Marín, G., Lucas-Pérez, M. E., Baixauli-Soler, S., Main, B. G., & Mínguez-Vera, A. (2022). Excess executive compensation and corporate governance in the United Kingdom and Spain: A comparative analysis. *Managerial and Decision Economics, 43*(7), 2817–2837. https://doi.org/10.1002/mde.3564

Turnbull, S. (1995). Case study: Innovations in corporate governance: The Mondragón experience. *Corporate Governance: An International Review, 3*(3), 167–180. https://doi.org/10.1111/j.1467-8683.1995.tb00112.x

World Bank. (2023). Retrieved October 23, 2023, from https://www.worldbank.org/en/search?q=Spain. https://www.world-exchanges.org/

Chapter 11
Hong Kong

Corporate Governance in Hong Kong: Issues, Systems, Characteristics, and Regulations

Cenaide Francieli Justen and Eliene Aparecida de Moraes

11.1 Introduction

Hong Kong is a non-member country of the Organization for Economic Co-operation and Development (OECD, 2022). In 2021, Hong Kong Exchange and Clearing ranked as the seventh largest stock exchange in the world in terms of market value of listed shares, with an amount of USD 5.43 trillion at the end of 2021 (WFE, 2023). In historical terms, during the armed conflicts between China and Great Britain and with the signing of the Treaty of Nanking, China was forced to hand over the island of Hong Kong to the British, and five trade ports were opened, beginning the process of economic opening. In 1918, 46.5% of Hong Kong's government revenue came from trade. In 1984, a joint declaration was signed by China and the United Kingdom, establishing that the Special Administrative Region (HKSAR) began to have its government with its independent powers, independent finances, freedom from Chinese taxes, a system of taxation, its currency, and free port status. However, it was after the 1997 Asian financial crisis that a search for improving Corporate Governance began with the aim of protecting the interests of interested parties. This historical context has resulted in a capital market in which most companies are concentrated in large family business groups (Chen et al., 2005). Approximately 75% of companies listed on the Hong Kong Stock Exchange in 2012 had one shareholder dominant, owning 30% or more of the issued shares (OECD, 2017).

Furthermore, Hong Kong's capital market is overseen and regulated by the Securities and Futures Commission (SFC), an independent statutory body

C. F. Justen (✉)
University of Vale do Rio dos Sinos, Porto Alegre, Brazil

E. A. de Moraes
University of Rio Verde, Rio Verde, Brazil

C. B. Macagnan (ed.), *Corporate Governance in Capital Markets*, CSR, Sustainability, Ethics & Governance,
https://doi.org/10.1007/978-3-031-94751-3_11

established in 1989 to regulate Hong Kong's securities and futures markets. In regulatory terms, it adopted the standard law system due to British influence (Miniaoui et al., 2022). Therefore, the chapter aims to describe the main characteristics of corporate governance in Hong Kong. To achieve this objective, a literature review was carried out covering the legislation that regulates the Hong Kong capital market, the corporate governance code, and other information related to the capital market or corporate governance in Hong Kong.

The results reveal that Hong Kong has been improving its corporate governance structure and practices, especially with the Securities and Futures Ordinance, Companies (Winding-Up and Miscellaneous Provisions) Ordinance, and Principles of Responsible Ownership. However, there are still challenges regarding the protection of minority shareholders, the independence of non-executive directors, female participation on the board of directors, and environmental, social, and corporate-ESG practices.

Given this context and to understand the stage of corporate governance in Hong Kong, this chapter describes the evolution of corporate governance in Hong Kong thanks to a systematic review of literature and governance regulation (e.g., company law, corporate governance code). Section 11.2 presents the evolution of the economic system, historical and legal aspects of the Hong Kong Stock Exchange and Securities Commission, corporate legislation that impacts companies' corporate governance, and the particularities of adopting international accounting standards. Section 11.3 discusses the corporate governance models permitted for publicly traded companies. Finally, final considerations and references are presented.

11.2 Evolution of Economic System and Corporate Governance

Following the 1997 Asian financial crisis, Hong Kong sought to improve its corporate governance mechanisms. This movement made significant progress with the Securities and Futures Ordinance, updated in 2003. Therefore, this section addresses the main aspects of corporate governance in Hong Kong, covering the historical and general aspects of the Hong Kong Stock Exchange and market regulations of capital; the updating and evolution of practices and corporate governance; and accounting aspects related to the internationalization of accounting standards.

These aspects are relevant, considering that in 2008, 9665 public companies were registered in the Hong Kong Commerce Register, whereas in 2014, the last year of publication of this statistic, this increased to 12,188. The total number of registered companies was 710,766 in 2008. It increased to 1,179,231 at the end of February 2014, an increase of 65.9% in 7 years, demonstrating substantial growth in company formation between 2008 and 2014. The high increase in the formation of public companies in a short period justified the study of the evolution of the economic system and corporate governance in Hong Kong.

11.2.1 Hong Kong Stock Exchange and the Securities and Exchange Commission

In Hong Kong, transactions involving equity instruments (shares) and financial instruments (derivatives, debt securities, etc.) are carried out on its only stock exchange, the Hong Kong Exchanges and Clearing Market (HKEX). It originated from the merger between the Stock Exchange of Hong Kong Limited (SEHK), the Hong Kong Futures Exchange Limited (HKFE), and the Hong Kong Securities Clearing Company Limited (HKSCC) on March 6, 2000. On March 27, 2000, HKEX started trading its shares on its stock exchange (HKEX, 2022). HKEX is the seventh-largest stock exchange in the world in terms of the market value of listed shares, with a value of USD 4.57 trillion at the end of 2022 (WFE, 2023). HKEX is the fourth-largest stock exchange in Asia based on market capitalization value, behind only the Shanghai Stock Exchange (USD 6.72), the Tokyo Stock Exchange (USD 5.38), and the Shenzhen Stock Exchange (USD 5.70) (WFE, 2023). HKEX is one of the fastest-growing stock exchanges in Asia, with 2601 as of October 2023, up from 1200 in 2008.

Chart 11.1 demonstrates the importance of the Hong Kong capital market through the percentage relationship between the market value of shares traded on the HKEX and the country's gross domestic product (GDP).

It is possible to see that the market value of shares traded on the HKEX throughout the period between 2010 and 2021 was almost always greater than 1000% of Hong Kong's GDP. HKEX is an attractive market for foreign and institutional investors due to the adoption of international accounting standards and the free exchange

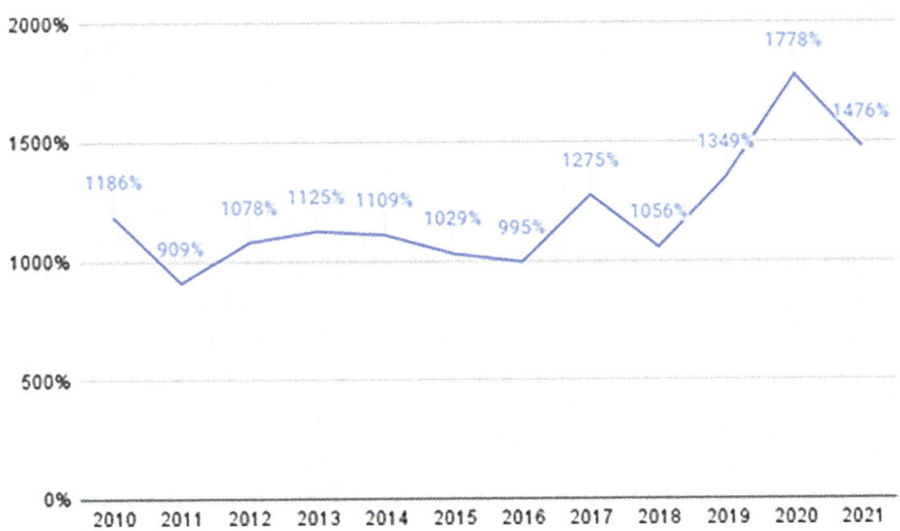

Chart 11.1 The percentage relationship between the market value of shares traded on HKEX and Hong Kong's GDP. *Source*: WFE (2023)

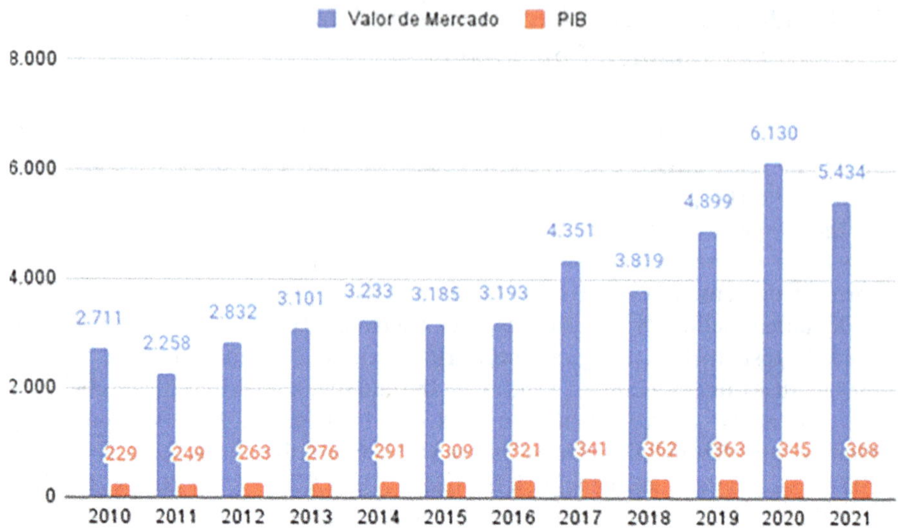

Chart 11.2 The market value of shares traded on HKEX and Hong Kong's GDP (in USD billion). *Source*: WFE (2023)

of information and capital (Kim et al., 2021). Chart 11.2 demonstrates the historical perspective of the market value of shares traded on the HKEX and the value of Hong Kong's GDP, in USD billion, between 2010 and 2021 to elucidate the relevance of the Hong Kong capital market.

It is noted that the market value of shares traded on HKEX showed an average growth of 8% during these 11 years. Hong Kong's GDP had an average growth of 4% in the same period. The increase in foreign investment (Vichitsarawong et al., 2010) and the low cost of listing on the stock market attract an increasing number of foreign companies (Du et al., 2013). At the end of October 2023, HKEX comprised 2601 listed companies, corresponding to $30,755.9 billion in capitalization (HKEX, 2023b).

HKEX has five different indices. The Hang Seng Index, launched on November 24, 1969, is the main performance indicator of the Hong Kong capital market. The actions are grouped into four sectors, namely: financial, public utility services, goods, and commerce. It is made up of 76 companies. The Hang Seng China Enterprises Index (HSCEI) reflects the performance of Mainland Chinese stocks listed in Hong Kong. It was launched on August 8, 1994, and comprises 50 companies. The Hang Seng Tech Index represents the performance of the 30 largest technology companies listed on the HKEX. Its launch took place on July 27, 2020. The MSCI China A 50 Connect Index was launched on August 20, 2021. This index captures the performance of the 50 largest companies, with A share, listed in Shanghai and Shenzhen through Northbound Stock Connect. The most representative sector of this index is financial. The CSI 300 Index demonstrates the performance of the top 300 shares of companies listed on the Shanghai and Shenzhen stock exchanges. Its launch occurred on April 8, 2005 (HKEX, 2022; HSI, n.d.).

The Hang Seng Index is the most relevant of the HKEX (HSI, n.d.). Most companies in the Hang Seng Index are linked to the technology and financial sectors.

Hong Kong's capital market is overseen and regulated by the Securities and Futures Commission (SFC), an independent statutory body established in 1989 to regulate Hong Kong's securities and futures markets. For (a) maintaining and promoting a fair, efficient, competitive, transparent, and orderly securities and futures industry; (b) helping the public understand the workings of the securities and futures industry; (c) providing protection for the investing public; (d) minimizing crime and misconduct in the industry; (e) reducing systemic risks in the sector; and (f) helping the government maintain Hong Kong's financial stability.

In regulatory terms, Hong Kong adopted the standard law system due to British influence (Miniaoui et al., 2022). In general, countries that use civil law have weaker protection for minority shareholders compared to countries that use the standard law system (La Porta et al., 2000). Therefore, the actions of the supervisory and regulatory bodies of the Hong Kong capital market are based on a set of regulations applied to the capital market. The most important ones are spelled out in Cap. 571 Securities and Futures Ordinance (04/01/2023), which changes and consolidates laws about financial products, the securities and futures market, the securities and futures industry, regulated activities, investor protection, and other related or incidental issues. Cap. 32 Companies (Winding-Up and Miscellaneous Provisions) Ordinance governing the liquidation of companies; for receivers and managers; for offering shares and debentures; for prospects; for disqualification orders; to prevent evasion of the Companies Ordinance; and for incidental and connected matters. The Principles of Responsible Ownership are principles and guidance to help investors determine how best to fulfill their ownership responsibilities.

Hong Kong is one of the largest financial centers in the world, playing an important role in the global economy. In this sense, it is essential that information about companies be disclosed, and that the information disclosed is reliable for investors to make decisions. To improve the reliability and credibility of reported information and allow investors to make comparative analyses of companies listed on the Hong Kong Stock Exchange with companies listed on other stock exchanges, the Hong Kong Accounting Board began requiring companies to adopt International Accounting Standards (IFRS) (Jaggi & Tsui, 2007). Before adopting IFRS in 2005, gains or losses arising from the revaluation of investment property were recognized in equity. After adopting IFRS, these revaluation gains or losses began to be recorded in the company's income statements (Chen & Tang, 2017). However, corporate practices do not fully comply with IFRS due to the lack of efficient and effective oversight mechanisms (Vichitsarawong et al., 2010).

Considering that in this section, the main aspects of the stock exchange, supervisory and regulatory bodies, and the legislation that governs the Hong Kong capital market were exposed, the next section addresses the predominance of the capital structure of companies listed on their exchanges of values.

11.2.2 National Corporate Legislation and International Accounting Standards (IFRS)

Due to conflicts of interest between management, directors, and shareholders, corporate governance plays an important role in reducing possible agency problems arising from the separation between control and ownership. After the Asian crisis, Hong Kong has been creating non-profit institutions that promote better corporate governance practices: (a) the Hong Kong Institute of Directors (HKID), (b) Asian Corporate Governance Association (ACGA), (c) Hong Kong Institute of Certified Public Accountants (HKICPA), (d) Hong Kong Institute of Chartered Secretaries (HKICS) and (e) Hong Kong Law Reform Commission (HKLRC) (HKEX, 2021).

This section covers the main aspects of Hong Kong's corporate legislation, discusses the recommendations of the Corporate Governance Code, and discusses the adoption of international accounting standards in the country.

11.2.2.1 Corporate Law in Hong Kong

The Companies Ordinance (Cap. 622), issued on July 12, 2012, consists of 921 sections, providing a modernized legal framework with standards for forming and operating companies in Hong Kong. The Companies Regulations came into force on March 3, 2014. The Companies Regulations were amended in 2018 (Amendment No. 2, or Amendment Ordinance) and have four main objectives: (a) improve corporate governance, (b) ensure better regulation, (c) facilitate business, and (d) modernize the law. The Companies Regulations enable companies to prepare two types of financial reports: simplified financial reports and comprehensive financial reports.

Simplified financial reporting is exempt from certain specific requirements relating to the preparation of financial statements, reporting rights, and auditors, and the applicable accounting standards are less complicated than standards applicable to listed companies or others not eligible for simplified reporting. However, auditing of these statements is still required. The criteria for determining eligibility for preparing simplified reports are that they are small businesses with total aggregate revenue not exceeding US$ 100 million, total aggregate assets not exceeding US$ 100 million, and numerous employees not exceeding 100. Companies listed on the Hong Kong Stock Exchange must prepare comprehensive financial reports. They must also prepare a more comprehensive management report, which includes an analytical and prospective business review, and have the option of sending a copy of the summary financial report instead of a copy of the entire financial report to its shareholders (Company Registry, 2023). Below, we will discuss some points of corporate law that are considered relevant to corporate governance in Hong Kong.

The Companies Regulations provide that the board of directors must present the financial statements for voting at the annual general meeting and that an executive who intentionally fails to comply with this requirement commits an offense and is subject to a fine of $300,000 and imprisonment for 12 months. The standard highlights that public limited companies must have at least two directors on the date of their incorporation.

Article 486 addresses situations in which parties are related to a director or former director of a company considering (a) a member of the director or former director's family, (b) a person who is in a cohabiting relationship with the director, or former director; (c) a minor child of a person covered by paragraph (b) who is not a child of the director or former director and lives with the director or former director; (d) a corporate body with which the director or former director is associated; (d) a person acting in the capacity of trustee of a particular trust, apart from a trust for an employee share scheme or a pension scheme; or (f) a person acting as a partner of the director or former director, the spouse of the director or former director, another person who is an entity linked to the director or former director (Company Registry, 2023). Furthermore, people employed or previously employed in good faith by that company or another company in the same group, or spouses, widowers, or minor children of these people. The director must declare any interest in a transaction with related parties to the other directors and inform the nature and extent of the interest in this type of transaction (Company Registry, 2023).

The rule is clear when it states that the company must not make loans to executives or corporate bodies controlled by the executives, enter credit transactions as a creditor of executives or related entities, or participate in questionable transactions (Company Registry, 2023). The term of the director's services contract must not exceed three years, and the company must publish a statement of the existence and duration of the agreement between the company and directors. A copy must be sent to the Directors' Services Committee-Hong Kong Securities for registration and filing by Articles 534 and 543 (Company Registry, 2023).

In Part 12, which relates to the administration and procedure of the company, the rule states that anything that can be done by a resolution passed at a general meeting of a company can be done without a meeting and the need for notice by a written resolution of the company's shareholders. A written resolution of a company has the same effect as if approved by a general meeting, except for the dismissal of an auditor before the end of the term of office (Company Registry, 2023). Directors or shareholders of the company may propose a written resolution. Shareholders may suggest resolutions in writing if they represent 5% of the total voting rights of all members entitled to vote in the deliberation or a smaller percentage, as provided for in the company's statutes, per Article 552 (Company Registry, 2023).

If members with voting rights properly appoint them, the Companies Regulations permit proxy voting. Deliberations at general meetings are approved when an ordinary resolution is made by a simple majority and a special resolution is made by a majority of at least 75% (Company Registry, 2023). According to Article 565, only directors can call a general meeting. However, directors can voluntarily call a general meeting when shareholders request it or call it when at least 5% of the total shareholders with voting rights request the meeting (Company Registry, 2023). In this case, the shareholders must declare the general nature of the business to be discussed at the meeting, and the directors must call it within 21 days after the date on which they become subject to the requirement. It cannot be held on a date later than 28 days after the date of the notice calling the meeting.

It is mandatory to send a notification informing the shareholder about the holding of a general meeting, whether in printed or electronic format (Company Registry, 2023). The notice must specify the date and time of the meeting, the physical location, and the virtual meeting technology to be used. It must also state that an annual general meeting and the notice must be available on the company website throughout the period commencing on the date of such notification and ending after the meeting. The notification must be sent to all shareholders, directors, and external auditors. According to Article 583, the general meeting can be held physically using virtual meeting technology or in a hybrid format.

In terms of disclosure of financial information, the Companies Regulations highlight that it must contain, in the explanatory notes to the annual consolidated statements, a statement of the holding's financial position for the current financial year and the movement in the holding's reserves. The subsidiary's financial statements must contain details of the ultimate parent company. The remuneration relating to the external auditor must be reported, understood as any amount paid by the company related to the auditor's expenses. The companies' regulations also provide for the disclosure of a report prepared by the directors that reports a review of the company's business, a description of the main risks and uncertainties faced, details of relevant events that affected the company and that occurred since the end of the fiscal year, and an indication of likely future developments in the company's business. And, if necessary, for a better understanding, this report should be in the business review: (a) analysis using financial key performance indicators, (b) discussion of the company's environmental policies and performance, (c) discussion of the company's compliance with relevant laws and regulations that have a significant impact on the company, and (d) an account of the company's key relationships with its employees, customers, suppliers, and others that have a considerable impact on the company and on which its success depends.

Finally, the Companies' Regulations require the disclosure of information on administrators' remuneration and any amounts paid to administrators in the form of benefits, retirement, payments about the termination of services provided by directors and advisors, and remuneration relating to services provided by counselors and directors.

11.2.2.2 Hong Kong Corporate Governance Code and International Accounting Standards

First, the main rules regarding the Hong Kong Corporate Governance Code are presented. Subsequently, the country's position regarding adopting international accounting standards issued by the International Accounting Standard Board (IASB) is presented. The Hong Kong Stock Exchange, a wholly owned subsidiary of HKEX, is responsible for issuing the Corporate Governance Code. The Corporate Governance Code is presented as two appendices to the listing rules: Main Board

Appendix 14 and GEM Appendix 15. There are no substantial differences between the two appendices.

The Hong Kong Code of Corporate Governance was reviewed in 2021 and came into force on January 1, 2022. It was divided into two sections: The first part covers mandatory disclosure requirements, and the second part covers the principles of good corporate governance, code provisions, and recommended best practices (HKEX, 2021). An attempt was made to present a summary description of the relevant issues regarding corporate governance addressed in the code.

To ensure transparency, the code highlights that issuers must include a narrative statement clarifying how the principles were applied to allow shareholder evaluation of the explanation. In addition, it must include a statement that reports whether the code's provisions have been complied with. If there is any deviation from the code's provisions, the deviation must be detailed during the financial year. The board of directors' composition must be categorized, containing the president's name, executive directors, non-executive directors, and independent non-executive directors. Likewise, the number of board meetings held during the fiscal year and the presence of each administrator, nominally at general meetings and the board of directors, as well as the identities of the president and chief executive, must be communicated, in addition to the deadline for the appointment of non-executive directors.

For committees that assist the board, information must be disclosed on the composition of the committees by independent non-executive directors, non-executive directors, and executive directors, indicating the names and identifying the chairperson of each committee. The number of meetings held by the committee during the year and the attendance record of members by name must also be disclosed. Furthermore, it must contain a summary of the work during the year, including a report on how it fulfilled its responsibilities in reviewing quarterly, semi-annual, and annual results for the audit committee a report on how it fulfilled its duties in reviewing quarterly, semi-annual, and yearly results. The remuneration committee established the remuneration policy for directors and executives, evaluated executive directors' performance, approved the policy for directors and executives, evaluated executive directors' performance, and approved the terms of service provision contracts for executive directors. Regarding the nomination committee, the nomination policy needs to be disclosed. The risk committee must have a report on how it fulfilled its responsibilities in reviewing risk management systems and internal controls and the effectiveness of the internal audit function.

In terms of risk management and internal control, the code indicates that an issuer must report in the corporate governance report that it has carried out a review of the effectiveness of its risk management systems and internal controls and must disclose whether it has an internal audit function, the frequency that the risk management systems and internal controls are reviewed, and the period covered, and that the risk management systems and internal controls are considered effective and adequate. The code highlights the issue of diversity, considering that a policy on diversity must be included in the company's corporate governance system, as well as the measurable objectives defined to implement the policy and the progress towards achieving these objectives. Disclosure and explanation should include when gender diversity will be achieved about the board and the numerical targets and timelines established for achieving gender diversity within the board.

Regarding shareholder rights, it is necessary to report how shareholders can call an extraordinary general meeting and the procedures by which questions can be put to the board and contact to allow these meetings to be directed appropriately. And be allowed sufficient contact to present proposals at shareholder meetings. Any significant changes to the issuer's constitutional documents must be reported so that shareholders can communicate their opinions on various matters, as well as measures taken to solicit and understand the views of shareholders and interested parties regarding the relationship with the investor.

The code highlights the relevance of the company's corporate purpose, strategy, and governance. It notes that the company must be led by an effective board that must take responsibility for its leadership and control and is collectively responsible for promoting its success by directing and supervising its business. Directors must make decisions objectively in the best interests of shareholders. The board must establish the company's purpose, values, and strategy, ensuring these and the shareholder culture are aligned. All directors must act with integrity, lead by example, and promote the desired culture. Directors must also include a discussion and analysis of group performance in the annual report, an explanation of the basis on which the issuer generates or preserves value over the long term, and the strategy for achieving the issuer's objectives.

The code also states that the board is responsible for governance functions and may delegate responsibility to a committee or committees. The board must at least develop and review the company's corporate governance policies and practices and make recommendations; review and monitor the training and ongoing professional development of counselors and senior management; review and monitor company policies and practices for compliance with legal requirements and regulations; develop, review, and monitor the code of conduct and compliance manual applicable to employees and directors; and monitor compliance. Furthermore, the board must have a balance of skills, experience, and diversity of perspectives appropriate to the requirements of the business. It must ensure that directors devote sufficient time and make contributions compatible with their roles and responsibilities on the board. Independent non-executive directors must be identified in all communications disclosing the names of directors. The board must conduct a regular evaluation of its performance.

Regarding appointments, elections, and dismissals, the code indicates that there must be a formal, transparent, and considered procedure for appointing new directors. There must be plans for the orderly succession of appointments, and all directors must be re-elected regularly. The reasons for the resignation or removal of any director must be explained. Directors must ensure that they can devote sufficient time and attention to the business and must not accept the appointment if they cannot do so. A nomination committee must be established with specific written terms of reference that address its authority and duties. This committee must review the board's structure, size, and composition at least annually and make recommendations on any proposed changes to the board to complement the company's corporate strategy.

Regarding directors' responsibilities, delegation, and board procedures, the code highlights that directors must always know their responsibilities, conduct, business activities, and development. Non-executive directors have the same duties of diligence, skill, and fiduciary duties as executive directors. Newly appointed directors must receive a comprehensive, formal, and personalized induction at appointments. After that, they must receive all necessary instruction and professional development to ensure they understand the company's operations and business and are fully aware of their responsibilities under corporate statutes and legislation, stock exchange listing rules, legal requirements, and other requirements. In regulatory requirements and business and governance policies, non-executive directors must attend board meetings to make independent judgments on strategy, policy, performance, accountability, resources, key appointments, and standards of conduct.

The code emphasizes that there must be a clear division between the responsibilities of the board chair and the chief executive to ensure a balance of power and authority so that power is not concentrated in any one individual. The chairperson and executive director's roles must be distinct and not held by the same person. The division of responsibilities between the chairperson and the chief executive must be set out in writing. Additionally, the code points out that before making decisions on behalf of shareholders, the board must provide management with clear instructions on the matters that require its approval. There must be a formal schedule of matters reserved explicitly for board approval. When the board delegates aspects of its management and administration functions to the board, it must also guide as to management powers, which management must report to and obtain prior approval from the board before making decisions or undertaking any commitments on behalf of the company.

When the board forms committees, they should be formed with specific written terms of reference that address their authority and duties. When committees are established to deal with specific matters, the board should give them specific directions that are sufficiently clear to enable them to perform their functions adequately. Committees' terms of reference should require them to inform the board of their decisions or recommendations unless there are legal or regulatory restrictions on their ability to do so.

Regarding the conduct of board proceedings and providing access to information, the code advises that directors must be guaranteed to participate in board proceedings meaningfully and effectively. Directors must promptly receive appropriate information in the form and quality that will enable them to make an informed decision and discharge their duties and responsibilities. The board must meet regularly, and meetings must be held at least four times a year at approximately quarterly intervals. Regular board meetings are expected to involve the active participation of most directors, who are entitled to be present in person or by electronic means of communication. Therefore, regular meetings do not include obtaining the board's consent by circling written resolutions.

The code provides for a company secretary who plays a supporting role for the board, ensuring a good flow of information within the board and that policies and procedures are complied with. The company secretary advises the board through the chairperson or chief executive on governance matters and must facilitate directors' induction and professional development. The secretary must be an employee of the company and have full knowledge of the issuer's business. When a company hires an external service provider as company secretary, it must disclose the identity of the person with sufficient seniority within the company with whom the service provider may come into contact (e.g., general counsel or chief financial officer).

The code provides recommendations on risk management and internal control. It states that the board is responsible for evaluating and determining the nature and extent of the risks it is willing to take to achieve the strategic objectives of adequate and effective internal control and risk management. These risks would include, among others, material ESG-related risks. The board must oversee management in the design, implementation, and monitoring of risk management and internal control systems, and management must confirm the effectiveness of these systems to the board. The board must continually oversee the company's risk management and internal control systems and ensure their efficacy and subsidiaries are reviewed annually and reported to shareholders. The review must cover all material controls, including financial, operational, and compliance controls. The board may disclose in the Corporate Governance Report that it has received confirmation from management about the effectiveness of the issuer's risk management systems and internal controls.

The code guides the audit committee, highlighting that the board must establish formal and transparent agreements to consider how it will apply financial reporting, risk management, and internal control principles and maintain an appropriate relationship with auditors. The listing rules for the exchange must specify the terms of reference for the audit committee. A duly appointed meeting secretary must keep complete minutes of audit committee meetings. Draft and final versions of meeting minutes should be sent to all audit committee members for comments and records within a reasonable time after the meeting.

Regarding remuneration, the code highlights that the company must have a formal and transparent policy on the remuneration of directors and other matters related to remuneration. Compensation levels must be sufficient to attract and retain directors to manage the company successfully without paying more than necessary. No director should be involved in deciding their remuneration. The remuneration committee must consult the chairperson of the board and the chief executive officer about its remuneration proposals for other executive directors. The remuneration committee should have access to independent professional advice if necessary.

The code provides recommendations on shareholder engagement, advising that the board should be responsible for maintaining an ongoing dialogue with shareholders, particularly using annual or other general meetings to communicate with them and encourage their participation. The company must have a dividend payment policy and disclose it in its annual report. The code encourages companies to include in their Corporate Governance Report details of shareholder information by type and aggregate shareholding, an indication of important dates in the next fiscal year, the percentage of public fluctuation based on publicly available information, and the knowledge of its directors as of the most recent date possible before the issuance of the annual report; and the number of shares held by each member of senior management.

Finally, the code indicates that the company must ensure that shareholders receive notice of shareholder meetings, are familiar with the detailed procedures for holding a vote, and must arrange to respond to shareholder questions at meetings. The chairperson of that general meeting must put forth a separate resolution for each substantially distinct issue. The company should avoid grouping resolutions unless they are interdependent and linked, and issuers should explain the reasons and material implications in the call notice.

Regarding accounting standards, domestic publicly traded companies are required to use the Hong Kong Financial Reporting Standards (HKFRS), which are practically identical to IFRS, with a single exception: a company domiciled in Hong Kong but incorporated outside of Hong Kong is permitted to use HKFRS or IFRS standards (IFRS, 2023). IFRS accounting standards are permitted for foreign companies. For example, in 2023, more than 250 Mainland Chinese companies will be listed on the Hong Kong Stock Exchange that uses IFRS or HKFRS standards. IFRS accounting standards are permitted for small and medium enterprises in Hong Kong (IFRS, 2023).

As one of China's two Special Administrative Regions, the other being Macau, Hong Kong has its own legal system, including its legal framework for developing accounting standards (IFRS, 2023). Under Section 18 of the Professional Accountants Ordinance, the Hong Kong Institute of Certified Public Accountants (HKICPA) is the only organization with legal authority to establish financial reporting, auditing, and ethical standards for professional accountants in Hong Kong. In 2023, it will have more than 47,000 members and around 14,000 registered students. The HKICPA was created on January 1, 1973, evolving from the Hong Kong Society of Accountants to contribute to developing the profession in Mainland China (CPA, 2023). The HKICPA is a statutory organization responsible for the registration of accounting professionals in Hong Kong and has six main functions: (i) qualification and registration of accountants, (ii) preparation and configuration of accounting standards, (iii) member support and development, (iv) providing the best professional practices, (v) maintaining the image and prestige of the accounting profession, and (vi) safeguarding the constitution, governance, and organization of the institute (CPA, 2023).

The HKICPA issues standards for financial reporting, auditing and reporting assurance, and ethical standards for accounting professionals. A board that oversees the HKICPA makes decisions regarding strategy, policy, and general direction while offering advice and support through oversight boards and committees. One of these is the Financial Reporting Standards Committee (FRSC), which is responsible for developing financial reporting standards to achieve convergence with IFRS issued by the IASB. In 2001, the HKICPA Board adopted the convergence of HKFRS with IFRS as a policy. Hong Kong Financial Reporting Standards include all Hong Kong

Financial Reporting Standards, Hong Kong Accounting Standards (HKASs), and Interpretations (IFRIC). The HKFRS establishes recognition, measurement, presentation, and disclosure requirements that address transactions and events relevant to general-purpose statements. They can also establish requirements for transactions and events mainly in specific sectors (CPA, 2023).

In the Preface to Hong Kong Financial Reporting Standards issued by the HKICPA, in item 8 of the Scope and Authority of HKFRSs section, it is highlighted that such standards were designed to be applied to the financial statements of all profit-making entities, including those carrying out commercial, industrial, financial, and similar activities, organized in corporate form or other forms. It is also highlighted that even though these standards are not designed to be applied to non-profit activities in the private sector, public sector, or government, these entities may consider them appropriate. Item 33 points out that although the Board has a policy to achieve convergence of HKFRS with IFRS, the Board may consider it appropriate to include additional disclosure requirements or, in some exceptional cases, deviate from an IFRS, highlighting that each HKFRS issued contains information on the degree of compliance with equivalent IFRS. HKFRS standards are standards that must be applied to publicly traded companies.

The HKFRS for Private Entities was also issued based on the IFRS for SMEs. However, the HKICPA chose to replace the term "SME" in the IFRS with "Private Entities" to better suit Hong Kong's circumstances. This set of accounting standards is optional for private entities, defined as follows: (a) companies that do not have public responsibility, that is, their debt or equity instruments are not traded on a public market, and (b) publish general-purpose financial statements for external users.

In addition, the HKICPA has issued the Financial Reporting Framework for Small and Medium-Sized Entities and the Financial Reporting Standard, accounting practice standards for small and medium-sized enterprises that, under Section 359 of the Companies Ordinance, qualify as exempt from reports.

This section summarizes the relevant issues addressed in the Hong Kong Corporate Governance Code and the current accounting standards used by companies in the country. The corporate governance model that Hong Kong companies use is in the following section.

11.3 Corporate Governance Model Applied in Hong Kong

HKEX outlined the corporate governance framework for Hong Kong. It is a single-level board structure, as seen in Fig. 11.1. Countries with a common law tradition, such as Australia, Singapore, the United Kingdom, and the United States, typically adopt single-level board structures. It is a structure considered typical of a shareholder-oriented corporate governance system.

The corporate governance structure adopted in Hong Kong separates the legal entity from its owners, and this occurs because there is a separation between

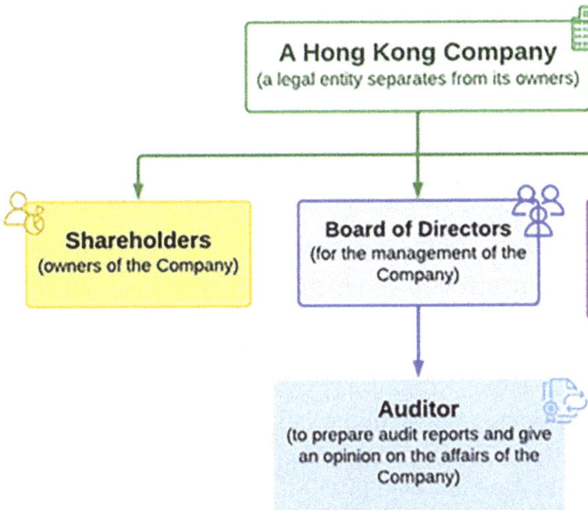

Fig. 11.1 Corporate Governance Structure in Hong Kong. *Source*: HKEX (2022)

ownership and management. That is, the owners are not responsible for managing the company. The owners become shareholders or partners who hire specialized people to manage the company. The board of directors has been hired to manage the company. The Company Secretary is an agent of the company who organizes and coordinates board and shareholder meetings. The auditor is hired to give an opinion on the adequacy and preparation of the financial statements and the company's business.

In the following sections, specific rules on the functioning of this corporate governance structure and their implications on several complex issues within organizational management were addressed, such as the composition of the board of directors, the constitution of committees, rights, and protection of minority shareholders, the concentration of ownership, and executive remuneration, among others.

11.3.1 *Sources of Funding, Separation Between Ownership and Control, and Rights of Minority Shareholders*

It is important to revisit history to understand the current context of the ownership structure of companies listed on the Hong Kong Stock Exchange. Therefore, it is noteworthy that for centuries, Hong Kong's business activities have been dominated by different ethnic groups (Fong, 2017). The historical perspective on Hong's ownership structure was made by dividing the periods for better understanding.

The First and Second Opium Wars between 1839–1842 and 1856–1860 promoted armed conflicts between China and Great Britain. The Treaty of Nanking was signed, which obliged China to pay war indemnity or compensation of US$ 21 million and hand over the island of Hong Kong to the British, opening five ports for trade (Guangzhou, Fuzhou, Xiamen, Ningbo, and Shanghai). The highest authority that London chose to run the colonial territory was the governor (Fong, 2017). Between 1880 and 1945, the Opium War took place, and in 1880, opium trafficking represented 39% of Chinese imports. As early as 1918, 46.5% of Hong Kong's government revenue came from the opium trade (Fong, 2017).

During World War II (1939–1945), Hong Kong was under the rule of the Japanese, who turned it into the military center of their campaign in Asia. The military government (administrative, civil, economic, judicial, and naval) enacted strict regulations, exercising power over residents. Commercial and economic activities began to be regulated by the Japanese, who took control of most factories. The Japanese military yen replaced the Hong Kong dollar, and people were impoverished by the forcibly imposed exchange rate. With the Japanese surrender in 1945, the British recovered Hong Kong (Fong, 2017). In the conflict between North Korea and South Korea, in the so-called Korean War (1950–1953), the United States banned trade with China, damaging commercial activity and hampering Hong Kong's economic growth.

In 1967, the Workers' Struggle took place, with terrible working conditions. The workers and/or workers revolted, followed by several workers' struggles framed by the Hong Kong Federation of Trade Unions (Fong, 2017). China committed to upholding the legal system for 50 years after the transfer of sovereignty by signing the Joint Declaration with the United Kingdom in 1984 as part of the "one country, two systems" policy in Hong Kong and establishing that the Special Administrative Region (HKSAR) would have independent powers (legislative, executive, and judiciary), independent finances, freedom from Chinese taxes and its taxation system, its currency, and free port status (Fong, 2017).

Finally, after the 1997 Asian Financial Crisis, it was discovered that structural weaknesses and the lack of Corporate Governance in Asian companies caused the crisis. Companies with low Corporate Governance showed greater drops in the stock market. From that moment on, a search began to improve Corporate Governance to protect the interests of interested parties (Fong, 2017).

Considering historical facts, there is a preponderance of British influence in Hong Kong, resulting in similarities in culture, economic model, and common law legal system (Miniaoui et al., 2022). The ownership structure of companies listed on the Hong Kong Stock Exchange is concentrated in large family business groups (Chen et al., 2005). Approximately 75% of companies listed on the Hong Kong Stock Exchange in 2012 had a dominant shareholder, owning 30% or more of the issued shares (OECD, 2017). Families often offer management positions to their family members without relevant and appropriate knowledge and skills (the same person occupying the positions of CEO and chairman of the board of directors) (Chen et al., 2005). There is a predominance of complex cross-properties with pyramidal structures, weakening transparency in disclosing profits to external investors (Vichitsarawong et al., 2010). This has caused an increase in the number of lawsuits involving shareholder fraud, merger disputes, clandestine listings, and/or disputes related to corporate governance (Michael & Goo, 2019). In fraudulent trading cases, the court may declare that the individual who knowingly took part in the transaction becomes responsible for the company's debts.

Regarding responsibility towards institutional investors, it is not mandatory to disclose voting policies, and the instructions require issuing votes of the beneficial owner of the shares. However, to mitigate conflicts of interest, analysts, brokers, rating agencies, and so on, must disclose their policies (OECD, 2021).

Besides, related to the protection of minority shareholders, Hong Kong has conditions that favor their expropriation, as discussed below. HKEX allows companies to issue two types of shares: ordinary or preferred (HKEX, 2023a). Ordinary shares give voting rights and receive dividends at the company's discretion. However, the payment of dividends is not mandatory even if the company records a profit for the year (HKEX, 2023a). Preferred shares are entitled to a preferential distribution of profits before any distribution to common shareholders. Preferred shareholders do not have voting rights and receive fixed dividends. The dividend does not increase even if the company's profit increases. Preferred shareholders have rights to corporate assets; in liquidation, they are ahead of ordinary shareholders but behind the company's creditors (HKEX, 2023a). Preferred shareholders may receive additional dividends if profits are sufficient. However, cumulative preferred shares transfer the right to profits to the following if profits are insufficient to pay the holders in any year. Article 139 highlights that publicly traded companies do not have the power to issue subscription bonuses (Company Registry, 2023; HKEX, 2023a).

The Companies Regulations, in Art. 180, highlight that the company may have more than one class of shares with different rights for each class, as long as this is provided for in the company's articles of association or if there was no such provision in the articles of incorporation, with the consent of the holders of shares of that class, in writing, representing at least 75% of the total voting rights of holders of shares in this class, or a special resolution passed at a separate general meeting of holders of shares in the class sanctioning the proposed variation (Company Registry, 2023; HKEX, 2023a).

In this regard, HKEX states in its listing rules Cap. 8A, despite believing in the "one share, one vote" principle, this remains the ideal system to empower shareholders and align their interests in a company. The exchange will consider listing requests from companies that seek to deviate from this principle. In these cases, HKEX will seek to safeguard the standards established in its listing rules and may authorize shares with weighted votes. Cap. 8A, item 02, defines weighted voting rights as the voting power associated with a share of a given class that is greater than or superior to the voting power associated with a common share or other right or governance arrangement disproportionate to the economic interest of the beneficiary in the issuer's equity securities.

Chapter 8A, item 4, states that a company that can apply for listing with a weighted share structure must satisfy at least one of the following requirements: (a) a market capitalization of at least HK$ 40,000,000,000 at the time of listing or (b) a market capitalization of at least HK$ 10,000,000,000 at the time of listing and revenue of at least HK$ 1,000,000,000 for the most recent audited financial year. Item 10 requires that a class of shares that confers weighted voting rights on a listed issuer must not confer on the beneficiary the right to more than ten times the voting power of the ordinary shares in any resolution presented at the general meetings of the issuer, and, after listing, the listed issuer may change the terms of a class of shares with weighted voting rights to increase the weighted voting rights associated with that class (Chapter 8A, item 16).

Furthermore, item 24 provides that any voting rights inherent to any class of shares must be disregarded and must not give the holder the right to more than one vote per share in any resolution to approve (a) changes to the constituent documents of the listed issuer, whatever their formulation, (b) variation of rights inherent to any class of shares, (c) the appointment or dismissal of an independent non-executive director; (d) the appointment or dismissal of auditors, and (e) the voluntary dissolution of the listed company. Even though the regulations prescribe some restrictions on shares with weighted voting power, several decisions that could lead to the expropriation of minority shareholders are still permitted.

Part 12 relates to the administration and procedure of the company, stating the rule states that anything that can be done by a resolution passed at a general meeting of a company can be done without a meeting and the need for notice by a written resolution of the company's shareholders. A written resolution of a company has the same effect as if approved by a general meeting, except for the dismissal of an auditor before the end of the term of office (Company Registry, 2023). Directors or shareholders of the company may propose a written resolution. Shareholders may suggest resolutions in writing if they represent 5% of the total voting rights of all members entitled to vote in the resolution or a smaller percentage, as provided for in the company's articles of association by Article 552 (Company Registry, 2023).

And according to Article 565, only directors can call a general meeting. However, directors can voluntarily call a general meeting when shareholders request it, or they must call it when at least 5% of the total shareholders with voting rights request the meeting. In this case, the shareholders must declare the general nature of the business to be discussed at the meeting, and the directors must call it within 21 days after the date on which they become subject to the requirement. It cannot be held on a date later than 28 days after the date of the notice calling the meeting. If the directors receive a request to call a meeting of at least 5% of the total shareholders with voting rights and do not do so, the shareholders who requested the meeting, or any of them who represent more than half of the total voting rights, may themselves convene the general meeting. In this case, the meeting must be convened no later than three months after the call requirement date. Any reasonable expenses incurred by members who requested the meeting due to the directors' failure to convene a meeting properly must be reimbursed by the company. The Company shall retain such refunded sums from any fees or other compensation due or to be due in connection with the services of the defaulting directors.

Companies Regulation also regulates, in its articles 724 and 725, that a court may consider that the company's business is being or has been conducted in a manner that is unfairly detrimental to the interests of shareholders in general or one or more shareholders, or that an actual or proposed act or omission by the company is or would be so harmful. In this case, the court may use resources, such as restricting the continuity of the company's business conduct, restricting the performance of acts to be carried out by the company, or even requesting the practice of acts that the company omitted or proposed to omit. Consequently, the company or any other person may be ordered to pay any damages and interest on those damages as the court deems appropriate to a shareholder whose interests have been unfairly prejudiced by the conduct of the company's business or by the act or omission (Company Registry, 2023). The following section describes the structure of the Hong Kong board of directors and its operating rules.

11.3.2 Shareholders Meeting, Board of Directors, and Committees

The publicly traded company must hold an annual general meeting concerning the financial year. It must send a copy of the accounting and financial reporting documents to all shareholders at least 21 days before the meeting date at which the copy is required (Company Registry, 2023). Suppose the company does not send the documents within the required deadline. In that case, the company and all individuals responsible for the company will be subject to a fine and imprisonment for 12 months. The general meeting makes the appointments of directors and advisors. However, it should not be done in a single deliberation. A director or advisor may be removed from office by resolution approved at a general meeting before the end of the term of office unless the director has held a position for life since August 31, 1984 (Company Registry, 2023).

The corporate governance structure in Hong Kong belongs to the Anglo-Saxon system (Chen et al., 2018; Cheung et al., 2011; He et al., 2012). Anglo-Saxon countries are common law countries where jurisprudence, customs, and practice are predominant (Miniaoui et al., 2022). Therefore, the board of directors reports directly to the chief executive of the Hong Kong Special Administrative Region (HKSAR) or the financial secretary under the delegated authority of the Hong Kong Stock Exchange (HKEX). In terms of size, the Hong Kong Board of Directors must have a minimum of three members and has no maximum member limit. Regarding its composition, the board of directors must contain at least three independent non-executive directors, representing at least one-third of the board. Finally, although there are no disclosure requirements on the gender composition of boards, the Listing Rules require the nominating committee of a listed company to have a diversity of policies for board members and to disclose the policy in its annual reports.

Female representation on the board of directors of the Hong Kong company increased from 11% in 2017 to approximately 12% in 2019. An average annual rate of 5% growth in participation on boards of directors in publicly traded companies. From this perspective, listing rules require the company's nomination committee and/or board listed on the stock exchange to have diverse policies for board members and disclose them in annual reports (OECD, 2021). They are improving their understanding of Corporate Social Responsibility initiatives and disclosures (increased monitoring functions) (Miniaoui et al., 2022).

The Exchange Listing Rules established the Hong Kong audit committee. The Hong Kong Institute of Certified Public Accountants promotes corporate governance practice, aiming to examine the role and legal responsibilities of independent directors, audit and remuneration committees, and education for directors (Vichitsarawong et al., 2010). In 1998, the code of best practice for the Hong Kong Stock Exchange (SEHK) listing rules included audit committee guidelines (Chen et al., 2005). In 2003, legislation began to require an audit committee for all companies listed on the stock exchange (He et al., 2012). Thus, the audit committee is responsible for monitoring the integrity of the issuer's financial statements and annual, semi-annual, and, if prepared for publication, quarterly reports and accounts, reviewing the judgments of significant financial reports contained therein, and so on. This committee must have at least three directors, with the majority being independent. Finally, the audit committee must meet at least two times a year (Chen et al., 2018; HKEX, 2021).

Another mandatory committee is the Appointment and Remuneration Committee (Vichitsarawong et al., 2010). They are responsible for making recommendations to the board on the company's succession plan, evaluating its performance, making appointments or dismissals of directors, and remunerating directors, among other things. Executive directors' compensation should be linked to corporate and individual performance (Chen et al., 2018). The nomination and remuneration committee must comprise at least three non-executive directors, with 50% of the members being independent directors (Miniaoui et al., 2022).

The Companies Ordinance, in its Article 465, provides that executives (directors and advisors) must exercise reasonable care, skills, and diligence in their functions, meaning having general knowledge, skills, and experience that can be reasonably expected from a person who performs the functions performed by the director about the company.

11.3.3 External Audit System

The Hong Kong Institute of Certified Public Accountants (HKICPA) is also responsible for issuing Auditing and Assurance Standards, known as the Hong Kong Standards on Quality Control, Auditing, Assurance, and Related Services (KHSQCs/HKSQMs). These standards are divided into (a) Hong Kong Auditing Standards (HKSAs), applied to the audit of historical financial information; (b) Hong Kong Standards on Review Engagement (HKSREs), applied to the review of historical financial information; (c) Hong Kong Standards on Assurance Engagements (HKSAEs), applied to assurance engagements dealing with matters other than historical financial information; (d) Hong Kong Standards on Circular Investment Reporting Undertakings (HKSIRs), applied to circular investment reporting undertakings; and (e) and Hong Kong Standards on Related Services (HKSRSs), applied to compilation work, work to apply agreed procedures to information and other related work (CPA, 2023).

Such standards establish basic principles on essential procedures and guide a company's responsibilities for its quality control according to Hong Kong labor standards (CPA, 2023). The standards issued by the HKICPA are consistent with the International Standards for Quality Control, Auditing, Review, Other Assurance, and Related Services issued by the International Auditing and Assurance Standards Board (IAASB). The HKSA is also aligned with International Standards on Auditing (ISA). The HKSA, or simply Hong Kong Auditing Standards, are established to audit financial statements by an independent auditor. The HKSA came into force for audits of financial statements for periods beginning on or after December 15, 2009.

Dealing with more specific legal aspects, such as the appointment of the external auditor, the Company Ordinance (Cap. 622) says that any person who meets the requirements of the law and is not a director or employee of the company, or whether a partner or employee of a director or employee of the company. The appointment of the external auditor must be made through deliberation at the annual general meeting held in the previous financial year (Company Registry, 2023). According to Art. 402, a person appointed as an external auditor does not assume the position until the appointment of the previous auditor is terminated. The term of office is generally one year, ending with the following general assembly (Company Registry, 2023). A court or the board of directors can also appoint an external auditor. When there is a vacancy in the position of external auditor, appointments by directors may take place, as may appointments by the court when the company does not hold a general meeting, and the directors or partners request one.

Regarding remuneration, the Companies Ordinance regulates that the remuneration of an external auditor appointed by the partners can be established through a resolution approved at a general meeting or in a manner specified. The board of directors may set the compensation of an external auditor when making the appointment, or it may do so in another way, such as by a general meeting or differently than it specifies. Similarly, the court itself may determine the compensation of an external auditor when making the appointment, by resolution at a general meeting, or in another manner that it specifies. Furthermore, by the Companies Ordinance, the external auditor's compensation includes any sums paid by the company for the auditor's related costs of performing his duties.

Suppose the auditor, after carrying out the audit, believes that the information for the period is inconsistent with the financial statements. In that case, he must state this opinion in the auditor's report and may convey this opinion to the shareholders at a general meeting, as per Art. 404 (Company Registry, 2023). In this sense, the individual auditor or every employee and agent of the individual auditor who is eligible for appointment as auditor of the company, audit firm, every partner, employee, and agent of the audit firm who is eligible for appointment as auditor of the company, or further, if the auditor who prepares the auditor's report is a legal entity, every director, member, employee, and agent of the auditor qualified for appointment as auditor of the company who commits offenses relating to the contents of the auditor's report, commits an offense, knowingly or recklessly, is subject to a fine of $150,000 (Company Registry, 2023).

According to Art. 411 of the Companies Ordinance (Cap. 622), the external auditor appointed by the company is entitled to participate in any of the general meetings held and to be heard on any part of the business of the meeting that concerns the person as auditor of the company. The standard also provides for the auditor's right to access accounting records, information, and explanations necessary to exercise his functions as the company's auditor.

Finally, the external auditor may resign from his mandate if he sends a written notification to the company, accompanied by a statement describing whether there were circumstances that should be brought to the partners' attention that impacted the decision to resign. Upon expiry of the term of office, the external auditor must send a notification to the company advising of the term of termination of service 14 days in advance. The company may also dismiss the auditor before his term of office expires. In this case, the company must, after the ordinary deliberation approved at the general meeting, notify the dismissed auditor and the relevant supervisory body within 15 days from the date on which the dismissal was approved (Company Registry, 2023).

11.4 Final Considerations

The Hong Kong Stock Exchange has been improving its corporate governance practices, especially after the 1997 Asian crisis, implementing corporate governance measures to stabilize its financial systems and improve regulation and supervision (Vichitsarawong et al., 2010). However, corporate governance mechanisms appear weak in companies (Chen et al., 2005), increasing the chance of controlling shareholders "squeezing" the interests of minority shareholders and subsequently delisting the company (He et al., 2012).

Furthermore, greater effort is needed to guarantee the true independence of non-executive directors. Hong Kong regulatory bodies must still address this significant issue (Cheung et al., 2013; Fong, 2017; He et al., 2012). This fragility arises from the institutional environment that began with the conflicts between China and Great Britain, alleviated by the signing of the 1984 declaration, establishing one country and two systems. The reformulations resulting from the Securities and Futures Law, updated in 2012, gave rise to obligations regarding the participation of non-executive members and independent members in the board of directors, the participation of women in management, the creation of the audit committee, appointment, and remuneration, performance evaluation of advisors, and so on.

Based on the publication of the ESG reporting guide set out in Appendix 27 of the Exchange Listing Rules, the management board is responsible for the governance and effective oversight of ESG issues and the assessment and management of relevant environmental and social risks. Ensuring long-term sustainable growth for shareholders and delivering long-term value for all stakeholders.

References

Chen, K. C. W., & Tang, F. (2017). Post-IFRS revaluation adjustments and executive compensation. *Contemporary Accounting Research, 34*(2), 1210–1231. https://doi.org/10.1111/1911-3846.12285

Chen, Z., Cheung, Y.-L., Stouraitis, A., & Wong, A. W. S. (2005). Ownership concentration, firm performance, and dividend policy in Hong Kong. *Pacific-Basin Finance Journal, 13*(4), 431–449. https://doi.org/10.1016/j.pacfin.2004.12.001

Chen, C., Wan, W. Y., & Zhang, W. (2018). Board Independence as a panacea to tunneling? An empirical study of related-party transactions in Hong Kong and Singapore. *Journal of Empirical Legal Studies, 15*(4), 987–1020. https://doi.org/10.1111/jels.12197

Cheung, Y.-L., Connelly, J. T., Jiang, P., & Limpaphayom, P. (2011). Does corporate governance predict future performance? Evidence from Hong Kong. *Financial Management, 40*(1), 159–197. https://doi.org/10.1111/j.1755-053x.2010.01138.x

Cheung, Y.-L., Jiang, K., Mak, B. S. C., & Tan, W. (2013). Corporate social performance, firm valuation, and industrial difference: Evidence from Hong Kong. *Journal of Business Ethics, 114*(4), 625–631. https://doi.org/10.1007/s10551-013-1708-0

Company Registry. (2023). *Companies ordinance (Cap. 622).* https://www.cr.gov.hk/en/legislation/companies-ordinance/cap622/companies-ordinance.htm

CPA. (2023). *Hong Kong Instituto of certified public accountants (HKICPA). About Us.* https://www.hkicpa.org.hk/en/About-us/Organization/Overview

Du, J., He, Q., & Yuen, S. W. (2013). Tunneling and the decision to go private: Evidence from Hong Kong. *Pacific-Basin Finance Journal, 22*(April 2013), 50–68. https://doi.org/10.1016/j.pacfin.2012.10.001

Fong, C. C. S. (2017). *Relationship between corporate governance & company performance of Hong Kong-based & China-based family-controlled property development companies Business & Management Conference, Geneva.*

Hang Seng Indexes Company Limited. (n.d.). All indexes. HSI. https://www.hsi.com.hk/eng/indexes/all-indexes. Retrieved July 15, 2025, from https://www.hsi.com.hk/eng/indexes/all-indexes

He, T. T., Li, W. X. B., & Tang, G. Y. N. (2012). Dividends behavior in state-versus family-controlled firms: Evidence from Hong Kong. *Journal of Business Ethics, 110*(1), 97–112. https://doi.org/10.1007/s10551-011-1150-0

HKEX. (2021). *Stock Exchange of Hong Kong Limited. Corporate governance code (CG code).* Appendix 14. https://en-rules.hkex.com.hk/sites/default/files/net_file_store/HKEX4476_3828_VER23680.pdf

HKEX. (2022). *Hong Kong exchanges and clearing market.* Corporate Governance. https://www.hkexgroup.com/Corporate-Governance?sc_lang=en

HKEX. (2023a). *Hong Kong exchange and clearing limited.* Equity Securities. https://www.hkex.com.hk/Products/Securities/Equities?sc_lang=en#collapse0

HKEX. (2023b). *Stock Exchange of Hong Kong Limited.* Monthly Market Highlights. https://www.hkex.com.hk/Market-Data/Statistics/Consolidated-Reports/HKEX-Monthly-Market-Highlights?sc_lang=en

IFRS. (2023). *IFRS foundation. Use of IFRS Accounting Standards by Jurisdiction.* https://www.ifrs.org/use-around-the-world/use-of-ifrs-standards-by-jurisdiction/view-jurisdiction/hong-kong-sar/.

Jaggi, B., & Tsui, J. (2007). Insider trading, earnings management, and corporate governance: Empirical evidence based on Hong Kong firms. *Journal of International Financial Management & Accounting, 18*(3), 192–222. https://doi.org/10.1111/j.1467-646x.2007.01012.x

Kim, D.-S., Yeo, E., & Zhang, L. (2021). Do cross-listed firms have a better governance structure and lower agency costs? Evidence from Chinese firms. *Sustainability, 13*(4), 1734. https://doi.org/10.3390/su13041734

La Porta, R., Lopez-De-Silanes, F., Shleifer, A., & Vishny, R. (2000). Investor protection and corporate governance. *Journal of Financial Economics, 58*(1–2), 3–27. https://doi.org/10.1016/s0304-405x(00)00065-9

Michael, B., & Goo, S. (2019). What do the Panama papers teach us about the administrative law of corporate governance reform in Hong Kong? *Tsinghua China Law Review, 11*(2), 1–32. https://doi.org/10.2139/ssrn.3101253

Miniaoui, Z., Chibani, F., & Hussainey, K. (2022). Corporate governance and CSR disclosure: International evidence for the period 2006–2016. *Journal of Risk and Financial Management, 15*(9), 398. https://doi.org/10.3390/jrfm15090398

OECD (2017). *OECD corporate governance factbook*. OECD Publishing, Paris. https://doi.org/10.1787/282ac02e-en.

OECD. (2021). *OECD corporate governance factbook*. Organization for Economic Co-operation and Development. https://www.oecd.org/corporate/corporate-governance-factbook.htm.

OECD. (2022). *Our global reach: Member countries*. Organization for Economic Co-operation and Development. https://www.oecd.org/about/

Vichitsarawong, T., Eng, L. L., & Meek, G. K. (2010). The impact of the Asian financial crisis on conservatism and timeliness of earnings: Evidence from Hong Kong, Malaysia, Singapore, and Thailand. *Journal of International Financial Management & Accounting, 21*(1), 32–61. https://doi.org/10.1111/j.1467-646x.2009.01035.x

WFE. (2023). *Statistics portal*. World Federation of Exchanges. https://www.world-exchanges.org/our-work/statistics

Index

C. B. Macagnan (ed.), *Corporate Governance in Capital Markets*, CSR, Sustainability, Ethics & Governance,
https://doi.org/10.1007/978-3-031-94751-3

D

E

F

G

H

GPSR Compliance
The European Union's (EU) General Product Safety Regulation (GPSR) is a set of rules that requires consumer products to be safe and our obligations to ensure this.

If you have any concerns about our products, you can contact us on

ProductSafety@springernature.com

In case Publisher is established outside the EU, the EU authorized representative is:

Springer Nature Customer Service Center GmbH
Europaplatz 3
69115 Heidelberg, Germany

www.ingramcontent.com/pod-product-compliance
Lightning Source LLC
Chambersburg PA
CBHW081813090925
32282CB00002B/21
* 9 7 8 3 0 3 1 9 4 7 5 0 6 *